Psychologically S

Psychologically Speaking

A book of quotations

Kevin Connolly
and Margaret Martlew

BPS
BOOKS

THE BRITISH
PSYCHOLOGICAL
SOCIETY

First published in 1999 by BPS Books (The British Psychological Society),
St Andrews House, 48 Princess Road East, Leicester LE1 7DR, UK.

A catalogue record for this book is available from the British Library.

ISBN 1 85433 302 X

Typeset by Ralph J. Footring, Derby

Printed by Biddles Ltd, Guildford and King's Lynn

For Colette, John, Oona, Sarah, Clare, Nicholas, Paul.

Contents

Preface

The idea for this collection arose in the course of conversation at a dinner party more than a decade ago. Someone had come across a particularly witty couple of sentences in a psychological monograph and quoted them to very good effect. Reflecting later, we felt sure that there must be lots of interesting, even entertaining material to be found and so our collection was begun. At first we collected whatever came our way and took our fancy, without any overall plan to guide us. Later we made lists of sources we thought should provide good pickings, mostly psychological luminaries of the twentieth century, and topics we thought should be included.

In compiling the collection we were forced to confront the question 'What is psychology?' As any psychologist knows, this is a tricky question. Whatever else, psychology is a broad church, perhaps the broadest among contemporary disciplines. After some reflection we decided to meet this challenge directly and not confine ourselves to psychology as mirrored by what is found between the covers of a textbook. In a real sense we are all psychologists: we live by our psychological knowledge and skill. Psychology, therefore, is found in the laboratory, the clinic, the workplace, the school, the street – indeed, wherever there are people. This approach has led us to rummage in all directions and happily draw material from wherever we found it, requiring only that it should be 'psychological'.

The collection is of quotations of psychological interest, not quotations from psychologists, though of course many are taken from the work of psychologists. Were it only the latter, two conclusions would quickly become inescapable. First, the prose style required in much contemporary psychological publishing does not readily lend itself to *bon mots*, even if the author is witty and possessed of a good turn of phrase. Second, it is certainly the case that if this or any other collection failed to include items taken from literature, poetry, philosophy, science and many other disciplines it would give an impoverished view of psychology.

As the collection grew, it became clear that a structure around which to organise it was needed. Several possibilities were considered before we settled on the present scheme, which groups the items into categories arranged alphabetically. The categories for the most part represent major concerns in psychology; a few are devoted to more peripheral topics and others reflect either our idiosyncrasies or our desire to give breadth and balance to the collection. In the case of topics (such as memory, intelligence and therapy) which are allotted a category of their own, the reader can turn directly to the category itself or can trace the topic in question using the subject index. The subject index is extensive and will usually generate more items on a topic than are contained in the category because of the cross-referencing system adopted. In addition, the author index allows the reader to chase up great psychologists such as William Shakespeare, Charles Darwin, William James and Sigmund Freud; or follow the ideas and contributions of some lesser mortals.

In compiling the collection, a number of criteria were used to select items: the succinctness with which a point is made, a clever definition, a neat description, the insight afforded, a sharp controversy exposed, the wit displayed, the daftness of some remarks and the naivety of others. The overall balance of the collection was also a consideration. Some topics were rich with examples whereas others were distinctly thin and required that we relax the selection criteria a little. Some topics may seem over-represented at the expense of others, and some readers will no doubt think that we have overlooked topics they believe to be of central importance. In some cases we might agree. However, if a good quotation cannot be found it cannot be included, and a poor one would serve no good purpose. In the case of some topics we searched long and hard without success. No doubt there are gems if only one knew where to look. Any suggestions or offerings from our readers would be most welcome; they will be carefully filed away against the possibility of any revision or further collection.

Most of us at some time or another have use for a quotation. Dorothy L. Sayers said, 'I always have a quotation for everything – it saves original thinking'. Similarly, Winston Churchill felt positively disposed to books of quotations when he wrote, 'quotations, when engraved upon memory, give you good thoughts. They also make you anxious to read the authors and look for more.' We hope that this collection meets these ends and also that from time to time it will give rise to a wry smile and occasionally a jolly good laugh.

Kevin Connolly, Margaret Martlew
University of Sheffield

Acknowledgements

The publishers would like to thank the following for permission to reproduce material in this volume:

Alan Brodie Representation and The Noel Coward Estate for the extract from *Private Lives* by Noel Coward; A.M. Heath & Co. Ltd, agents for the Orwell Estate, for extracts from *Animal Farm* by George Orwell; Carcanet for extracts from *Complete Poems* by Robert Graves; Chatto & Windus for the extract from *Round and Round the Garden* by Alan Ayckbourn; Egmont Children's Books Ltd for extracts from A.A. Milne; Faber and Faber for extracts from *Collected Poems* by W.H. Auden, *Forty Years On, Getting On, The Madness of King George* and *Writing Home* by Alan Bennett, *Collected Poems* by Philip Larkin, *The Spirit Level* by Seamus Heaney, and *Collected Poems 1909–1962* and *Old Possum's Book of Practical Cats* by T.S. Eliot; Gerald Duckworth and Company Ltd for extracts by Dorothy Parker; Harvard University Press for extracts from *Acts of Meaning* by Jerome Bruner, © 1990 by the President and Fellows of Harvard College; J.M. Dent for the extract from 'Do not go Gentle into that Good Night' from *Collected Poems* by Dylan Thomas; John Murray (Publishers) Ltd for the extract from *Summoned by Bells* by John Betjeman; Jonathan Cape for the extract from *The Second Sex* by Simone de Beauvoir, translated by H.M. Parshley; Pantheon Books for the extract from *Songs by Tom Lehrer* (recording), 1953, by Tom Lehrer; Penguin Books and James MacGibbon for the extract from *The Collected Poems of Stevie Smith* (Penguin 20th Century Classics) by Stevie Smith; Scientific American for extracts from 'The origins of alienation' by Urie Bronfenbrenner, August 1974; Martin Secker and Warburg for the extract from *My Left Foot* by Christie Brown and for the extract from *Trainspotting* by Irvine Welsh; The Society of Authors, on behalf of the Bernard Shaw Estate, for extracts from *Major Barbara* and *You Never Can Tell* by George Bernard Shaw; Taylor & Francis Books Ltd for the extract from *The Family and Individual Development* by D.W. Winnicott; Tavistock Publications for the extract from *Knots* by R.D. Laing; W.W. Norton & Company, Inc., for the extract from *Our Inner Conflicts: A Constructive Theory of Neurosis* by Karen Horney, © 1945 by W.W. Norton & Company, Inc., renewed © 1972 by Renate Mintz, Marianne von Eckardt and Bridgitte Horney Swarenski.

Every effort has been made to trace and acknowledge ownership of copyright. The publishers will be glad to make suitable arrangements with any copyright holders whom it has not been possible to contact.

A note on conventions

We have not attempted to provide detailed bibliographic information: our aim has simply been to give the reader sufficient to track down a quotation. Whenever possible we have given either the author's life dates or the date of first publication of a source. Life dates are more usual in the case of literary authors, whose work often appears in several editions. For scientific authors, date of first publication of a work is generally preferred, with some exceptions such as Darwin and Freud. Where a poem has no title, the title of the collection is given.

Abbreviations
anon., anonymous
attrib., attributed
c., circa
cent., century
cit., cited in
ed., editor
edn, edition
n.d., not dated
vol., volume
[ ] editors' note

ABILITIES

1 The rarity of commanding ability, and the vast abundance of mediocrity, is no accident, but follows of necessity, from the very nature of these things.
FRANCIS GALTON (1822–1911) *Hereditary Genius*

2 ... since as far as we know, the full range of human talents is represented in all major races of man and all socioeconomic levels, it is unjust to allow the mere fact of an individual's racial or social background to affect the treatment accorded to him.
A.R. JENSEN *Harvard Educational Review*, 1969

3 ... it is not only unrealistic but misleading to think of man's intellectual gifts and capabilities purely in cognitive terms.
STEPHEN WISEMAN *Intelligence and Ability*, 1973

4 It takes little talent to see what lies under one's nose, a good deal of it to know in which direction to point that organ.
W.H. AUDEN (1907–1973) *Dyer's Hand*

5 There is no substitute for talent. Industry and all the virtues are of no avail.
ALDOUS HUXLEY (1894–1963) *Point Counter Point*

6 You must make use of people according to their abilities, and realize that absolutely no one is perfect.
FRANÇOISE de MAINTENON (1635–1719) letter to Count d'Aubigue, September 1679

7 And all may do, what has by man been done.
EDWARD YOUNG (1630–1765) *Night Thoughts*

8 Knowledge may give weight, but accomplishments give lustre, and many more people see than weigh.
LORD CHESTERFIELD, PHILIP STANHOPE (1694–1773) *Letters to His Son*

9 But know that in the soul
Are many lesser faculties, that serve
Reason as chief.
JOHN MILTON (1608–1674) *Paradise Lost*

10 What a piece of work is man! how noble in reason! how infinite in faculties! in form and movement how express and admirable! in action how like an angel! in apprehension how like a god! the beauty of the world, the paragon of animals.
WILLIAM SHAKESPEARE (1564–1616) *Hamlet*

11 In a world as empirical as ours, a youngster who does not know what he is good *at* will not be sure what he is good for.
E.Z. FRIEDENBERG *The Vanishing Adolescent*, 1959

12 No bird soars too high if he soars with his own wings.
WILLIAM BLAKE (1757–1827) 'The Marriage of Heaven and Hell'

13 You have flair.... It's handed out at birth.... And as always happens in these cases, it's always given to the very people who in my opinion do least to earn it.
ALAN AYCKBOURN *Joking Apart*, 1979

14 Some men are born mediocre, some men achieve mediocrity, and some men have mediocrity thrust upon them.
JOSEPH HELLER *Catch-22*, 1961

15 Of science and logic he chatters
As fast and as fine as he can:
Though I am no judge of such matters
I'm sure he's a talented man.
W.M. PRAED (1802–1839) 'The Talented Man'

16 It always seemed to me a sort of clever stupidity only to have one sort of talent – almost like a carrier-pigeon.
GEORGE ELIOT (1819–1880) *Mill on the Floss*

2

1 In sober truth, whatever homage may be professed, or even paid, to real or supposed mental superiority, the general tendency of things throughout the world is to render mediocrity the ascendant power among mankind.
JOHN STUART MILL (1806–1873) *An Essay on Human Understanding*

2 ... it is undeniable that a gift for mathematics is one of the most specialised talents and that mathematicians as a class are not particularly distinguished for general ability or versatility.
G.H. HARDY *A Mathematician's Apology*, 1940

3 Natural abilities are like natural plants, that need priming by study.
FRANCIS BACON (1561–1626) *Essays*

4 Man's capacities have never been measured, nor are we to judge of what he can do by any precedents, so little has been tried.
H.D. THOREAU (1817–1862) *Walden*

5 No one knows what he can do till he tries.
PUBLILIUS SYRUS (c. 50 BC) *Sententiae*

6 As we advance in life we learn the limits of our abilities.
J.A. FROUDE (1818–1894) *Short Studies: Education*

7 The superior man is distressed by his want of ability.
CONFUCIUS (c. 551–c. 478 BC) *Analects*

ACCIDENTS

8 Accidents occur in the best regulated families.
CHARLES DICKENS (1812–1870) *David Copperfield*

9 The driver who is steady, conscientious and alert, who is able to orient himself to the total environment in which he operates, rather than just the immediate task, may be the one to whom virtually all accidents are preventable.
W.N. McBAIN *Journal of Applied Psychology*, 1970

10 Accidents, try to change them – it's impossible. The accidental reveals the man.
PABLO PICASSO (1881–1973) interview, *Vogue*, November 1956

11 My only solution for the problem of habitual accidents ... is to stay in bed all day. Even then, there is always the chance that you will fall out.
ROBERT BENCHLEY (1889–1945) *Chips off the Old Benchley*

12 Accident, n. An inevitable occurrence due to the action of immutable natural laws.
AMBROSE BIERCE (1842–1914) *Devil's Dictionary*

13 now and then
there is a person born
who is so unlucky
that he runs into accidents
which started out to happen
to somebody else
don marquis (1878–1937) 'archy says'

ACHIEVEMENT

14 Man, unlike any other thing organic or inorganic in the universe, grows beyond his work, walks up the stairs of his concepts, emerges ahead of his accomplishments.
JOHN STEINBECK (1902–1968) *The Grapes of Wrath*

15 That low man seeks a little thing to do
Sees and does it:
This high man, with a great thing to pursue
Dies ere he knows it.
ROBERT BROWNING (1812–1889) *A Grammarian's Funeral*

16 People are beginning to see that the first requisite to success in life is to be a good animal.
HERBERT SPENCER *Education*, 1861

1 University wasn't quite what I expected. I thought people would be brainier than they were. But instead of intellectuals, it was just those who had done the most homework at school.
ALAN DAVIES, interview, *The Guardian*, 19 August 1997

2 The trouble with the rat race is, even if you win, you are still a rat.
CHER *The Independent*, 21 December 1996

3 There is always time for failure.
JOHN MORTIMER *Clinging to the Wreckage*, 1982

4 It is not the clear-sighted who rule the world. Great achievements are accomplished in a blessed, warm mental fog.
JOSEPH CONRAD (1857–1924) *Victory*

5 By their fruits ye shall know them.
Bible, Matthew

ACTION

6 A cultural psychology, almost by definition, will not be preoccupied with 'behavior' but with 'action', its intentionally based counterpart, and more specifically with situated action – action situated in a cultural setting, and in the mutually interacting intentional states of the participants.
J.S. BRUNER *Acts of Meaning*, 1990

7 In no case may we interpret an action as the outcome of the exercise of a higher psychic faculty, if it can be interpreted as the outcome of the exercise of one which stands lower in the psychological scale.
C. LLOYD MORGAN *An Introduction to Comparative Psychology*, 1894

8 That Action is best, which procures the greatest Happiness for the greatest number.
FRANCIS HUTCHESON (1694–1746) *Inquiry into the Original of an Idea of Beauty and Virtue*

9 There are degrees of attraction and degrees of reasonableness of an action; but seldom, if ever, is an action dictated other than by emotion or reason alone. The more attractive a course of action, the more effortless will it be because the emotional impetus, springing uncalled from the intuitive appraisal, carries us into action.
M.B. ARNOLD *Emotion and Personality*, 1960

10 Our nature consists in movement; absolute rest is death.
BLAISE PASCAL (1623–1662) *Pensées*

11 Suit the action to the word.
WILLIAM SHAKESPEARE (1564–1616) *Hamlet*

12 The quality of life is determined by its activities.
ARISTOTLE (384–322 BC) *Nicomachean Ethics*

13 The act is a *whole* and is stimulated or inhibited as a whole.
GRACE de LAGUNA *Speech, Its Function and Development*, 1927

14 Action is consolatory. It is the enemy of thought and the friend of flattering illusions.
JOSEPH CONRAD (1857–1924) *Nostromo*

15 Every action of every living creature involves some trial and error, and for any trial to be new, it must be in some degree random. Even if the new action is only a member of some well-explored *class* of actions, it must still, by its very newness, become in some measure a validation or exploration of the proposition 'this is the way to do it'.
GREGORY BATESON *Mind and Nature*, 1979

16 Objects are known only through the subject, while the subject can know himself or herself only by acting on objects materially and mentally.
JEAN PIAGET *American Psychologist*, 1978

17 The test of any man lies in action.
PINDAR (518–438 BC) *Odes*

18 From the moment of birth we are immersed in action, and can only fitfully guide it by taking thought.
A.N. WHITEHEAD (1861–1941) *Science and the Modern World*

4

1 Not always actions show the man: we find
Who does a kindness is not therefore kind.
ALEXANDER POPE (1688–1744) *Moral Essays*

2 To know is easy, to act is difficult.
CHINESE PROVERB

3 The great end of life is not knowledge, but action.
T.H. HUXLEY (1825–1895) *Technical Education*

4 I acted and my action made me wise.
THOM GUNN 'Fighting terms', 1954

5 Never confuse movement with action.
ERNEST HEMINGWAY (1899–1961)
cit. A.E. Hotchner *Papa Hemingway*, 1966

ADAPTATION

6 Adaptations are generally those features of plants and animals that astonish and delight us and lead us to exclaim at the intricate cleverness of nature ... we make the often unthinking assumption that these adaptations are 'for something', that they have goals, that they are end-directed.
HENRY PLOTKIN *The Nature of Knowledge*, 1994

7 The human way of life maximises adaptation through awareness and choice, and these abilities depend on human biology.
S.L. WASHBURN in J.D. Roslansky *Uniqueness of Man*, 1969

8 ... we may conclude that those who cannot change their system when occasion requires it will no doubt continue prosperous as long as they glide with the stream of fortune; but when that turns against them they are ruined, from not being able to follow that blind goddess through all her variations.
NICCOLÒ MACHIAVELLI (1469–1527) *The Prince*

9 My own belief is that man has the capacity as well as the desire to develop his potentialities and become a decent human being.... I believe that man can change and go on changing as long as he lives. And this belief has grown deeper with understanding.
KAREN HORNEY *Our Inner Conflicts*, 1945

10 If we want things to stay as they are, things will have to change.
GIUSEPPE DI LAMPEDUSA (1896–1957) *The Leopard*

11 Man is a pliable animal, a being who gets accustomed to everything.
FEODOR DOSTOYEVSKY (1821–1881) *The House of the Dead*

12 We are shaping the world faster than we can change ourselves, and we are applying to the present the habits of the past.
WINSTON CHURCHILL (1874–1965) cit. J. Walsh *Time*, July 1993

13 ... all adaptation is knowledge.
HENRY PLOTKIN *The Nature of Knowledge*, 1994

14 New truth is always a go-between, a smoother-over of transitions.
WILLIAM JAMES *Pragmatism*, 1908

15 The sloth is as much at a loss to proceed on his journey across a smooth and level floor, as a man would be who had to walk a mile in stilts upon a line of feather beds.
CHARLES WATERTON *Wanderings in South America*, 1825

16 Adaptations to real-life situations, such as performance in school classrooms, require more than cognitive abilities.
SANDRA SCARR *American Psychologist*, 1981

17 Thus if we enquire into the state of all dumb creatures, we shall find those fare best that are left to nature's conduct.
DESIDERIUS ERASMUS (1466–1536) *The Praise of Folly*

1 What constitutes adaptive thought behavior in one culture is not necessarily adaptive in another culture. Moreover, thoughts and actions that would shape behavior in appropriate ways in one context might not shape them in appropriate ways in another context.
R.J. STERNBERG *Metaphors of Mind*, 1990

2 If I am doing mathematical logic, I take great pains to work within one of these logical systems which are believed to be foolproof. On the other hand, as a working mathematician, I behave quite differently in everyday life.
MARVIN MINSKY *The New Yorker*, December 1981

3 Our body is a machine for living. It is organised for that, it is its nature.
LEO TOLSTOY (1828–1910) *War and Peace*

ADDICTION

4 Every form of addiction is bad, no matter whether the narcotic be alcohol or morphine or idealism.
CARL JUNG (1875–1961) *Memories, Dreams and Reflections*

5 In a consumer society there are inevitably two kinds of slaves: the prisoners of addiction and the prisoners of envy.
IVAN ILLICH *Tools for Conviviality*, 1973

6 All sin tends to be addictive, and the terminal point of addiction is what is called damnation.
W.H. AUDEN (1907–1973) *A Certain World*

ADOLESCENCE

7 To some extent behavior symptomatic for the marginal man can be found in the adolescent. He too is oversensitive, easily shifted from one extreme to the other, and particularly sensitive to the shortcomings of his younger fellows. Indeed, his position is sociologically the same as that of the marginal man; he does not wish to belong any longer to a group which is, after all, less privileged than the group of adults, but at the same time he knows that he is not fully accepted by the adults.
KURT LEWIN *American Journal of Sociology*, 1939

8 I would there were no age between sixteen and three-and-twenty, or that youth would sleep out the rest, for there is nothing in the between but getting wenches with child, wronging the ancientry, stealing, fighting.
WILLIAM SHAKESPEARE (1564–1616) *The Winter's Tale*

9 A major problem in our postindustrial society is the existence of an alienated, infantilized, and disliked group of citizens called adolescents.
I.A. HYMAN *American Psychologist*, 1979

10 The imagination of a boy is healthy, and the mature imagination of a man is healthy; but there is a slice of life between in which the soul is in a ferment, the character undecided, the way of life uncertain, the ambition thicksighted: thence proceeds mawkishness.
JOHN KEATS (1795–1821) Preface to *Endymion*

11 Adolescence is the peak period of private and public self-consciousness and of social anxiety.
A.H. BUSS *Self-Consciousness and Social Anxiety*, 1980

12 One thing that must be recognized at the start by those who explore in this area of psychology is that fact that the adolescent boy or girl does not want to be understood.
D.W. WINNICOTT *The Family and Individual Development*, 1965

13 The adolescent is coping with problems of identity, autonomy, and sexuality.
LOIS W. HOFFMAN *American Psychologist*, 1979

6

1 I have read somewhere that children from twelve to fourteen years of age – that is, in the transition stage from childhood to adolescence – are singularly inclined to arson and even murder. As I look back upon my boyhood ... I can quite appreciate the possibility of the most frightful crime being committed without object or intent to injure but just because – out of curiosity, or to satisfy an unconscious craving for action.
LEO TOLSTOY (1828–1910) *Childhood, Boyhood, Youth*

2 The children of indomitable progressives are often puzzled in adolescence how to assert their individuality.
NOEL ANNAN *Times Literary Supplement*, 11 March 1983

ADVERSITY

3 Adversity reminds men of religion.
LIVY (59 BC–17 AD) *History of Rome*

4 Sweet are the uses of adversity,
Which, like the toad, ugly and
    venomous,
Wears yet a precious jewel in his head.
WILLIAM SHAKESPEARE (1564–1616) *As You Like It*

5 By trying we can easily learn to endure adversity. Another man's, I mean.
MARK TWAIN (1835–1910) *Following the Equator*

6 Great men rejoice in adversity just as brave soldiers triumph in war.
SENECA (4 BC–65 AD) *De Providentia*

7 The greatest object in the universe, says a certain philosopher, is a good man struggling with adversity: yet there is a still greater, which is the good man that comes to relieve it.
OLIVER GOLDSMITH (1730–1774) *The Vicar of Wakefield*

AFFECTION

8 Most people would rather get than give affection.
ARISTOTLE (384–322 BC) *Nicomachean Ethics*

9 Affection is created by habit, community of interests, convenience and the desire of companionship. It is a comfort rather than an exhilaration.
SOMERSET MAUGHAM (1874–1965) *The Summing Up*

10 Human nature is so constructed that it gives affection most readily to those who seem least to demand it.
BERTRAND RUSSELL (1872–1970) *The Conquest of Happiness*

11 A mixture of admiration and pity is one of the surest recipes for affection.
ANDRÉ MAUROIS (1885–1967) *Ariel*

12 Affection is a coal that must be
    cool'd
Else, suffer'd, it will set the heart on
    fire.
WILLIAM SHAKESPEARE (1564–1616) 'Venus and Adonis'

13 Affection is the mortal illness of lonely people.
GARY INDIANA *Crazy Horse*, 1989

AGE AND AGEING

14 There is more felicity on the far side of baldness than young men can possibly imagine.
LOGAN PEARSALL SMITH (1865–1946) *Afterthoughts*

15 No pleasure is worth giving up for the sake of two more years in a geriatric home in Weston-super-Mare.
KINGSLEY AMIS *The Times*, 21 June 1994

16 But at my back I always hear
Time's winged chariot drawing near.
And yonder all before us lie
Deserts of vast eternity.
ANDREW MARVELL (1621–1678) 'To His Coy Mistress'

1 Age will not be defied.
FRANCIS BACON (1561–1626) *Essays*

2 I recently turned sixty. Practically a third of my life is over.
WOODY ALLEN *The Observer*, 10 March 1996

3 'Seven years and seven months!,' Humpty Dumpty repeated thoughtfully. 'An uncomfortable sort of age. Now if you'd asked *my* advice, I'd have said, "Leave off at seven" – but it's too late now.'
'I never ask advice about growing', Alice said indignantly.
'Too proud?' the other enquired.
Alice felt even more indignant at this suggestion. 'I mean,' she said, 'that one can't help growing older.'
LEWIS CARROLL (1832–1898) *Alice Through the Looking Glass*

4 The young feel tired at the end of an action –
The old, at the beginning.
T.S. ELIOT (1888–1965) *The Family Reunion*

5 Jane will be quite an old maid soon, I declare. She is almost three and twenty! Lord, how ashamed I should be of not being married before three and twenty!
JANE AUSTEN (1775–1817) *Pride and Prejudice*

6 Your old men shall dream dreams, your young men shall see visions.
Bible, Joel

7 When I was young I was told, 'You'll see, when you're fifty'. I am fifty and I haven't seen a thing.
ERIK SATIE cit. Pierre-Daniel Templier, *Erik Satie*, 1969

8 Do not try to live forever. You will not succeed.
GEORGE BERNARD SHAW (1856–1950) *The Doctor's Dilemma*

9 If youth knew; if age could.
HENRI ESTIENNE (1531–1598) *Les Premices*

10 So year by year your tense unfinished faces
Sink further from the light. No one pretends
To want to help you now. For interest passes
Always towards the young and more insistent.
PHILIP LARKIN (1922–1985) 'Neurotics'

11 Time carries all things, even our wits, away.
VIRGIL (70–19 BC) *Eclogues*

12 I was twenty-five and too old to be unusual.
JAMES D. WATSON *The Double Helix*, 1968

13 Become old early if you would be old long.
PROVERB

14 At fifty, one can no longer love.
NAPOLEON BONAPARTE (1769–1821) *The St. Helena Journal*, 7 April 1817

15 The stethoscope tells what everyone fears
You're likely to go on living for years
With a nurse-maid waddle and a shop-girl simper
And the style of your prose growing limper and limper.
THEODORE ROETHKE (1908–1963) 'Academic'

16 Senescence begins
And middle age ends
The day your descendants
Outnumber your friends.
OGDEN NASH (1902–1971) 'Crossing the Border'

17 Cognitive ageing is endlessly fascinating because it continually demands abandonment or radical revision of mainstream models in order to provide plausible functional explanations for change and individual differences.
PAT RABBITT *The Psychologist*, 1999

18 Grow old along with me!
The best is yet to be,
The last of life, for which the first was made:
Our times are in his hand
Who saith, 'A whole I planned,
Youth shows but half; trust God: see all, nor be afraid'!
ROBERT BROWNING (1812–1889) 'Rabbi Ben Ezra'

1 That age is best which is the first,
When youth and blood are warmer;
But being spent, the worse and worst
Times still succeed the former.
ROBERT HERRICK (1591–1674) 'To the
Virgins, To Make Much of Time'

2 I am not really conscious of a decline
in my mental energy. But I have
intimations that my thoughts move in
the old grooves and do not push out
into new grooves, and that my ways of
expression are becoming stereotyped.
HAROLD NICOLSON *Diaries*, 31 December
1949

3 What is passable in youth, is
detestable in later age.
JANE AUSTEN (1775–1817) *Emma*

4 All of us who are lucky must put up
with ageing as best we can, but to do
anything useful about it we must
recognise and understand all of the
extraordinarily unpleasant things that it
does to us and the ways in which these
contract the scope of our lives.
PAT RABBITT *The Psychologist*, 1999

AGGRESSION

5 The tendency to aggression is an
innate, independent, instinctual
disposition in man.
SIGMUND FREUD (1856–1939) *Civilisation
and its Discontents*

6 There is every reason to think that
hereditary influences must operate to
modify the operations of either the
centres that increase or those that
decrease the tendencies that we call
'aggression'.
J.Z. YOUNG *An Introduction to the Study of
Man*, 1971

7 There is not one single kind of
behavior which can be called
'aggressive' nor is there any single
process which represents 'aggression'.
R.N. JOHNSON *Aggression in Man and
Animals*, 1972

8 ... aggression, far from being the
diabolical, destructive principle that
classical psychoanalysis makes it out to
be, is really an essential part of the life-
preserving organization of instincts.
KONRAD LORENZ *On Aggression*, 1963

9 Aggression, like every other part of
human behavior we take for granted, is
a challenging engineering problem!
STEVEN PINKER *How the Mind Works*, 1997

10 The very emphasis of the
Commandment: Thou shalt not kill,
makes it certain that we are descended
from an endlessly long chain of
generations of murderers whose love of
murder was in their blood as it is
perhaps also in our own.
SIGMUND FREUD (1856–1939) *Reflections on
War and Death*

11 Curiously enough, appeasement
gestures have evolved in a large variety
of animals under the selective pressure
exerted by behaviour patterns releasing
aggression. In trying to appease a
member of its species, the animal does
everything to avoid aggression.
KONRAD LORENZ *On Aggression*, 1963

ALCOHOL

12 Alcohol is a very necessary
article.... It makes life bearable to
millions of people who could not endure
their existence if they were quite sober.
It enables Parliament to do things at
eleven at night that no sane person
would do at eleven in the morning.
GEORGE BERNARD SHAW (1856–1950) *Major
Barbara*

13 Love makes the world go round?
Not at all. Whisky makes it go round
twice as fast.
COMPTON MACKENZIE (1883–1972) *Whisky
Galore*

14 My first masters taught me this
habit, for breakfast, they said, gave a
man a good mind. So they started the
day by drinking.
FRANÇOIS RABELAIS (1494–1553) *Gargantua*

1 Drink, sir, is a great provoker of three things ... nose painting, sleep and wine. Lechery, sir, it provokes, and unprovokes; it provokes the desire, but it takes away the performance.
WILLIAM SHAKESPEARE (1564–1616) *Macbeth*

2 Man, being reasonable, must get drunk;
The best of life is but intoxication.
LORD BYRON (1788–1824) *Don Juan*

3 We drink one another's healths, and spoil our own.
JEROME K. JEROME (1859–1927) *Idle Thoughts of an Idle Fellow*

4 Though I personally favor both alcohol and neurologizing, in moderation, the point here does not assume that either is a good thing.
D.O. HEBB *Psychological Review*, 1955

5 Abstinence is the thin end of the pledge.
ANON.

6 Drunkenness is simply voluntary insanity.
SENECA (4 BC–65 AD) *Moral Epistles to Lucilius*

7 The sway of alcohol over mankind is unquestionably due to its power to stimulate the mystical faculties of human nature.
WILLIAM JAMES *Varieties of Religious Experience*, 1902

8 I feel quite sure that drunkenness must be placed among the factors in the production of idiocy.
J. LANGDON DOWN *Mental Afflictions of Childhood and Youth*, 1887

ALIENATION

9 Although alienation ultimately affects the individual, it has its roots in the institutions of the society and among these institutions the family plays a particularly critical role.
URIE BRONFENBRENNER *Scientific American*, 1974

10 School prepares for the alienating institutionalization of life by teaching the need to be taught. Once this lesson is learned, people lose their incentive to grow in independence; they no longer find relatedness attractive, and close themselves off to the surprises which life offers.
IVAN ILLICH *Deschooling Society*, 1971

11 Everyone is quick to blame the alien.
AESCHYLUS (525–456 BC) *The Suppliants*

12 My need for sympathy has often induced me to seek it from people who, instead of strengthening me, unnerved me.
VINCENT VAN GOGH (1853–1890) *Dear Theo*

13 The evil and cure lie not in the victims of alienation but in the social institutions that produce alienation, and their failure to be responsive to the most human needs and values of a democratic society.
URIE BRONFENBRENNER *Scientific American*, 1974

14 The man who regards his own life and that of his fellow-creatures as meaningless is not merely unfortunate but almost disqualified for life.
ALBERT EINSTEIN *The World as I See It*, 1934

15 ... the alienation of children and youth and its destructive developmental sequelae reflect a breakdown of the interconnections among the various segments of the child's life – family, school, peer group, neighbourhood....
URIE BRONFENBRENNER *American Psychologist*, 1979

ALTRUISM

16 ... but self-sacrifice in *itself* is not of value. It is of value only if it is important for the actualisation of the individual; it is of value only if the rescue of others is of such importance to the individual that his own self-realization demands this sacrifice.
KURT GOLDSTEIN *Human Nature in the Light of Psychopathology*, 1940

1 The 'altruist' expects reciprocation from society for himself or his closest relatives.
E.O. WILSON *On Human Nature*, 1978

2 Self-sacrifice enables us to sacrifice other people without blushing.
GEORGE BERNARD SHAW (1856–1950) *Man and Superman*

3 Self-preservation, nature's first great law.
ANDREW MARVELL (1621–1678) 'Hodge's Vision from the Monument'

4 It is evident that the ordinary social life of well meaning persons is a tissue of altruistic actions.... In every aspect of social life civilized behaviour is exhibited by the caring for others.
JOHN ECCLES *The Human Psyche*, 1980

5 The parent who conveys his values to the child didactically as tidy principles, and no more, accomplishes only that learning in the child. Generalised altruism would appear to be best learned from parents who do not only try to inculcate the principles of altruism, but who also manifest altruism in everyday interactions.
M.R. YARROW *et al. Developmental Psychology*, 1973

6 Guilt, self-destruction, sexual strivings, and conflict about homosexuality are the fundamental forces underlying generosity and altruism.
SIGMUND FREUD (1856–1939) *Group Psychology and the Analysis of the Ego*

7 'Soft-core' altruism ... is ultimately selfish.... Its psychological vehicles are lying, pretense, and deceit, including self-deceit, because the actor is most convincing who believes that his performance is real.
E.O. WILSON *On Human Nature*, 1978

8 'Tis also pleasant to be deemed magnanimous
The more so in achieving our own ends.
LORD BYRON (1788–1824) *Don Juan*

9 Much as we might wish to believe otherwise, universal love and the welfare of the species as a whole are concepts which simply do not make evolutionary sense.
RICHARD DAWKINS *The Selfish Gene*, 1976

10 I do nobody harm, I say none harm, I think none harm, but wish everybody good. And if this be not enough to keep a man alive, in good faith I long not to live.
THOMAS MORE (1478–1535) letter to his daughter, Margaret Roper, May 1535, cit. W. Roper *A Man of Singular Virtue*, 1626

11 I'd lay down my life for two brothers or eight cousins.
J.B.S. HALDANE *New Scientist*, 8 September 1974

12 He who would do good must do it in Minute Particulars.
General Good is the plea of the scoundrel, hypocrite and flatterer.
WILLIAM BLAKE (1757–1827) 'Jerusalem'

13 Greater love hath no man than this: that a man lay down his life for his friends.
Bible, John

14 Greater love hath no man than this: that he lay down his friends for his life.
JEREMY THORPE, said about Prime Minister Macmillan's Cabinet reshuffle, 13 July 1962, cit. S. Freeman, B. Penrose *Rinkagate*, 1996

AMBITION

15 ... thou wouldst be great,
Art not without ambition, but without
The illness should attend it.
WILLIAM SHAKESPEARE (1564–1616) *Macbeth*

16 Ambition
Is like the sea wave, which the more you drink
The more you thirst – yea – drink too much, as men
Have done on rafts of wreck – it drives you mad.
ALFRED, LORD TENNYSON (1808–1892) *The Cup*

17 Such joy ambition finds.
JOHN MILTON (1608–1674) *Paradise Lost*

1 Ambition has its disappointments to sour us, but never the good fortune to satisfy us.
BENJAMIN FRANKLIN (1706–1790) *On True Happiness*

2 All ambitions are lawful except those which climb upward on the miseries or credulities of mankind.
JOSEPH CONRAD (1857–1924) *A Personal Record*

3 Ambition, in a private man a vice,
Is, in a prince, the virtue.
PHILIP MASSINGER (1583–1640) *The Bashful Lover*

4 My ambition is enormous but vague. I am too disinterested in my activities ever to achieve distinction.
W.N.P. BARBELLION *The Journal of a Disappointed Man*, 1919

5 Ambition can creep as well as soar.
EDMUND BURKE (1729–1797) *Letters on a Regicide Peace*

ANALOGIES

6 Analogies decide nothing, that is true, but they can make one feel more at home.
SIGMUND FREUD (1856–1939) *New Introductory Lectures on Psychoanalysis*

7 Analogies are useful but limited: they may reflect common constraints, but not common causes.
STEPHEN J. GOULD *The Mismeasure of Man*, 1981

ANGER

8 A soft answer turneth away wrath.
Bible, Proverbs

9 The greatest remedy for anger is delay.
SENECA (4 BC–65 AD) *De Ira*

10 Anger is never without argument, but seldom with a good one.
GEORGE SAVILE, MARQUESS OF HALIFAX (1633–1695) *Of Anger*

11 He that is slow to anger is better than the mighty.
Bible, Proverbs

12   Anger is like
A full-hot horse, who being allowed his way,
Self-mettle tires him.
WILLIAM SHAKESPEARE (1564–1616) *Henry VIII*

13 Anger is momentary madness.
HORACE (65–8 BC) *Epistles*

14 Anybody can become angry – that is easy; but to be angry with the right person, and to the right degree, and at the right time, and for the right purpose, and in the right way – that is not within everybody's power and is not easy.
ARISTOTLE (384–322 BC) *Nicomachaen Ethics*

ANIMALS AND MAN

15 There is clearly some sense in which human action and society are related to animals, for we have a long animal social past, our bodies and minds are the outcome of evolution and we are in fact animals, not vegetables or gods.
VERNON REYNOLDS *The Biology of Human Action*, 1980

16 Among the multitude of animals which scamper, fly, burrow and swim around us, man is the only one who is not locked into his environment. His imagination, his reason, his emotional subtlety and toughness make it possible for him not to accept the environment but to change it.
J. BRONOWSKI *The Ascent of Man*, BBC TV 1975

1 There are one hundred and ninety-three living species of monkeys and apes. One hundred and ninety-two of them are covered with hair. The exception is a naked ape self-named *Homo sapiens*.
DESMOND MORRIS *The Naked Ape*, 1967

2 Animals lack cruelty, but they also lack mercy.
ROSEMARY DINNAGE *The Observer*, 25 April 1979

3 I trust that I shall not be thought rash if I express a belief that experiments on the higher nervous activities of animals will yield not a few directional indications for education and self-education in man.
IVAN PAVLOV *Lectures on Conditioned Reflexes*, 1928

4 With every passing year chimpanzees seem to become more able. There is every reason to believe that this rise in ability will persist, not because the IQs of chimpanzees are rising but rather because experimenters are becoming more clever, and methods for training performances are undergoing continuing refinement.
HOWARD GARDNER *Artful Scribbles*, 1980

5 God makes the animals, man makes himself.
G.C. LICHTENBERG (1742–1799) *Aphorisms*

6 The behaviour and mental life of people, the proper subject matter of psychology, is far too complex to be understood in the impoverished terms suitable for understanding the behaviour of rats and pigeons in a small number of highly contrived and artificial situations.
N.J. MACKINTOSH *Quarterly Journal of Experimental Psychology*, 1997

7 Human behavior differs from animal behavior in the same qualitative manner as the entire type of adaptability and historical development of man differs from the adaptability and development of animals, because the process of man's mental development is part of the general historic development of mankind.
L.S. VYGOTSKY *Psychological Research in the USSR, Vol. I*, 1966

8 When you see the sign 'African Primates Meeting' you expect someone to produce bananas.
DESMOND TUTU *Daily Telegraph*, 24 June 1996

9 Cats and monkeys – monkeys and cats – all human life is there.
HENRY JAMES (1843–1916) *The Madonna of the Future*

10 Drinking when we are not thirsty and making love all the year round, madam; that is all there is to distinguish us from other animals.
PIERRE BEAUMARCHAIS (1732–1799) *The Marriage of Figaro*

11 Animals, whom we have made our slaves, we do not like to consider our equal.
CHARLES DARWIN (1809–1882) *Notebook B, 1837–1838*

12 The animal kingdom exhibits a series of mental developments which may be regarded as antecedents to the mental development of man, for the mental life of animals shows itself to be throughout, in its elements and in the general laws governing the combination of the elements, the same as the mental life of man.
WILHELM WUNDT *Outline of Psychology*, 1902

13 The statements of enthusiasts who discover consciousness and resemblance to man on every side should not be too readily accepted.
JACQUES LOEB *Comparative Physiology of the Brain and Comparative Psychology*, 1905

14 ... in so far as we are animals our business is at all costs to survive.
ALDOUS HUXLEY (1894–1963) *The Doors of Perception*

1 The basic structure of man's behavioural equipment resembles that of infra-human species but has in the course of evolution undergone special modifications that permit the same ends to be reached by a much greater diversity of means.
JOHN BOWLBY *Attachment and Loss, Vol. 1: Attachment*, 1969

2 The animals other than man live by appearance and memories and have little connected experience; but the human race lives also by art and reasonings.
ARISTOTLE (384–322 BC) *Metaphysics*

3 Human beings should regard it as an honour to be classed as political animals.
FRANS de WAAL *Chimpanzee Politics: Power and Sex and Apes*, 1982

4 The main difference between man and animal is man's ability to laugh.
PETER USTINOV *Quotable Ustinov*, 1995

5 The lack of language habits forever differentiates brute from man.
J.B. WATSON *Behaviorism*, 1924

6 Man is the only one that knows nothing, that can learn nothing without being taught. He can neither speak nor walk nor eat, and in short he can do nothing at the prompting of nature only, but weep.
PLINY THE ELDER (23–79) *Natural History*

7 Nothing can be more obvious than that all animals were created solely and exclusively for the use of man.
THOMAS LOVE PEACOCK (1785–1866) *Headlong Hall*

8 When not waiting, insects wander aimlessly. And yet, strangely enough, this aimless wandering is always an indirect way to something important. It is by aimless wandering that an insect efficiently covers vast quarters of space to find food, or a mate, or a place to lay eggs. People, by contrast, generally move directly from one place to another, usually to do something unimportant.
V.G. DETHIER *To Know a Fly*, 1962

9 I have known very many dogs and can say with firm conviction that all of all creatures the one nearest to man in the fineness of its perceptions and in its capacity to render true friendship, is a bitch. Strange that in English her name has become a term of abuse.
KONRAD LORENZ *Man Meets Dog*, 1954

ANXIETY

10 [Anxiety] represents an emotional state that does not refer to anything definite ... the source of anxiety is nothing and nowhere. Anxiety deals with nothingness. It is the inner experience of being faced with nothingness.
KURT GOLDSTEIN *Human Nature in the Light of Psychopathology*, 1940

11 Anxiety, defined as the anticipation of painfully intense stimuli, appears to exercise an important influence in actually shaping human and infrahuman behavior alike.
H.O. MOWRER *Psychological Review*, 1939

12 The distinctive quality of human anxiety arises from the fact that man is a valuing animal, who interprets his life and world in terms of symbols and meanings.
ROLLO MAY *The Meaning of Anxiety*, 1950

13 Whatever else anxiety is, it is undoubtedly an emotion; sometimes, reading the work of psychologists, one is tempted to think that it is the only emotion.
J.A. GRAY *The Neuropsychology of Anxiety*, 1982

14 Anxiety (or dread) itself needs no description; everyone has personally experienced this sensation or to speak more correctly this affective condition, at some time or other.
SIGMUND FREUD (1856–1939) *A General Introduction to Psychoanalysis*

15 Anxiety (fear) is the conditioned form of the pain reaction....
H.O. MOWRER *Psychological Review*, 1939

1 When anxiety besets groups or nations, it may force individuals into very strange situations and lead them to renounce reason and freedom to a degree that seems unbelievable to the objective observer.
KURT GOLDSTEIN *Human Nature in the Light of Psychopathology*, 1940

2 Our whole life is taken up with anxiety for personal security, with preparations for living, so that we really never live at all.
LEO TOLSTOY (1828–1910) *My Religion*

3 Just as the capacity for physical pain has evolved to protect us from immediate and future tissue damage, the capacity for anxiety has evolved to protect us from future dangers and other kinds of threats.
R.M. NESSE, G.C. WILLIAMS *Evolution and Healing*, 1995

4 When you're lying awake with a dismal headache, and repose is taboo'd by anxiety,
I conceive you may use any language you choose to indulge in without impropriety.
W.S. GILBERT (1836–1911) *Iolanthe*

APPEARANCES

5 It is only shallow people who do not judge by appearances.
OSCAR WILDE (1854–1900) *Picture of Dorian Gray*

6 Underneath this flabby exterior is an enormous lack of character.
OSCAR LEVANT *Memoirs of an Amnesiac*, 1965

7 A businessman is the only one who always seeks to make it appear, when he attains the object of his labours, ie. the making of a great deal of money, that it was not really the object of his labours.
H.L. MENCKEN (1880–1956) *Smart Set*

8 No power on earth, however, can abolish the merciless class distinction between those who are physically desirable and the lonely, pallid, spotted silent, unfancied majority.
JOHN MORTIMER *Clinging to the Wreckage*, 1982

9 Love and pregnancy and riding upon a camel cannot be hid.
ARABIAN PROVERB

10 I am resolved to grow fat and look young till forty, and then slip out of the world with the first wrinkle and the reputation of five and twenty.
JOHN DRYDEN (1631–1700) *The Maiden Queen*

11 The dancing child is always a very different person from her everyday self.... One is continually fooled by the depths of sophistication in the dancing of some pensive, dull child, or the lazy grace of some noisy little hoodlum.
MARGARET MEAD *Coming of Age in Samoa*, 1928

12 This Englishwoman is so refined She has no bosom and no behind.
STEVIE SMITH (1902–1971) 'This Englishwoman'

13 We dont bother much about dress and manners in England, because as a nation we dont dress well and we've no manners.
GEORGE BERNARD SHAW (1856–1950) *You Never Can Tell*

14 Men seldom make passes At girls who wear glasses.
DOROTHY PARKER (1893–1967) 'News Item'

15 Most women are not as young as they are painted.
MAX BEERBOHM (1872–1956) *The Yellow Book*

16 The man whose habitual expression is supercilious, or distrustful, or apologetic, is making a statement of belief about himself in relation to other people though he may not hold the belief in verbal form.
D.W. HARDING *Experience into Words*, 1963

1 Nowher so besy a man as he ther
n'as
And yet he seemed besier than he was.
GEOFFREY CHAUCER (1340–1400)
Canterbury Tales

2 There is no trusting appearances.
RICHARD BRINSLEY SHERIDAN (1751–1816)
The School for Scandal

3 ... they [the Anemolians] were set out
with all those things, that among the
Utopians were either the badges of
slavery, the marks of infamy, or
children's rattles ... that though they
[the Utopians] paid some reverence to
those that were the most meanly clad ...
yet when they saw the ambassadors,
themselves so full of gold chains, they
looking upon them as slaves, made
them no reverence at all.
THOMAS MORE (1478–1535) *Utopia*

4 Men should be what they seem.
WILLIAM SHAKESPEARE (1564–1616) *Othello*

5 He was careful of his appearance
altogether, and carried a razor and boot-
brush that he would not sell, though he
had sold his 'papers' and even his
pocket knife long since. Nevertheless,
one would have known him for a tramp
a hundred yards away. There was
something in his drifting style of walk,
and the way he had of hunching his
shoulders forwards, essentially abject.
GEORGE ORWELL (1903–1950) *Down and
Out in Paris and London*

6 Appearances are not held to be a
clue to the truth. But we seem to have
no other.
IVY COMPTON-BURNETT *Manservant and
Maidservant*, 1947

7 Twenty years of romance makes a
woman look like a ruin; but twenty
years of marriage make her something
like a public building.
OSCAR WILDE (1854–1900) *A Woman of No
Importance*

8 Men with small foreheads are fickle,
whereas if they are rounded or bulging
out the owners are quick-tempered.

Straight eyebrows indicate softness of
disposition, those that curve out toward
the temples, humour and dissimulation.
The staring eye indicates impudence,
the winking indecision. Large and
outstanding ears indicate a tendency to
irrelevant talk or chattering.
ARISTOTLE (384–322 BC) *Historia Animalium*

9 You look wise. Pray correct that
error.
CHARLES LAMB (1775–1834) *Essays of Elia*

10 To me, fair friend, you never can be
old,
For as you were when first your eye I
ey'd,
Such seems your beauty still.
WILLIAM SHAKESPEARE (1564–1616)
Sonnets

11 Nonsense child! Nature never
makes a ferret in the shape of a mastiff.
You'll never persuade me that I can't tell
what men are by their outsides. If I
don't like a man's looks, depend upon it
I shall never like *him*.
GEORGE ELIOT (1819–1880) *Adam Bede*

APPETITES

12 Doth not the appetite alter? A man
loves the meat in his youth that he
cannot endure in his age.
WILLIAM SHAKESPEARE (1564–1616) *Much
Ado About Nothing*

13 New dishes beget new appetites
THOMAS FULLER (1654–1734) *Gnomologia*

14 Subdue your appetites, my dears,
and you've conquered human nature.
CHARLES DICKENS (1812–1870) *Nicholas
Nickleby*

15 Let the appetite be subject to
reason.
CICERO (106–43 BC) *De Officiis*

APPLYING PSYCHOLOGY

1 I learned that when a science does not usefully apply to practical problems there is something wrong with the theory of the science.
J.J. GIBSON *A History of Psychology in Autobiography, Vol. 5*, 1967

2 Like intelligent discussion or debate, applied research does not necessarily reduce disagreement.
D.K. COHEN, M.S. GARET *Harvard Education Review*, 1975

3 Wherever man is struggling mightily to make something of himself there is a fertile place for the researcher to be.
B. MAHER *Clinical Psychology and Personality: The Selected Papers of George Kelly*, 1969

4 Practical sciences proceed by building up: theoretical sciences by resolving into components.
THOMAS AQUINAS (1225–1274) *Commentary on Ethics*

5 In a practical science, so much depends upon particular circumstances that only general rules can apply.
ARISTOTLE (384–322 BC) *Nicomachean Ethics*

6 In psychology, as in the management of pigs, it is one thing to know the body of principles, the science; it is quite another to possess the art of putting these principles into practice.
WILLIAM GLOVER *Know Your Own Mind*, 1918

7 Egad, I think the interpreter is the hardest to understand of the two!
RICHARD BRINSLEY SHERIDAN (1751–1816) *The Critic*

8 For I have to admit in my case the truth of the charge so often made against British thinkers in general, namely, that their primary and fundamental interest is in questions of practice or conduct and that they derive from this their speculative or theoretical interests.
WILLIAM McDOUGALL *Character and the Conduct of Life*, 1932

9 I happen to believe in applied research because I think it keeps you honest, it keeps you working on things that are important instead of on trivial things.
D. McCLELLAND cit. David Cohen *Psychologists on Psychology*, 1977

ARGUMENT

10 Experimentation must give way to argument, and argument must have recourse to experimentation.
GASTON BACHELARD (1884–1962) *The New Scientific Spirit*

11 Like the best of rows, it moved rapidly from the particular to the general.
IAN McEWAN *Black Dogs*, 1992

12 O yes! give me a handful of generalities and analogies, and I'll undertake to justify Burke and Hare, and prove them benefactors of their species.
GEORGE ELIOT (1819–1880) *Felix Holt*

13 Every man will dispute with great good humour upon a subject in which he is not interested.
SAMUEL JOHNSON (1709–1784) cit. James Boswell *The Life of Samuel Johnson*

14 Never maintain an argument with heat and clamour, though you think or know yourself to be in the right.
LORD CHESTERFIELD, PHILIP STANHOPE (1694–1773) *Letters to His Son*

15 Con was a thorn to brother Pro –
On Pro we often sicked him.
Whatever Pro would claim to know
Old Con would contradict him!
CHRISTOPHER MORLEY (1890–1957) 'The Twins'

1   Heat is in proportion to the want of true knowledge.
LAURENCE STERNE (1713–1768) *Tristram Shandy*

2   Iteration, like friction, is likely to generate heat instead of progress.
GEORGE ELIOT (1819–1880) *Mill on the Floss*

3   He draweth out the thread of his verbosity finer than the staple of his argument.
WILLIAM SHAKESPEARE (1564–1616) *Love's Labour's Lost*

ART

4   The elegant rationality of science and the metaphoric nonrationality of art operate with deeply different grammars; perhaps they even represent a profound complementarity.
J.S. BRUNER *On Knowing: Essays for the Left Hand*, 1962

5   Don't translate my works to those of children…. They are worlds apart…. Never forget the child knows nothing of art…. The artist on the contrary is concerned with formal compositions of his pictures, whose representational meaning comes about with intention, through associations of the unconscious.
PAUL KLEE cit. F. Klee *The Diaries of Paul Klee 1898–1918*, 1968

6   What is essential in a work of art is that it should rise far above the realm of personal life and speak from the spirit and heart of the poet as man to the spirit and heart of mankind.
CARL JUNG (1875–1961) *Modern Man in Search of a Soul*

7   Make figures with such action as may be sufficient to show what the figure has in mind; otherwise your art will not be worthy of praise.
LEONARDO DA VINCI (1452–1519) *The Notebooks of Leonardo da Vinci*

8   As in psychology, so with the visual arts: sophistication seems if anything to have decreased over the years.
L. HUDSON *Bodies of Knowledge*, 1982

9   The artist's first aim is to set himself free and, by communicating his work to other people suffering from the same arrested desires, he offers them the same liberation. He represents his most personal wishful phantasies as fulfilled; but they only become a work of art when they have undergone a transformation which softens what is offensive in them, conceals their personal origin and, by obeying the laws of beauty, bribes other people with a bonus of pleasure.
SIGMUND FREUD (1856–1939) *The Claim of Psychoanalysis to Scientific Interest*

10   Art is … pattern informed by sensibility.
HERBERT READ *The Meaning of Art*, 1955

11   … as we gaze at a painting of a landscape, different aspects of the painter's message are processed by different regions of our brain…. Perhaps different artists could be characterised by their ability to appeal to different parts of our visual system.
M. LIVINGSTONE, D. HUBEL in R.L. Gregory *et al. The Artful Eye*, 1995

12   Painting is a science and should be pursued as an inquiry into the laws of nature. Why, then, may not landscape painting be considered as a branch of natural philosophy, of which pictures are but experiments?
JOHN CONSTABLE (1776–1837) *4th Hampstead Lecture*, 1836

13   Art being a thing of the mind, it follows that any scientific study of art will be psychology. It may be other things as well, but psychology it will always be.
MAX FRIEDLANDER cit. E. Gombrich *Art and Illusion*, 1977

14   Science is about progress, art about change. Science is now better than that of Galileo, but our art is only different from that of Leonardo.
LEWIS WOLPERT *Independent on Sunday*, 23 February 1997

1 The brain's representations are the inspiration and substance of art.
RICHARD GREGORY *The Artful Eye*, 1995

2 Art is man's nature.
EDMUND BURKE (1729–1797) *An Appeal from the New to the Old Whigs*

3 It may well be that one reason humans enjoy art is precisely because it requires this extra interpretive effort. Natural images, with all the rich sources of information which make the perception of object structure unambiguous, are just too easy. We like the intellectual challenge that many forms of art offer.
DAVID PERRET *et al.* in R.L. Gregory *et al.* *The Artful Eye*, 1995

ARTIFICIAL INTELLIGENCE

4 Nor will this seem in any way strange to those who know the different kinds of automata, or moving machines that the industry of man can fabricate. If there were such machines which had the organs and appearance of a monkey or some other animal, we should have no way of recognizing that they were not entirely of the same nature as the animal.
RENÉ DESCARTES (1596–1650) *Discourse on Method*

5 Of course, people differ from computer programs in a number of ways, not the least of which is their considerably greater complexity and range of mental functioning. In using the computational metaphor, these differences may tend to receive rather short shrift.
R.J. STERNBERG *Metaphors of Mind*, 1990

6 In brief, all things are artificial; for Nature is the art of God.
THOMAS BROWNE (1605–1682) *Religio Medici*

7 But I do wish to propound one principle which is, so to speak, a kind of electronic Occam's Razor: We should not invoke any entities or forces to explain mental phenomena if we can achieve an explanation in terms of a possible electronic computer.
M.G. KENDALL *The Review of the International Statistical Institution*, 1966

8 Research on the performance of adaptive systems must take on a taxonomic, and even a sociological aspect. We have a great deal to learn about the variety of strategies, and we should neither disdain nor shirk the painstaking, sometimes pedestrian, tasks of describing that variety.
H.A. SIMON in D. Norman *Perspectives on Cognitive Science*, 1981

9 The question we wanted to ask is this: 'Can a digital computer, as defined, think?'. That is to say: 'Is instantiating or implementing the right computer program with the right inputs and outputs sufficient for, or constitutive of, thinking?'. And to this question the answer is clearly, 'no'.
JOHN SEARLE *Minds, Brains and Science*, 1984

10 These languages [higher-level languages] have a number of interesting peculiarities, beginning with the fact that nobody speaks them.
H. KENNER *The State of the Language*, 1980

11 I conceive likewise, as I have already said, that Art may go so far as to frame an engine, that shall articulate words like those, which I pronounce; but then I conceive the same, that it would only pronounce those, that were design'd it should pronounce, and that it would always pronounce them in the same order.
G. de CORDEMAY *A Philosophical Discourse Concerning Speech*, 1668

12 Computer programming is too useful to cognitive science to be left solely in the hands of the artificial intelligentzia.
P. JOHNSON-LAIRD in D. Norman *Perspectives in Cognitive Science*, 1981

1 So, whether or not mind ever fully enters computers, we should mind out for ourselves and teach them to look after us.
RICHARD GREGORY *Mind in Science*, 1981

2 A machine cannot think any more than a book can remember.
L.S. HEARNSHAW *The Shaping of Modern Psychology*, 1987

3 People's supposed imperfections are there for a reason. It may be possible that in the distant future we will build machines that improve upon what people can do: but machines will have to equal people first, *and I mean equal very very literally.*
R. SCHANK in D. Norman *Perspectives in Cognitive Science*, 1981

4 The fact that 'the mind of the machine' has been featured in *Playboy* suggests that this phrase is so paradoxical as to be positively titillating.
MARGARET BODEN *Artificial Intelligence and Natural Man*, 1977

5 While artificial systems are necessarily explicit in stating the relations between a symbol and its referent, natural systems are not. The gene carries no explicit symbols for the details of the structure that it yields.
M. STUDDERT-KENNEDY, U. BELLUGI *Signed and Spoken Language*, 1980

6 Although machines can perform certain things as well as or perhaps better than any of us can do, they infallibly fall short in others, by the which means we may discover that they did not act from knowledge, but only from the disposition of their organs. For while reason is a universal instrument which can serve all contingencies, these organs have need of some special adaptation for every particular action. From this it follows that it is morally impossible that there should be sufficient diversity in any machine to allow it to act in all events of life in the same way as our reason causes us to act.
RENÉ DESCARTES (1596–1650) *Discourse on Method*

7 If linguistic intelligence is merely the ability to carry out formal operations of a certain complexity, for instance the parsing of sentences or the proof of theorems in a formal system, then it seems clear that linguistic intelligence is a comparatively unimportant part of humanity and that it is shared by inert artifacts like computers. It is rather in the interpretation of formal systems, their application to the world and to our concerns, that we really display the powers of mind, and from this point of view formal systems are simply games we play with and tools we use.
A.J.P. KENNY *The Nature of Mind*, 1972

8 But we should not let our inability to discern a locus of intelligence lead us to conclude that programmed computers therefore cannot think. For it may be so with *man*, as with *machine*....
MARVIN MINSKY *Proceedings of the Institute of Radio Engineers*, 1961

ASPIRATIONS

9 We are all of us in the gutter, but some of us are looking at the stars.
OSCAR WILDE (1854–1900) *Lady Windemere's Fan*

10 Who digs hills because they do aspire,
Throws down one mountain to cast up a higher.
WILLIAM SHAKESPEARE (1564–1616) *Pericles*

11 I'd like to be a queen of people's hearts, in people's hearts, but I don't see myself being Queen of this country.
DIANA, PRINCESS OF WALES, interview, BBC TV, 20 November 1995

12 It is always easier to fight for one's principles than to live up to them.
ALFRED ADLER cit. Phyllis Bottome *Alfred Adler*, 1939

13 The young have aspirations that never come to pass, the old have reminiscences of what never happened.
SAKI (1870–1916) *Reginald at the Carlton*

1 Striving to better, oft we mar what's well.
WILLIAM SHAKESPEARE (1564–1616) *King Lear*

2 Whenever a man does a thoroughly stupid thing, it is always from the noblest of motives.
OSCAR WILDE (1854–1900) *The Picture of Dorian Gray*

ASSESSMENT

3 Psychological assessment is a rational, problem-solving process, guided by principles, theories, and empirically established relationships among personality characteristics and between personality characteristics and test variables.
NORMAN TALLENT *The Practice of Psychological Assessment*, 1992

4 A basic justification for assessment is that it provides information of value to the planning, execution, and evaluation of treatment. It seems self-evident that interventions are more rational, faster, and more effective if based on prior diagnosis of the problem, whether we are talking about repairing a car, the human body, a conflict between nations, or the human problems that bring people into psychotherapy.
S.J. KORCHIN, D. SCHULDBERG *American Psychologist*, 1981

5 It appears that the actual utility of assessment (behavioral and traditional) in planning and conducting treatment programs is unclear and has not been empirically demonstrated....
A.T. PROUT in H.M. Knoff *The Assessment of Child and Adolescent Personality*, 1986

6 ... the school does not really change people; rather, it sorts, labels and grades children for the labour market. In other words, schools do not make children cleverer; they merely certify for employers which ones are cleverer.
P. SOROKIN cit. A. Heath *Social Mobility*, 1927

7 Belonging to the 'in group' may be given greater weight than grade point average in classifying a student as an 'excellent student', or 'getting into a lot of trouble' may be more important than 'performing up to ability level' in deciding that a student is an 'underachiever'.
A. CICOUREL, J.I. KITSUSE *The Educational Decision Makers*, 1963

8 Treating of a disease resulting from an assemblage of symptoms, some of which do not appear to have yet engaged the general notice of the profession, particular care is required whilst endeavouring to mark its diagnostic character.
JAMES PARKINSON *An Essay on the Shaking Palsy*, 1817

9 The Station Psychologist gave his opinion that an element of incendiarism was inseparable from adolescence. Indeed, if checked, it might produce morbid neuroses. For his part he thought that the prisoner had performed a perfectly normal act and, moreover, had shown more than normal intelligence in its execution.
EVELYN WAUGH (1903–1966) *Love Among the Ruins*, 1953

ATTACHMENT

10 Attachment has its roots in early interaction.
L.A. SROUFE *American Psychologist*, 1979

11 ... when the patterning of attachment to parent develops unfavourably during an individual's childhood and adolescence, the patternings of both his sexual and parental behaviour are likely to develop unfavourably also.
JOHN BOWLBY *Animal Behavior*, 1980

1 The beast and bird their common
   charge attend
The mothers nurse it and the sires
   defend;
The young dismisses, to wander earth
   or air,
There stops the instinct, and there ends
   the care.
A longer care man's helpless kind
   demands,
That longer care contracts more lasting
   bands.
ALEXANDER POPE (1688–1744) 'Essay on
Man'

2 The principle of the bond, formed by
having something in common which has
to be defended against outsiders, remains the same, from cichlids defending
a common territory or brood, right up to
scientists defending a common opinion
and – most dangerous of all – the
fanatics defending a common ideology.
KONRAD LORENZ *On Aggression*, 1963

3 It is because of this marked tendency
to monotropy that we are capable of deep
feelings, for to have a deep attachment to
a person (or a place or a thing) is to have
taken them as the terminating object of
our instinctual responses.
JOHN BOWLBY *A Secure Base: Clinical
Applications of Attachment Theory*, 1988

4 Who knows not that the first scene
of infancy is for the most part pleasant
and delightsome? What, then, is it in
children that makes us so kiss, hug,
and play with them ... but their
ingredients of ignorance and folly?
DESIDERIUS ERASMUS (1466–1536) *The
Praise of Folly*

ATTENTION

5 Everyone knows what attention is. It
is the taking possession by the mind, in
a clear and vivid form of one out of what
seem several simultaneous possible
objects or trains of thought.... It implies
withdrawal from some things in order to
deal effectively with others.
WILLIAM JAMES *Principles of Psychology*,
1890

6 We know, from ordinary life, that we
are not able to direct our attention
perfectly steadily and uniformly to one
and the same object.... At times the
attention turns towards the object most
intensely, and at times the energy flags.
WILHELM WUNDT *An Introduction to
Psychology*, 1912

7 My attention span is not what it was,
since the thoughts of middle age are
short thoughts.
GORE VIDAL *Two Sisters*, 1970

8 'Attention' is a word with a great
many very varied meanings, applicable
to a very wide range of phenomena,
many of them obviously central to an
understanding of human and animal
behaviour and probably even to the
design of intelligent artifacts.
NEVILLE MORAY *Attention*, 1969

9 Depend upon it, Sir, when a man
knows he is to be hanged in a fortnight,
it concentrates the mind wonderfully.
SAMUEL JOHNSON (1709–1784) cit. James
Boswell *The Life of Samuel Johnson*

10 The shortest way to do many things
is to do only one thing at once.
SAMUEL SMILES (1812–1904) *Self-Help*

11 The climax of mental integration
would seem to be 'attention'.... The
'willed' act is but a culmination of
attention.
CHARLES SHERRINGTON *Man on His Nature*,
1940

12 Einstein was found to show a fairly
continuous alpha rhythm while carrying
out rather intricate mathematical
operations.... Suddenly his alpha waves
dropped out and he appeared restless.
When asked if there was anything
wrong, he replied he had found a
mistake in the calculations he had
made the day before. He asked to
telephone Princeton immediately.
WILDER PENFIELD, H. JASPER *Epilepsy and
the Functional Anatomy of the Human Brain*,
1954

13 The true art of memory is the art of
attention.
SAMUEL JOHNSON (1709–1784) *The Idler*

1 He that is everywhere is nowhere.
THOMAS FULLER (1654–1734) *Gnomologia*

2 How did the party go in Portman Square?
I cannot tell you; Julia was not there.

And how did Lady Gaster's party go?
Julia was next to me and I do not know.
HILAIRE BELLOC (1870–1953) 'Juliet'

3 i never think at all when i write
nobody can do two things at the same time
and do them both well
don marquis (1878–1937) 'archy on the radio'

4 Consider this. As between reading, listening and speaking, one falls asleep most easily reading, next most easily listening, and only with the greatest difficulty while writing or speaking.
J.S. BRUNER *Towards a Theory of Instruction*, 1966

5 It is interesting to watch the knowing looks and grave countenance of an infant while examining any new object; the sight, the feeling, the taste, and for aught we know, the reasoning powers are all at work; never disturb a child thus occupied; it is exercising the power of attention.
MRS J. BAKEWELL *The Mother's Practical Guide*, 1845

ATTITUDES

6 Not much more than a hundred years ago the term 'attitude' was used exclusively with reference to a person's posture. To describe someone as adopting 'a threatening attitude' or a 'defiant attitude' was to refer to his physical mien.... nowadays 'attitude' increasingly connotes the psychological rather that the immediately physical orientation of a person.
MARIE JAHODA, N. WARREN *Attitudes*, 1966

7 An individual experiencing temporary fear, grief, or anger all too often carries his body in an attitude which the world recognizes as the outward manifestation of that particular emotion. If he persists in this dramatization ... thus forming ... 'a habit pattern', the muscular arrangement becomes set.... Now what the individual feels is no longer an emotion, a single response to an immediate situation, henceforth he lives, moves and has his being in an attitude.
IDA ROLF *Systematics*, 1963

8 An attitude contains a more or less coherent ordering of a variety of data.... What the person says at one point is understandably connected with what he has stated earlier.... It is on this basis that we undertake to foretell how a person is likely to respond to a new development.
S.E. ASCH *Social Psychology*, 1952

9 ... it is inaccurate and misleading to say that different people have different 'attitudes' concerning the same 'thing'.... We do not simply 'react to' a happening or to some impingement from the environment in a determined way.... We behave according to what we bring to the occasion and what each of us brings to the occasion is more or less unique.
A. HASTORF, H. CANTRIL *Journal of Abnormal and Social Psychology*, 1954

10 The concept of attitudes is one of the oldest theoretical ideas in social psychology and, in manifold ways, has supported a huge body of sometimes disparate research. Despite this history, the exact meaning of the notion has remained somewhat obscure.
J. POTTER, M. WETHERALL *Discourse and Social Psychology*, 1987

11 Public opinion, a vulgar, impertinent, anonymous tyrant who deliberately makes life unpleasant for anyone who is not content to be the average man.
W.R. INGE (1860–1954) *Outspoken Essays*

ATTRACTION

1 In older married couples, one often discovers features which give man and wife the semblance of brother and sister; in the same way, one may notice in a master and dog who have spent some time together likenesses in manner which are touching and comical at the same time.
KONRAD LORENZ *Man Meets Dog*, 1954

2   Her voice was ever soft,
Gentle and low; an excellent thing in
     woman.
WILLIAM SHAKESPEARE (1564–1616) *King Lear*

3 Had Cleopatra's nose been shorter, the whole face of the world would have changed.
BLAISE PASCAL (1623–1662) *Pensées*

4 The fair sex should always be fair;
     and no man
Till thirty, should perceive there's a
     plain woman.
LORD BYRON (1788–1824) *Don Juan*

5 Mrs Allen was one of that numerous class of females whose society can raise no other emotion than surprise at there being any men in the world who could like them well enough to marry them.
JANE AUSTEN (1775–1817) *Northanger Abbey*

6 Never shall a young man,
Thrown into despair
By those great honey-coloured
Ramparts at your ear,
Love you for yourself alone
And not your yellow hair.
W.B. YEATS (1865–1939) 'For Anne Gregory'

7 She was a remarkably silly girl and as such had commanded Basil's immediate attention.
EVELYN WAUGH (1903–1966) *Put Out More Flags*

ATTRIBUTION

8 … there is a pervasive tendency for actors to attribute their actions to situational requirements, whereas observers tend to attribute the same actions to stable personal dispositions.
E.E. JONES, R.E. NESBETT in E.E. Jones *et al. Attribution: Perceiving the Causes of Behavior*, 1972

9 … attribution processes are to be understood, not only as a means of providing the individual with a veridicial view of his world, but as a means of encouraging and maintaining his effective exercise of control in that world.
H.H. KELLEY in E.E. Jones *et al. Attribution: Perceiving the Causes of Behavior*, 1972

10 Who friendship with a knave has
     made,
Is judged a partner in the trade.
JOHN GAY (1685–1732) *The Beggar's Opera*

11 Do not do unto others as you would they should do unto you. Their tastes may not be the same.
GEORGE BERNARD SHAW (1856–1950) *Maxims for Revolutionists*

12 How is it that a lame man does not annoy us while a lame mind does? Because a lame man recognizes that we are walking straight, while a lame mind says it is we who are limping.
BLAISE PASCAL (1623–1662) *Pensées*

13 Individualistic as opposed to societal attributions lead people to believe that there is little the government can do about poverty and the redistribution of wealth ('the poor are always with us'; 'the cream will always come to the top').
ADRIAN FURNHAM, ALAN LEWIS *The Economic Mind*, 1986

14 From time immemorial pigs have always enjoyed the reputation of being swine.
JAROSLAV HASEK (1883–1923) *The Red Commissar*

1 He is a small modest man – with a great deal to be modest about.
WINSTON CHURCHILL (1874–1965), said of the then Prime Minister, Clement Attlee, cit. *Chicago Sunday Tribune Magazine of Books*, 27 June 1954

2 They keep blaming the boots when it is the feet that are at fault.
SAMUEL BECKETT (1906–1989) *Waiting for Godot*

3 Young men think old men are fools; but old men *know* young men are fools.
GEORGE CHAPMAN (1559–1634) *All Fools*

4 The name 'worm' is an indefinite though suggestive term popularly applied to any elongated creeping thing that is not obviously something else.
A.C. CHANDLER, C.P. READ *An Introduction to Parasitology*, 1961

AUTHORITY

5 The authoritarian theory proceeds from the assumption that human relations' concerns are irrelevant in business, and that most people are mutually dependent, indolent, self-centred and uncooperative. They are assumed to require strong direction and control by external forces if discipline is to be maintained. If most people employed in industry were in fact immature and dependent, the authoritarian theory would be appropriate; but there is no basic evidence that such behavior is inherent in human nature.
N.R.F.MAIER, J.J. HAYES *Creative Management*, 1962

6 Lear: Dost thou know me fellow?
Kent: No, sir; but you have that in your countenance which I would fain call Master.
Lear: What's that?
Kent: Authority.
WILLIAM SHAKESPEARE (1564–1616) *King Lear*

7 Some system of authority is a requirement of all communal living, and it is only the man dwelling in isolation who is not forced to respond, through defiance or submission, to the commands of others.
STANLEY MILGRAM *Obedience to Authority*, 1974

8 ... the worst concomitants of precision: meanness and authoritarianism.
EDWARD BLISHEN *Times Literary Supplement*, 1983

B

BEAUTY

1   The awful thing is that beauty is mysterious as well as terrible. God and the devil are fighting here, and the battlefield is the heart of man.
FEODOR DOSTOYEVSKY (1821–1881) *The Brothers Karamazov*

2   Just as lines and edges are low-level aesthetic primitives because they are powerful triggers of neural activity low down in the cortical pathways in the primary visual cortex, so the human form is a higher level aesthetic primitive because it stimulates activity further along the cortical pathways in neuronal systems specialized for analysing the human body, probably in the temporal lobe.
RICHARD LATTO in R.L. Gregory *et al. The Artful Eye*, 1995

3   Mathematics possess not only truth, but some supreme beauty – a beauty cold and austere, like that of sculpture.
BERTRAND RUSSELL (1872–1970) *Mysticism and Logic*

4   A thing of beauty is a joy for ever:
Its loveliness increases: it will never
Pass into nothingness.
JOHN KEATS (1795–1821) 'Endymion'

5   Beauty is no quality in things themselves. It exists merely in the mind which contemplates them.
DAVID HUME (1711–1776) *Essays, Moral, Political, and Literary*

6   Beauty is the lover's gift.
WILLIAM CONGREVE (1670–1729) *The Way of the World*

7   It is thought a sign of a sluggish and sordid mind, not to preserve carefully one's natural beauty.
THOMAS MORE (1478–1535) *Utopia*

8   I never saw an ugly thing in my life; for let the form of an object be what it may – light, shade, and perspective will always make it beautiful.
JOHN CONSTABLE (1776–1837) cit. Charles Leslie *The Life of John Constable*, 1843

9   If only, in aesthetics, we could forget for a while about the beautiful and get down instead to the dainty and the dumpy.
J.L. AUSTIN *Philosophical Papers*, 1961

10   I always say beauty is only sin deep.
SAKI (1870–1916) *Reginald's Choir Trust*

11   Fourier is a mathematical poem.
LORD KELVIN (1824–1907) *Treatise on Natural Philosophy*

12   Exuberance is beauty.
WILLIAM BLAKE (1757–1827) 'The Marriage of Heaven and Hell'

13   You can only perceive real beauty in a person as they grow older.
ANOUK AIMEE *The Guardian*, 24 August 1988

14   Beauty is not in the eye of the beholder but embedded in his genes.
TOM WOLFE *Independent on Sunday*, 2 February 1997

15   Beauty is one of the rare things that do not lead to a doubt of God.
JEAN ANOUILH *Becket*, 1961

BEHAVIOUR

1 A rat running a maze; a cat getting out of a puzzle box; a man driving home to dinner; a child hiding from a stranger; a woman doing her washing or gossiping over the telephone; a pupil marking a mental test sheet; a psychologist reciting a list of nonsense syllables; my friend and I telling one another our thoughts and feelings – *these are behaviors (qua molar)*.
E.C. TOLMAN *Purposive Behavior in Man and Animals*, 1932

2 For behaviour, men learn it, as they take diseases, one of another.
FRANCIS BACON (1561–1626) *Advancement of Learning*

3 Behavior is a man's way of changing his circumstances, not proof that he has submitted to them.
G.A. KELLY in B. Maher *Clinical Psychology and Personality*, 1969

4 ... we can only *infer* the existence and the nature of thoughts or feelings from the activities of the organisms which appear to exhibit them.
G.J. ROMANES *Animal Intelligence*, 1882

5 Not even the specialist has yet been – and I doubt that he ever will be – able to make other than trivial predictions about human behaviour by direct reference to the fact that such behaviour is (as it is) ultimately controlled by nerve cells, chemicals and electricity.
NICHOLAS HUMPHREY *Consciousness Regained*, 1983

6 Human behavior – like the deepest capacities for emotional response which drive and guide it – is the circuitous technique by which human genetic material has been and will be kept intact.
E.O. WILSON *On Human Nature*, 1978

7 Behaviour seemeth to me as a garment of the mind, and ought to have the conditions of a garment. For it ought to be made in fashion; it ought not to be too curious; it ought to be shaped so as to set forth any good making of the mind, and hide any deformity; and above all, it ought not to be too strait, or restrained for exercise or motion.
FRANCIS BACON (1561–1626) *Advancement of Learning*

8 By behaviour I mean the total of the movements made by the intact animal.
N. TINBERGEN *The Study of Instinct*, 1951

9 When people are on their best behaviour they aren't always at their best.
ALAN BENNETT *Writing Home*, 1994

BEHAVIOURISM

10 Vain wisdom all, and false philosophy.
JOHN MILTON (1608–1674) *Paradise Lost*

11 The behaviorist sweeps aside all medieval conceptions. He drops from his scientific vocabulary all subjective terms such as sensation, perception, image, desire, and even thinking and emotion.
J.B. WATSON *Behaviorism*, 1924

12 Behaviourism is indeed a kind of flat-earth view of the mind ... it has substituted for the erstwhile anthropomorphic view of the rat, a ratomorphic view of man.
ARTHUR KOESTLER *The Ghost in the Machine*, 1967

13 I believe that everything important in psychology (... that is everything save such matters as involve society and words) can be investigated in essence through the continued experimental and theoretical analysis of the determiners of rat behaviour at a choice point.
E.C. TOLMAN *Psychological Review*, 1938

1 Give me a dozen healthy infants, well-formed, and my own specified world to bring them up in and I'll guarantee to take anyone at random and train him to become any type of specialist I might select – doctor, lawyer, artist, merchant-chief and, yes, even beggar-man and thief.
J.B. WATSON *Behaviorism*, 1924

2 Philosophical behaviorism is not a metaphysical theory: it is the denial of a metaphysical theory. Consequently, it asserts nothing.
PAUL ZIFF *Analysis*, 1958

3 A scientific analysis of behavior must, I believe, assume that a person's behavior is controlled by his genetic and environmental histories rather than by the person himself as an initiating, creative agent.
B.F. SKINNER *About Behaviorism*, 1974

4 The call to studying 'objective' behavior rather than subjective experience made psychology sound more scientific. Moreover, the behaviorist research program gave psychologists lots to do.
P. THAGARD *Conceptual Revolution*, 1992

5 I believe as firmly as ever in the future of behaviorism – behaviorism as a companion of zoology, physiology, psychiatry, and physical chemistry.
J.B. WATSON in *A History of Psychology in Autobiography, Vol. 3*, 1936

6 ... behaviorism by no means recommends itself on grounds of inherent plausibility.
J.A. FODOR *Psychological Explanation*, 1968

7 Of course, Behaviourism 'works'. So does torture. Give me a no-nonsense, down-to-earth behaviourist, a few drugs, and simple electrical appliances, and in six months I will have him reciting the Athanasian Creed in public.
W.H. AUDEN (1907–1973) *A Certain World*

8 Behaviourist psychology is pretty empty as an intellectual pursuit but it does have an important ideological role..... It provides a kind of palatable ideology for the application of these techniques of coercion.
NOAM CHOMSKY in D. Cohen *Psychologists on Psychology*, 1977

9 Behaviourism could be accurately and briefly described as a psychology which leaves out psychology.
G.D. MARTIN *Language, Truth and Poetry*, 1975

10 I think the behaviorists are right in holding that talk of ideas is bad business even for psychology.
W.V. QUINE in S. Saporta *Psycholinguistics*, 1961

11 Let us limit ourselves to those things that can be observed, and formulate laws concerning only those things.
J.B. WATSON *Behaviorism*, 1924

12 This brings me to the school of 'behaviourism'. My original reaction to this was to regard it as no more than a South Sea Bubble. John Watson and John Law, I asked myself, which of these made people lose their senses most? But I have since noticed that, whilst the title has gained an ever-widening adherence, the extravagances that originally brought it into fame have been silently discarded.
CHARLES SPEARMAN in *A History of Psychology in Autobiography, Vol. 1*, 1930

13 As a scientific attempt to understand behaviour, the behaviourist's approach was impeccable in intention and design. The problem, quite simply, was that it didn't work.
NICHOLAS HUMPHREY *The Inner Eye*, 1986

BELIEF

14 A belief is an attitude which incorporates a large amount of cognitive structuring.... The individual uses his belief as a basis for predicting what will happen in the future.
J.B. COOPER, J.L. McGAUGH *Integrating Principles of Social Psychology*, 1956

1   Public administrative organizations shape *beliefs* about their work and their impact on society rather more effectively than they cope with poverty, ignorance, crime, and emotional disturbance.
MURRAY EDLEMAN *Political Language*, 1977

2   Faith, to my mind, is a stiffening process, a sort of mental starch, which ought to be applied as sparingly as possible.
E.M. FORSTER (1879–1970) *Two Cheers for Democracy*

3   Irrationally held truths may be more harmful than reasoned errors.
T.H. HUXLEY (1825–1895) *Science and Culture*

4   *Doublethink* means the power of holding two contradictory beliefs in one's mind simultaneously, and accepting both of them.
GEORGE ORWELL (1903–1950) *Nineteen Eighty-Four*

5   Faith consists in believing not what seems true, but what seems false to our understanding.
VOLTAIRE (1694–1778) *Philosophical Dictionary*

6   Clov: Do you believe in the life to come?
Hamm: Mine was always that.
SAMUEL BECKETT (1906–1989) *Endgame*

7   Credulity is the man's weakness but the child's strength.
CHARLES LAMB (1775–1834) *Essays of Elia*

8   For what a man would like to be true, that he more readily believes.
FRANCIS BACON (1561–1626) *Novum Organum*

9   Who knows much believes the less.
ANON.

10   Yet to replace the idea of God as something like a man by a wholly impersonal entity is so mysterious and indeed terrifying that I personally really cannot seriously contemplate it.
J.Z. YOUNG *Programs of the Brain*, 1978

11   What a man believes may be ascertained, not from his creed, but from the assumptions on which he habitually acts.
GEORGE BERNARD SHAW (1856–1950) *Man and Superman*

12   The belief that we have come from somewhere is closely linked with the belief that we are going somewhere.
E.H. CARR *What is History*, 1961

BLUSHING

13   The young blush much more freely than the old but not during infancy, which is remarkable, as we know that infants at a very early age redden from passion.
CHARLES DARWIN (1809–1882) *The Expression of the Emotions in Man and Animals*

14   Better a red face than a black heart.
PORTUGUESE PROVERB

15   I always take blushing either for a sign of guilt or ill breeding.
WILLIAM CONGREVE (1670–1729) *The Way of the World*

16   Her blush is guiltiness, not modesty.
WILLIAM SHAKESPEARE (1564–1616) *Much Ado About Nothing*

17   Man is the only animal that blushes. Or needs to.
MARK TWAIN (1835–1910) *Following the Equator*

18   There is a good deal to be said for blushing, if one can do it at the proper moment.
OSCAR WILDE (1854–1900) *A Woman of No Importance*

19   The man that blushes is not quite a brute.
EDWARD YOUNG (1683–1765) *Night Thoughts*

1 Blushing is the most peculiar and most human of human expressions. Monkeys redden from passion but it would take an overwhelming amount of evidence to make us believe that any animal can blush.
CHARLES DARWIN (1809–1882) *The Expression of the Emotions in Man and Animals*

BOREDOM

2 Boredom, after all, is a form of criticism.
WILLIAM PHILLIPS *A Sense of the Present*, 1967

3 There is no such thing on earth as an uninteresting subject; the only thing that can exist is an uninterested person.
G.K. CHESTERTON (1874–1936) *Heretics*

4 I have measured out my life with coffee spoons:
T.S. ELIOT (1888–1965) 'The Love Song of J. Alfred Prufrock'

5 Man is the only animal that can be bored.
ERICH FROMM *The Sane Society*, 1955

6 ... every child's life is punctuated by spells of boredom: that state of suspended anticipation in which things are started and nothing begins....
ADAM PHILLIPS *On Kissing, Tickling and Being Bored*, 1993

7 One can be bored until boredom becomes a mystical experience.
LOGAN PEARSALL SMITH (1865–1946) *Afterthoughts*

8 The effect of boredom on a large scale in history is underestimated. It is a main cause of revolutions, and would soon bring to an end all the static Utopias and the farmyard civilisation of the Fabians.
W.R. INGE *The End of an Age*, 1948

9 Boredom has always played more of a role in human history than we are prepared to admit. And we should never underrate the boredom induced by empty ideas pretentiously paraded.
J.S. BRUNER *Actual Minds, Possible Worlds*, 1986

10 Boredom: the desire for desires.
LEO TOLSTOY (1828–1910) *Anna Karenina*

BRAIN

11 No supposition seems to me more natural than that there is no process in the brain correlated with association or with thinking; so that it would be impossible to read off thought-processes from brain-processes.... It is thus perfectly possible that certain psychological phenomena *cannot* be investigated physiologically, because physiologically nothing corresponds to them.
LUDWIG WITTGENSTEIN (1889–1951) *Zettel*

12 We know the human brain is a device to keep the ears from grating on one another.
PETER De VRIES *Comfort Me with Apples*, 1956

13 Man reigns over nature through the architectural perfection of his cerebrum. Such is his patent, his indisputable title of nobility and of dominion over other animals.
RAMON y CAJAL *Reflections on My Life*, 1937

14 I believe myself then able to prove – 1. That each cerebrum is a distinct and perfect whole as an organ of thought. 2. That a separate and distinct process of thinking or ratiocination may be carried on in each cerebrum simultaneously.
A.L. WIGAN *The Duality of Mind*, 1844

15 We are not interested in the fact that the brain has the consistency of cold porridge.
ALAN TURING cit. A.P. Hodges *Alan Turing: The Enigma*, 1983

16 My brain: it's my second favorite organ.
WOODY ALLEN *Sleeper*, 1973

1 In trying to understand the functional principles governing the human nervous system, we must remind ourselves that our brain has evolved from earlier kinds of brains – that our kind of brain was not built from scratch especially for us, but has capacities and limitations that are due to its historical origins.
P.S. CHURCHLAND *Neurophilosophy: Toward a Unified Science of the Mind–Brain*, 1986

2 The deepest scientific problem with which the nervous system confronts us is how it manages to work at all.
GUNTHER STENT *Paradoxes of Progress*, 1978

3 We must recollect that all our provisional ideas in psychology will presumably one day be based on an organic substructure.
SIGMUND FREUD (1856–1939) *On Narcissism: An Introduction*

4 The wasting of the brain which leads to baldness.
HIPPOCRATES (c. 460–377 BC) *Epidemics*

5 Though the Life Force supplies us with its own purpose it has no other brains to work with than those it has painfully and imperfectly evolved in our heads
GEORGE BERNARD SHAW (1856–1950) *The Irrational Knot*

6 One of the most sobering, even humiliating, facts in the whole of brain physiology is that scarcely a single phenomenon discovered by study of the electrical activity of the brain – the EEG – was foreseen or predicted by physiologists and indeed few of these electrical effects are really understood today.
W. GREY WALTER *Listener*, 1959

7 If it is for mind that we are searching the brain, then we are supposing the brain to be more than a telephone-exchange. We are supposing it a telephone-exchange along with the subscribers as well.
CHARLES SHERRINGTON *Man on his Nature*, 1940

8 If the essential feature of the brain is that it contains information then the task is to learn to translate the language that it uses.
J.Z. YOUNG *Programs of the Brain*, 1978

9 The brain ... is the citadel of sense-perception.
PLINY THE ELDER (23–79) *Natural History*

10 I was taught that the human brain was the crowning glory of evolution so far, but I think it is a very poor scheme for survival.
KURT VONNEGUT *The Observer*, 27 December 1987

11 ... the search for a truly 'objective' understanding of nature is unlikely to succeed, because of the admittedly evolutionary rather than divine origin of the human nervous system, with which this project has to be conducted.
GUNTHER STENT *Paradoxes of Progress*, 1978

12 Brain, n. An apparatus with which we think that we think.
AMBROSE BIERCE (1842–1914) *Devil's Dictionary*

13 Human uniqueness lies in the flexibility of what our brain can do.
STEPHEN J. GOULD *The Mismeasure of Man*, 1981

14 The brain, as an organ of thought, is available for our use only because it was formed and developed before our time.
S. WALKER *Animal Thought*, 1983

BRAIN DAMAGE

15 ... after some brain shock, a person may be able to speak, but the wrong word often vexatiously comes to his lips, just as if his Broca shelves had been jumbled.
W.H. THOMSON *Brain and Personality*, 1907

1 Mon *je*, my I, had abruptly become an onlooker, a spectator of my body ... what I saw, a few weeks after the shock, as accounting for my behaviour was the complete continuity of my awareness, of my 'I', my conscious *je*. My brain had been damaged, not myself. My speech centre had suffered impairment, not my thought centre; my right hand had become awkward, but the flaw in the instrument did not upset the workman.
RAYMOND ARON *Encounter*, February 1984

2 You are with me now as you are
    everyday
Seeking some glimmer of recognition
Some sign of recovery. You take my
    hand.
I try to say: 'I love you.'
Instead I squawk,
Eyes bobbing like dead buds in a
    watertank.
I try to say: 'Have pity on me, pity on
    yourself
Put a bullet between the buds.'
Instead I gurgle.
ROGER McGOUGH 'Head Injury', 1971

3 A characteristic means by which patients with brain injuries avoid catastrophic situations is a tendency toward orderliness.... The brain injured patients whom I had under my observation for many years kept their closets in model condition. Everything had its definite place and was so arranged that the patient could find it and take it out as easily as possible. Everything, in other words, was 'in order', from the patients point of view.
KURT GOLDSTEIN *The Organism*, 1938

BULLIES AND VICTIMS

4 Everyone pushes a falling fence.
PROVERB

5 There is no end to the violations committed by children on children, quietly talking alone.
ELIZABETH BOWEN (1899–1973) *The House in Paris*

6 A bully is always a coward.
PROVERB

7 insects are not always
going to be bullied
by humanity
some day they will revolt
i am already organising
a revolutionary society to be
known as the worms turnverin
don marquis (1878–1937) 'certain maxims of archy'

8 Any victim demands allegiance.
GRAHAM GREENE (1904–1991) *The Heart of the Matter*

CHARACTER

1 No class of [men] have better sentiments or feel more constantly the differences between the higher and the lower path in life than the hopeless failures, the sentimentalists, the drunkards, the schemers, the 'dead-beats', whose life is one long contradiction between knowledge and action, and who, with full command of theory, never get to holding their limp characters erect.
WILLIAM JAMES *Text Book of Psychology*, 1892

2 Character is not a fashionable concept.
MALCOLM BRADBURY *Stepping Westward*, 1965

3 Slice him where you like, a hellhound is always a hellhound.
P.G. WODEHOUSE (1881–1975) *The Code of the Woosters*

4 Muscles are in a most intimate and peculiar sense the organs of the will. They have built all the roads, cities, and machines in the world, written all the books, spoken all the words, and, in fact done everything that man has accomplished with matter. Character might be in a sense defined as a plexus of motor habits.
G. STANLEY HALL *Youth: Its Education, Regimen and Hygiene*, 1921

5 It is well for the world that in most of us, by the age of thirty, the character has set like plaster, and will never soften again.
WILLIAM JAMES *Principles of Psychology*, 1890

6 There is a character of a gentleman; so there is a character of a scholar, which is no less easily recognized. The one has an air of books about him, as the other has of good breeding. The one wears his thoughts as the other does his clothes, gracefully; and even if they are a little old-fashioned, they are not ridiculous: they have had their day.
WILLIAM HAZLITT (1778–1830) *On the Conversation of Authors*

7 A man's character is his fate.
HERACLITUS (c. 540–c. 475 BC) *On the Universe*

8 Nature is often hidden, sometimes overcome, seldom extinguished.
FRANCIS BACON (1561–1626) *Essays*

9 He who says there is no such thing as an honest man, you may be sure is himself a knave.
BISHOP GEORGE BERKELEY (1685–1753) *Maxims Concerning Patriotism*

10 Any man who hates dogs and babies can't be all bad.
L.C. ROSTEN, said of W.C. Fields in a speech at Masquers' Club Dinner, February 1939

11 I believe it can be shown that there are patterns in people's money behaviour which can be related to their character makeup, and that there is a sufficient constant correlation between character and behaviour to justify speaking of money types.
T. WISEMAN *The Money Motive*, 1974

12 The true index of a man's character is the health of his wife.
CYRIL CONNOLLY (1903–1974) *The Unquiet Grave*

13 We are asked to believe that an individual's character structure is, in all essentials, determined by the time his last diaper is changed.... If the chances for peace in the world depend to such a degree upon infant fixations ought we not to disband ... and register as wet nurses to the mewling citizens of tomorrow.
G.W. ALLPORT *Psychological Review*, 1947

1 Some people are moulded by their admirations, others by their hostilities.
ELIZABETH BOWEN (1899–1973) *The Death of the Heart*

2 Simplicity of character is no hindrance to subtlety of intellect.
JOHN MORLEY *Life of Gladstone*, 1903

3 Knowledge has outstripped character development, and the young today are given an education rather than an upbringing.
ILYA EHRENBURG *Saturday Review*, 30 September 1967

CHILD ABUSE

4 When one learns that as late as 1900 there were still people who believed venereal disease could be cured 'by means of sexual intercourse with children' one begins to recognize the dimensions of the problem more fully.
L. de MAUSE *The History of Childhood*, 1976

5 Where the chances of harming a child's normal development are concerned, it [child sexual abuse by parents] ranks higher than abandonment, neglect, physical maltreatment or any other form of abuse. It would be a total mistake to underrate the implication or frequency of its actual occurrence.
ANNA FREUD in P.B. Mrazek, C.H. Kempe *Sexually Abused Children and their Families*, 1981

6 Freud's announcement of his new discoveries [seduction theory] ... on the etiology of hysteria met with no reasoned refutation or scientific discussion, only disgust and disavowal. The idea of sexual violence in the family was so emotionally charged that the only response it received was irrational distaste. Faced with his colleagues' hostility to his discoveries, Freud sacrificed his major insight.
J.M. MASSON *Freud, The Assault on Truth*, 1984

7 Even children of respected, high-minded puritanical families fall victim to real rape much more frequently than one had dared to suspect. Either parents themselves seek substitution for their lack of [sexual] satisfaction in this pathological manner or else trusted persons ... abuse the ignorance and innocence of children. The obvious objection that we are dealing with sexual fantasies of the child himself, that is, with hysterical lies, unfortunately is weakened by the multitude of confessions of this kind, on the part of patients in analysis, to assaults on children.
SANDOR FERENCZI, International Psychoanalytic Congress, Wiesbaden, 1932

8 What folly it is that daughters are always supposed to be
In love with Papa. It wasn't the case with me
I couldn't take to him at all
But he took to me.
What a sad case to befall a child of three.
STEVIE SMITH (1902–1971) 'Papa Love Baby'

CHILD REARING

9 Severe and frequent whipping is I think a very bad Practice; it inflames the skin, it puts the Blood into a Ferment, and there is besides, a Meanness, a degree of Ignominy attending it, which makes it very unbecoming: still there may be Occasions which will render it necessary: but I earnestly advise that all the milder Methods be first try'd. A coarse clamorous manner of enforcing Obedience is also to be avoided; it is vulgar, and nothing vulgar should be seen in the Behaviour of Parents to the Children, because through the Eyes and Ears it taints their tender Minds; still, let Parents make their Children later see and feel the Power they have over them.
J. NELSON *An Essay on the Government of Children under Three General Heads: Viz, Health, Manners and Education*, 1753

1 Maternal Advice

1. Never command unless you mean to be obeyed.

2. As early as possible, establish an absolute and entire authority over your child.

3. Never make a promise, which you do not intend performing.

4. Never attempt to deceive your child by look, word, or deed.

5. Never frighten your child into the performance of its duties.

6. Beware of incessantly finding fault.

7. Never praise or blame your child to visitors in its presence: the first will excite pride and vanity, the last anger and enmity.

8. Be not *unequal* in your government.

9. Never use the rod, under the *influence of passion* – and never, but through necessity – and but for sins.

10. Never give your child what it cries or teases you for.

11. Provoke not your child to wrath by delaying *unnecessarily* to answer it when it speaks to you. Defer not to give the information desired.

12. Refuse not to gratify their childish desires, if they be innocent and of little consequence.

ANON. *The Mother's Magazine*, 1844

2 Train up a child in the way he should go: and when he is old, he will not depart from it.
Bible, Proverbs

3 We could do worse than conclude, as have many before us, that from love and respect for home we derive our deepest loyalties to nation.
IAN McEWAN *The Child in Time*, 1987

4 There is a sensible way of treating children. Treat them as though they were young adults. Dress them, bath them with care and circumspection. Let your behavior always be objective and kindly firm. Never hug or kiss them, never let them sit on your lap. If you must kiss them on the forehead when they say goodnight. Shake hands with them in the morning. Give them a pat on the head if they make an extra-ordinary good job of a difficult task.
J.B. WATSON *Psychological Care of Infant and Child*, 1928

5 Speak roughly to your little boy,
And beat him when he sneezes;
He only does it to annoy,
Because he knows it teases.
LEWIS CARROLL (1832–1898) *Alice's Adventures in Wonderland*

6 If it became a tradition that small children were never subjected to complete or prolonged separation from their parents in the same way that regular sleep and orange juice have become nursery traditions, I believe many cases of neurotic character development would be avoided.
JOHN BOWLBY *International Journal of Psycho-Analysis*, 1940

7 The proper time to influence the character of a child is about a hundred years before he is born.
W.R. INGE *The Observer*, 21 July 1929

8 From the day your baby is born, you must teach him to do without things. Children today love luxury too much. They have execrable manners, flaunt authority, have no respect for their elders.
SOCRATES (469–399 BC) cit. H. Handler, A. Samelson *Childhood*, 1990

9 Nothing has a stronger influence psychologically on their environment, and especially on their children, than the unlived life of the parents.
CARL JUNG (1875–1961) *Paracelsus*

10 The first duties of Children are in great measure mechanical: an obedient Child makes a Bow, comes and goes, speaks or is silent, just as he is bid, before he knows any other Reason for so doing than that he is bid.
J. NELSON *An Essay on the Government of Children under Three General Heads: Viz. Health, Manners and Education*, 1753

11 Train up a fig tree in the way it should go, and when you are old sit under the shade of it.
CHARLES DICKENS (1812–1870) *David Copperfield*

1 He that loveth his son will continue to lay stripes upon him,
That he may have joy of him in the end,
He that chastiseth his son shall have profit of him,
And shall glory of him among his acquaintance.
He that teacheth his son shall provoke his enemy to jealousy;
And before friends he shall rejoice of him.
Bible, Ecclesiasticus

2 ... the most important and also the most difficult task in raising a child is helping him to find meaning in life.
BRUNO BETTELHEIM *The Uses of Enchantment*, 1978

3 I will content myself with saying that children are helpless and easily victimised, and that therefore no one should be given unlimited power over them.
QUINTILIAN (c. 35–100) *Institutio Oratoria*

4 Break their wills betimes; begin this great work before they can run alone, before they can speak plain or perhaps speak at all. Let him have nothing he cries for, absolutely nothing, great or small. Make him do as he is bid, if you whip him ten times running to effect it. Break his will now and his soul will live and he will probably bless you to all eternity.
JOHN WESLEY (1703–1791) cit. John Julius Norwich *Christmas Crackers*, 1980

5 Love children especially, for like the angels they too are sinless, and they live to soften and purify our hearts, and, as it were guide us. Woe to him who offends a child.
FEODOR DOSTOYEVSKY (1821–1881) *The Brothers Karamazov*

6 If there is anything that we wish to change in the child, we should first examine it and see whether it is not something that could better be changed in ourselves.
CARL JUNG (1875–1961) *Collected Works, Vol. 17*

CHILDHOOD

7 The ideal child is: A child who never cries unless actually stuck by a pin, illustratively speaking ... who soon builds up a wealth of habits that tide him over dark and rainy days – who puts on such habits of politeness and neatness and cleanliness that adults are willing to be around him at least part of the day ... who eats what is set before him – who sleeps and rests when put to bed for sleep and rest – who puts away two-year-old habits when the third year has to be faced ... who finally enters manhood so bulwarked with stable work and emotional habits that no adversity can quite overwhelm him.
J.B. WATSON *Psychological Care of Infant and Child*, 1928

8 [We] need to distinguish between the biological existence of children and the social construction of 'childhood'.
JOSHUA MEYROWITZ *No Sense of Place*, 1985

9 Childhood is Last Chance Gulch for happiness. After that you know too much.
TOM STOPPARD *Where Are They Now?*, 1973

10 As Freud thought, individuals never lose access to the emotional states and strivings of their childhood.
HOWARD GARDNER *Leading Minds*, 1996

11 Famous men are usually the product of an unhappy childhood.
WINSTON CHURCHILL (1874–1965) cit. H. Berrington *British Journal of Political Science*, 1974

12 The childhood shows the man,
As morning shows the day.
JOHN MILTON (1608–1674) *Paradise Regained*

13 The more I see of children – and I am thankful to say I do manage to see a good deal of them – the more I realise that their world is quite unlike ours.
VANESSA BELL (1879–1961) *Sketches in Pen and Ink*

1 With the establishment of a good relationship to the world of skills and tools, and with the advent of sexual maturity, childhood proper comes to an end.
ERIK ERIKSON *Childhood and Society*, 1950

2 Grown-ups never understand anything for themselves, and it is tiresome for children to be always and forever explaining things to them.
ANTOINE de SAINT-EXUPERY (1900–1944) *Le Petit Prince*

3 Childhood is not from birth to a
    certain age and at a certain age
The child is grown, and puts away
    childish things,
Childhood is the kingdom where nobody
    dies.
Nobody that matters, that is.
EDNA St VINCENT MILLAY (1892–1950) 'Childhood is the Kingdom Where Nobody Dies'

4 Know you what it is to be a child?... It is to believe in love, to believe in loveliness, to believe in belief ... it is to turn pumpkins into coaches, and mice into horses, lowness into loftiness, and nothing into everything, for each child has its fairy godmother in its own soul.
FRANCIS THOMPSON (1859–1907) *Shelley*

5 There is always one moment in childhood when the door opens and lets the future in.
GRAHAM GREENE (1904–1991) *The Power and the Glory*

6 On those occasions the hard-pressed parent may find some solace in the time-honoured analogy between childhood and disease – a physically and mentally incapacitating condition, distorting emotions, perceptions and reason, from which growing up is the slow and difficult recovery.
IAN McEWAN *The Child in Time*, 1987

7 In the turquoise-coloured fields of childhood there's nothing except childhood.
MIROSLAV HOLUB 'Brief reflection on childhood', 1982

8 But when I was a child I took everything for granted,
Including the stupidity of older people.
T.S. ELIOT (1888–1965) *The Family Reunion*

9 Childhood has no forebodings: but then it is soothed by no memories of outlived sorrow.
GEORGE ELIOT (1819–1880) *Mill on the Floss*

10 Childhood is a process *sui generis*, a series of developmental stages in which each manifestation has its importance as a transition, not as a final result.
ANNA FREUD *The Psychoanalytic Treatment of Children*, 1946

11 Childhood n. The period of human life intermediate between the idiocy of infancy and the folly of youth – two removes from the sin of manhood and three from the remorse of age.
AMBROSE BIERCE (1842–1914) *Devil's Dictionary*

12 Two lads that thought there was no
    more behind,
But such a day tomorrow as to-day,
And to be boy eternal.
WILLIAM SHAKESPEARE (1564–1616) *The Winter's Tale*

13 Childhood is measured out by
    sounds and smells
And sights, before the dark of reason
    grows.
JOHN BETJEMAN (1906–1984) *Summoned by Bells*

14 Childhood is a disease – a sickness that you grow out of.
WILLIAM GOLDING (1911–1993) *The Guardian*, 22 June 1990

CHILDREN

1 A child is a person who is going to carry on what you have started. He is going to sit wherever you are sitting, and when you are gone, attend to those things which you think are important. You may adopt all the policies you please, but how they are carried out depends on him. He will assume control of your cities, states and nations. He is going to move in and take over your churches, schools, universities and corporations. All your books are going to be judged, praised or condemned by him. The fate of humanity is in his hands.
ABRAHAM LINCOLN (1809–1865) attrib.

2 Children 'fall apart' repeatedly, and unlike Humpty Dumpty, grow together again.
ERIK ERIKSON in M.J.E. Senn *Symposium on Healthy Personality*, 1950

3 There is a reason to doubt that children are infinitely resilient, even given the flexibility of our species.
L.A. SROUFE *American Psychologist*, 1979

4 In about their tenth or eleventh year, children get to hear about sexual matters. A child who has grown up in a comparatively uninhibited social atmosphere, tells other children what he knows, because this makes him feel mature and superior.
SIGMUND FREUD (1856–1939) *On the Sexual Theories of Childhood*

5 A policy which gives priority to investment in children would give practical recognition to the fact that they are the seed-corn of the future. Their development determines the fabric of tomorrow's society.
MIA KELMER-PRINGLE *Investment in Children*, 1982

6 Children are born true scientists.
R. BUCKMASTER FULLER (1895–1983) *R. Buckmaster Fuller on Education*

7 In order to make the world safer for democracy, we must make democracy safe for the healthy child.
ERIK ERIKSON in M.J.E. Senn *Symposium on the Healthy Personality*, 1950

8 Children are not resilient, children are malleable.
BRUCE PERRY in J. Osofsky *Children in a Violent Society*, 1997

9 She was not really bad at heart,
But only rather rude and wild:
She was an aggravating child.
HILAIRE BELLOC (1870–1953) 'Rebecca'

10 [Love] to children it is an absolute necessity of their nature and when it is denied them they are no longer children.
MARY CARPENTER cit. H. Cunningham *The Children of the Poor*, 1991

11 Children are given to us to discourage our better emotions.
SAKI (1870–1916) *Reginald*

12 Child care writers of the post-war era sentimentally ignored the fact that children are at heart selfish, and reasonably so, for they are programmed for survival.
IAN McEWAN *The Child in Time*, 1987

13 It is their birthright that the environment to which they must adapt is one that promotes healthy psychological development.
L.A. SROUFE *American Psychologist*, 1979

14 Do not be afraid of having children. This world has not been created to be a cemetery.
POPE JOHN XXIII *New York Times*, 30 December 1959

15 When you are very old you know that children have the right idea. If only they had the authority.
PETER USTINOV *Quotable Ustinov*, 1995

16 A willingness to devote adequate resources to the care of children is the hallmark of a civilised society.
MIA KELLMER-PRINGLE *The Needs of Children*, 1980

1 In order to understand the child, we must know his reactions; but in order to understand his reactions we must also know the child.
K. KOFFKA *The Growth of the Mind*, 1924

2 Children have no scruples over allowing animals to rank as their full equals. Uninhibited as they are in the avowal of their bodily needs, they no doubt feel themselves more akin to animals than their elders, who may well be a puzzle to them.
SIGMUND FREUD (1856–1939) *Totem and Taboo*

3 Children appeared in Europe along with the pocket watch and the Christian moneylenders of the Renaissance. Before our century neither the poor nor the rich knew of children's dress, children's games or children's immunity from the law. Children belonged to the bourgeoisie.
IVAN ILLICH *Deschooling Society*, 1971

4 ... a society which neglects its children, however well it may function in other respects, risks eventual disorganisation and demise.
URIE BRONFENBRENNER *Two Worlds of Childhood*, 1970

5 Children sweeten labours, but they make misfortunes more bitter: they increase the cares of life, but they mitigate the remembrance of death.
FRANCIS BACON (1561–1626) *Essays*

CIVILISATION

6 It is human to have a long childhood; it is civilised to have an even longer childhood.
ERIK ERIKSON *Childhood and Society*, 1950

7 Civilisation is an active deposit which is formed by the combustion of the Present with the Past.
CYRIL CONNOLLY (1903–1974) *The Unquiet Grave*

8 To be able to fill leisure intelligently is the last product of civilisation.
BERTRAND RUSSELL (1872–1970) *The Conquest of Happiness*

9 Civilisation advances by extending the number of important operations which we can perform without thinking about them.
A.N. WHITEHEAD (1861–1947) *Introduction to Mathematics*

10 Human beings do not carry civilisation in their genes. All that we do carry in our genes are certain capacities – the capacity to learn to walk upright, to use our brains, to speak, to relate to our fellow men, to construct and use tools, to explore the universe, and to express that exploration in religion, in art, in science, in philosophy.
MARGARET MEAD *New York Times Magazine* 19 April 1964

11 I ... walked to Greenwich, in my way seeing a coffin with a dead body therein, dead of the plague ... the parish have not appointed anyone to bury it, but only set a watch ... that nobody should go thither or come thence; this disease making us more cruel to one another than we are to dogs.
SAMUEL PEPYS (1633–1703) *Diary*, 22 August 1665

12 By the mere fact that he forms part of an organised crowd, a man descends several rungs in the ladder of civilisation.
GUSTAVE LE BON *The Crowd: A Study of the Popular Mind*, 1896

13 Between the spirit of the individual and the spirit of civilization there is always a mutual relationship.
E. R. JAENSCH *Eidetic Imagery*, 1930

14 Cast on this globe, without physical powers, and without innate ideas; unable by himself to obey the constitutional laws of his organization, which call him to the first rank in the system of being; MAN can find only in the bosom of society the eminent station that was destined for him in nature, and would be, without the aid of civilization, one of the most feeble and least intelligent of animals; – a truth which, although it has often been insisted upon, has not as yet been rigorously demonstrated.
J. ITARD *The Wild Boy of Aveyron*, 1802

1 The principal task of civilisation, its actual *raison d'être* is to defend us against nature.
SIGMUND FREUD (1856–1939) *The Future of an Illusion*

CLOTHING

2 What does it signify how we dress here, where nobody knows us.
ELIZABETH (Mrs) GASKELL (1810–1865) *Cranford*

3 The need of dress is eminently a 'higher' or spiritual need.
THORSTEN VEBLEN *The Theory of the Leisure Class*, 1899

4 It is perhaps no mere chance that a period of unexcelled scientific progress should have followed the abandonment of ornamental clothing at the beginning of the last century.
J.C. FLUGEL *The Psychology of Clothes*, 1930

5 His socks compelled one's attention without losing one's respect.
SAKI (1870–1916) *Chronicles of Clovis*

6 One of the greatest of sex allurements would be lost, and the extreme importance of clothes would disappear at once if the two sexes were to dress alike; such identity of dress has, however, never come about among any people.
HAVELOCK ELLIS (1859–1939) cit. Phyllis Grosskurth *Havelock Ellis*, 1980

7 They say that women, in a bombing-raid,
Retire to sleep in brand-new underwear,
Lest they be tumbled out of doors, displayed
In shabby garments to the public stare.
NORMAN CAMERON (1905–1953)
'Punishment Enough'

COGNITION

8 *Thinking, believing* and *remembering* are not names that refer to simple processes for which we need a theory. They are part of the theory, part of a symbolic scheme we have constructed to represent human action and interaction.
DAVID OLSON *Human Development*, 1977

9 The study of cognition is only one fraction of psychology, and it cannot stand alone.
U. NEISSER *Cognitive Psychology*, 1967

10 To me, logic and learning and all mental activity have always been incomprehensible as a complete and closed picture and have been understandable only as a process by which man puts himself *en rapport* with his environment.
NORBET WIENER *I Am a Mathematician*, 1956

11 The facts show convincingly that the structure of activity does not remain static during different stages of historical development and that the most important forms of cognitive processes – perception, generalisation, deduction, reasoning, imagination and analysis of one's own inner life – vary as the conditions of social life change and the rudiments of knowledge are mastered.
A.R. LURIA *Cognitive Development*, 1976

12 ... cognition is a fundamentally cultural process.
EDWIN HUTCHINS *Cognition in the Wild*, 1996

13 Cognitive psychology is not the whole of psychology, nor is computer modelling the whole of cognitive psychology.
L.S. HEARNSHAW *The Shaping of Modern Psychology*, 1987

14 ... the more global a cognitive process is, the less anybody understands it.
J.A. FODOR *The Modularity of Mind*, 1983

15 No theory that fails to acknowledge the possibility of development can be taken seriously as an account of human cognition.
U. NEISSER *Cognition and Reality*, 1976

COGNITIVE DISSONANCE

1 Almost everybody enjoys a magician. And the magician only creates dissonance – you see before you an event which you know to be impossible on the basis of previous knowledge.... If the art of magic is essentially producing dissonance, and if human nature abhors dissonance, why is the art of magic still flourishing?
R.B. ZAJONC *Public Opinion Quarterly*, 1960

2 Under conditions of uncertainty, people are at their most vulnerable to social influence and are strongly dependent on social comparison for understanding reality and checking the veracity of their perceptions and opinions.
DOMINIC ABRAMS *The Psychologist*, November 1997

3 The 'cognitive dissonance' hypothesis of North American psychology ... would appear to be based upon a culture-specific discomfort Americans have with noticing themselves being inconsistent from one occasion to another, or possessing mutually inconsistent aims ... even in a situation in which two cannot simultaneously be accomplished.
NANCY MUCH in J. Smith *et al. Rethinking Psychology*, 1995

4 We have a group who believed the world was going to end on a specific date.... They would be picked up at a specific time by flying saucers. They were all sitting around waiting and, of course, nobody came. And, after four to six hours of turmoil and desperation, they reached the conclusion that God had saved the world because they had sat up all night praying. And then ... they went out proselytising very hard.
LEON FESTINGER cit. David Cohen *Psychologists on Psychology*, 1977

COGNITIVE SCIENCE

5 The computer metaphor potentially provides a mechanistic theory of reasoning and for the cognitive psychologist 'cognition' is computation.
MIKE OAKSFORD *The Psychologist*, June 1997

6 In cognitive science the normal procedure is to isolate some psychological phenomenon, make a theoretical model of the postulated mental processes, and then test the model, by a computer simulation, to make sure it works as the author thought it would. If it fits at least some of the psychological facts then it is thought to be a useful model. The fact that it is rather unlikely to be the correct one seems to disturb nobody.
FRANCIS CRICK *What Mad Pursuit*, 1988

7 Cognitive science was born in a re-action against behaviorism. Behaviorism had made the claim that internal mental structure was either irrelevant or non-existent – that the study of behavior could be conducted entirely in an object characterization of behavior itself. Cognitive science's reaction was not simply to argue that the internal mental world was important too; it took as its domain of study the internal mental environment largely separated from the external world. Interaction with the world was reduced to read and write operations conducted at either end of extensive processing activity. This fits the computer metaphor very well, but it made the organization of the environment in which thinking took place seem largely irrelevant. Both behaviorism and cognitivism must be wrong.
EDWIN HUTCHINS *Cognition in the Wild*, 1996

8 We approach the problems of human psychology as humans, and it seems a pity to waste that advantage.
MARY MIDGLEY *Heart and Mind*, 1981

1 Of course, not all experiments necessarily reveal God's truth, but some undoubtedly will produce results that should cause cognitive scientists with computational orientations to alter their theories and thus their programs.
R. SCHANK in D. Norman *Perspectives on Cognitive Science*, 1981

2 The computer was not made in the image of the person. The computer was made in the image of the formula manipulations of abstract symbols. And the last 30 years of cognitive science can be seen as attempts to remake the person in the image of the computer.
EDWIN HUTCHINS *Cognition in the Wild*, 1996

3 Cognitive Science needs to be aware of its metaphors, to be concerned with what they hide, and to be open to alternative metaphors – even if they are inconsistent with the current favorites.
G. LAKOFF, M. JOHNSON in D. Norman *Perspectives on Cognitive Science*, 1981

COMMON SENSE

4 In our daily lives we all predict and explain other people's behavior from what we think they know and what we think they want. Beliefs and desires are the explanatory tools of our own intuitive psychology, and intuitive psychology is still the most useful and complete science of behavior there is.
STEVEN PINKER *How the Mind Works*, 1997

5 ... if we face our problems honestly and without regard to, or fear of, difficulty, the theoretical psychology of the future will catch up with, and eventually surpass, common sense.
D.O. HEBB *Psychological Review*, 1953

6 Common sense is the very antipodes of science.
E.B. TITCHENER *Systematic Psychology*, 1929

7 But folk psychology, though it changes, does not get displaced by scientific paradigms. For it deals with the nature, causes, and consequences of those intentional states – beliefs, desires, intentions, commitments – that most scientific psychology dismisses in its efforts to explain human action.
J.S. BRUNER *Acts of Meaning*, 1990

8 Science is nothing but trained and organized common sense.
T.H. HUXLEY (1825–1895) *Collected Essays*

9 Investigators began to act on the assumption that if you want to find out something about someone, the best way to do it is to ask him ... and to take the answer at face value ... there is much in favor of such a commonsense approach. It is conservative; it does not presume that the psychologist can know more about a person than the person himself can know or will tell. It is parsimonious.... It is demystifying.
R.N. WOLFE in K.H. Craik *et al. Fifty Years of Personality Psychology*, 1993

10 Common sense is nothing more than a deposit of prejudices laid down in the mind before you reach eighteen.
ALBERT EINSTEIN cit. Lincoln Barnett *The Universe and Dr Einstein*, 1950

11 Common sense is the best distributed commodity in the world, for every man is convinced that he is well supplied with it.
RENÉ DESCARTES (1596–1650) *Discourse on Method*

12 The same principles which at first lead to scepticism, pursued to a certain point bring men back to common sense.
BISHOP GEORGE BERKELEY (1685–1753) *Three Dialogues Between Hylas and Philonus*

13 From the psychologist's point of view it would be a pure mystery if a person's behaviour should ever be deter-mined, as the layman believes, directly by the concrete properties of the actual situation. The layman's belief is in full agreement with everyday experience ... I shall confess at once that I choose the layman's belief whole-heartedly.
WOLFGANG KOHLER *Gestalt Psychology*, 1930

14 ... there's nothing common about common sense.
STEVEN PINKER *How the Mind Works*, 1997

1 In general, straightforward common-sense statements will be found more convincing than technical descriptions, statistical exhibits, or academic arguments.
R.M. YERKES *Memoirs of the National Academy of Science*, 1921

2 John Locke invented common sense, and only Englishmen have had it ever since!
BERTRAND RUSSELL (1872–1970) cit. D.C. Dennet, *Darwin's Dangerous Idea*, 1995

3 The common sense is that which judges the things given to it by the other senses.
LEONARDO DA VINCI (1452–1519) *Notebooks of Leonardo da Vinci*

4 Nothing is more flatly contradicted by experience than the belief that a man, distinguished in one or even several departments of science, is more likely to think sensibly about ordinary affairs than anyone else.
WILFRED TROTTER *The Collected Papers of Wilfred Trotter FRS*, 1941

COMMUNICATION

5 If you cannot – in the long run – tell everyone what you have been doing, your doing has been worthless.
ERWIN SCHRÖDINGER *Science and Humanism*, 1951

6 In every social situation we can find a sense in which one participant will be an observer with something to gain from assessing expressions, and another will be a subject with something to gain from manipulating this process.
ERVING GOFFMAN *Strategic Interaction*, 1969

7 ... all communication necessitates context, ... without context, there is no meaning, and ... contexts confer meaning because there is classification of contexts.
GREGORY BATESON *Mind and Nature*, 1979

8 The medium is the message.
MARSHALL McLUHAN *Understanding Media*, 1964

9 I had done it! It had started – the thing that was to give my mind its chance of expressing itself. True, I couldn't speak with my lips, but now I would speak through something more lasting than spoken words – written words. That one letter, scrawled on the floor with a broken bit of yellow chalk gripped between my toes, was my road to a new world, my key to mental freedom.
CHRISTY BROWN *My Left Foot*, 1954

10 Many Writers perplexe their Readers, and Hearers with meere *Non-sense*. Their writings need sunshine.
BEN JONSON (1572–1637) *Timber: or Discoveries*

11 When he discovered Australia, Cook sent a sailor ashore to inquire of the natives the name of a strange animal they had brought to the ship from the land. The sailor reported that it was known as a *kangaroo*. Many years passed before it was learned that when the natives were asked about the name of the animal, they replied 'kangaroo' and were simply asking, 'What did you say?'
R. MUELLER *Buzzwords*, 1974

12 All culture and all communication depend on the interplay between expectation and observation, the waves of fulfilment, disappointment, right guesses, and wrong moves that make up our daily life.
E.H. GOMBRICH *Art and Illusion*, 1960

13 Your face, my Thane, is a book Where men may read strange matters.
WILLIAM SHAKESPEARE (1564–1616) *Macbeth*

14 There is no emotion of the mind, which nature does not make an effort to manifest by some of those signs (tones, looks, gestures), and therefore a total suppression of those signs is of all other states the most apparently unnatural.
THOMAS SHERIDAN *Courses of Lectures on Elocution*, 1796

15 Who can refute a sneer?
REVEREND WILLIAM PALEY *Principles of Moral and Political Philosophy*, 1785

1 I protest ... against the cutting off of intellectual originality by the difficulties of the means of communication in the modern world, but even more against the axe which has been put to the root of originality because the people who have elected communication as a career so often have nothing more to communicate.
NORBERT WIENER *The Human Use of Human Beings*, 1950

2 Quite possibly, textual communication entails all *the major skills for rational human behavior in general.*
R. de BEAUGRANDE, W.V. DRESSLER *Introduction to Text Linguistics*, 1981

3 One always speaks badly when one has nothing to say.
VOLTAIRE (1697–1778) *Commentaries on Corneille*

4 The man of science appears to be the only man who has something to say, just now – and the only man who does not know how to say it.
JAMES BARRIE cit. A. Quiller Couch *The Art of Writing*, 1916

5 The ill and unfit choice of words wonderfully obstructs the under-standing.
FRANCIS BACON (1561–1626) *Novum Organum*

COMPASSION

6 What value has compassion that does not take its object in its arms.
ANTOINE de SAINT-EXUPERY (1900–1944) *The Wisdom of the Sands*

7 You weep for what you know. A red-haired child
Sick in a fever, if you touch him once,
Though but so little as with a finger-tip,
Will set you weeping; but a million sick
You would as soon weep for the rule of three
Or compound fractions.
ELIZABETH BARRETT BROWNING (1806–1861) 'Aurora Leigh'

COMPETENCE

8 It is easier to appear worthy of positions that we have not got, than of those we have.
DUC FRANCOIS DE LA ROCHEFOUCAULD (1613–1680) *Maxims*

9 He [Francis Galton] had the advantage of competence without the limitation of being an expert.
E.G. BORING *A History of Experimental Psychology*, 1950

10 By competence, I just mean that system of internal principles and structures that we use for our behavior. I would be perfectly happy with the term knowledge.
NOAM CHOMSKY cit. D. Cohen *Psychologists on Psychology*, 1977

COMPLEXITY

11 A man, viewed as a behaving system, is quite simple. The apparent complexity of his behavior over time is largely a reflection of the complexity of the environment in which he finds himself.
H.A. SIMON *The Sciences of the Artificial*, 1969

12 ... the most complex types of behavior that I know; the logical and orderly arrangement of thought and action.
K.S. LASHLEY in L.A. Jeffress *Cerebral Mechanisms of Behavior*, 1951

13 All complex human functions display a principle of relative stability. Built up to operate in a world of rapid change, they retain their constancy until some step is passed, and then a little change produces a big effect.
F.C. BARTLETT *Proceedings of the 12th International Congress of Psychology*, Edinburgh, 1950

14 It is far more difficult to be simple than to be complex.
JOHN RUSKIN (1819–1900) *Modern Painters*

1 Complex sciences, because of their complexity, offer so many 'natural experiments' that the disadvantage of not being able to set up controlled experiments in a laboratory may be largely offset.
C.F.A. PANTIN *The Relation Between the Sciences*, 1968

2 As a general rule, if we wish to discover the causes of complicated phenomena, and their interplay and laws, we must investigate separately the effects of any individual cause and then consider the joint operation of many causes.
E. H. WEBER (1795–1878) *The Sense of Touch*

3 ... the ability to reduce everything to simple fundamental laws does not imply the ability to start from these laws and reconstruct the universe.
P. W. ANDERSON *Science*, 1972

4 Where chaos begins, classical science stops.
JAMES GLEICK *Chaos*, 1987

5 ... the claim that the mind searches for simplicity ... leads to the prediction that the richer the patterns that the cognitive system can find in a stimulus, the more simply it can be encoded, and hence the better it will be remembered.
NICK CHATER *The Psychologist*, 1997

6 ... the *pattern which connects is a metapattern*. It is a pattern of patterns. It is that metapattern which defines the vast generalization that, indeed, *it is patterns that connect.*
GREGORY BATESON *Mind and Nature*, 1979

7 The understanding of complicated phenomena depends upon an analysis by which they are resolved into their simple elementary components.
JACQUES LOEB *Comparative Physiology of the Brain and Comparative Psychology*, 1905

8 We need nowadays to be able to think not just about simple processes but about complex systems.
C.H. WADDINGTON *Tools for Thought*, 1977

COMPUTERS

9 I don't give a damn about computers. I'm interested in people. I write about the *human mind* – not about computers.
MARGARET BODEN, interview, *The Psychologist*, 1991

10 Men are more easily made than machinery.
LORD BYRON (1788–1824) 'An Ode to the Framers of the Frame Bill'

11 To err is human but to really foul things up requires a computer.
ANON.

12 Why did all the sensorimotor apparatus fall off the person when the computer replaced the brain? It fell off because the computer was never a model of the person to begin with.
EDWIN HUTCHINS *Cognition in the Wild*, 1996

13 Computers do not crunch numbers: they manipulate symbols.
MARGARET BODEN *Artificial Intelligence and Natural Man*, 1977

14 Even if we regard the central nervous system as a 'computer' it is none the less the outcome of a long process of biological evolution.... It is difficult to believe that the engineer ... is necessarily the best guide to the vicissitudes of organic evolution.
O.L. ZANGWILL *An Introduction to Modern Psychology*, 1950

CONDITIONING

15 Conditioning is an objective substitute for introspection, a form of language which enables an experimenter to know what discrimination an animal can make, what it does and does not perceive.
E.G. BORING *A History of Experimental Psychology*, 1950

1 The therapy that used conditioning to induce inhibition of some behavioral trait brought Victorian moral language into a technically more refined age.
ROGER SMITH *Inhibition*, 1992

2 It is obvious that the different kinds of habits based on training, education and discipline of any sort are nothing but a long chain of conditioned reflexes.
IVAN PAVLOV *Lectures on Conditioned Reflexes*, 1928

3 In Paris I had bought three books by Henri Bergson: ... and late one afternoon, sitting on deck, I was reading one of them. Suddenly I was startled by a very loud blast of a bugle. A member of the crew had come up behind me and had taken this customary way of announcing that dinner was served. After dinner I came back and began to read again. I went down the same page, and as I approached the point at which I heard the blare of the bugle, I could feel perceptual and emotional responses slowly building up. The very thing Pavlov would have predicted! The summer was over and serious business lay ahead.
B.F. SKINNER *Particulars of My Life*, 1976

CONFLICT

4 Unresolved conflict leads to anxiety, depression, hostility, unrealistic fantasies, and even delusions and hallucinations.... I have become more and more convinced that conflict *itself*, not any particular kind of conflict, represents the most serious kind of malfunction of the brain short of physical damage, and the most common even among 'normal' people.
WILLIAM T. POWERS *Behavior: The Control of Perception*, 1974

5 Each of us has interests which conflict with the interests of everybody else. That's our original sin, and can't be helped.
B.F. SKINNER *Walden Two*, 1948

6 Who overcomes
By force, hath overcome but half his foe.
JOHN MILTON (1608–1674) *Paradise Lost*

7 The wise and good man neither himself fights with any person nor does he allow another, as far as he can prevent it.
EPICTETUS (c. 55–135) *Discourses*

8 Stating that he would not stand it,
Stating in emphatic language
What he'd do before he'd stand it.
LEWIS CARROLL (1832–1898) 'Hiawatha's Photographing'

CONFORMITY

9 Why do we follow the majority? Is it because they are more right? No but they are stronger.
BLAISE PASCAL (1623–1662) *Pensées*

10 We think so because other people all think so,
Or because – or because – after all we do think so,
Or because we were told so, and think we must think so,
Or because we once thought so, and think we still think so,
Or because having thought so, we think we *will* think so.
HENRY SIDGWICK (1838–1900) *Henry Sidgwick*

11 If all pulled in one direction the world would keel over.
YIDDISH PROVERB

12 Conformity is one side of a man, uniqueness is the other.
CARL JUNG (1875–1961) *Contributions to Analytical Psychology*

13 As soon as you can say what you think, and not what some other person has thought for you, you are on the way to being a remarkable man.
J.M. BARRIE (1860–1937) *Tommy and Grizel*

14 Most people are other people. Their thoughts are someone else's opinions, their lives a mimicry, their passions a quotation.
OSCAR WILDE (1854–1900) *De Profundis*

46

1 Fascist governments have not found the five-year-old too young to regiment into uniform, to marshall in battalions preparatory to group behavior which will be required in later years.
ARNOLD GESELL *The First Five Years of Life*, 1940

2 Every public action which is not customary, either is wrong or, if it is right, is a dangerous precedent. It follows that nothing should ever be done for the first time.
F.M. CORNFORD (1874–1943) *Micro-cosmographia Academica*

3 If you live along with all the other
people
and are just like them, and conform,
and are nice
you're just a worm –
and if you live with all the other people
and you don't like them and won't be
like them and won't conform
then you're just the worm that has
turned,
in either case, a worm.
D.H. LAWRENCE (1885–1930) 'Worm Either Way'

4 The best thing to do is to behave in a manner befitting one's age. If you are sixteen or under, try not to go bald.
WOODY ALLEN *Without Feathers*, 1976

5 The American ideal, after all, is that everyone should be as much alike as possible.
JAMES BALDWIN *Notes of a Native Son*, 1955

6 Every Jack sticks to his own Jill: every tinker esteems his own trull: and the hob-nailed suitor prefers Joan the milk-maid before any of my lady's daughters. These things are true, and are ordinarily laughed at, and yet, however ridiculous they seem, it is hence only that all societies receive their cement and consolidation.
DESIDERIIUS ERASMUS (1466–1536) *The Praise of Folly*

CONNECTIONISM

7 ... connectionist networks are not particularly realistic models of the brain, despite the hopeful label 'neural networks'....
STEVEN PINKER *How the Mind Works*, 1997

8 Connectionism has galvanized psychologists, computer scientists and neuroscientists alike and it would be overly pessimistic to argue that no serious advances will come of such a concerted research effort.
P.T. QUINLAN *Connectionism and Psychology*, 1991

9 Only connect.
E.M. FORSTER (1879–1970) *Howards End*

10 ... when there is a choice between getting a job done and mirroring the brain, connectionists often opt for getting the job done.
STEVEN PINKER *How the Mind Works*, 1997

CONSCIENCE

11 Conscience is the voice of the soul, the passions are the voice of the body.
JEAN-JACQUES ROUSSEAU (1712–1778) *Émile*

12 A man's conscience and his judgement is the same thing, and as the judgement, so the conscience, may be erroneous.
THOMAS HOBBES (1588–1679) *Leviathan*

13 Conscience is the internal perception of the rejection of a particular wish operating within us.
SIGMUND FREUD (1856–1939) *Totem and Taboo*

14 All a man can bring is his own conscience.
JOSEPH CONRAD (1857–1924) *Under Western Eyes*

15 Conscience: the inner voice which warns us that someone may be looking.
H.L. MENCKEN (1880–1956) *A Little Book in C Major*

46

1 By calling a variety of actions bad, evil, or naughty, we encourage the child to identify them all in one category, and to react in the future with anxiety to everything thus labelled. This, very briefly and not altogether adequately, is my account of the growth of conscience.
HANS EYSENCK in T. Likona *Moral Development and Behavior*, 1976

2 Why does man regret, even though he may endeavour to banish any such regret, that he has followed the one natural impulse, rather than the other; and why does he further feel that he ought to regret his conduct? Man in this respect differs profoundly from the lower animals.
CHARLES DARWIN (1809–1882) *Descent of Man*

3 The conscience can be, and is, constantly narcotised as much by relatively good deeds as by relatively bad deeds.
ARNOLD BENNETT (1867–1931) *Self and Self Management*

4 Thus conscience doth make cowards of us all.
WILLIAM SHAKESPEARE (1564–1616) *Hamlet*

5 My conscience is of courtly Mold
Fit for the highest Station:
Where's the Hand when touch'd with Gold,
Proof against Temptation.
JOHN GAY (1685–1732) *Polly*

6 ... conscience looks backwards and judges past actions, inducing that kind of dissatisfaction, which if weak we call regret, and if severe remorse.
CHARLES DARWIN (1809–1882) *Descent of Man*

7 Conscience and cowardice are really the same things. Conscience is the trade-name of the firm.
OSCAR WILDE (1854–1900) *The Picture of Dorian Gray*

CONSCIOUSNESS

8 The youth of today and mature scientists in increasing numbers are turning to meditation, oriental religions, and personal use of psychedelic drugs. The phenomena encountered in these ASCs [altered states of consciousness] provide more satisfaction and are more relevant to the formulation of philosophies of life and deciding on appropriate ways of living, than 'pure reason'.
C.T. TART *Science*, June 1972

9 Consciousness reigns but it doesn't govern.
PAUL VALÉRY (1871–1945) cit. W.H. Auden *A Certain World*, 1970

10 My relationship to my surroundings is my consciousness.... For the animal, its relation to others does not exist as a relation. Consciousness is therefore, from the very beginning, a social product and remains so as long as men exist at all.
KARL MARX cit. S. Avinieri *The Social and Political Thought of Karl Marx*, 1968

11 Consciousness ... is the phenomenon whereby the universe's very existence is made known.
ROGER PENROSE *The Emperor's New Mind*, 1989

12 Human consciousness is a perpetual pursuit of a language and a style.
HENRI FOCILLON cit. K. Aichity, *A Writer's Time*, 1986

13 Our normal waking consciousness, rational consciousness as we call it, is but one special type of consciousness, whilst all about it, parted from it by the flimsiest of screens, there lie potential forms of consciousness entirely different. We may go through life without suspecting their existence; but apply the requisite stimulus, and at a touch they are there in all their completeness, definite types of mentality which probably somewhere have their field of application and adaptation.
WILLIAM JAMES *Varieties of Religious Experience*, 1902

1 I learned to distinguish between these states which reigned alternately in my mind ... each one returning to dispossess the other with the regularity of a fever and ague: contiguous and yet so foreign to one another, so devoid of means of communication, that I could no longer understand, or even picture to myself, in one state what I had desired or dreaded or even done in the other.
MARCEL PROUST (1871–1922) *Remembrance of Things Past*

2 Consciousness can never be anything else than conscious existence and existence of men in their actual life process.
KARL MARX cit. L.S. Fraser *Marx and Engels*, 1959

3 ... belief in the existence of consciousness goes back to the ancient days of superstition and magic.
J.B. WATSON *Behaviorism*, 1924

4 The question of where mind or consciousness enters in the phylogenetic scale and of the nature of conscious experience as distinct from physiological processes are pseudo-problems, arising from misconceptions of the nature of the data revealed by introspection. A comparative study of the behavior of animals is a comparative study of mind, by any meaningful definition of the term.
K.S. LASHLEY *Quarterly Review of Biology*, 1949

5 Consciousness, then, is our mode of analysis of the outside world into objects and actions.
J. BRONOWSKI (1908–1974) *The Origins of Knowledge and Imagination*

6 Physics is the study of the structure of consciousness.
G. ZUKAV *The Dancing Wu Li Masters*, 1979

7 Consciousness is reflected in a word as the sun in a drop of water. A word relates to consciousness as a living cell relates to an organism, as an atom relates to the universe.
L.S. VYGOTSKY *Thought and Language*, 1962

8 Consciousness will always be one degree above comprehensibility.
G.C.H. EHRENSVARD *Man on Another World*, 1905

9 An analysis of the very concept of explanation would begin and end with a renunciation as to our explaining our own conscious activity.
NIELS BOHR *Atomic Physics and Human Knowledge*, 1958

10 It is nothing less than pure assumption to say that consciousness, which is admitted to be present, has practically no effect whatever upon behaviour. And we must ask any evolutionist who accepts this conclusion, how he accounts on evolutionary grounds for the existence of a useless adjunct to a neural process.
C. LLOYD MORGAN *Animal Behaviour*, 1900

CONSTRUCTS

11 Constructs are not merely ways of labelling our universe, they are ways of trying to understand and anticipate it.
DON BANNISTER in B.M. Foss *New Horizons in Psychology*, 1966

12 Abstraction and generalisation of human activity are not the exclusive prerogatives of professional psychologists. What they do any person may do. Indeed every person does! Each individual the psychologists study abstracts and generalizes on his own for he is even more vitally interested than they can ever be in the task of understanding himself and his relationship to other persons and values.
G.A. KELLY *The Abstraction of Human Concepts*, 1961

13 Constructs are essentially predictive. Thus when we construe a man as *honest* rather than *dishonest* we are essentially predicting that if we lend him money we will get it back.... It is precisely because our constructs are predictors that our construct systems are in a continual state of change for each of us.
D. BANNISTER in B.M. Foss *New Horizons in Psychology*, 1966

CONTRARINESS

1 Adam was but human – this explains it all. He did not want the apple for the apple's sake; he wanted it only because it was forbidden. The mistake was in not forbidding the serpent; then he would have eaten the serpent.
MARK TWAIN (1835–1910) *Pudd'nhead Wilson*

2 The Rum Tum Tugger is a curious beast;
His disobliging ways are a matter of habit.
If you offer him fish then he always wants a feast;
Where there isn't any fish then he won't eat rabbit.
T.S. ELIOT (1888–1965) *Old Possum's Book of Practical Cats*

COPING

3 ... it is precisely those individuals in whom a certain need has always been satisfied who are best equipped to tolerate deprivation of that need in the future; furthermore, those who have been deprived in the past will react to current satisfactions differently from one who has never been deprived.
ABRAHAM H. MASLOW *Psychological Review*, 1943

4 The ability to maintain self-command under trying circumstances is important, as is therefore the coolness and moral resoluteness needed if this is to be done.
ERVING GOFFMAN *Interaction Ritual*, 1967

5 The strength of people's convictions in their own effectiveness determines whether they will even try to cope with difficult situations.
ALBERT BANDURA *Social Learning Theory*, 1977

6 Tranquility is nothing else than the good ordering of the mind.
MARCUS AURELIUS (121–180) *Meditations*

7 Though nothing can bring back the hour
Of splendour in the grass, of glory in the flower;
We will grieve not, rather find
Strength in what remains behind.
WILLIAM WORDSWORTH (1770–1850)
'Intimations on Immortality'

8 Our torments also may in length of time
Become our elements.
JOHN MILTON (1608–1674) *Paradise Lost*

9 And almost every one when age,
Disease, or sorrows strike him,
Inclines to think there is a God,
Or something very like him.
A.H. CLOUGH (1819–1861) 'There is No God'

10 The notion that we can transfer our guilt and sufferings to some other being who will bear them for us is familiar to the savage mind. It arises from a very obvious confusion between the physical and the mental, between the material and the immaterial. Because it is possible to shift a load of wood, stones or what not, from our own back to the back of another, the savage fancies that it is equally possible to shift the burden of his pains and sorrows to another, who will suffer them in his stead. Upon this idea he acts, and the result is an endless number of very unamiable devices for palming off upon someone else the trouble which a man shrinks from bearing himself.
JAMES G. FRAZER (1854–1941) *The Golden Bough*

COURAGE

11 There are various forms of *courage*, namely, the capacity to envisage immediate danger and yet proceed with the course of action that brings the danger on. The variations are established by the nature of the risk, for example, whether physical, financial, social or spiritual.... Note that the interests served by courageous action may be quite selfish; the issue is the actor's readiness to face great risk.
ERVING GOFFMAN *Interaction Ritual*, 1967

1 'I'm very brave generally,' he went on in a low voice: 'only today, I happen to have a headache.'
LEWIS CARROLL (1832–1898) *Alice Through the Looking Glass*

2 Ah, were I courageous enough
To shout *Stuff your pension!*
But I know, all too well, that's the stuff
That dreams are made on.
PHILIP LARKIN (1922–1985) 'Toads'

3 Healthy children will not fear life if their elders have integrity enough not to fear death.
ERIK ERIKSON *Childhood and Society*, 1950

4 Cowards die many times before their deaths;
The valiant never taste of death but once.
WILLIAM SHAKESPEARE (1564–1616) *Julius Caesar*

5 He went out into the blizzard and we have not seen him since. We knew that poor Oates was walking to his death, but though we tried to dissuade him, we knew it was the act of a brave man and an English gentleman. We all hope to meet the end with a similar spirit, and assuredly the end is not far.
CAPTAIN R.F. SCOTT (1868–1912) *Diary*

6 Those who have courage to love should have courage to suffer.
ANTHONY TROLLOPE (1815–1882) *The Claverings*

7 My valour is certainly going! – it is sneaking off! – I feel it oozing out as if it were at the palms of my hands!
RICHARD BRINSLEY SHERIDAN (1751–1816) *The Rivals*

COURTSHIP

8 Dating is a social engagement with the threat of sex at its conclusion.
P.J. O'ROURKE *Modern Manners*, 1984

9 Courtship is to marriage, as a very witty prologue to a very dull play.
WILLIAM CONGREVE (1670–1729) *The Old Bachelor*

10 I conclude that musical notes and rhythms were first acquired by the male or female progenitors of mankind for the sake of charming the opposite sex.
CHARLES DARWIN (1809–1882) *The Descent of Man*

11 Woe betide the man who dares to pay a woman a compliment today....
Forget the flowers, the chocolates, the soft word – rather woo her with a self-defence manual in one hand and a family planning leaflet in the other.
ALAN AYCKBOURN *Round and Round the Garden*, 1975

CREATIVITY

12 All scientists know of colleagues whose minds are so well equipped with the means of refutation that no new idea has the temerity to seek admittance. Their contribution to science is accordingly very small.
PETER MEDAWAR *A Note on the Scientific Method*, 1949

13 Discovery is not a result of logical thought, even though the end result is intimately bound to the rules of logic.
ALBERT EINSTEIN (1879–1955) cit. Einstein Museum, Bern

14 The requirements of creativity are that the tendency to eccentricity must be bridled by at least an intermittent sense of the possible.
EDITORIAL *The Independent*, 28 March 1998

15 Fruitful ideas usually change emphasis, or change the kinds of facts taken into consideration.
COLWYN TREVARTHEN in M.V. Cranach *et al. Human Ethology*, 1979

16 Modern education has made great strides in encouraging inventiveness, but it still has a long way to go before it can completely rid itself of the urge to suppress creativity.
DESMOND MORRIS *The Human Zoo*, 1969

17 Man unites himself with the world in the process of creation.
ERICH FROMM *The Art of Loving*, 1957

1   ... he who would create aesthetically must first of all, not only observe, but also feel.
CHARLES SPEARMAN *The Creative Mind* 1930

2   Nothing can be created out of nothing.
LUCRETIUS (96–55 BC) *De Rarum Novarum*

3   Creativity is traditionally something mysterious.
P.E. VERNON *et al. The Psychology and Education of Gifted Children*, 1977

4   Too often thinking is equated with rationality.... Yet we know that creative thinking, in art as well as science, does not seem to follow this route.
J. GETZELS, M. CSIKSZENTMIHALYI *The Creative Vision*, 1976

5   I sometimes begin a drawing with no preconceived problem to solve, with only the desire to use pencil on paper and make lines, tones and styles, with no conscious aim, but as my mind takes in what is so produced a point arrives where some idea becomes conscious and crystallizes, and then a control and ordering begins to take place.
HENRY MOORE cit. B. Gheselin *The Creative Process*, 1955

6   The formulation of a problem is often more essential than its solution, which may be merely a matter of mathematical or experimental skill. To raise new questions, new problems, to regard old problems from a new angle, requires creative imagination and marks real advance in science.
ALBERT EINSTEIN in A. Einstein, L. Infeld *The Evolution of Physics*, 1938

7   I have been speculating last night what makes a man a discoverer of undiscovered things; and a most perplexing problem it is. Many men who are very clever – much cleverer than the discoverers – never originate anything.
CHARLES DARWIN (1809–1882) cit. Emma Darwin *A Century of Family Letters, 1792–1896*

8   True creativity often starts where language ends.
ARTHUR KOESTLER *The Act of Creation*, 1964

9   Society is creative when it is ruled by creative spirits.
CECIL COLLINS (1908–1989) *The Vision of the Fool*

10   The passion for destruction is also a creative passion.
MICHAEL BAKUNIN cit. A. Alvarez *The Savage God*, 1974

11   The discoveries of science, the works of art are explorations – more, are explorations of hidden likeness. The discoverer or the artist presents in them aspects of nature and fuses them into one. This is the act of creation, in which an original thought is born and it is the same act in original science and original art.
J. BRONOWSKI (1908–1974) *Science and Human Values*, 1956

12   In the case of British New Guinea it appears pretty evident that art flourishes where food is abundant. One is perhaps justified in making the general statement that the finer the man the better the art, and that the artistic skill of a people is dependent upon the favourableness of their environment.
A.C. HADDON *Evolution in Art*, 1895

13   For masterpieces are not single and solitary births; they are the outcome of many years' thinking in common, of thinking by the body of the people, so that the experience of the mass is behind the single voice.
VIRGINIA WOOLF (1882–1941) *A Room of One's Own*

CRIME AND DELINQUENCY

1 I came to the conclusion many years ago that almost all crime is due to the repressed desire for aesthetic expression.
EVELYN WAUGH (1903–1966) *Decline and Fall*

2 All things can corrupt perverted minds.
OVID (43 BC–17 AD) *Tristia*

3 Bad company is a disease;
Who lies with dogs, shall rise with fleas.
R. WATKYNS (1610–1664)

4 Catholics and Communists have committed great crimes, but at least they have not stood aside, like an established society, and been indifferent. I would rather have blood on my hands than water like Pilate.
GRAHAM GREENE (1904–1991) *The Comedians*

5 Errors look so very ugly in persons of small means – one feels they are taking quite a liberty in going astray; whereas people of fortune may naturally indulge in a few delinquencies.
GEORGE ELIOT (1819–1880) *Scenes from Clerical Life*

6 Crime isn't a disease. It's a symptom.
RAYMOND CHANDLER (1888–1959) *The Long Goodbye*

CROWDS

7 A crowd has no intellect, only passions.
J.M. COETZEE *The Master of Petersburg*, 1994

8 The multitude is always ready to listen to the strong-willed man, who knows how to impose himself upon it.
GUSTAVE LE BON *The Crowd: A Study of the Popular Mind*, 1896

9 … the crowd is always intellectually inferior to the isolated individual, but … from the point of view of feelings and of the acts these feelings provoke, the crowd may according to circumstances, be better or worse than the individual.
GUSTAVE LE BON *The Crowd: A Study of the Popular Mind*, 1896

10 A crowd is a slow, stupid creature, far less intelligent than any one of its members.
IAN McEWAN *Black Dogs*, 1992

11 You cannot make a man by standing a sheep on its hindlegs. But by standing a flock of sheep in that position you can make a crowd of men.
MAX BEERBOHM (1872–1956) *Zuleika Dobson*

12 'Suppose there are two mobs?' suggested Mr. Snodgrass.
'Shout with the largest,' replied Mr. Pickwick.
CHARLES DICKENS (1812–1870) *Pickwick Papers*

13 For a man to refrain even from good words, and hold his peace, it is commendable; but for a multitude it is great mastery.
CHARLES LAMB (1775–1834) *Essays of Elia*

14 Every aristocracy that has ever existed has behaved, in all essential points, exactly like a small mob.
G.K. CHESTERTON (1874–1936) *Heretics*

15 An individual in a crowd is a grain of sand amid other grains of sand, which the wind stirs up at will.
GUSTAVE LE BON *The Crowd: A Study of the Popular Mind*, 1896

16 A crowd is a device for indulging ourselves in a kind of temporary insanity by all going crazy together.
E.D. MARTIN (1880–1941) *The Behavior of Crowds*

CRUELTY

1 Cruelty, like every other vice, requires no motive outside itself – it only requires opportunity.
GEORGE ELIOT (1819–1880) *Scenes from Clerical Life*

2 The wish to hurt, the momentary intoxication with pain, is the loophole through which the pervert climbs into the minds of ordinary men.
J. BRONOWSKI (1908–1974) *The Face of Violence*

3 Cruelty has a human heart.
WILLIAM BLAKE (1757–1827) 'Songs of Innocence and Experience'

4 I must be cruel to be kind.
WILLIAM SHAKESPEARE (1564–1616) *Hamlet*

5 Being cruel to be kind is just ordinary cruelty with an excuse made for it.
IVY COMPTON-BURNETT (1884–1969) *Daughters and Sons*

CULTURE

6 In the encounter with another culture the individual gains new experiential knowledge by coming to understand the roots of his or her own ethnocentrism and by gaining new perspectives and outlooks on the nature of culture.... Paradoxically, the more one is capable of experiencing new and different dimensions of human diversity, the more one learns of oneself.
P.S. ADLER *Journal of Humanistic Psychology*, 1975

7 Culture shock is precipitated by the anxiety that results from losing all our familiar signs and symbols of social intercourse. These signs or symbols include the thousand and one ways in which we orient ourselves to the situations of daily life.... These cues which may be words, gestures, facial expressions, customs, or norms are acquired by all of us in the course of growing up and are as much a part of our culture as the language we speak or the beliefs we accept.
K. OBERG *Practical Anthropology*, 1960

8 Man's nature, his passions, and anxieties are a cultural product.
ERICH FROMM *Escape from Freedom*, 1941

9 Traditional African societies have by and large normally been grouped into the general category of 'primitive'. And one of the most important differentiating characteristics of the category is normally taken to be the fact of being 'non-literate'; another is of being 'simple'. People have found it only too easy to slip from this into an assumption that 'non-literate' involved something like our concept of 'illiterate' and, further, that 'simple' implied simple intellectually or artistically as well as simple in technology. Neither of these assumptions is in fact logically or empirically defensible.
RUTH FINNEGAN *Oral Literature in Africa*, 1970

10 The past is a foreign country. They do things differently there.
L.P. HARTLEY(1895–1972) *The Go-Between*

11 It is not enough for a country to breed talent. It must eventually deserve it.
PETER USTINOV *Quotable Ustinov*, 1995

12 Psychology follows culture, but often at a discreet distance.
WILLIAM KESSEN *American Psychologist*, 1979

13 The impact of human uniqueness upon the world has been enormous because it has established a new kind of evolution to support the transmission across generations of learned knowledge and behavior.
STEPHEN J. GOULD *The Mismeasure of Man*, 1981

14 Culture has the power to impose itself on nature from within.
S. TOULMIN *New York Review of Books*, June 1977

1 No man ever looks at the same world with pristine eyes. He sees it edited by a definite set of customs and institutions and ways of thinking.
RUTH BENEDICT *Patterns of Culture*, 1935

2 The structures of mind and culture are most effectively understood as developmental processes.
C.J. LUMSDEN, E.O. WILSON *Genes, Mind, and Culture*, 1981

D

CURIOSITY

3 Curiosity is one of the permanent and certain characteristics of a vigorous intellect.
SAMUEL JOHNSON (1709–1784) *The Rambler*

4 ... I believe there exists & I feel within me, an instinct for truth, or knowledge or discovery, of something of the same nature as the instinct of virtue, & that our having such an instinct is reason enough for scientific researches without any practical results *ever* ensuing from them.
CHARLES DARWIN (1809–1882) *The Correspondence of Charles Darwin, Vol. 4*, 1847–1850

5 Curiosity in children ... is but an appetite after knowledge; and therefore ought to be encouraged in them, not only as a good sign, but as the great Instrument Nature has provided, to remove that Ignorance they were born with; and which, without this busie Inquisitiveness, will make them dull and useless creatures.
JOHN LOCKE (1632–1704) *Some Thoughts Concerning Education*

6 Disinterested intellectual curiosity is the life blood of real civilisation.
G. M. TREVELYAN (1876–1962) *English Social History*

7 Curiosity is, in great and generous minds, the first passion and the last.
SAMUEL JOHNSON (1709–1784) *The Rambler*

DATA

8 Psychologists have constructed for themselves an *alter ego*, a significant other, or an imaginary companion in their pursuits – the data. The whole range of human characteristics can be projected into that significant other....
JAAN VALSINER *Culture and the Development of Children's Actions*, 1997

9 ... data are in part a product of the mind of the observer....
C.H. COOMBS *A Theory of Data*, 1964

10 The process of attaching meaning to numbers is known as *measurement* and numbers that have meaning are often called *data*.
R.M. THORNDIKE *Data Collection and Data Analysis*, 1982

11 The fact is the actual occurrence of the event; the datum is the recording of the event.
G. McCAIN, E.M. SEGAL *The Game of Science*, 1969

12 This article is mainly based on missing data.
URIE BRONFENBRENNER *American Psychologist*, 1979

DEATH

1   There had been a time when I would have regarded it as plainly untragic to be ill and dying in your late sixties, hardly worth struggling against or complaining about. You're old, you die. Now I was beginning to see that you hung on at every stage – forty, sixty, eighty – until you were beaten.
IAN McEWAN *Black Dogs*, 1992

2   If this is dying, then I don't think much of it.
LYTTON STRACHEY (1880–1932) cit. Michael Holroyd *Lytton Strachey*, 1967

3   If there wasn't death I think you couldn't go on.
STEVIE SMITH (1902–1971) *The Observer*, 9 November 1969

4   My death will break the more direct relations between my present experiences and future experiences, but it will not break various other relations. This is all there is to the fact that there will be no one living who will be me. Instead of saying, 'I shall be dead', I should say, 'There will be no future experiences that will be related, in certain ways, to these present experiences'.
DEREK PARFIT *Reasons and Persons*, 1984

5   Death must be distinguished from dying with which it is often confused.
SYDNEY SMITH (1771–1845) *Table Talk*

6   Life is a great surprise. I do not see why death should not be an even greater one.
VLADIMIR NABOKOV (1899–1977) *Pale Fire*

7   There is a remedy for everything but death, which will be sure to lay us out flat some time or other.
MIGUEL DE CERVANTES (1547–1616) *Don Quixote*

8   Our final experience, like our first, is conjectural. We move between two darknesses.
E.M. FORSTER (1879–1970) *Some Aspects of the Novel*

9   Just try and set death aside. It sets you aside, and that's the end of it!
IVAN TURGENEV (1818–1883) *Fathers and Sons*

10   All men think all men are mortal but themselves.
EDWARD YOUNG (1683–1765) *Night Thoughts*

11   Do not go gentle into that good night,
Old age should burn and rave at close of day;
Rage, rage against the dying of the light.
DYLAN THOMAS (1914–1953) 'Do Not Go Gentle Into That Good Night'

12   The act of dying too is one of the acts of life.
MARCUS AURELIUS (121–180) *Meditations*

13   Ever since dying came into fashion life hasn't been safe.
YIDDISH PROVERB

14   Tear up your mourning and hang up your brightest colours in his honour and let us all praise God that he had not to die in a stuffy bed of a trumpery cough, weakened by age and saddened by the disappointments that would have attended his work had he lived.
GEORGE BERNARD SHAW, letter to Michael Collins' sister after his assassination, cit. Brendan Behan *Brendan Behan's Other Island*, 1962

15   While I thought that I was learning how to live, I have been learning how to die.
LEONARDO DA VINCI (1452–1519) *The Notebooks of Leonardo da Vinci*

16   There is nothing over which a free man ponders less than death; his wisdom is, to meditate not on death but on life.
BARUCH SPINOZA (1632–1677) *Ethics*

17   Before I became old I tried to live well; now that I am old, I shall try to die well; but dying well means dying gladly.
SENECA (4 BC–65 AD) *Moral Epistles to Lucilius*

1 Waldo is one of those people who would be enormously improved by death.
SAKI (1870–1916) *Beasts and Superbeasts*

2 Death destroys a man; the idea of death saves him.
E.M. FORSTER (1879–1970) *Howards End*

3 Let me die a youngman's death
not a clean and inbetween
the sheets holywater death
not a famous-last-words
peaceful out of breath death.
ROGER McGOUGH 'Let me Die a Youngman's Death', 1967

4 The grave's a fine and private place,
But none, I think, do there embrace.
ANDREW MARVELL (1621–1678) 'To His Coy Mistress'

5 A man's dying is more the survivors' affair than his own.
THOMAS MANN (1875–1955) *The Magic Mountain*

6 Death is not the greatest of ills; it is worse to want to die, and not be able to.
SOPHOCLES (496–406 BC) *Electra*

7 It's not that I'm afraid to die, I just don't want to be there when it happens.
WOODY ALLEN *Getting Even*, 1971

8 There is only one liberty, to come to terms with death. After which everything is possible.
ALBERT CAMUS (1913–1960) *Notebooks*

9 Then I found myself listening to
The amplified grave ticking of hall clocks
Where the phone lay unattended in a calm
Of mirror glass and sunstruck pendulums.
And found myself then thinking: if it were nowadays,
This is how Death would summon Everyman.
SEAMUS HEANEY 'A Call', 1996

DECEPTION

10 Hypocrisy is a sort of homage that vice pays to virtue.
DUC FRANÇOIS DE LA ROCHEFOUCAULD (1613–1680) *Maxims*

11 You can fool too many of the people too much of the time.
JAMES THURBER (1894–1961) *Fables of our Time*

12 That may smile, and smile, and be a villain;
WILLIAM SHAKESPEARE (1564–1616) *Hamlet*

13 Sir Christopher Wren
Said 'I am going to dine with some men
If anyone calls
Say I am designing St. Paul's'.
E. CLERIHEW BENTLEY (1875–1956) *Biography for Beginners*

14 The cruellest lies are often told in silence.
ROBERT LOUIS STEVENSON (1850–1894) *Virginibus Puerisque*

15 … look like the innocent flower
But be the serpent under't.
WILLIAM SHAKESPEARE (1564–1616) *Macbeth*

16 Oh what a tangled web we weave,
When first we practise to deceive!
WALTER SCOTT (1771–1832) *Marmion*

17 It is not the lie that passeth through the mind, but the lie that sinketh in, and settleth in it, that doth the hurt.
FRANCIS BACON (1561–1626) *Essays*

18 It is not in human nature to deceive others, for a long time, without in a measure, deceiving ourselves.
JOHN HENRY (CARDINAL) NEWMAN (1801–1890) *Parochial and Plain Sermons, 1837–1842*

19 A little inaccuracy sometimes saves tons of explanation.
SAKI (1870–1916) *The Square Egg*

20 The broad mass of a nation … will more easily fall victim to a big lie than to a small one.
ADOLF HITLER (1889–1945) *Mein Kampf*

1 There is no worse lie than a truth misunderstood by those who hear it.
WILLIAM JAMES *Varieties of Religious Experience*, 1902

2 My evidence contains a misleading impression, not a lie. It was being economical with the truth.
SIR ROBERT ARMSTRONG, Cabinet Secretary reporting to Select Committee, 1986

3 A truth that's told with bad intent
Beats all the lies you can invent.
WILLIAM BLAKE (1757–1827) 'Auguries of Innocence'

DECISION MAKING

4 Emotions have powerful effects on decisions. Moreover, the outcomes of decisions have powerful effects on emotions.
B.A. MELLERS, A. SCHWARTZ, A. COOKE *Annual Review of Psychology*, 1998

5 It is frequently the case that nobody knows all that is to be known about an issue, and different people often know different things about it. This means that to one degree or another they all conceive of the problem differently.... The upshot is that, in the aggregate most decision problems are very ill defined and the decision options are not at all clear.
L.R. BEACH *The Psychology of Decision Making*, 1997

6 I must have a prodigious quantity of mind; it takes me as much as a week sometimes, to make it up.
MARK TWAIN (1835–1910) *The Innocents Abroad*

7 For though with judgement we on things reflect,
Our will determines, not our intellect.
E. WALLER (1606–1687) *Divine Love*

8 There is no more miserable human being than one in whom nothing is habitual but indecision.
WILLIAM JAMES *Principles of Psychology*, 1890

9 Decisions are typically made according to rules or habits, without much thinking. But the creation of these rules and habits results from earlier decisions.
N. HASLAM, J. BARON in R.J. Sternberg, P. Ruzgis *Personality and Intelligence*, 1994

10 If someone tells you he is going to make 'a realistic decision', you immediately understand that he has resolved to do something bad.
MARY McCARTHY *On the Contrary*, 1962

11 ... decisions seldom are made in isolation – the decision maker always must be mindful of the preferences and opinions of other people. However, in all cases, he or she must make up his or her mind and then differences with others must be resolved in some manner.
L.R. BEACH *The Psychology of Decision Making*, 1997

12 While the doctor is reflecting the patient dies.
ITALIAN PROVERB

DEPRESSION

13 I *am* convinced that depression is largely a social phenomenon....
GEORGE W. BROWN in J.E. Barret *et al. Stress and Mental Disorder*, 1979

14 Depression is evidence of growth and health in the emotional development of the individual.
DONALD WINNICOTT *The Family and Individual Development*, 1965

15 A suicidal depression is a kind of spiritual winter, frozen, sterile, unmoving.
A. ALVAREZ *The Savage God*, 1974

16 Melancholy mark'd him for her own.
THOMAS GRAY (1716–1771) 'Elegy Written in a Country Churchyard'

17 If there be a hell upon earth, it is to be found in a melancholy man's heart.
ROBERT BURTON (1577–1640) *The Anatomy of Melancholy*

1 Depression is the common cold of psychopathology and has touched the lives of us all, yet it is probably the most dimly understood and most in-adequately investigated of all the major forms of psychopathology.
MARTIN SELIGMAN *Helplessness*, 1975

DESIRE

2 Whenever we confront an unbridled desire we are surely in the presence of a tragedy in-the-making.
QUENTIN CRISP *Manners from Heaven*, 1984

3 ... desires are given not chosen....
W.H. AUDEN (1907–1973) in C.C. Abbott *Poets at Work*, 1948

4 There are two tragedies in life. One is not to get your heart's desire. The other is to get it.
GEORGE BERNARD SHAW (1856–1950) *Man and Superman*

5 In order to possess, one must first have desired.
MARCEL PROUST (1871–1922) *Remembrance of Things Past*

6 O Western wind, when wilt thou blow
That the small rain down can rain?
Christ, that my love were in my arms
And I in my bed again.
ANON.

7 Desire is the very essence of man.
BARUCH SPINOZA (1632–1677) *Ethics*

8 There is nothing like desire for preventing the thing one says from bearing any resemblance to what one has in one's mind.
MARCEL PROUST (1871–1922) *Remembrance of Things Past*

DESPAIR

9 O the mind, mind has mountains; cliffs of fall
Frightful, sheer, no-man fathomed. Hold them cheap
May who ne'er hung there.
GERARD MANLEY HOPKINS (1844–1889) 'No Worst, There Is None'

10 Utter despair, impossible to pull myself together; only when I have become satisfied with my sufferings can I stop.
FRANZ KAFKA (1883–1924) *Diaries of Franz Kafka*

11 In a really dark night of the soul it is always three in the morning, day after day.
F. SCOTT FITZGERALD (1896–1946) *The Crack-Up*

12 Despair is the price one pays for setting oneself an impossible aim.
GRAHAM GREENE (1904–1991)*The Heart of the Matter*

13 Which way shall I fly
Infinite wrath, and infinite despair?
Which way I fly is hell; myself am hell;
And, in the lowest deep, a lower deep,
Still threat'nins to devour me, open wide,
To which the hell I suffer seems a heaven.
JOHN MILTON (1608–1674) *Paradise Lost*

14 Fade far away, dissolve, and quite forget
What thou among the leaves has never known,
The weariness the fever, and the fret,
Here where men sit and hear each other groan.
Where youth grows pale, and spectre thin, and dies
Where but to think is to be full of sorrow
And leaden-eyed despairs.
JOHN KEATS (1795–1821) 'Ode to a Nightingale'

15 He who has never hoped can never despair.
GEORGE BERNARD SHAW (1856–1950) *Caesar and Cleopatra*

1 Despair is better treated with hope not dope.
RICHARD ASHER *Lancet*, 1958

DEVELOPMENT

2 [Development] consists of a series of childhoods which call for a variety of subenvironments depending on the environment experienced during previous stages.
ERIK ERIKSON in B. Schaffner *Group Processes*, 1956

3 A journey of a thousand miles must begin with a single step.
LAO-TZE (6th cent. BC) *Tao Te Ching*

4 The future is now.
MARGARET MEAD *Culture and Commitment*, 1970

5 The maladapted child in ways creates its own environment and may contribute to its own developmental anomalies.
D. CICCHETTI, R. RIZLEY *New Directions in Child Development*, 1981

6 The growth or decline of any human being however uninteresting he may in himself be, is not uninteresting, surely. It is a process quite good to watch.
MAX BEERBOHM (1872–1956) *A Peep into the Past*

7 One's prime is elusive.
MURIEL SPARK *The Prime of Miss Jean Brodie*, 1961

8 Intellectual growth contains its own rhythm and speeding up cannot be continued indefinitely
JEAN PIAGET *Biology and Knowledge*, 1971

9 'Where shall I begin please your majesty?' he asked.
'Begin at the beginning' the king said, gravely, 'and go on till you come to the end: then stop.'
LEWIS CARROLL (1832–1898) *Alice's Adventures in Wonderland*

10 Heredity proposes ... development disposes.
PETER MEDAWAR *The Art of the Soluble*, 1967

11 Development is genetically guided but variable and probabilistic because influential events in the life of every person can be neither predicted nor explained by general laws.
SANDRA SCARR *Contemporary Psychology*, 1982

12 ... in this final hour ... he, his intentions, and his acts – the whole variations and complexities of his individuality – were in essence the very same as those that marked his earliest days. He has ripened; that was all.
BRAM STOKER (1847–1912) *The Lair of the White Worm*

13 Development is not always progressive and constructive.
R.W. OPPENHEIM in K. J. Connolly and H. F. R. Prechtl *Maturation and Development*, 1981

14 The question is how development occurs in the particular animal under prevailing conditions, not what heredity specifically contributes or environment specifically contributes, or how much either contributes proportionally, to the process.
T.C. SCHNEIRLA cit. D.B. Harris *The Concept of Development*, 1957

15 Development is fluid and it is never too late for changes to take place.
MICHAEL RUTTER in J. Bruner, A. Garton *Human Growth and Development*, 1978

16 Order in behavioral development, however, is quite as consonant with interactionism as with predeterminism.
J. McVICKER HUNT *The Challenge of Incompetence and Poverty*, 1969

17 There is nothing permanent except change.
HERACLITUS (c. 540–c. 460 BC) cit. Aristotle *De Caslo*

18 Ontogenesis is a brief and rapid recapitulation of phylogenesis.
ERNST HAECKEL (1834–1919) *The Riddle of the Universe*

1 ... you will be astonished to find how the whole mental disposition of your children changes with advancing years. A young child and the same when nearly grown, sometimes differ almost as much as do a caterpillar and butterfly.
CHARLES DARWIN (1809–1882) in F. Darwin *The Life and Letters of Charles Darwin*, 1911

2 The zone of proximal development defines those functions that have not yet matured but are in the process of maturation, functions that will mature tomorrow but are currently in an embryonic state.... The actual developmental level characterizes mental development retrospectively, while the zone of proximal development characterizes mental development prospectively.
L.S. VYGOTSKY *Mind in Society*, 1978

3 It is the hereditary ballast which conserves and stabilises the growth of each individual infant.
ARNOLD GESELL *Infancy and Human Growth*, 1928

4 The body is at its best between the ages of thirty and thirty-five: the mind is at its best about the age of forty-nine.
ARISTOTLE (384–322 BC) *Rhetoric*

5 The old believe everything; the middle-aged suspect everything; the young know everything.
OSCAR WILDE (1854–1900) *The Chameleon*

6 He used to be a child: he has become an adult. That is a difference of quality. For the child is irrational, the adult is rational.
SENECA (4 BC–65 AD) cit. T. Wieddmann *Adults and Children in the Roman Empire*, 1989

7 Most of an organism, most of the time is developing from one pattern to another not from homogeneity into a pattern.
ALAN TURING *Proceedings of the Royal Society B*, 1952

8 To say, then, that a theory of development is 'culture free' is not to make a wrong claim, but an absurd one.
J. BRUNER *Actual Minds, Possible Worlds*, 1986

9 'Do you know who made you?' 'Nobody, as I know on', said the child, with a short laugh.... 'I 'spect I grow'd.'
HARRIET BEECHER STOWE (1811–1896) *Uncle Tom's Cabin*

10 ... much of American developmental psychology is the science of the behavior of children in strange situations with strange adults.
URIE BRONFENBRENNER *Child Development*, 1974

11 Not to go back, is somewhat to advance,
And men must walk at least before they dance.
ALEXANDER POPE (1688–1744) 'Imitations of Horace'

12 Indeed much of what we know about security and competence is merely the other side of the coin of *in*security and *in*competence. Namely we are aware that most children who do *not* experience discord, rejection and other serious hazards do *not* develop gross disorders of development.
MICHAEL RUTTER in J. Bruner, A. Garton *Human Growth and Development*, 1978

DISABILITY

13 My disability has not been a severe handicap. Theoretical physics is a good subject for handicapped people because it is all in the mind.
STEPHEN HAWKING, interview, BBC radio, 1 February 1988

14 All children are individuals, and this applies as much to those who are handicapped as to those who are not handicapped.
VICKY LEWIS *Development and Handicap*, 1987

1 but one day soon you must feel
the silent stopwatch chill your ear
in the doctor's rooms, and be wired
back into a slightly thinned world
with a faint plastic undertone to it
and, if the rumours are true, snatches
of static, music, police transmission:
it's a BARF minor Car Fourteen
  Prospect.
LES MURRAY 'Hearing Impairment' *The
Daylight Moon,* 1987

2 Notwithstanding what hath been
said of the dignity and superior nature
of this faculty [vision], it is worthy of our
observation that there is very little of
the knowledge acquired by sight that
may not be communicated to a man
born blind.
THOMAS REID (1710–1796) *An Enquiry into
the Human Mind on the Principles of Common
Sense*

3 Certainly, the dull are usually
backward; but the backward are not
necessarily dull.
CYRIL BURT *Mental and Scholastic Tests,*
1921

4 So long as there are two deaf people
upon the face of the earth and they get
together, so long will signs be in use.
J. SCHUYLER LONG *The Sign Language,*
1910

5 O, loss of sight, of thee I most
  complain!
Blind among enemies, O worse than
  chains,
Dungeons, or beggary, or decrepit age.
JOHN MILTON (1608–1674) *Samson
Agonistes*

6 The gradations of mental incapacity
are as numerous and delicate as are
those of mental capacity....
J. LANGDON DOWN *Mental Afflictions of
Childhood and Youth,* 1887

7 Dyslexia. An ambiguous word, never
satisfactorily defined.
PETER LAWRENCE *Is My Child Stupid,* 1988

8 Dyslexia lures KO.
GRAFFITTI

9 Study of [handicapped] children can
clarify the processes underlying
development. They can point to other
routes to development, and they can
identify features of development which
may have been overlooked in the study
of non-handicapped children.
VICKY LEWIS *Development and Handicap,*
1987

DISADVANTAGE

10 If children are labelled 'culturally
deprived' then it follows that the parents
are inadequate, the spontaneous realiz-
ation of their culture, its images and
symbolic representations are of reduced
value and significance. Teachers will
have lower expectations of the children,
which the children will undoubtedly ful-
fil. All that informs the child, that gives
meaning and purpose to him outside of
the school, ceases to be valid and
accorded significance and opportunity
for enhancement within the school.
BASIL BERNSTEIN in D. Rubenstein, C.
Stoneman *Education for Democracy,* 1970

11 ... recovery from gross deprivation
or distortion of the socialization process
in early life takes many years. It is not
surprising that society has not yet
found a way of meeting adequately the
treatment needs of these children.
SULA WOLFF *Children Under Stress,* 1969

12 That girls are raped, that two boys
  knife a third,
Were axioms to him, who'd never heard
Of any world where promises were kept
Or one could weep because another
  wept.
W.H. AUDEN (1907–1973) *The Shield of
Achilles*

13 ... even in the worst family
circumstances, a few 'good' factors can
do much to balance the serious
maladaptive and disruptive influences.
If we knew more about these protective
factors we would be in a better position
to help children at risk.
MICHAEL RUTTER, NICOLA MADGE *Cycles of
Disadvantage,* 1976

1   Poor children enter [task] situations at a disadvantage. They may be easily bored by the tasks; they lack experience with formal learning situations, and they may not possess certain vocabulary relevant to the tasks. All these factors combine to lower poor children's chances of success. But this does not necessarily indicate a deficiency in poor children's learning ability.
H. GINSBURG *The Myth of the Deprived Child*, 1972

DISSATISFACTION

2   'You look as if you wished the place in Hell;
My friend said, 'judging from your face'. O well,
I suppose its' not the place's fault', I said.
'Nothing, like something, happens anywhere.'
PHILIP LARKIN (1922–1985) 'I Remember, I Remember'

3   Nought's had, all's spent
Where our desires are got without content.
WILLIAM SHAKESPEARE (1564–1616) *Macbeth*

4   Complaining is a contempt upon one's self: it is an ill sign both of a man's head and of his heart. A man throweth himself down whilst he complaineth: and when a man throweth himself down nobody careth to take him up again.
GEORGE SAVILE, MARQUESS OF HALIFAX (1633–1695) *Miscellaneous Thoughts and Reflections*

5   Dissatisfaction with his lot seems to be the characteristic of man in all ages and climates. So far, however, from being an evil, as at first might be supposed, it has been the great civiliser of our race.... But the same discontent which has been the source of all our improvements, has been the parent of no small progeny of follies and absurdities.
CHARLES MACKAY *Extraordinary Popular Delusions and the Madness of Crowds*, 1852

6   How my achievements mock me!
WILLIAM SHAKESPEARE (1564–1616) *Troilus and Cressida*

DOUBT AND CERTAINTY

7   William James used to preach the 'will to believe'. For my part, I should wish to preach the 'will to doubt' ... what is wanted is not the will to believe, but the wish to find out, which is the exact opposite.
BERTRAND RUSSELL (1872–1970) *Sceptical Essays*

8   I knew that nought was lasting, but now even
Change grows too changeable, without being new.
LORD BYRON (1788–1824) *Don Juan*

9   A proof tells us where to concentrate our doubts.
ANON.

10   It is not certain that everything is uncertain.
BLAISE PASCAL (1623–1662) *Pensées*

11   I do not believe.... I know.
CARL JUNG (1875–1961) in Laurens van der Post *Jung and the Story of our Time*, 1976

12   It is certain because it is impossible.
TERTULLIAN (155–222) *De Carne Cristi*

13   We have learnt to distrust those who come with absolute certainties, whether in religion, science, politics or philosophy.
J.Z. YOUNG *Philosophy and the Brain*, 1987

14   If a man begin with certainties, he shall end in doubts; but if he be content to begin with doubts, he shall end in certainties.
FRANCIS BACON (1561–1626) *The Advancement of Learning*

15   Ten thousand difficulties do not make one doubt.
JOHN HENRY (CARDINAL) NEWMAN (1801–1890) *Apologia Pro Vita Sua*

1 Only charlatans are certain.... Doubt is not a very agreeable state but certainty is a ridiculous one.
VOLTAIRE (1692–1778) *The Ignorant Philosopher*

DRAWING

2 ... the child's eye at a surprisingly early period loses its primal 'innocence', grows 'sophisticated' in the sense that instead of seeing what is really presented it sees, or pretends to see, what knowledge and logic tell it is there. In other words his sense-perceptions have for artistic purposes become corrupted by a too large admixture of intelligence.
JAMES SULLY *Studies of Childhood*, 1895

3 Drawings are produced by actions in which meaning and pragmatics may be actively involved in determining the form, direction and sequence of strokes.
PETER VAN SOMMERS *Drawing and Cognition*, 1984

4 While children's drawings possess undoubted aesthetic appeal for the adult and may resemble great works of art, these drawings may mean something very different for the child.... Whether children's drawings possess repleteness or expression cannot be determined simply by examining works produced spontaneously. All works of art, even those produced by children and chimpanzees, or by accident, possess these properties for perceivers if the perceivers attend to all physical aspects of the works and apprehend a mood expressed.
ELLEN WINNER *Invented Worlds: The Psychology of the Arts*, 1982

5 The pattern of development in children's drawings is determined by what it is that children are trying to do when they are learning to draw.
JOHN WILLATS *Art and Representation*, 1997

6 Once I drew like Raphael, but it has taken me a whole lifetime to learn to draw like children.
PABLO PICASSO (1881–1973) cit. F. de Meredien *Le Dessain d'Enfant*, 1974

7 ... children tend to lose their flexibility in portraying things in the very act of generating earlier versions of them. That is not to say that children's drawings never change, but rather that their drawings often evolve by the modulation or amendment of existing devices, rather than through a revolutionary re-thinking of the basic representational strategy.
PETER VAN SOMMERS *Drawing and Cognition*, 1984

8 No occupation conduces more surely than drawing to a habit of clear thinking, and accurate and true expression.
A.S. BALLIN, E.A. WELLDON *The Kindergarten System Explained*, n.d.

DREAMS

9 To a certain extent the dream is a restorative for the brain, which during the day is called upon to meet the severe demands for trained thought, made by the conditions of a higher civilisation.
FRIEDRICH NIETZSCHE (1844–1900) *Human, All Too Human*

10 A tissue of thoughts, usually a very complicated one, which has built up during the day and has not been completely dealt with – 'a day's residue' – continues during the night to retain the quota of energy – the 'interest' – claimed by it, and threatens to disturb sleep. This 'day's residue' is transformed by dream-work into a dream and made innocuous to sleep.
SIGMUND FREUD (1856–1939) *Jokes and their Relation to the Unconscious*

11 Thus through relating his dreams the patient himself furnished the most important means of gaining access to the unconscious and disturbing complexes with which his symptoms were connected.
CARL JUNG (1875–1961) *The Psychology of the Unconscious*

1 Dreams in general originate from those incidents which have most occupied the thoughts during the day.
HERODOTUS (484–424 BC) *Histories*

2 I have had a dream, past the wit of man to say what dream it was.
WILLIAM SHAKESPEARE (1564–1616) *A Midsummer Night's Dream*

3 We live, as we dream – alone.
JOSEPH CONRAD (1857–1924) *Heart of Darkness*

4 The dream is the reflection of the waves of the unconscious life in the floor of the imagination.
H.F. AMIEL (1821–1888) *Journal*, 1889

5 And I awoke in struggles, and cried aloud, 'I will sleep no more!'
THOMAS de QUINCY (1785–1859) *Confessions of an Opium Eater*

6 A dream which is not interpreted is like a letter which is not read.
The Talmud

7 But I, being poor, have only my dreams;
I have spread my dreams under your feet;
Tread softly because you tread on my dreams.
W.B. YEATS (1865–1939) 'He Wishes for the Clothes of Heaven'

8 ... the art of working profitably with dreams is something that anyone can learn should they really wish to do so.
ANTHONY STEVENS *Private Myths*, 1995

9 Dreams are meaningful only in the context of the dreamer's life.
DONALD BROADRIBB *The Dream Story*, 1987

10 I do not know whether I was a man dreaming I was a butterfly or whether I am now a butterfly dreaming I am a man.
CHUANG TZU (369–286 BC)

11 Dreams are always set in the past.
ADAM PHILLIPS *On Kissing, Tickling and Being Bored*, 1993

DRUGS

12 Those who have never been brain-washed or addicted to a drug find it hard to understand their fellow men who are driven by such compulsions.
RICHARD DAWKINS *The Extended Phenotype*, 1982

13 I've tried it [writing] long ago, with hashish and peyote. Fascinating, yes, but no good, no. This, as we find in alcohol, is an *escape* from awareness, a cheat, a momentary substitution, and in the end a destruction of it. With luck, someone might have a fragmentary Kubla Khan vision. But with no meaning. And with the steady destruction of the observing and remembering mind.
CONRAD AIKEN cit. G. Plimpton *The Writer's Chapbook*, 1989

14 These effects of mescalin are the sort of effects you could expect to follow the administration of a drug having the power to impair the efficiency of the cerebral reducing valve. When the brain runs out of sugar, the undernourished ego grows weak.... As Mind at Large seeps past the no longer watertight valve, all kinds of biologically useless things start to happen.
ALDOUS HUXLEY (1894–1963) *The Doors of Perception*

15 Thou hast the keys of Paradise, oh just, subtle, and mighty opium.
THOMAS de QUINCY (1785–1859) *Confessions of an Opium Eater*

16 Drug use and procrastination often go hand in tourniquet.
WILL SELF *Junk Mail*, 1995

17 Doctors who insist that drugs alone can work cures are either modest, overworked or incompetent. A maniac quietened by a depressant but otherwise untreated represents an advantage to the society of the mental hospital; but it does not necessarily follow that the patient shares in this.
C.R.B. JOYCE in B.M. Foss *New Horizons in Psychology*, 1966

1 If nervous systems are susceptible to drug-like influences via the normal sense organs, should we not positively expect that natural selection would have favoured the exploitation of such possibilities, would have favoured the development of visual, olfactory, or auditory 'drugs'?
RICHARD DAWKINS *The Extended Phenotype*, 1982

2 It is, perhaps, not impossible that those mental diseases caused by poisons that are formed in the body just as special substances, for instance, alcohol, hashish, and other intoxicating substances, produce temporary mental diseases.
JACQUES LOEB *Comparative Physiology of the Brain and Comparative Psychology*, 1905

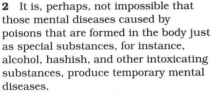

EARLY EXPERIENCE

3 The first messages written on the *tabula rasa* may not necessarily be the most difficult to erase.
JEROME KAGAN in A.M. Clark and A.D.B. Clark *Early Experience: Myth and Reality*, 1976

4 Society would benefit immeasurably if every child could have a good beginning.
MURIEL BEADLE *A Child's Mind*, 1971

5 The Battle of Waterloo was won on the playing fields of Eton.
ARTHUR WELLESLEY, DUKE OF WELLINGTON (1769–1852) attrib.

6 For the pure cleane witte of a sweete yong babe, is like the newest wax, most able to receive the best and fayrest printing.
ROGER ASCHAM (1515–1568) *Scholemaster*

7 A maggot must be born i' the cheese to like it.
GEORGE ELIOT (1819–1880) *Adam Bede*

8 My very first conscious memory dates from when I was four. I was being taken for a walk by the nursemaid. I was dressed in knickerbockers, with a fawn-coloured coat, and on my head a red tam-o'shanter – you know, the round cap with a little tail protruding from its centre, like the remains of a cut umbilical cord. And then out of the hawthorn hedge there hopped a fat toad. What a creature, with its warty skin, its big eyes bulging up, and its awkward movements! That comic toad helped to determine my career as a naturalist.
JULIAN HUXLEY *Memories*, 1970

1 The child is the father of the man.
WILLIAM WORDSWORTH (1770–1850) 'My Heart Leaps'

2 I think we may observe, that when children are first born, all objects of sight, that do not hurt the eyes, are indifferent to them; and they are no more afraid of a blackamoor, or a lion, than of their nurse or a cat. What is it then, that afterwards, in certain mixtures of shapes and colour, comes to affright them? Nothing but the apprehension of harm, that accompany these things. Did a child suck every day a new nurse, I make account it would be no more affrighted with the changes of faces at six months old than at sixty.
JOHN LOCKE (1632–1704) *Some Thoughts Concerning Education*

3 The imitativeness of our early years makes us acquire the passions of our parents, even when these passions poison our lives.
STENDHAL (1783–1842) *Love*

4 Although the crudity of modern psychological methods permits any reasonable person to maintain the hypothesis of the stability of early characteristics, one should at least accommodate to the existing empirical information and entertain the remote possibility that the profiles sculpted within the family during the first two to three years are not necessarily permanent.
JEROME KAGAN *American Psychologist*, 1979

5 The practice of coitus was familiar to me at the age of six and seven, after which I suspended it and did not resume it till I was twenty-four; it was a common enough practice among the village children.
ERNEST JONES *Free Associations: Memories of a Psycho-Analyst*, 1959

6 Every adult, whether he is a follower or a leader, a member of a mass or an elite, was once a child. He was once small. A sense of smallness forms a substratum of his mind, ineradicably. His triumphs will be measured against this smallness, his defeats will substantiate it.
ERIK ERIKSON *Childhood and Society*, 1950

7 Give me a girl at an impressionable age and she is mine for life.
MURIEL SPARK *The Prime of Miss Jean Brodie*, 1961

8 The character of a child is already plain, even in its mother's womb. Before I was born my mother was in great agony of spirit and in a tragic situation. She could take no food except iced oysters and champagne. If people ask me when I began to dance I reply, 'In my mother's womb, probably as a result of the oysters and champagne – the food of Aphrodite!'
ISADORA DUNCAN (1878–1927) *My Life*

9 In my beginning is my end.
T.S. ELIOT (1888–1965) 'East Coker'

EATING

10 One should eat to live, and not live to eat.
MOLIÈRE (1622–1673) *Le Bourgeois Gentilhomme*

11 The whole of nature ... is a conjugation of the verb to eat, in the active and the passive.
W.R. INGE (1860–1954) *Outspoken Essays*

12 And let your soul delight itself in fatness.
Bible, Isiah

13 We each day dig our graves with our teeth.
SAMUEL SMILES (1812–1904) *Duty*

14 Tell me what you eat and I will tell you what you are.
ANTHELME BRILLAT-SAVARIN (1755–1826) *Physiologie du Gout*

15 A scientist says: Roast beef made England what she is today.
Moral: Eat more vegetables.
ANON.

16 Gluttony is an emotional escape, a sign that something is eating us.
PETER DE VRIES *Comfort Me with Apples*, 1956

1 Abstain from beans. There be sundry interpretations of this symbol. But Plutarch and Cicero think beans to be forbidden of Pythagorus, because they be windy and do engender impure humours and for that cause provoke bodily lust.
RICHARD TAVENER (1505–1575) *Proverbs*

2 There is no love sincerer than the love of food.
GEORGE BERNARD SHAW (1856–1950) *Man and Superman*

3 Man is the only animal that can remain on friendly terms with the victims he intends to eat until he eats them.
SAMUEL BUTLER (1835–1902) *The Notebooks of Samuel Butler*

ECONOMIC PSYCHOLOGY

4 The love of money is the root of all evil.
Bible, Timothy

5 As individuals express their life, so they are. What they are, therefore coincides with their production, both with what they produce and how they produce. The nature of individuals thus depends on the material conditions determining their production.
KARL MARX (1818–1883) cit. S. Avinieri *The Social and Political Thought of Karl Marx*, 1968

6 ... there are not more useful members in a commonwealth than merchants. They knit mankind together in a mutual intercourse of good offices, distribute the gifts of nature, find work for the poor, and wealth to the rich, and magnificence to the great.
JOSEPH ADDISON (1672–1719) *The Spectator*

7 The world is too much with us; late and soon
Getting and spending we lay waste our powers.
WILLIAM WORDSWORTH (1770–1850) 'The World Is Too Much With Us'

8 Psychologists and economists apparently agree that goods are purchased in pursuit of the satisfaction of some need or want. So ... it is assumed that a prospective consumer has a 'problem' which the consumption of a certain good or combination of goods assuages....
ADRIAN FURNHAM, ALAN LEWIS *The Economic Mind*, 1986

9 The blind unplanned wisdom of the market ... is overwhelmingly superior to the well researched, rational, systematic, well-meaning, co-operative, science-based, forward looking, statistically respectable plans of government.
KEITH JOSEPH *Stranded in the Middle Ground*, 1976

10 In the unconscious mental life money can represent not only possessions but everything that one can take or give: therefore it can represent relations to objects in general and everything through which the bodily Ego feeling and with it self-regard can be increased or diminished.
OTTO FENICHEL cit. H. Fenichel, O. Rapaport *The Collected Papers of Otto Fenichel*, 1944

EDUCATION

11 It should be clear that education is far more strongly influenced by political, moral and economic factors than by psychological research. Innovations will not be accepted and implemented if they run counter to current beliefs, threaten social institutions, and require more financial support than the public is willing to give.
H. GINSBURG *The Myth of the Deprived Child*, 1972

12 There is much to be said for apathy in education.
E.M. FORSTER (1879–1970) *Maurice*

1 Ignorance is like a delicate exotic fruit; touch it and the bloom is gone. The whole theory of modern education is radically unsound. Fortunately, in England, at any rate, education produces no effect whatsoever.
OSCAR WILDE (1854–1900) *The Importance of Being Earnest*

2 Our first wish is that all men should be educated fully to full humanity; that he should be able to know the truth and not be deluded by what is false; to love good and not be seduced by evil; to do what should be done and not permit what should be avoided; to talk wisely about everything with everybody when there is need, and not be dumb in any matter.
JOHN COMENIUS (1592–1670) in J. Piaget *John Amos Comenius on Education*, 1967

3 Above all, the memory of children should be trained and exercised; for this is, as it were, a treasury of learning, and it is for this reason that the mythologists have made Memory the mother of the Muses, thereby intimating and hinting that there is nothing in the world like memory for creating and fostering.
PLUTARCH (c. 50–120) *Moralia*

4 Pedagogical practice has not kept pace with psychological principle.
WILLIAM GLOVER *Know Your Own Mind*, 1918

5 The high degree of cooperation and social culture which man needs for his very existence demands spontaneous social effort, and the dominant purpose of education is to evoke it.
ALFRED ADLER *Problems of Neurosis*, 1964

6 Reading maketh a full man; conference a ready man; and writing an exact man.
FRANCIS BACON (1561–1626) *Essays*

7 Whereas then a rattle is a suitable occupation for infant children, education serves as a rattle for young people when older.
ARISTOTLE (384–322 BC) *Politics*

8 The examination system, and the fact that instruction is treated mainly as training for a livelihood, leads the young to regard knowledge from a purely utilitarian point of view as the road to money, not as the gateway to wisdom.
BERTRAND RUSSELL (1872–1970) *Principles of Social Reconstruction*

9 By education most have been misled:
So they believe, because they so were bred.
The priest continues what the nurse began,
And thus the child imposes on the man.
JOHN DRYDEN (1631–1700) 'The Hind and the Panther'

10 Intelligence appears to be the thing that enables a man to get along without education. Education appears to be the thing that enables a man to get along without the use of his intelligence.
A.E. WIGGAM *The New Decalogue of Science*, 1923

11 A child miseducated is a child lost.
JOHN F. KENNEDY State of the Union Address, 11 January 1962

12 I call therefore a complete and generous education that which fits a man to perform justly, skilfully and magnanimously all the offices both public and private, of peace and war.
JOHN MILTON (1608–1674) *Of Education*

13 It is to be hoped that the influences of infant schools on the morals of the poor will be felt with gratifying force in the improved conduct of the rising generation.
MRS J. BAKEWELL *The Mother's Practical Guide*, 1845

14 In the old days a technical education consisted of the acquirement of 'good practice'. Good practice now never stays for long, for it is a highly perishable quality.
J.D. BERNAL, interview, *Science Journal*, March 1965

15 Education is simply the soul of a society as it passes from one generation to another.
G.K. CHESTERTON (1874–1936) *The Observer*, 6 July 1924

1 I would urge that in considering these deep issues of educability we keep our perspective broad and remember that the human race has a biological past from which we can read lessons from the culture of the present.
J.S. BRUNER *American Psychologist*, 1972

2 Education kills by degrees.
ANON.

3 In a general way the whole of education is dominated by this threefold rhythm. Till the age of thirteen or fourteen there is the romantic stage, from fourteen to eighteen the stage of precision, and from eighteen to two and twenty the stage of generalization.
A.N. WHITEHEAD (1861–1947) *The Aims of Education*

4 To live for a time close to great minds is the best kind of education.
JOHN BUCHAN (1875–1940) *Memory Hold the Door*

5 The education of the average American child of the upper middle class is such as to guard him solicitously against the awareness of death and doom.
NORBERT WIENER *The Human Use of Human Beings*, 1954

6 Give me a child of twelve who knows nothing at all, and at fifteen I will give him back to you as wise as the one you have instructed from the beginning.
JEAN-JACQUES ROUSSEAU (1712–1778) *Émile*

7 When they have passed their fifth birthday they should for the next two years learn simply by observation whatever they may be required to learn. Education after that may be divided into two stages – from the seventh year to puberty and from puberty to the completion of twenty-one years.
ARISTOTLE (384–322 BC) *Poetics*

8 ... sufficient is now known of child psychology to produce a scheme of scientific instruction which represents not merely the views of advocates of particular subjects, but is biologically sound because it is in accord with the principles of mental growth.
SIR RICHARD GREGORY *British Association for the Advancement of Science Report*, 1922

9 What we look for here is, first, religious and moral principles: secondly, gentlemanly conduct: thirdly, intellectual ability.
THOMAS ARNOLD (1795–1842) address to the scholars at Rugby

10 Children have to be educated, but they have also to be left to educate themselves.
ERNEST DIMNET *The Art of Thinking*, 1928

11 Education is an admirable thing, but it is well to remember from time to time that nothing that is worth knowing can be taught.
OSCAR WILDE (1854–1900) *The Critic as Artist*

12 Soap and education are not as sudden as a massacre but they are more deadly in the long run.
MARK TWAIN (1835–1910) *Sketches Old and New*

13 Education ... has produced a vast population able to read but unable to distinguish what is worth reading.
G. M. TREVELYAN *English Social History*, 1942

14 'Tis Education forms the common mind
Just as the twig is bent, the tree's inclin'd.
ALEXANDER POPE (1688–1744) 'Epistles to Several Persons'

15 Education is what survives when what has been learnt has been forgotten.
B. F. SKINNER *New Scientist*, 21 May 1964

16 Instruction, after all, does not begin at school.
L.S. VYGOTSKY *Thought and Language*, 1962

17 The discipline of colleges and universities is in general contained, not for the benefit of the students, but for the interest, or more properly speaking, for the ease of the masters.
ADAM SMITH (1723–1790) *Wealth of Nations*

1 The belief that all genuine education comes about through experience does not mean that all experiences are genuinely or equally educative.
JOHN DEWEY (1859–1952) *Experience and Education*

2 Perhaps our greatest hope of achieving equality of educational opportunity lies in the possibility of finding significant patterns of individual differences in the development of abilities and taking advantage of these differences to create the optimal interaction between pupil and instruction.
A.R. JENSEN *American Education Research Journal*, 1968

3 The proper study of mankind is books.
ALDOUS HUXLEY (1894–1963) *Chrome Yellow*

4 ... the idea of 'readiness' is a mischievous half-truth. It is a half-truth largely because it turns out that one *teaches* readiness or provides opportunities for its nurture, one does not simply wait for it.
J.S. BRUNER, *Towards a Theory of Instruction*, 1966

EGOCENTRISM

5 I am extraordinarily patient, provided I get my own way in the end.
MARGARET THATCHER *The Observer*, 4 April 1989

6 No man thinks there is much ado about nothing when the ado is about himself.
ANTHONY TROLLOPE (1815–1882) *The Bertrams*

7 if a swiss cheese
could think
it would think that
a swiss cheese
was the most important
thing in the world
just as everything that
can think at all
does think about itself
don marquis (1898–1937) 'archygrams'

8 What care I if good God be,
If he be not good to me.
STEVIE SMITH (1902–1971) *Collected Poems*, 1975

9 For most of us, if we do not talk of ourselves, or at any rate of the individual circles of which we are the centres, we can talk of nothing. I cannot hold with those who wish to put down the insignificant chatter of the world.
ANTHONY TROLLOPE (1815–1882) *Framley Parsonage*

EMBARRASSMENT

10 He who frequently becomes embarrassed in the presence of others is regarded as suffering from a foolish unjustified sense of inferiority and in need of therapy.
ERVING GOFFMAN *Interaction Ritual*, 1967

11 In common usage one is primarily ashamed of *oneself*, while one is primarily embarrassed about one's *presented* self.
A. MODIGLIANI *Embarrassment and Social Influence*, 1966

12 One person's embarrassment is ... another person's empowerment.
KATHRYN FLEET *The Observer*, 24 August 1997

13 Whatever else, embarrassment has to do with the figure the individual cuts before others.... The crucial concern is the impression one makes on others.
ERVING GOFFMAN *American Journal of Sociology*, 1967

EMOTION

14 The secret of life is never to have an emotion that is unbecoming.
OSCAR WILDE (1854–1900) *A Woman of No Importance*

1 As one observantly wanders around the world, passing from language to language, culture to culture, one notices how diverse are the catalogues of emotions that are recognized in the practices and stories of the peoples one meets.
ROM HARRÉ in J. Smith *et al. Rethinking Psychology*, 1995

2 Animals manifestly enjoy excitement, and suffer from ennui and may exhibit curiosity.
CHARLES DARWIN (1809–1882) *Descent of Man*

3 *Emotional intelligence* is an organizing framework for categorizing abilities relating to understanding, managing, and using feelings.... Moreover, individual differences in understanding, regulating and using feelings constitute the major aspects of personality. Emotions ... provide an important keystone to understanding the personality–intelligence connection.
P. SALOVEY, J.D. MAYER *Personality and Intelligence*, 1994

4 My theory ... is that *the bodily changes follow directly the perception of the exciting fact, and that our feelings of the same changes as they occur* IS *the emotion* ... we feel sorry because we cry, angry because we strike, afraid because we tremble....* Without the bodily states following on the perception, the latter would be purely cognitive in form, pale, colourless, destitute of emotional warmth.
WILLIAM JAMES *Text Book of Psychology*, 1892

5 I am aware of no evidence for the existence of a special condition called 'emotion' which follows different principles of action from other conditions of the organism. I can therefore see no reason for a psychological study of 'emotion' as such.
ELIZABETH DUFFY *Journal of General Psychology*, 1941

6 It is conceivable that colour values and other values important in aesthetics, such as brightness or sharpness of light, reflectance, texture, and aspects of mass such as balance and weight, have direct relations to the brain chemistry of emotion.
COLWYN TREVARTHEN in R.L. Gregory *et al. The Artful Eye*, 1995

7 Man is gifted with pity and other kindly feelings; he has also the power of preventing many kinds of suffering. I conceive it to fall well within his province to replace Natural Selection by other processes that are more merciful and not less effective.
FRANCIS GALTON (1822–1911) *Memories of My Life*

8 A trifle consoles us because a trifle upsets us.
BLAISE PASCAL (1623–1662) *Pensées*

9 Emotions occur precisely when adaptation is hindered for any reason whatever. The man who can run away does not have the emotion of fear. Fear occurs only when flight is impossible. Anger is displayed only when one cannot strike his enemy.
E. CLAPAREDE in M.L. Reymert *Feelings and Emotions*, 1928

10 We owe all the emotional side of our mental life, our joys and sorrows, our happy and unhappy hours, to our vasomotor system. If the impressions which fall upon our senses did not possess the power of stimulating it, we would wander through life unsympathetic and passionless, all impressions of the outer world would only enrich our experience, increase our knowledge, but would arouse neither joy nor anger, would give us neither care nor fear.
C. LANGE cit. W.B. Cannon *American Journal of Psychology*, 1927

11 Long childhood makes a technical and mental virtuoso out of man, but it also leaves a lifelong residue of emotional immaturity in him.
ERIK ERIKSON *Childhood and Society*, 1950

12 ... emotions are mental devices for guaranteeing commitment.
MARK RIDLEY *The Origins of Virtue*, 1996

1 And so, universally it seems, emotional speech is naturally linked to certain forms of pitch, loudness and rhythm; whilst conversely these forms of sound acquire the property of reproducing the emotions. An amazing example of intimacy in such association is afforded by the operas which marry the words of Gilbert to the notes of Sullivan.
CHARLES SPEARMAN *The Creative Mind*, 1930

2 Surprise is an extraordinarily useful phenomenon to students of the mind, for it allows us to probe what people take for granted.
J.S. BRUNER *Actual Minds, Possible Worlds*, 1986

3 At three years of age the child's whole emotional life plan has been laid down, his emotional disposition set. At that age the parents have already determined for him whether he is to grow into a happy person, wholesome and good-natured, whether he is to be a whining, complaining neurotic, an anger driven, vindictive, over-bearing slave driver or one whose every move in life is definitely controlled by fear.
J.B. WATSON *Psychological Care of Infant and Child*, 1928

4 The whale has a twofold distinction among the fishes: first, when seen from a distance, it looms large among them; and, second, on close examination, it is found to be no fish at all. Something like that I predict for the theory of emotions among the theories in the psychological textbooks and periodicals.
M.F. MEYER *Psychological Review*, 1933

5 'Emotion' has no distinguishing characteristics.
ELIZABETH DUFFY *Journal of General Psychology*, 1941

6 The more closely I scrutinize my states, the more persuaded I become that whatever moods, affections, and passions I have are in truth constituted by, and made up of, those bodily changes we ordinarily call their expression or consequence; and the more it seems to me that if I were to become corporeally anaesthetic, I should be excluded from the life of the affections, tender and harsh alike, and drag out an existence of merely cognitive or intellectual form.
WILLIAM JAMES *Mind*, 1884

7 ... emotion has survived as the arrogant child of psychology: the more it is ignored and relegated to a place in the corner as 'merely a semantic', the more arrogant and brutish it becomes to theory.
D.K. CANDLAND *Emotion: Bodily Change*, 1962

8 The neural basis of affect we can suppose need not entail much neural superstructure.
CHARLES SHERRINGTON *Man on His Nature*, 1940

9 Emotions are everywhere the same: but the artistic expression of them varies from age to age and from one country to another. We are brought up to accept the conventions current in the society into which we are born.
ALDOUS HUXLEY (1894–1963) *Music in India and Japan*

10 Wit is the epitaph of an emotion.
FRIEDRICH NIETZSCHE (1844–1900) *Menschliches*

11 If I am correct in my assertion that the cognitive system is subservient to the regulatory system, with pure cognition an artificial situation grafted onto a biological organism, then emotions play a critical role in behavior.
D.A. NORMAN *Perspectives on Cognitive Science* 1981

12 Both laughter and weeping are sudden emotions, custom taking them both away. For no man laughs at old jests; or weeps for an old calamity.
THOMAS HOBBES (1588–1679) *Leviathan*

13 Emotional ambivalence in the proper sense of the term – that is, the simultaneous existence of love and hate towards the same object – lies at the root of many important cultural institutions.
SIGMUND FREUD (1856–1939) *Totem and Taboo*

1 There is a sort of fascination in all sincere unpremeditated eloquence, which opens to one the inward drama of the speaker's emotions.
GEORGE ELIOT (1819–1880) *Adam Bede*

2 The indulgence of the emotions (when not violent or excessive) is about the least expensive of our mental exercises and may go on when we are unfit for any of the higher intellectual moods, least of all for the crowning work of storing up new knowledge or new aptitudes.
ALEXANDER BAIN *Education as Science*, 1880

3 There is a road from the eye to the heart that does not go though the intellect.
G.K. CHESTERTON (1874–1936) *The Defendant*

4 Her sister came in looking miserable, the two-year-old observed her; her own face changed; she began to look miserable, and then began to cry. Could it be that by the simple act of imitating her sister's facial expression she was directly creating corresponding feeling in herself?
NICHOLAS HUMPHREY *The Inner Eye*, 1986

5 ... all emotion is evoked by the apprehension of importance. Where nothing matters, there is no emotion.
MARGARET DONALDSON *Human Minds*, 1992

6 In a rage, it is notorious how we 'work ourselves up' to a climax by repeated outbreaks of expression. Refuse to express a passion, and it dies. Count ten before venting your anger, and its occasion seems ridiculous. Whistling to keep up courage is no mere figure of speech. On the other hand, sit all day in a moping posture, sigh, and reply to everything with a dismal voice, and melancholy lingers.
WILLIAM JAMES (1842–1910) *Mind*, 1884

EMPATHY

7 One can only understand people after one has noted the books they read, the pictures they hang on their walls, the diversions they seek, and the company they keep.
W.A. HUNT *The American Psychologist*, 1951

8 You never really understand a person until you consider things from his point of view – until you climb into his skin and walk around in it.
HARPER LEE *To Kill a Mocking Bird*, 1960

9 About suffering they were never wrong,
The Old Masters: how well they understood
Its human position: how it takes place
While someone else is eating or opening
a window or just walking dully along.
W.H. AUDEN (1907–1973) 'Musée des Beaux Arts'

10 ... we are also unique in that most simple of behaviours, by our compulsion to look each other in the face. In this is revealed our innate desire to enter into other minds, and our intense social being.... Our species may almost be defined by our inquisitiveness about others' lives and minds and thoughts.
J. COLE *About Face*, 1997

11 If, however, each person were able to feel an identity with other persons and with his environment, to see himself as part of a larger unity, he would have that sense of oneness that supports the selfless actions necessary to regulate population growth, minimize pollution, and end wars.
A.J. DEIKMAN *Archives of General Psychiatry*, 1971

1 [Given] the similitude of the thoughts and passions of one man, to the thoughts and passions of another, whosoever looketh into himself, and considereth what he doth, when he does think, opine, reason, hope, fear, etc. and upon what grounds; he shall thereby read and know, what are the thoughts and passions of all other men upon the like occasions.
THOMAS HOBBES (1588–1679) *Leviathan*

2 I never knew any man in my life who could not bear another's misfortunes perfectly like a Christian.
ALEXANDER POPE (1688–1744) *Thoughts on Various Subjects*

3 No stranger to trouble myself I am learning to care for the unhappy.
VIRGIL (70–19 BC) *Aeneid*

4 Ultimately the concern for the other's existence is an intrinsic property of man's nature, and man is not to be understood without a consideration of his belonging together with the 'other'. This is the foundation of understanding language. It is the basis of all friendship, of all love, where with surprise and astonishment we recognise what is taking place in the 'other' is identical to what is taking place in us.
KURT GOLDSTEIN *Journal of Psychology*, 1957

5 Were a man to know what his fellow truly thinks; could he feel in his own body those impulses which drive the other to his idiomatic acts and words – what an insight he would gain.
NORMAN DOUGLAS *An Almanac*, 1945

6 We have brought our skill in understanding the feelings of others to a high state of perfection and in the presence of another person we are always almost involuntarily practising this skill.
FRIEDRICH NIETZSCHE (1844–1900) *Daybreak*

7 Never attack an opponent until you understand him so well that you can defend him.
R.B. MACLEOD *Perception, Essays in honor of James J. Gibson*, 1974

ENVIRONMENT

8 It is a mistake to separate the cultural environment from the natural environment, as if there were a world of mental products distinct from the world of material products. There is only one world, however diverse, and all animals live in it, although we human animals have altered it to suit ourselves.
J.J. GIBSON *The Ecological Approach to Visual Perception*, 1979

9 Pick any animal species at random, study its behavior in its normal habitat throughout its life cycle, and you will discover an intricate set of behaviors, many of them of almost incredible matching relationship to the demands of the environment, like a lock and key.
R.B. LOCKARD *American Psychologist*, 1971

10 The problem for the management of child development is to find out how to govern the encounters children have with their environments to foster both an optimally rapid rate of intellectual development and a satisfying life.
J. McVICKER HUNT *Intelligence and Experience*, 1961

11 The Greeks were impressed by the fact that Egyptians did not appear to practice infanticide.... They connected this with the fact that Egypt was a rich and fertile country and could afford a growing population.
P. SLOTENDIJK *Critique of Cynical Reason*, 1988

12 In behavior genetics, *environmental* means *nongenetic*, that is, all influences that are not encoded in DNA.
ROBERT PLOMIN *Development, Genes and Psychology*, 1986

13 Perhaps we still do not fully realize the importance of housing in matters of morals and character, for even now there are horrible slums, in which hope ebbs away from human lives in an environment of leaking roofs, broken windows, rats, bugs, and the remains of the day-before-yesterday's meal.
B. SEEBOHM ROWNTREE, G.R. LAVERS *English Life and Leisure*, 1951

1 Bad as our urban conditions often are, there is not a slum in the country which has a third of the infantile death-rate of the royal family in the middle ages.
J.B.S. HALDANE *Daedalus or Science and the Future*, 1923

2 Even in a palace life may be lived well.
MARCUS AURELIUS (121–180) *Meditations*

3 germs are very
objectionable to men
but a germ
thinks of a man
as only the swamp
in which
he has to live
don marquis (1878–1937) 'random thoughts by archy'

4 It is excessively unfortunate that so many of our social traditions and general habits, our clothes, our food, our city life, work in the direction of *creating* ill health and sex-dislocation.
MARIE STOPES *Change of Life in Men and Women*, 1936

ENVY

5 Glamour cannot exist without personal social envy being a common and widespread emotion.
JOHN BERGER *Ways of Seeing*, 1973

6 Betrayed by the head porter,
    ostracized by dons,
Missing the pros, he was sentenced by
    the cons,
A lamentable case of academic *mores*
Prompted by puritan envy and trumped-
    up stories.
R. BOTTRALL cit. Roma Gill *William Empson*, 1974

EQUALITY

7 We hold these truths to be sacred and undeniable; that all men are created equal and independent.
THOMAS JEFFERSON (1743–1826) *Declaration of Independence*

8 I am fond of pigs. Dogs look up to us. Cats look down on us. Pigs treat us as equals.
WINSTON CHURCHILL (1874–1965) attrib.

9 When our forefathers declared it to be self-evident that 'all men are created equal', they uttered biological and psychological nonsense.
J. McVICKER HUNT *The Challenge of Incompetence and Poverty*, 1969

10 All animals are equal, but some animals are more equal than others.
GEORGE ORWELL (1903–1950) *Animal Farm*

ERRORS

11 ... science is not just a matter of making mistakes, but of making mistakes in public.
DANIEL DENNET in J. Khalfa *What is Intelligence*, 1994

12 Posterity is as likely to be wrong as anybody else.
HEYWOOD BOUN (1888–1939) *Sitting on the World*

13 A life spent making mistakes is not only more honourable but more useful than a life spent doing nothing.
GEORGE BERNARD SHAW (1856–1950) *The Doctor's Dilemma*

14 Error is just as important a condition of life as truth.
CARL JUNG (1875–1961) *Psychological Reflections*

15 If all else fails, immortality can always be assured by a spectacular error.
J.K. GALBRAITH (1908–) attrib.

1 Errors, like straws, upon the surface flow;
He who would search for pearls must dive below.
JOHN DRYDEN (1631–1700) *All For Love*

2 As she frequently remarked when she made any such mistake, it would all be the same a hundred years hence.
CHARLES DICKENS (1812–1870) *Nicholas Nickleby*

3 To err is human, to persist in error is devilish.
ST AUGUSTINE (354–430) *Confessions*

4 If we were not provided with the knack of being wrong, we could never get anything useful done.
LEWIS THOMAS *The Medusa and the Snail*, 1979

5 A man should never be ashamed to own that he has been in the wrong, which is but saying, in other words, that he is wiser today than he was yesterday.
JONATHAN SWIFT (1667–1745) *Thoughts on Various Subjects*

6 There are infinite possibilities of error, and more cranks take up unfashionable untruths than unfashionable truths.
BERTRAND RUSSELL (1872–1970) *Unpopular Essays*

7 It is the capacity for making mistakes which is the mark of the higher stages of intelligence.
H.H. PRICE *Thinking and Experience*, 1953

8 You see that our study of errors has not been fruitless.
SIGMUND FREUD (1856–1939) *Introductory Lectures on Psycho-Analysis*

EVIL

9 The evil that I'm talking about lives in all of us. It takes hold in an individual, in private lives, within a family, and then it's the children who suffer most. And then, when conditions are right, in different countries, at different times, a terrible cruelty, a viciousness against life erupts, and everyone is surprised by the depth of hatred within himself. Then it sinks back and waits. It's something in our hearts.
IAN McEWAN *Black Dogs*, 1992

10 Evils which are patiently endured when they seem inevitable become intolerable when once the idea of escape from them is suggested.
A. de TOCQUEVILLE (1805–1859) *The Old Regime and the French Revolution*

11 Propagandist tendency in any art, in poetry or in painting, means its final desecration and is altogether evil.
KONRAD LORENZ *On Aggression*, 1963

12 Those of us who believe in the innate goodness of people and who believe in the methods and percepts of scientific thought find 'evil' a difficult concept.
DOROTHY ROWE in D. Pilgrim *Psychology and Psychotherapy*, 1983

EVOLUTION

13 The action of this principle is exactly like that of the centrifugal governor of the steam engine, which checks and corrects any irregularities almost before they become evident; and in like manner no unbalanced deficiency in the animal kingdom can ever reach any conspicuous magnitude, because it would make itself felt at the very first step, by rendering existence difficult and extinction almost sure to follow.
ALFRED RUSSEL WALLACE (1823–1913) *Journal and Proceedings of the Linnaean Society*, 1858

14 All our unique features are ultimately expressions of our unique inventiveness.
JARED DIAMOND in M.P. Murphy, A.J. O'Neill *What is Life?*, 1995

15 Social values are necessarily built in large part around inherent traits in human nature written into the species by evolution.
ROGER SPERRY *Perspectives in Biology and Medicine*, 1972

1 If we are to carry out any grand analysis of human social behaviour, it will have to be in evolutionary terms, and we shall have to focus our attention almost entirely upon the precise manner in which both nepotistic and reciprocal transactions are conducted in the usual environments in which humans have evolved their social patterns.
R.D. ALEXANDER *Darwinism and Human Affairs*, 1979

2 Roughly speaking, the heredity of other animals is a mechanism like that of a hand organ: it is made to play a few tunes; you can play these tunes at once with little or no training; and you never play any others. The heredity of man on the other hand, is a mechanism more like that of a piano: it is not made to play particular tunes; you can do nothing at all on it without training; but a trained player can draw from it an infinite variety of music.
C.H. COOLEY *Human Nature and the Social Order*, 1922

3 Human language is an embarrassment for evolutionary theory because it is vastly more powerful than one can account for in terms of selective fitness.
DAVID PREMACK *Cognition*, 1985

4 Darwin's expression, 'the struggle for existence' is sometimes erroneously interpreted as the struggle between different species. In reality, the struggle Darwin was thinking of and which drives evolution forward is the competition between near relations. What causes species to disappear or become transformed into a different species is the profitable 'invention' that falls by chance to one or a few of its members in the everlasting gamble of hereditary change. The descendants of these lucky ones gradually outstrip all the others until the particular species consists only of individuals who possess the new invention.
KONRAD LORENZ *On Aggression*, 1963

5 Are God and Nature then at strife,
That Nature lends such evil dreams?
So careful of the type she seems,
So careless of the single life.
ALFRED, LORD TENNYSON (1809–1892) 'In Memoriam'

6 So evolutionary theory does make predictions, at least to the extent of telling us that some sorts of world are not possible worlds hence not worlds we should plan for. In this sense, evolutionary theory is anti-utopian. But, whatever its restrictions, it does not bind us into a straitjacket of consistent maximisation. Nor does it require us to accept narrow selfishness as the only human motive that can survive.
H.A. SIMON *Reason in Human Affairs*, 1983

7 From an evolutionary point of view, man has stopped moving, if he ever did move.
PIERRE TEILHARD DE CHARDIN (1881–1955) *The Phenomenon of Man*

8 Things cannot be other than they are.... Everything is made for the best purpose. Our noses were made to carry spectacles, so we have spectacles. Legs were clearly intended for breeches, and we wear them.
VOLTAIRE (1697–1778) *Candide*

9 We must however acknowledge, as it seems to me, that man with all his noble qualities ... still bears in his bodily frame the indelible stamp of his lowly origin.
CHARLES DARWIN (1809–1882) *The Descent of Man*

10 I am coming more and more to the conviction that the rudiments of every human behavioural mechanism will be found far down in the evolutionary scale and also represented even in primitive activities of the nervous system.
K.S. LASHLEY in L.A. Jeffress *Cerebral Mechanisms of Behavior*, 1951

11 A plausible argument could be made that evolution is the control of development by ecology.
L. VAN VALEN *Science*, 1973

1 In the case of such systems as language or wings it is not easy even to imagine a course of selection that might have given rise to them.
NOAM CHOMSKY *Language and Problems of Knowledge*, 1988

2 The world has not only evolved, it is evolving.
Th. DOBZHANSKY *The Biology of Ultimate Concern*, 1969

3 Consider the auk:
Becoming extinct because he forgot how to fly, and could only walk.
Consider man, who may well become extinct
Because he forgot how to walk and learned how to fly before he thought.
OGDEN NASH (1902–1971) 'Consider the Auk'

4 Man's body may have been developed from that of a lower animal form under the law of natural selection; but ... we possess intellectual and moral faculties that could not have been so developed, but must have another origin.
ALFRED RUSSEL WALLACE (1823–1913) *Darwinism*

5 Evolution, however, is a phenomenon that does not occur in individuals – they die – but in populations.
C.H. WADDINGTON *The Evolution of an Evolutionist*, 1975

6 Just as our bodies still keep the reminders of our old functions and conditions in many old-fashioned organs, so our minds, too, which apparently have outgrown those archaic tendencies, nevertheless bear the marks of the evolution passed through, and the very ancient re-echoes, at least dreamily, in phantasies.
CARL JUNG (1875–1961) *Psychology of the Unconscious*

7 It is likely that the first human brains evolved to impose symbolic meaning on the external world, and the scientific virus later infected a minority of their descendants, where it now flourishes in nerve circuits that originally evolved to carry other ideas.
LEWIS WOLPERT *The Unnatural Nature of Science*, 1992

8 Why has not man a microscopic eye? For this plain reason, man is not a fly.
ALEXANDER POPE (1688–1744) 'An Essay on Man'

9 It is possible that there is, after all, something unique about man and the planet he inhabits.
Th. DOBZHANSKY *Perspectives in Biology and Medicine*, 1972

10 In attempting to understand the elements out of which mental phenomena are compounded, it is of the greatest importance to remember that from the protozoa to man there is nowhere a very wide gap either in structure or in behaviour. From this fact it is a highly probable inference that there is also nowhere a very wide mental gap.
BERTRAND RUSSELL (1872–1970) *The Analysis of Mind*

11 Darwinian Theory: 'a scientific mistake, untrue on its facts, unscientific in its methods, and mischievous in its tendency.'
LOUIS AGASSIZ *American Journal of Science and Arts*, 1860

12 In proportion as physical characteristics become less important, mental and moral qualities will have an increasing importance to the well-being of the race. Capacity for acting in concert, for protection of food and shelter; sympathy, which leads all in turn to assist each other; the sense of right, which checks depredation upon our fellows ... all qualities that from earliest appearance must have become objects of natural selection.
ALFRED RUSSEL WALLACE (1823–1913) *Journal of the Royal Anthropological Society*, 1864

EXCESS

13 Assassination is the extreme form of censorship.
GEORGE BERNARD SHAW (1856–1950) *The Rejected Statement*

1 The road of excess leads to the Palace of Wisdom.
WILLIAM BLAKE (1757–1827) 'The Marriage of Heaven and Hell'

2 Moderation is a fatal thing. Nothing succeeds like excess.
OSCAR WILDE (1854–1900) *A Woman of No Importance*

EXPERIENCE

3 Experience is not what happens to a man; it is what a man does with what happens to him.
ALDOUS HUXLEY (1894–1963) *Texts and Pretexts*

4 How much a dunce that has been sent to roam,
Excels a dunce that has been kept at home.
WILLIAM COWPER (1731–1800) 'The Progress of Error'

5 A sadder and a wiser man,
He rose the morrow morn.
SAMUEL TAYLOR COLERIDGE (1772–1834) 'The Ancient Mariner'

6 Accuse not Nature, she hath done her part;
Do thou but thine.
JOHN MILTON (1608–1674) *Paradise Lost*

7 Experience is never limited, and it is never complete.
HENRY JAMES (1843–1916) *The Art of Fiction*

8 Experience is a good teacher, but she sends in terrific bills.
MINNA ANTRIM *Naked Truth and Veiled Allusions*, 1902

9 To most men, experience is like the stern lights of a ship, which illume only the track it has passed.
SAMUEL TAYLOR COLERIDGE (1772–1834) *Table Talk*

10 All our experiences are strictly private; but some experiences are less private than others.
ALDOUS HUXLEY (1894–1963) *Literature and Science*

11 None of us can help the things life has done to us. They're done before you realise it, and once they're done they make you do other things until at last everything comes between you and what you'd like to be, and you've lost your true self forever.
EUGENE O'NEILL (1888–1953) *Long Day's Journey into Night*

12 ... personal experience may be expected to prove an invaluable aid to doing psychology.
NICHOLAS HUMPHREY *Consciousness Regained*, 1983

13 Even God cannot change the past.
AGATHON (447–401 BC) cit. Aristotle *Nichomachean Ethics*

14 The assaying of tea is an art and not a science. It is the man and not his instruments, which is the most important. There can be no substitute for my experience and intuited knowledge.
TIMOTHY MO *An Insular Possession*, 1986

15 No story is the same to us after a lapse of time; or rather, we who read it are no longer the same interpreters.
GEORGE ELIOT (1819–1880) *Adam Bede*

16 Experience is a comb, which nature gives to men when they are bald.
PROVERB

17 Experience is the name everyone gives to their mistakes.
OSCAR WILDE (1854–1900) *Lady Windermere's Fan*

EXPERIMENTS

18 Psychologists rush to experiment now as they once rushed to construct flimsily grounded systems.
R.B. AMMONS in G.S. Seward and J.P. Seward *Current Psychological Issues*, 1960

19 ... experiment in psychology is at least as old as Aristotle.
C.S. MYERS *Textbook of Experimental Psychology*, 1909

1 It would be much better if some of our well-trained experimentalists were encouraged to do a little pioneering.
FRANK BEACH *American Psychologist*, 1950

2 The empiricist ... thinks he believes only what he sees, but he is much better at believing than at seeing.
GEORGE SANTAYANA (1863–1952)
Skepticism and Animal Faith

3 ... psychology is to a large extent submerged by the natural sciences model. The most prominent effect of this is the dominance of experiments.
L. VAN LANGEEHOVE in J. Smith *et al.*
Rethinking Psychology, 1995

4 The case against psychological experiments with animals by the 'animal liberationists' is false at almost every point; worse, it is deliberately so.
J.A. GRAY in H. Beloff, A.M. Colman
Psychological Survey 6, 1987

5 There are other sources of psychological knowledge, which become accessible at the very point where the experimental method fails us.
WILHELM WUNDT *Principles of Physiological Psychology*, 1904

6 I love fools' experiments. I am always making them.
CHARLES DARWIN (1809–1882) cit. Francis Darwin *The Life of Charles Darwin*, 1902

7 An experiment should astonish you.
P. JOHNSON-LAIRD in D.A. Norman
Perspectives in Cognitive Science, 1982

8 The meaning of particular words – even of such words as meaning – must be discovered, like everything else in this world, by experiment, and not by intuition.
K.J.W. CRAIK *The Nature of Psychology*, 1966

9 Experiment is observation made in specifiable and controllable circumstances and it seeks to eliminate that dependence on the personal judgement, the tact, the intuition of the observer which is the weakness of the observational method.
WILFRED TROTTER *The Collected Papers of Wilfred Trotter FRS*, 1941

10 The vast bulk of barren experiments which has dogged the growth of psychology took origin in the confusion which treated measurement as sufficient unto itself.
SUSAN ISAACS *Intellectual Growth in Young Children*, 1930

11 Physiological experiment on animals is justifiable for real investigation, but not for mere damnable and detestable curiosity.
CHARLES DARWIN (1809–1882) letter to E. Ray Lankester

12 'Objectivity' means intellectual honesty; it doesn't mean ruling the experimenter out of experimentation, especially when it comes to the interpretation of data.
MYRTLE B. McGRAW *Neuromuscular Maturation of the Human Infant*, 1943

13 The existence of experimental methods makes us think we have the means of solving the problems which trouble us, though the problems and methods pass one another by.
LUDWIG WITTGENSTEIN (1889–1951)
Philosophical Investigations

EXPLANATION

14 When we say that a man eats *because* he is hungry, smokes a great deal *because* he has the tobacco habit, fights *because* of the instinct of pugnacity, behaves brilliantly *because* of his intelligence, or plays the piano well *because* of his musical ability, we seem to be referring to causes. But on analysis these phrases prove to be merely redundant descriptions.
B.F. SKINNER *Science and Human Behavior*, 1953

15 The question why one explanation or another should seem satisfactory involves the prior question why any explanation at all should be sought after and found satisfactory.
K.J.W. CRAIK *The Nature of Explanation*, 1943

1 The fallacy of differentiating a science or an art according to its application and the moral intention of the agent is obvious enough with regard to pharmacy and artillery; it is equally real, though to many people apparently it is less obvious, with regard to magic.
JAMES G. FRAZER (1854–1941) Preface in B. Malinowski *Argonauts of the Pacific*

2 No more things should be presumed to exist than are absolutely necessary.
WILLIAM OF OCCAM (c. 1280–1349) *Quodlibeta*

3 Description is the first stage in constructing explanations.
J. KATZ *Linguistic Philosophy*, 1972

4 Man masters nature not by force but by understanding. That is why science has succeeded where magic failed: because it has looked for no spell to cast on nature.
J. BRONOWSKI (1908–1974) *Science and Human Values*

5 The very essence of explanation is generalisation.
K.J.W. CRAIK *The Nature of Explanation*, 1943

6 We must do away with explanations, and description alone must take its place.
LUDWIG WITTGENSTEIN (1889–1951) *Philosophical Investigations*

7 'Why,' said the Dodo, 'the best way to explain it is to do it.'
LEWIS CARROLL (1832–1898) *Alice's Adventures in Wonderland*

8 In the last analysis magic, religion and science are nothing but theories of thought; and as science has supplanted its predecessors, so it may hereafter be itself superseded by some more perfect hypothesis, perhaps some totally different way of looking at the phenomena – of registering the shadows on the screen – of which we in this generation can form no idea.
JAMES G. FRAZER (1854–1941) *The Golden Bough*

FACES

9 Physiologists have estimated that the face musculature is such that over twenty thousand different facial expressions are somatically possible.
RAY L. BIRDWHISTELL *Kinesics and Context*, 1970

10 ... most scientists consider the universality of facial expressions of emotion to be well established.... While robust, the evidence is limited to just a handful of emotions: anger, disgust, sadness, enjoyment and fear/surprise.
PAUL EKMAN, Afterword in Charles Darwin *The Expression of the Emotions in Man and Animals, 3rd edn*, 1997

11 Minds differ more than faces.
VOLTAIRE (1694–1778) *Philosophical Dictionary*

12   There's no art
To find the mind's construction in the
          face;
WILLIAM SHAKESPEARE (1564–1616) *Macbeth*

13 On becoming very intimate with Fitz-Roy, I heard that I had run a very narrow risk of being rejected, on account of the shape of my nose! He was an ardent disciple of Lavater, and was convinced that he could judge a man's character by the outline of his features; and he doubted whether anyone with my nose could possess sufficient energy and determination for the voyage. I think he was afterwards well-satisfied that my nose had spoken falsely.
CHARLES DARWIN (1809–1882) cit. P. Ekman ed. *The Expression of the Emotions in Man and Animals, 3rd edn*, 1997

1 ... face and facial expression define our uniqueness and individuality and act to conceal as well as to reveal. We would be exposed and threatened if the intimacy we allow a few were to be available to all. The face fascinates in part by its mystery and by our creative acts of interpretation.
J. COLE *About Face*, 1997

FACTS

2 Facts are mainly theories to which we have become sufficiently accustomed.
ERNST MACH cit. K.F. Reigel *Structure and Transformations*, 1975

3 To speculate without facts is to attempt to enter a house of which one has not the key, by wandering aimlessly round and round, searching the walls and now and then peeping through the windows. Facts are the key.
JULIAN HUXLEY *Essays in Popular Science*, 1937

4 The fatal futility of fact.
HENRY JAMES (1843–1916) *The Spoils of Poynton*

5 Till facts are grouped and called there can be no prediction. The only advantage of discovering laws is to foretell what will happen and to see the bearing of scattered facts.
CHARLES DARWIN (1809–1882) *Species Notebook*

6 Without theories and hypotheses, our tale of positive facts would be pretty insignificant, and would grow very slowly.
RAMON y CAJAL *Reflections on My Life*, 1937

7 For psychology, particularly for child psychology, it follows as a necessary corollary that we are always to draw interpretations and conclusions from the entire context and never from a single fact.
ALFRED ADLER *The Practice and Theory of Individual Psychology*, 1925

8 Now, what I want is, Facts ... Facts alone are wanted in life.
CHARLES DICKENS (1812–1870) *Hard Times*

9 My mind seems to have become a kind of machine for grinding general laws out of large collections of facts.
CHARLES DARWIN (1809–1882) *The Origin of Species*

10 It is always possible to convince an objective sceptic by facts, but never a fanatic follower.
H.J. JACOBY *Analysis of Handwriting*, 1939

11 'Spirits' may not exist – but the universal belief in their existence may have had its origin, not in normal facts only, but in abnormal facts. And these facts, at the lowest estimate, must suggest that man may have faculties, and be surrounded by agencies, which physical science does not take into account in its theory of the universe and of human nature.
ANDREW LANG *Cock Lane and Common Sense*, 1894

12 Science is built up of facts, as a house is built up of storeys; but an accumulation of facts is no more a science than a heap of stones is a house.
JULES POINCARÉ (1854–1912) *Science and Hypothesis*

13 I worked on true Baconian principles, and without any theory collected facts.
CHARLES DARWIN (1809–1882) cit. Gavin de Beer *Autobiographies: Charles Darwin, Thomas Henry Huxley*, 1974

FALSIFICATION

14 Falsification is crucial to us for one overwhelming reason. Man, we know, is infinitely capable of belief. Surprising that he has not been described as *Homo credens*.
J.S. BRUNER *Actual Minds, Possible Worlds*, 1986

1 If it could be demonstrated that any complex organ existed which could not possibly have been formed by numerous, successive slight modifications, my theory would absolutely break down.
CHARLES DARWIN (1809–1882) *Origin of Species*

2 It must be possible for an empirical scientific system to be refuted by experience.
KARL POPPER *The Logic of Scientific Discovery*, 1935

3 Milton's Satan in 'Paradise Lost' may have been the forerunner of Karl Popper's falsificationism.
J.S. BRUNER *Actual Minds, Possible Worlds*, 1986

4 False views, if supported by some evidence, do little harm, for everyone takes a salutary pleasure in proving their falseness.
CHARLES DARWIN (1809–1882) *The Descent of Man*

FAMILIES

5 The family is one of nature's masterpieces.
G. SANTAYANA (1863–1952) *The Life of Reason*

6 'What is a wife?' asked one, after a thoughtful pause.
'I am wife to Daddy.'
'And is Daddy your wife?'
'No Daddy is my husband.'
'Then who are you?'
PAMELA GLENCONNER *The Sayings of Children*, 1918

7 With the exception of the police and the military, the family is perhaps the most violent social group, and the home the most violent social setting in our society.
R.J. GELLES, M.A. STRAUS *Journal of Social Issues*, 1979

8 I'm beginning to lose patience
With my personal relations:
They are not deep,
They are not cheap.
W.H. AUDEN (1907–1973) 'Shorts'

9 The awe and dread with which the untutored savage contemplates his mother-in-law are amongst the most familiar facts of anthropology.
JAMES G. FRAZER (1854–1941) *The Golden Bough*

10 If we give ourselves the time, our genomes will together teach us that we are all profoundly related, that we are all one human family.
ROBERT POLLACK *Signs of Life*, 1994

11 The family – that dear octopus from whose tentacles we never quite escape.
DODIE SMITH (1896–1990) *Dear Octopus*

12 Families with no tradition for sacrifice do not survive for many generations.
STEPHEN J. GOULD *Natural History*, 1976

13 He that hath wife and children hath given hostages to fortune; for they are impediments to great enterprises, either of virtue or mischief.
FRANCIS BACON (1561–1626) *Essays*

14 It cannot be too strongly emphasized that the integration of the family derives from the integrative tendency of each individual child.
DONALD WINNICOTT *The Family and Individual Development*, 1965

15 All happy families resemble one another, but each unhappy family is unhappy in its own way.
LEO TOLSTOY (1828–1910) *Anna Karenina*

16 It is a melancholy truth that even great men have their poor relations.
CHARLES DICKENS (1812–1870) *Bleak House*

1 Here is the mother all boobed and bodicey
Who started the children upon their odyssey.
Here sits the father stern as a rock
Who rules the world with his iron cock.
Those two children white as mice
Who saw the ghost in the attic, twice,
And who are we to suppose this vignette
Not threaded with love like a string quartet?
KIT WRIGHT 'Victorian Family Photograph', 1983

FATE

2 We may become the makers of our fate when we have ceased to pose as its prophets.
KARL POPPER *The Open Society and Its Enemies*, 1945

3 Human reason needs only to will more strongly than fate and she *is* fate.
THOMAS MANN (1875–1955) *The Magic Mountain*

4 Events will take their course, it is no good
Our being angry at them; he is happiest
Who wisely turns them to the best account.
EURIPIDES (484–406 BC) *Bellerphon*

5 I do not believe in a fate that falls on men however they act; but I do believe in a fate that falls on them unless they act.
G.K. CHESTERTON (1874–1936) *Generally Speaking*

6 Men at some times are masters of their fates;
The fault, dear Brutus, is not in our stars, But in ourselves, that we are underlings.
WILLIAM SHAKESPEARE (1564–1616) *Julius Caesar*

7 Men are not prisoners of fate, but only prisoners of their own minds.
FRANKLIN DELANO ROOSEVELT (1882–1945), speech, 15 April 1939

FATHERS

8 Fathers are no longer, if they ever were, merely a biological necessity – a social accident. They are an important influence on their child's development. And a close relationship between father and child benefits the father as well as the child. Children need their fathers, but fathers need their children, too.
ROSS D. PARKE *Fathering*, 1981

9 The father by instinct supplies the roughness, the sterness which stiffens in the child the centres of resistance and independence, right from the earliest days.
D.H. LAWRENCE (1885–1930) *Fantasia of the Unconscious*

10 It is a wise child that knows his own father.
HOMER (8th cent. BC) *Odyssey*

11 The fundamental defect of fathers, in our competitive society, is that they want their children to be a credit to them.
BERTRAND RUSSELL (1872–1970) *Sceptical Essays*

12 Most fathers seem to present a more playful, jazzing up approach. As one watches this interaction, it seems that the father is expecting a more heightened, playful response from the baby. And he gets it! Amazingly enough, an infant by two or three weeks displays as entirely different attitude (more wide-eyed, playful and bright faced) towards his father than his mother.
T.B. BRAZELTON *Seminars in Perinatology*, 1979

13 How many a father have I seen,
A sober man, among his boys,
Whose youth was full of foolish noise.
ALFRED, LORD TENNYSON (1809–1892) 'In Memoriam'

14 The rev'rend gray-beards rav'd and stormed,
That beardless laddies
Should think they better were inform'd
Than their auld daddies.
ROBERT BURNS (1759–1796) 'Epistle to Simpson: Postscript'

1 Fathers, provoke not your children lest they be discouraged.
Bible, Colossians

2 Fathers tend to spend more of their available time playing with their children than mothers do, and to play differently. Their physical and robust approach complements and contrasts with mothers' verbal, paced style. Children profit from this diversity of experience.
ROSS D. PARKE *Fathering*, 1981

3 A father is a banker provided by nature.
ANON.

FATIGUE

4 As soon as the bodily exertion has closed for the day, the man lies down and his muscles have rest; but when the mentally fatigued man lies down, his enemy continues to harass him during his weary hours of sleeplessness.
FRANCIS GALTON (1822–1911) *Journal of the Royal Anthropological Institute*, 1888

5 A man can wear out a particular part of his mind by continually using it and tiring it, just as he can wear out the elbows of his coat.
WINSTON CHURCHILL (1874–1965) *Painting as a Pastime*

6 Too tired to yawn, too tired to sleep: Poor Tired Tim! It's sad for him.
WALTER DE LA MARE (1873–1956) 'Tired Tim'

7 Restlessness appears to be the commonest sign of partial fatigue: that is, of the attention being wearied while the muscles are craving to be employed.
FRANCIS GALTON (1822–1911) *Journal of the Royal Anthropological Institute*, 1888

FEAR

8 Fear is conditioned by, and directed against, very definite aspects of the environment.... Fear sharpens the senses, whereas anxiety renders them unusable; fear drives to action, anxiety paralyses.
KURT GOLDSTEIN *Human Nature in the Light of Psychopathology*, 1940

9 Fear, when strong, expresses itself in cries, in efforts to hide or escape, in palpitations and tremblings; and these are just the manifestations that would accompany an actual experience of the evil feared.
HERBERT SPENCER *Principles of Psychology*, 1855

10 Fear is the main source of superstition and one of the main sources of cruelty. To conquer fear is the beginning of wisdom.
BERTRAND RUSSELL (1872–1970) *An Outline of Intellectual Rubbish*

11 There are times when fear is good
It must keep its watchful place
At the heart's controls. There is
Advantage in the wisdom won from pain.
AESCHYLUS (525–456 BC) *The Eumenides*

12 For it is not death and pain that is a fearful thing, but the fear of death and pain.
EPICTETUS (c. 55–135) *Discourses*

13 I have seen the moment of my greatness flicker,
And I have seen the eternal Footman hold my coat, and snicker,
And in short, I was afraid.
T.S. ELIOT (1888–1965) 'The Love Song of J. Alfred Prufrock'

14 Present fears
Are less than horrible imaginings.
WILLIAM SHAKESPEARE (1564–1616) *Macbeth*

15 To fear love is to fear life, and those who fear life are already three parts dead.
BERTRAND RUSSELL (1872–1970) *Marriage and Morals*

1   No passion so effectually robs the mind of all its powers of acting and reasoning as fear.
EDMUND BURKE (1729–1797) *On the Sublime and the Beautiful*

2   The fear that kills.
WILLIAM WORDSWORTH (1770–1850) 'Resolution and Independence'

3   I will show you fear in a handful of dust.
T.S. ELIOT (1888–1965) 'The Waste Land'

4   ... man, like other animals, responds with fear to certain situations not because they carry a *high* risk of pain or danger, but because they signal an *increase* of risk.
JOHN BOWLBY *Animal Behaviour*, 1980

5   Children's fears are home grown just like their loves and temper outbursts. The parents do the emotional planting and cultivating.
J.B. WATSON *Psychological Care of Infant and Child*, 1928

6   Instead of being at the mercy of wild beasts, earthquakes, landslides, and inundations, modern man is battered by the elemental forces of his own psyche. This is the World Power that vastly exceeds all other powers on earth. The Age of Enlightenment, which stripped nature and human institutions of gods, overlooked the God of Terror who dwells in the human soul.
CARL JUNG (1875–1961) *The Development of Personality*

7   How does one kill fear, I wonder? How do you shoot a spectre through the heart, slash off its spectral head, take it by its spectral throat?
JOSEPH CONRAD (1857–1924) *Lord Jim*

8   The man who has ceased to fear has ceased to care.
F.H. BRADLEY (1846–1924) *Aphorisms*

9   The thing I fear most is fear.
MICHEL DE MONTAIGNE (1533–1592) *Essays*

10   May we not suspect that the vague but very real fears of children, which are quite independent of experience, are the inherited effects of real dangers and abject superstitions during ancient savage times?
CHARLES DARWIN (1809–1882) *Mind*, 1877

11   When I speak of fear, I do not mean merely or mainly personal fear: the fear of death or decrepitude or penury or any other such merely mundane misfortune. I am thinking of a more metaphysical fear. I am thinking of the fear that enters the soul through experience of the major evils to which life is subject: the treachery of friends, the death of those whom we love, the discovery of the cruelty that lurks in the average human nature.
BERTRAND RUSSELL (1872–1970) *Autobiography*

12   To the man who is afraid everything rustles.
SOPHOCLES (496–406 BC) *Fragment*

13   A man may destroy everything within himself, love and hate and belief, and even doubt; but as long as he clings to life he cannot destroy fear.
JOSEPH CONRAD (1857–1924) *Tales of Unrest*

FEELINGS

14   In this era of 'information processing psychology' it may seem quaint to talk of mental states: it is more fashionable to speak of representations, frames, scripts or semantic networks. But while I find it lucid enough to speak in such terms about memories of things, sentences, or even faces, it is much harder so to deal with feelings, insights and understandings – and all the attitudes, dispositions, and ways of seeing things that go with them. We usually put such issues aside, saying that one must first understand the simpler things. But what if feelings and viewpoints are the simpler things? If such dispositions are the elements of which the others are composed, then we must deal with them directly.
MARVIN MINSKY in D. Norman *Perspectives on Cognitive Science*, 1982

1 It is only with the heart that one can see rightly: what is essential is invisible to the eye.
ANTOINE de SAINT-EXUPERY (1900–1944) *Le Petit Prince*

2 Enough of science and of art:
Close up those barren leaves.
Come forth, and bring with you a heart
That watches and receives.
WILLIAM WORDSWORTH (1770–1850) 'The Tables Turned'

3 The longer I am in politics the more I realise that facts are not the determining thing. Feelings are what counts – feelings which are totally out of accord with some of the facts.
MARGARET THATCHER *New York Times*, 12 February 1975

4 In all men, thought and action start from a single source, namely feeling.
EPICTETUS (c. 55–135) *Discourses*

5 Feelings have proved to be one of the most fascinating attractions along the path of dalliance.
B.F. SKINNER in Rom Harre *Problems of Scientific Revolution*, 1975

FOOLISHNESS

6 A fool must now and then be right by chance.
WILLIAM COWPER (1731–1800) *Conversations*

7 Who knows a fool must know this brother;
One fop will recommend another.
JOHN GAY (1685–1732) *Fables*

8 Most fools think they are only ignorant.
BENJAMIN FRANKLIN (1706–1790) *Poor Richard's Almanack*

9 The learn'd is happy nature to explore,
The fool is happy that he knows no more.
ALEXANDER POPE (1688–1744) *An Essay on Man*

10 If the fool would persist in his folly he would become wise.
WILLIAM BLAKE (1757–1827) 'The Marriage of Heaven and Hell'

FORGETTING

11 What we should be most afraid of, perhaps, is the fact that, since the invention of printing, magnetic tape and computer cards, the Collective Mind has lost the vital ability to *forget*.... This problem is nowhere more acute than in science itself, where the sheer accumulation of facts threaten to impede rather than assist the progress of new ideas.
COLIN BLAKEMORE *Mechanisms of the Mind*, 1977

12 Darker grows the valley, more and more forgetting.
GEORGE MEREDITH (1828–1909) 'Love in the Valley'

13 But each day brings its petty dust
Our soon chok'd souls to fill,
And we forget because we must,
And not because we will.
MATTHEW ARNOLD (1822–1888) 'Absence'

14 Men are men: the best sometime forget.
WILLIAM SHAKESPEARE (1564–1616) *Othello*

15 I've a grand memory for forgetting.
ROBERT LOUIS STEVENSON (1850–1894) *Kidnapped*

16 Old men forget: yet all shall be forgot,
But he'll remember with advantages
What feats he did that day.
WILLIAM SHAKESPEARE (1564–1616) *Henry V*

17 I feel assured there is no such thing as ultimate forgetting: traces once impressed upon the memory are indestructible.
THOMAS de QUINCY (1785–1859) *Confessions of an Opium Eater*

1 'The horror of that moment, the King went on, 'I shall never, *never* forget!' 'You will, though,' the Queen said, 'if you don't make a memorandum of it.'
LEWIS CARROLL (1832–1898) *Alice Through the Looking Glass*

2 There is a wicked inclination in most people to suppose an old man decayed in his intellects. If a young or middle-aged man, when leaving a company, does not recollect where he left his hat, it is nothing: but if the same inattention is discovered in an old man, people will shrug up their shoulders, and say 'His memory is going'.
SAMUEL JOHNSON (1709–1784) cit. James Boswell *The Life of Samuel Johnson*

FREEDOM

3 No man who knows aught, can be so stupid as to deny that all men naturally were born free.
JOHN MILTON (1608–1674) *The Tenure of Kings and Magistrates*

4 Freedom not to do one thing requires that you do another, imperatively. And there you have it, chains.... You take freedom and you shut yourself up with your idea, just that particular one and no other. And there you are again, in chains.
PABLO PICASSO (1881–1973) cit. Helene Parmolin *Picasso: The Artist and His Models and Other Recent Works*, 1965

5 I am as free as nature first made man,
Ere the base laws of servitude began,
When wild in woods the noble savage ran.
JOHN DRYDEN (1631–1700) *The Conquest of Granada*

6 We stand today more alone and more focussed on ourselves than we have ever been. We sense in this condition a powerful freedom to be what we want, yet, at the same time, we are unhappy. Freedom to succeed is also freedom to fail. The self must often bear the blame for such failure.
MICHAEL LEWIS *Shame*, 1992

FREUD

7 Freud's great contribution to Western thought has been described as the application of the principle of cause and effect to human behavior.
B.F. SKINNER *Scientific Monthly*, 1954

8 He [Freud] was ill-informed in the field of contemporary psychology and seems to have derived only from hearsay any knowledge he had of it.
ERNEST JONES *Life and Works of Sigmund Freud*, 1953–1957

9 But Freud doesn't appeal to our reason. He seduces us. He is a fine prose writer. He gives us a way of finding a (maybe erroneous) narrative for our lives. He may be utterly wrong scientifically, with devastating consequences, but there is something artistically appealing about him.
NICCI GERARD *The Observer*, 1 June 1997

10 What a misfortune it is that so profoundly influential a theorist [Freud] should have spent so little time observing his own children, and should have had so slight a sexual interest in his own wife!
L. HUDSON *Bodies of Knowledge*, 1982

11 Freud put the 'anal' into psychoanalysis.
GRAFFITTI

12 It can indeed be argued that much of Freud's work was really semantic and that he made a revolutionary discovery in semantics, namely that neurotic symptoms are meaningful, disguised communications, but that, owing to his scientific training and allegiance, he formulated his findings in the conceptual framework of the physical sciences.
CHARLES RYCROFT *Psychoanalysis and Beyond*, 1985

13 Freud fails to do justice to the positive aspects of life. He fails to recognize that the basic phenomenon of life is an incessant process of coming to terms with the environment; he only sees escape and craving for release.
KURT GOLDSTEIN *The Organism*, 1938

1 He wasn't clever at all: he merely told
the unhappy Present to recite the Past
like a poetry lesson till sooner
or later it faltered at the line where

long ago the accusations had begun
and suddenly knew by whom it had
      been judged,
how rich life had been and how silly,
and was life-forgiven and more humble,

able to approach the Future as a friend
without a wardrobe of excuses, without
a set mask of rectitude or an
embarrassing over-familiar gesture.
W.H. AUDEN (1907–1973) 'In Memory of
Sigmund Freud (d. Sept 1939)'

2 ... the central curiosity in Freud's
life: how someone who was deeply
imbued in high nineteenth century
ideas, who throughout his life adhered
to the strictest notions of decorum –
ideas and notions, it must be said, that
some of us today find almost
incomprehensible – should be the first
to draw man's attention to the
pervasiveness, from the earliest days, of
sexuality.
RICHARD WOLLHEIM On Art and the Mind,
1974

3 The trouble with Freud is that he
has never played the Glasgow Empire
Saturday night.
KEN DODD The Times, 7 August 1965

4 The significance of Freud's life and
thought is too important, as a historical
expression of forces deeper than Freud
himself realised, to be left to the
Freudians.
PHILIP RIEFF New York Times Book Review,
30 May 1965

5 In science, the universe did not
change when Einstein thought of
relativity but man did change a little
after Freud.
MARIE JAHODA Models of Man, 1980

FRIENDSHIP

6 To find a friend one must close one
eye. To keep him – two.
NORMAN DOUGLAS An Almanac, 1945

7 Fellowship is heaven, and lack of
fellowship is hell: fellowship is life and
lack of fellowship is death.
WILLIAM MORRIS (1834–1896) A Dream of
John Ball

8 ... I had found a companion and
confidant in myself. There was a secret
in this world and it belonged to me and
to somebody who lived in the same body
with me. There were two of us, and we
could talk with one another.... It was a
great solace to me to find a sympathizer
in my own breast.
EDMUND GOSSE (1849–1928) Autobiography

9 Of two close friends, one is always
the slave of the other.
MIKHAIL LERMONTOV (1814–1841) A Hero of
our Time

10 A fav'rite has no friend.
THOMAS GRAY (1716–1771) 'On the Death of
a Favorite Cat'

11 At school, friendship is a passion ...
what earthquakes of the heart and whirl-
winds of the soul are confined in that
simple phrase, a schoolboy's friendship!
BENJAMIN DISRAELI (1804–1881) Coningsby

12 It is easier to forgive an Enemy
than to forgive a Friend.
WILLIAM BLAKE (1757–1827) 'Jerusalem'

13 For there is no man, that imparteth
his joys to his friend, but that he joyeth
the more, and no man, that imparteth
his grief to his friend, but he grieveth
the less.
FRANCIS BACON (1561–1626) Essays

14 Love is blind: friendship closes its
eyes.
PROVERB

15 Better lose a jest than a friend.
THOMAS FULLER (1654–1734) Gnomologia

1 Our feelings towards our friends reflect our feelings towards ourselves.
ARISTOTLE (384–322) *Nicomachean Ethics*

2 Acquaintance, n. A person whom we know well enough to borrow from, but not well enough to lend to.
AMBROSE BIERCE (1842–1914) *The Devil's Dictionary*

FRUSTRATION

3 Frustration does not always lead to aggression.... Frustration may result in the seeking of other means of reaching the goal or giving up the goal...; or it may elicit emotional reactions such as anxiety or depression.
A.H. BUSS *Self-Consciousness and Social Anxiety*, 1980

4 ONCE I LIVED IN CAPITALS
MY LIFE INTENSELY PHALLIC

but now i'm sadly lowercase
with the occasional *italic*
ROGER McGOUGH 'italic', 1987

5 Sick men long most to drink, who know they may not.
OVID (43 BC–17 AD) *Ars Amatoria*

GAMES

6 A game is an ongoing series of complementary ulterior transactions progressing to a well-defined, predictable outcome.
ERIC BERNE *Games People Play*, 1966

7 It may seem a superfluous question to ask, Why is this game played? But the Ethnologist is bound to do so, for he knows from experience that practically everything man does has a meaning, and it is his business to endeavour to find out whether there is any reason for the performance of any action, and if so to discover its significance.
A.C. HADDON in C. F. Jayne *String Figures and How to Make Them*, 1906

8 My childhood was chiefly, if not exhaustively, bellicose. I used blowpipes improvised at the last minute among the bushes; I crouched behind the few parked cars, firing my repeater rifle; I led attacks with fixed bayonets.... This orgy of war games produced a man who managed to do eighteen months of military service without touching a gun, devoting his long hours in the barracks to the grave study of medieval philosophy.
UMBERTO ECO *Misreadings*, 1961

9 To form the character of the child over three and up to six years old there will be a need of games.... Children of this age have games which come by natural instinct; and they generally invent them of themselves whenever they meet together.
PLATO (429–347 BC) *Laws*

1 Pastimes and games are substitutes for the real living of real intimacy.
ERIC BERNE *Games People Play*, 1966

GENETICS

2 ... genes do not determine one's destiny....
ROBERT PLOMIN *Development, Genes and Psychology*, 1986

3 The singularity of the human self becomes comprehensible in the light of genetics.
Th. DOBZHANSKY *American Psychologist*, 1967

4 It is an advance to realise that heredity does not operate like Fate in the tragedy of Sophocles; that genes do not drive an Oedipus to kill his father and marry his mother.
J.L. FULLER in G.S. Seward, J.P. Seward *Current Psychological Issues*, 1960

5 Man does not transmit a single acquired memory to his progeny. The son of the greatest mathematician does not inherit even the multiplication table.
EUGENE MARAIS (1872–1936) *The Soul of the White Ant*

6 From what is already known about heredity, should we not naturally expect to find the children of well-to-do, cultured and successful parents better endowed than the children who have been reared in slums and poverty?
L.S. TERMAN *The Intelligence of School Children*, 1921

7 ... no behaviour can be independent of an animal's heredity.
D.O. HEBB *British Journal of Animal Behaviour*, 1953

8 So in regard to mental qualities, their transmission is manifest in our dogs, horses and other domestic animals. Besides special tastes and habits, general intelligence, courage, bad and good tempers, etc. are certainly transmitted.
CHARLES DARWIN (1809–1882) *The Descent of Man*

9 The genes hold culture on a leash. The leash is very long, but inevitably values will be constrained in accordance with their effects on the human gene pool.
E.O. WILSON *On Human Nature*, 1978

10 ... the more learning is basic, the less will there be any simple relationship between genes and behaviors.
S.L. WASHBURN *American Psychologist*, 1976

11 There are no genes for behaviour.
I.I. GOTTESMAN *Journal of Child Psychology and Psychiatry*, 1966

12 A society can grant equality of opportunity to its members, or it can withhold such equality; genetic diversity is biologically given and could not be stamped out even if this were desirable.
Th. DOBZHANSKY in D. Glass *Genetics* 1968

13 ... except for a few cases of pathological deficiency, the factor of heredity plays a very small part in human life, as compared with the factor of environment.
W.C. BAGLEY *The Educational Process*, 1912

14 All the evidence to date suggests the ... overwhelming importance of genetic factors in producing the great variety of intellectual differences which we observe in our culture, and much of the difference observed between certain racial groups.
HANS EYSENCK *Race, Intelligence and Education*, 1971

15 Man is not exempt from the laws of nature, and if human marriages were directed, psychologically distinct strains could undoubtedly be formed as readily as in rats or dogs.
J.L. FULLER in G.S. Seward, J.P. Seward *Current Psychological Issues*, 1960

16 ... quantitative genetic theory, the foundation for the methods used in behavioral genetics, is a theory of scope and power rarely seen in the behavioral sciences.
ROBERT PLOMIN *Development, Genes and Psychology*, 1986

1 It is easy to say that human language is a genetically determined faculty; it is certainly much less easy for the biologist to demonstrate the genetic determinism of the simplest behavioral ability.
JEAN-PIERRE CHANGEUX in M. Piatelli-Palmarini *Language and Learning*, 1980

2 Inheritance of intelligence implies no more than inheritance of body size.
J.L. FULLER, W.R. THOMPSON *Behavior Genetics*, 1960

GENIUS

3 Genius seems to consist in the power of applying the originality of youth to the experience of maturity.
MICHAEL POLANYI *The Study of Man*, 1959

4 Criticism is the due of genius.
L.L. WHYTE *The Unconscious Before Freud*, 1962

5 Genius is the ability to renew one's emotions in daily experience.
PAUL CEZANNE (1839–1906) cit. R. Kendall *Cezanne by Himself*, 1988

6 There are many kinds of genius; each age has its different gifts.
DESIDERIUS ERASMUS (1466–1536) *The Works of Hilary*

7 The tendency to very high pitched voice which is so remarkably common in men of intellectual ability may possibly be due to a slight paralysis of the vocal chords.
HAVELOCK ELLIS (1859–1939) *A Study of British Genius*

8 No great genius has ever been without some madness.
ARISTOTLE (384–322 BC) cit. Seneca *Moral Essays*

9 The public is wonderfully tolerant. It forgives everything except genius.
OSCAR WILDE (1854–1900) *Intentions*

10 In contrast to stable, limited talent which is inherited, true *genius* occurs almost invariably as a non-repeatable, non-inheritable phenomenon. In addition degeneracy is a demonstrably important factor. The posterity of persons of genius almost always shows a tendency to die out rapidly; frequently the man of genius has no direct descendants.
E. KRETSCHMER *A Textbook of Medical Psychology*, 1934

11 Genius is a talent for producing that for which no definite rule can be given, and not an aptitude in the way of cleverness for what can be learned according to some rule; and that consequently originality must be its primary property.
IMMANUEL KANT (1724–1804) *Critique of Pure Reason*

12 When a true genius appears in the world, you may know him by this sign, that the dunces are all in confederacy against him.
JONATHAN SWIFT (1667–1745) *Thoughts on Various Subjects*

13 Genius is one per cent inspiration and ninety-nine per cent perspiration.
THOMAS A. EDISON (1847–1931) *Life*

14 One science only will one genius fit:
So vast is art, so narrow human wit.
ALEXANDER POPE (1688–1744) *An Essay on Criticism*

15 Genius can only breathe freely in an atmosphere of freedom.
JOHN STUART MILL (1806–1873) *On Liberty*

16 Beware of notions like genius and inspiration; they are a sort of magic wand and should be used sparingly by anybody who wants to see things clearly.
J. ORTEGA Y GASSET *Notes on the Novel*, 1925

17 Men of genius are far more abundant than is supposed.
EDGAR ALLAN POE (1809–1849) *Marginalia*

18 The concept of genius as akin to madness has been carefully fostered by the inferiority complex of the public.
EZRA POUND (1885–1972) *The ABC of Reading*

1 A person of genius should marry a person of character. Genius does not herd with genius.
OLIVER WENDELL HOLMES (1809–1894) *The Professor at the Breakfast Table*

2 Patience is a necessary ingredient of genius.
BENJAMIN DISRAELI (1804–1881) *Contarini Fleming*

3 The secret of science is to ask the right question, and it is the choice of problem more than anything else that marks the man of genius in the scientific world.
HENRY TIZARD in C.P. Snow *A Postscript to Science and Government*, 1962

4 Genius is power, talent is applicability.
RALPH WALDO EMERSON (1803–1882) *Journals*

GESTALT PSYCHOLOGY

5 I believe that Gestalt theory's concern with the importance of human values has been vindicated in a backhand way by the modern academic behaviorists.... The modern behaviorists now tell us that if we want to understand and change a person's behavior, we have to have some idea of what that person thinks and feels. Isn't that marvelous! They call it 'cognitive behaviorism'. When I said the same thing 40 years ago, they called it the pollution of scientific psychology with mysticism.
ROBERT SHERRILL in G.A. Kimball *et al. Portraits of Pioneers in Psychology*, 1991

6 By the end of the 1920s, Gestalt psychologists had been invited to lecture at the Bauhaus, and in 1930 the Bauhaus offered an entire course in psychology, with the emphasis on Gestalt psychology, as a part of the regular curriculum.
JOHN WILLATS *Art and Representation*, 1997

7 According to the most general definition of *gestalt*, the process of learning, of reproduction, of striving, of emotional attitude, of thinking, acting, and so forth, may be included as subject matter of *gestalttheorie* in so far as they do not consist of independent elements, but are determined in a situation as a whole.
WOLFGANG KOHLER *Gestalt Psychology*, 1930

8 ... the Gestalt school dissolved into the fog of subjectivism. With the death of the school, many of its early and genuine insights were unfortunately lost to the mainstream of experimental psychology.
DAVID MARR *Vision*, 1982

GESTURE

9 Acts of speaking are often accompanied in our culture by movements of the arms and hands that are termed *gestures*. These movements that occur only during speech, are synchronized with linguistic units, ... perform text functions like speech, dissolve like speech in aphasia, and develop together with speech in children. Because of these similarities, a strong case can be made for regarding gestures and speech as parts of a common psychological system.
D. McNEILL *Psychological Review*, 1985

10 The gesture is the initial visual sign which contains the child's future writing as an acorn contains a future oak.
L.S. VYGOTSKY *Mind in Society*, 1978

11 ... however far apart in colour, habits, manners, and religion people may be, the universal language of gesture can forge links between them. For gesture-language is practically the same in all human beings, and it follows that it must correspond to the primary level of existence, comprising instincts and emotions on the one hand and an elementary knowledge of objects on the other.
CHARLOTTE WOLFF *The Psychology of Gesture*, 1945

GOSSIP

1 There is only one thing worse in the world than being talked about, and that is not being talked about.
OSCAR WILDE (1854–1900) *The Picture of Dorian Gray*

2 If it is abuse – why one is always sure to hear of it from one damned good-natured friend or other!
RICHARD BRINSLEY SHERIDAN (1751–1816) *The Critic*

3 Gossip needs no carriage.
RUSSIAN PROVERB

4 Love and Scandal are the best sweetners of tea.
HENRY FIELDING (1707–1754) *Love in Several Masques*

5 I'm called away by particular business.
But I leave my character behind me.
RICHARD BRINSLEY SHERIDAN (1751–1816) *The School for Scandal*

6 At ev'ry word a reputation dies.
ALEXANDER POPE (1688–1744) 'The Rape of the Lock'

7 Whoever gossips to you will gossip of you.
SPANISH PROVERB

GRANDPARENTS

8 Every one needs to have access to both grandparents and grandchildren in order to become a full human being.
MARGARET MEAD *Blackberry Winter*, 1972

9 ... my grandfather could enjoy me without owning me: I was his 'wonder' because he wanted to end his days as a wonderstruck old man; he decided to regard me as an unusual boon from fate, as a free gift which could always be revoked: what could he have demanded of me? My very presence satisfied him.
JEAN-PAUL SARTRE (1905–1980) *Words*

10 ... the grandmother is not a suitable custodian of the care and rearing of her grandchild: She is a disturbing factor against which we are obliged to protect the child according to the best of our ability.
H. VOLLMER *American Journal of Orthopsychiatry*, 1937

11 In fact, he [Charles Darwin] was obviously in the same category as God and Father Christmas. Only, with our grandfather, we also felt, modestly, that we ought to disclaim any virtue of our own in having produced him.
GWEN RAVERAT (1885–1957) *Period Piece*

GREATNESS

12 Untimely death is an essential part of iconization; the person is forever young, caught at the height of beauty – and unfinished, always with uncertainty about the potential unfulfilled.
HELEN HASTE *The Psychologist*, November 1997

13 But be not afraid of greatness: some men are born great, some achieve greatness, and some have greatness thrust upon them.
WILLIAM SHAKESPEARE (1564–1616) *Twelfth Night*

14 Great minds tend toward banality.
ANDRÉ GIDE (1869–1951) *Pretexts*

15 Great discoverers are not necessarily great men. Who changed the world more than Columbus? What was he? An adventurer. He had character, it is true, but he was not a great man.
SIGMUND FREUD (1856–1939) cit. Ernest Jones, *Life and Work of Sigmund Freud*, 1953–1957

GRIEF

16 No one ever told me that grief felt so like fear.
C.S. LEWIS (1898–1963) *A Grief Observed*

1 Pure and simple sorrow is as impossible as pure and complete joy.
LEO TOLSTOY (1828–1910) *War and Peace*

2 When sorrows come, they come not single spies,
But in battalions.
WILLIAM SHAKESPEARE (1564–1616) *Hamlet*

3 It is idle to grieve if you get no help from grief.
SENECA (4 BC–65 AD) *Moral Epistles to Lucilius*

4 To me the meanest flower that blows can give
Thoughts that do often lie too deep for tears.
WILLIAM WORDSWORTH (1770–1850) 'Intimations on Immoratality'

5 For a keener grief it is to call to mind that lost happiness than to suffer the presence of the unhappiness that cometh after.
GEOFFREY OF MONMOUTH (c. 1100–c. 1154) *History of the Kings of Britain*

6 Tears, idle tears, I know not what they mean,
Tears from the depth of some divine despair
Rise in the heart, and gather to the eyes,
In looking on the happy Autumn fields,
And thinking of the days that are no more.
ALFRED, LORD TENNYSON (1809–1892) *The Princess*

7 Grief and disappointment give rise to anger, anger to envy, envy to malice, malice to grief again, till the whole circle be completed.
DAVID HUME (1711–1776) *A Treatise of Human Nature*

8 ... he who remains passive when over-whelmed with grief loses his best chance of recovering his elasticity of mind.
CHARLES DARWIN (1809–1882) *The Expression of the Emotions in Man and Animals*

9 Happiness is beneficial for the body but it is grief that develops the mind.
MARCEL PROUST (1871–1922) *Rememberance of Things Past*

10 Sorrow concealed, like an oven stopp'd,
Doth burn the heart to cinders where it is.
WILLIAM SHAKESPEARE (1564–1616) *Titus Andronicus*

11 Work is the best antidote to sorrow my dear Watson.
ARTHUR CONAN DOYLE (1859–1930) *The Return of Sherlock Holmes*

GROUPS

12 We all know we are unique individuals, but we tend to see others as representatives of groups.
DEBORAH TANNEN *You Just Don't Understand*, 1992

13 Every social group is organized and held together by some psychological tendency or group of tendencies, which give the group a bias in its dealings with external circumstances. The bias constructs the special persistent features of a group culture ... what the individual will observe in his environment and what he will connect from his past life with the direct response.
F.C. BARTLETT *Remembering*, 1932

14 We live in a social environment which is in constant flux. Much of what happens to us is related to the activities of groups to which we do or do not belong; and the changing relations between these groups require constant readjustments of our understanding of what happens and constant causal attributions about the why and how of the changing conditions of our lives.
H. TAJFEL *Journal of Social Issues*, 1969

15 ... it seems to be generally felt that public disagreement among members of a team not only incapacitates them for united action but also embarrasses the reality sponsored by the team.
ERVING GOFFMAN *The Presentation of the Self in Everyday Life*, 1959

1 Commitment by its nature, frees us from ourselves and, while it stands us in opposition to some, it joins us with others similarly committed.
MICHAEL LEWIS *Shame*, 1992

2 Effective social action by the individual depends upon a high degree of conformity to the group.... Yet the provision of a wide range of information to individuals and insistence on their privilege and duty of choice is essential if the group is to maintain the flexibility and variety of action that are needed for effective adaptation to circumstances.
J.Z. YOUNG *An Introduction to the Study of Man*, 1970

3 There is no dogma so queer, no behaviour so eccentric or even outrageous, but a group of people can be found who think it divinely inspired.
ALDOUS HUXLEY (1894–1963) *The Olive Tree*

4 As organization men see it, through an extension of the group spirit, through educating people to sublimate their egos, organizations can rid themselves of their tyrants and create a *harmonious* atmosphere in which the group will bring out the best in everyone.
WILLIAM WHYTE *The Organization Man*, 1956

5 Love, friendship, respect, do not unite people as much as a common hatred for something.
ANTON CHEKHOV (1860–1904) *Notebooks, 1892–1904*

6 In men this blunder still you find, All think their little set mankind.
HANNAH MORE (1745–1833) 'Florio'

7 A closed group ... is an intolerant entity.
I. EIBL-EIBESFELDT *Love and Hate*, 1971

8 The majority never has right on its side.
HENRIK IBSEN (1828–1906) *An Enemy of the People*

9 When several fairly primitive individuals, such as small boys, laugh together at one or several others not belonging to the same group, the activity, like that of other redirected appeasement ceremonies, contains quite a large measure of aggression directed towards non-members of the group.
KONRAD LORENZ *On Aggression* 1963

10 The convention is that the scientific community is those people who are able to speak its language.
JOHN ZIMAN *Public Knowledge: The Social Dimension of Science*, 1968

11 One's enough. Two's company. Three's a crowd.
ANON.

12 A stable hierarchy is a guarantee of peace and harmony in the group.
FRANS de WAAL *Chimpanzee Politics: Power and Sex and Apes*, 1982

13 It takes an out-group to make an in-group.
E.G. BORING in *A History of Psychology in Autobiography, Vol. 4*, 1952

14 A nation is the average of its people urged on by the few.
ARTHUR MEE *Children's Newspaper*, 12 January 1935

15 Tell me what company thou keepest, and I'll tell, thee what thou art.
MIGUEL DE CERVANTES (1547–1616) *Don Quixote*

GROWTH

16 The real measure of the individual, accordingly, whether lower animal or man, must include the element of growth as a creative power.
G.E. COGHILL *Anatomy and the Problem of Behaviour*, 1929

17 Growth is the only evidence of life.
JOHN HENRY (CARDINAL) NEWMAN (1801–1890) *Apologia Pro Vita Sua*

GUILT

1   It is not the conscience which raises a blush, for a man may sincerely regret some slight fault committed in solitude, or he may suffer the deepest remorse for an undetected crime, but he will not blush.... It is not the sense of guilt, but the thought that others think or know us to be guilty which crimsons the face.
CHARLES DARWIN (1809–1882) *The Expression of the Emotions in Man and Animals*

2   Guilt is the awareness of dislodgement of the self from one's core role structure.
G.A. KELLY *The Psychology of Personal Constructs*, 1955

3   No such thing
as innocent
bystanding
SEAMUS HEANEY 'Mycenae Lookout', 1996

4   The experience of total helplessness in the midst of a disaster seems to be related to later feelings of depression.... Survivors later develop a great deal of anger, usually directed towards those they perceive as responsible for the accident. They may also develop considerable guilt revolving around their own decision to travel on that particular trip, guilt about what they did or did not do to survive the trauma and guilt about surviving when many others were killed or maimed.
WILLIAM YULE in C.F. Saylor *Children and Disaster*, 1993

5   The offender never forgives.
RUSSIAN PROVERB

6   Life without industry is guilt, and industry without art is brutality.
JOHN RUSKIN (1819–1900) *Lectures on Art*

7   Had laws not been, we never had been blam'd;
For not to know we sinn'd is innocence.
WILLIAM DAVENANT (1606–1668) 'Dryden Miscellany'

H

HABIT

8   Habits and skills are Plans that were originally voluntary but that have become relatively inflexible, involuntary, automatic. Once the Plan that controls a sequence of skilled actions becomes fixed through overlearning, it will still function in much the same way as an innate Plan in instinctive behavior.
G.A. MILLER, E. GALANTER, K.H. PRIBRAM *Plans and the Structure of Behavior*, 1960

9   Habit and routine free the mind for more constructive work.
THEODORE ROOSEVELT (1858–1919) attrib.

10   Habit is also opposed to changes: for it renders even our errors dear to us.... What seems intrinsically right, is so merely thro habit.
NOAH WEBSTER (1758–1843) *Dissertations on the English Language*

11   Habit is thus the enormous fly-wheel of society, its most precious conservative agent. It alone is what keeps us all within the bounds of ordinance, and saves the children of fortune from envious uprisings of the poor.... It dooms us all to fight out the battle of life upon lines of our nurture or our early choice, and to make the best of a pursuit that disagrees because there is no other for which we are fitted, and it is too late to begin again.
WILLIAM JAMES *Principles of Psychology*, 1890

1 The basic characteristic of habit is that every experience enacted and undergone modifies the one who acts and undergoes, while this modification affects, whether we wish it or not, the quality of subsequent experiences. For it is a somewhat different person who enters into them.
JOHN DEWEY (1859–1952) *Experience and Education*

2 The only unimpeachable definition of a word is that it is a human habit, an habitual act on the part of a human individual which has, or may have, the effect of evolving some idea in the mind of another individual. A word may thus be rightly compared with such an habitual act as taking off one's hat or raising one's finger to one's cap.
OTTO JESPERSEN *Language*, 1922

3 There's nothing like being used to a thing.
RICHARD BRINSLEY SHERIDAN (1751–1816) *The Rivals*

4 Unnatural generally only means uncustomary, and everything which is usual appears natural.
JOHN STUART MILL (1806–1873) *The Subjection of Women*

5 It seems, in fact, as though the second half of a man's life is made up of nothing, but the habits he has accumulated during the first half.
FEODOR DOSTOYEVSKY (1821–1881) *The Possessed*

6 The great thing then, in all education, is to make our nervous system our ally instead of our enemy.... For this we must make automatic and habitual, as early as possible, as many useful actions as we can.
WILLIAM JAMES *Principles of Psychology*, 1890

7 Habit is everything – even in love.
VANVENARGUES *Reflection and Maxims*, 1746

8 'Tis not, therefore, reason which is the guide of life, but custom. That alone determines the mind, in all instances, to suppose the future comparable to the past.
DAVID HUME (1711–1776) *A Treatise of Human Nature*

9 Habit is overcome by Habit.
THOMAS à KEMPIS (c. 1380–1471) *The Imitation of Christ*

10 Psychologically speaking, habits and customs are the most economical means of getting cumulative value from the common experiences of life.
JOHN DEWEY (1859–1952) *Lectures in China, 1919–1920*

11 Most human beings have an almost infinite capacity for taking things for granted.
ALDOUS HUXLEY (1894–1963) *Themes and Variations*

HABITUATION

12 Goodness, what a view, you lucky devil. Though I suppose as you live with it every day you don't see it.
BORIS PASTERNAK (1890–1960) *Doctor Zhivago*, 1958

13 When you're with somebody for a very long time, you end up just not seeing each other. You forget to value each other as you should.
LOUIS de BERNIÉRES, interview, *The Guardian*, 23 August 1997

14 Beauty is all very well at first sight; but who ever looks at it when it has been in the house three days.
GEORGE BERNARD SHAW (1856–1950) *Man and Superman*

15 If it were in our power to keep the cherry blossom on the tree, we should cease to admire it.
JAPANESE PROVERB

HALLUCINATIONS

1   Voices in my head,
Chanting, 'Kisses. Bread.
Prove yourself. Fight. Shove.
Learn. Earn. Look for love.
VIKRAM SETH 'Voices', 1990

2   Art thou not, fatal vision, sensible
To feeling as to sight? or art thou but
A dagger of the mind, a false creation,
Proceeding from the heat-oppressed
    brain?
WILLIAM SHAKESPEARE (1564–1616)
Macbeth

3   I know a thing or two about ghosts,
because I grew up with all the best
ghosts in English Literature; my father
used to tell me about them, when I was
a small boy, and I loved the
uncanniness and fear, as happy, well-
protected children do.
ROBERTSON DAVIES *Murther and Walking
Spirits*, 1991

HANDS

4   [The hand] is, in everyday use, often
simultaneously or successively
expressive, executive and perceptive.
J.M. KENNEDY in E.C. Carterette *et al.*
Handbook of Perception, Vol. 8, 1978

5   ... the working hand is the tool of the
eye.
G. REVESZ *Psychology and the Art of the
Blind*, 1950

6   Now it is the opinion of Anacagoras
that the possession of these hands is
the cause of man being of all animals
the most intelligent. But it is more
rational to suppose that man has hands
because of his superior intelligence. For
the hands are instruments, and the
invariable plan of nature in distributing
the organs is to give each to such
animal as can make use of it; nature
acting in this matter as any prudent
man would do ... we must conclude that
man does not owe his superior
intelligence to his hands, but his hands

to his superior intelligence. For the
most intelligent of animals is the one
who would put the most organs to good
use, and the hand is not looked upon as
one organ but as many; for it is as it
were an instrument for further
instruments.
ARISTOTLE (384–322 BC) in J.B. Barnes *The
Complete Works of Aristotle*, 1984

7   The hands are a sort of feet, which
serve us in our passage towards
Heaven, curiously distinguished into
joints and fingers, and fit to be applied
to any thing which reason can imagine
or desire.
THOMAS TRAHERNE (1637–1674)
Meditations of the Six Days of Creation

8   Cold hands, warm heart.
PROVERB

9   It is a moot point whether the
human hand created the human brain,
or the brain created the hand. Certainly
the connection is intimate and
reciprocal.
A.N. WHITEHEAD (1861–1947) *The Aims of
Education*

10   Revere those hairy wrists
And leg-of-mutton fists
Which pulverised the trolls
And carved deep Donts in stone,
Great hands which under knolls
Are now disjointed bone,
But what has been has been.
W.H. AUDEN (1907–1973) 'Precious Five'

11   The hand is the cutting edge of the
mind.
J. BRONOWSKI (1908–1974) *The Ascent of
Man*

12   To write creatively I must work by
hand.
J.A. SCOTT KELSO *Dynamic Patterns*, 1995

13   One of the basic developmental
problems of the human infant is to use
his hand adaptively, to grasp food, and
to manage implements for conveying
food through the short but troublesome
route from hand to mouth.
ARNOLD GESELL, F.L. ILG *Feeding Behavior
of Infants*, 1947

HAPPINESS

1 Leisure activities play an important part in happiness, because it is under the individual's own control what they do. Sport and leisure activities are a good source of happiness, but we also found that people who watched soap operas are happier than those who do not.
MICHAEL ARGYLE cit. *The Guardian*, 5 October 1998

2 How to gain, how to keep, how to recover happiness is in fact for most men at all times the secret motive of all they do, and of all they are willing to endure.
WILLIAM JAMES *Varieties of Religious Experience*, 1902

3 Can any man say with certainty he was happy at a particular moment of time which he remembers as being delightful? Remembering it certainly makes him happy, because he realises how happy he could have been, but at the actual moment when the alleged happiness was occurring, did he really feel happy?
EUGENE DELACROIX (1798–1863) *Journal*

4 ... cheerfulness keeps up a kind of day-light in the mind, and fills it with a steady and perpetual serenity.
JOSEPH ADDISON (1672–1719) *The Spectator*

5 No matter what happiness may be it is something of positive value and unhappiness is something of negative value. We believe that free men everywhere have an inalienable right to life, liberty and the pursuit of – an uninhibited hypothalamus.
P.T. YOUNG *American Psychologist*, 1967

6 But a lifetime of happiness! No man alive could bear it: it would be hell on earth.
GEORGE BERNARD SHAW (1856–1950) *Man and Superman*

7 Happiness is a mystery like religion, and should never be rationalised.
G.K. CHESTERTON (1874–1936) *Heretics*

8 A man is happy so long as he chooses to be happy.
ALEXANDER SOLZHENITSYN *Cancer Ward*, 1968

9 Happiness is the only sanction of life; where happiness fails, existence remains a mad and lamentable experiment.
G. SANTAYANA (1863–1952) *The Life of Reason*

10 Happiness is no laughing matter.
RICHARD WHATELEY (1787–1863) *Apophthegrams*

11 For if unhappiness develops the forces of the mind, happiness alone is salutary to the body.
MARCEL PROUST (1871–1922) *Time Regained*

12 Happiness is an imaginary condition....
THOMAS SZASZ *The Second Sin*, 1974

13 What is happiness? The feeling that power *increases* – that resistance is being overcome.
FRIEDRICH NIETZSCHE (1844–1900) *The Anti-Christ*

14 Ask yourself whether you are happy, and you cease to be so.
JOHN STUART MILL (1806–1873) *Autobiography*

15 Happiness is not an ideal of reason but of imagination.
IMMANUEL KANT (1724–1804) *Fundamental Principles of the Metaphysics of Ethics*

16 A large income is the best recipe for happiness I ever heard of.
JANE AUSTEN (1775–1817) *Mansfield Park*

17 The first and indispensable requisite of happiness is a clear conscience, unsullied by the reproach or remembrance of any unworthy action.
EDWARD GIBBON (1737–1796) *The Autobiography*

18 How happy could I be with either, Were t'other dear Charmer away!
JOHN GAY (1685–1732) *The Beggar's Opera*

1   There is no duty we so much underrate
as the duty of being happy.
ROBERT LOUIS STEVENSON (1850–1894)
Virginibus Puerisque

2   When we are happy we are always good, but when we are good we are not always happy.
OSCAR WILDE (1854–1900) *The Picture of Dorian Gray*

HATRED

3   Hatred rarely does harm to its object. It is the hater who suffers.... Rancour in the bosom is the foe of personal happiness.
LORD BEAVERBROOK *The Divine Propagandist*, 1962

4   Sadness is very close to hate.
MICHAEL ONDAATJE *The English Patient*, 1992

5   No one is born hating another person because of the colour of his skin, or his background, or his religion. People must learn to hate, and if they can learn to hate, they can be taught to love, for love comes more naturally to the human heart than its opposite.
NELSON MANDELA *Long Walk to Freedom*, 1994

6   Now hatred is by far the longest pleasure;
Men love in haste, but they detest at leisure.
LORD BYRON (1788–1824) *Don Juan*

7   It is part of human nature to hate the man you have hurt.
TACITUS (56–120) *Agricola*

8   The worst sin towards our fellow creatures is not to hate them, but to be indifferent to them: that's the essence of inhumanity.
GEORGE BERNARD SHAW (1856–1950) *The Devil's Disciple*

HELPLESSNESS

9   The human need to control and influence the environment has been considered one of the great driving motivations behind our actions and behavior.... Repeated experience with uncontrollable events can lead one to the conclusion that he or she is helpless and will be unable to control the outcome of any future events ... learned helplessness is characterized by a cluster of symptoms including motivational deficits, decreased persistence, cognitive defects, and, in humans, sadness and lowered self esteem. In addition ... [it has been] linked with a number of diseases.
MICHAEL GAZZANIGA *Nature's Mind*, 1992

10   Assigning only a psychological cause does not necessarily consign a phenomenon to a metaphysical or parapsychological status. Death from helplessness is real enough.
MARTIN SELIGMAN *Helplessness*, 1975

HOME

11   Home is the place where, when you have to go there,
They have to take you in.
ROBERT FROST (1874–1963) 'The Death of the Hired Man'

12   Home is so sad. It stays as it was left,
Shaped to the comfort of the last to go
As if to win them back.
PHILIP LARKIN (1922–1985) 'Home is so Sad'

13   Home is where one starts from. As we grow older
The world becomes stranger, the pattern more complicated
Of dead and living.
T.S. ELIOT (1888–1965) 'East Coker'

14   The Edwardian slum child, like his forbears, felt an attachment to family life that a later age may find hard to understand. Home, however poor, was the focus of all his love and interests, a sure fortress against a hostile world.
ROBERT ROBERTS *The Classic Slum*, 1971

1 Home is where you come to when you have nothing better to do.
MARGARET THATCHER cit. *The Independent*, 11 May 1991

HOMOSEXUALITY

2 In the nineteenth century, the idea appeared that homosexual behavior made a particular kind of person; homosexuality, in essence, defined an individual's identity, and this identity was labelled as a sickness. Today, political movements offer alternatives to this rigid, negative construct.
D.E.S. FRABLE *Annual Review of Psychology*, 1997

3 Since 'unnatural' means 'removed from nature', only the most civilised, because the least natural, class of society can be expected to tolerate such a product of civilisation.
VITA SACKVILLE-WEST (1892–1962) cit.
Nigel Nicolson *Portrait of a Marriage*, 1973

4 I am the love that dare not speak its name.
LORD ALFRED DOUGLAS (1870–1945) 'Two Loves'

HOPE

5 Hope springs eternal in the human breast;
Man never is, but always to be blest.
ALEXANDER POPE (1688–1744) *An Essay on Man*

6 One can imagine an animal angry, frightened, unhappy, happy, startled: But hopeful? Can only those hope who can talk? Only those who have mastered the use of language. That is to say, the phenomena of hope are modes of this complicated form of life.
LUDWIG WITTGENSTEIN (1889–1951)
Philosophical Investigations

7 We must rediscover the distinction between hope and expectation.
IVAN ILLICH *Deschooling Society*, 1971

8 Hope is itself a species of happiness, and, perhaps, the chief happiness which this world affords.
SAMUEL JOHNSON (1709–1784) cit. James Boswell *The Life of Samuel Johnson*

9 What reinforcement we may gain from hope,
If not, what resolution from despair.
JOHN MILTON (1608–1674) *Paradise Lost*

10 Extreme hopes are born of extreme misery.
BERTRAND RUSSELL (1872–1970) *Unpopular Essays*

11 I can't tell if a straw ever saved a drowning man, but I know that a mere glance is enough to make despair pause. For in truth we who are creatures of impulse are not creatures of despair.
JOSEPH CONRAD (1857–1924) *Chance*

12 The natural flights of the human mind are not from pleasure to pleasure but from hope to hope.
SAMUEL JOHNSON (1709–1784) *The Rambler*

HUMAN NATURE

13 ... man is essentially a battlefield, he is a dark cellar in which a maiden aunt and a sex-crazed monkey are locked in mortal combat, the affair being refereed by a rather nervous bank clerk.
DON BANNISTER in B.M. Foss *New Horizons in Psychology*, 1966

14 Thus there are many ways to study man psychologically. Yet to study him most fully is to take him as an individual. He is more than a bundle of habits; more than a nexus of abstract dimensions; more too than a representative of his species. He is more than a citizen of the state, and more than a mere incident in the gigantic movements of mankind. He transcends them all.
G.W. ALLPORT *Personality: A Psychological Perspective*, 1937

1 The understanding of human nature seems to us indispensable to every man.
ALFRED ADLER *Understanding Human Nature*, 1927

2 Science cannot solve the ultimate mystery of Nature. And it is because in the last analysis we ourselves are part of the mystery we are trying to solve.
MAX PLANCK in J.D. Barrow, F.J. Tipter *The Anthropic Cosmological Principle*, 1986

3 Though men are not dogs, they should humbly try to remember how much they resemble dogs in their brain functions, and not boast themselves as demigods.
WILLIAM SARGANT *Battle for the Mind*, 1957

4 There are many wonderful things, and nothing is more wonderful than man.
SOPHOCLES (c. 496–c. 406 BC) *Antigone*

5 ... man is more than the sum of his reflexes, instincts and immediate reactions of all sorts. He is all these plus his creative potential for the future.
G.E. COGHILL *Anatomy and the Problem of Behaviour*, 1929

6 Broadly speaking we are in the middle of a race between human skill as a means, and human folly as an end.
BERTRAND RUSSELL (1872–1970) *The Impact of Science on Society*

7 Chaos of thought and passion, all confus'd;
Still by himself abused or disabused;
Created half to rise, and half to fall;
Great lord of all things, yet a prey to all.
ALEXANDER POPE (1688–1744) *An Essay on Man*

8 The natural man has only two primal passions, to get and beget.
WILLIAM OSLER (1849–1919) *Science and Immortality*

9 ... it would be very singular that all nature, all the planets, should obey eternal laws, and that there should be a little animal, five feet high, who, in contempt of these laws, could act as he pleased, solely according to his caprice.
VOLTAIRE (1697–1778) *The Ignorant Philosopher*

10 And much it grieved my heart to think
What man has made of man.
WILLIAM WORDSWORTH (1770–1850) 'Lines Written in Early Spring'

11 To say, for example, that a man is made up of certain chemical elements is a satisfactory description only for those who intend to use him as a fertiliser.
H.J. MULLER *Science and Children*, 1943

12 Consider your origins: you were not made to live as brutes, but to follow virtue and knowledge.
DANTE (1265–1321) *Divine Comedy: Inferno*

13 ... human nature is almost unbelievably malleable, responding accurately and contrastingly to cultural conditions.
MARGARET MEAD *Sex and Temperament in Primitive Societies*, 1935

14 Man is, indeed a mechanism, but he is a mechanism which, within his limitations of life, sensitivity and growth, is creating and operating himself.
G.E. COGHILL *Anatomy and the Problem of Behaviour*, 1929

15 If the organism were a sum of parts which one could study separately, there would be no difficulty in combining the parts to form a science of the whole. But all attempts to understand the organism as a whole directly from these phenomena have met with very little success. They have not been successful, we may conclude, because the organism is not a sum of parts.
KURT GOLDSTEIN *Human Nature in the Light of Psychopathology*, 1963

16 Human nature is, then, not unitary but multiform; the number of human natures is almost as great as the number of humans.
Th. DOBZHANSKY *American Psychologist*, 1967

17 Human beings, whether individuals, families or larger groups, do not like to be intimately scrutinized.
JOHN BOWLBY in K.J. Connolly, J.S. Bruner *The Growth of Competence*, 1974

1 Without Contraries there is no progression. Attraction and Repulsion, Reason and Energy, Love and Hate are necessary to Human Existence.
WILLIAM BLAKE (1757–1827) 'The Marriage of Heaven and Hell'

2 I am not thought, I am not action, I am not feeling; I am something that thinks and acts and suffers.
THOMAS REID (1710–1796) *Essays on the Active Powers of the Human Mind*

3 I should describe the human race as a strange species of bipeds who cannot run fast enough to collect the money which they owe themselves
don marquis (1878–1937) *archy's life of mehitabel*

4 Our humanity rests upon a series of learned behaviors, woven together into patterns that are infinitely fragile and never directly inherited.
MARGARET MEAD *Male and Female*, 1949

5 ... human nature is too important to be left to the behaviorists and psychoanalysts.
U. NEISSER *Cognition and Reality*, 1976

6 Human nature is so well disposed towards those who are in interesting situations, that a young person who either marries or dies is sure of being kindly spoken of.
JANE AUSTEN (1775–1817) *Emma*

7 The more one analyses people, the more all reasons for analysis disappear. Sooner or later one comes to that dreadful universal thing called human nature.
OSCAR WILDE (1854–1900) *The Decay of Lying*

8 How many natures lie in human nature?
BLAISE PASCAL (1623–1662) *Pensées*

9 The problem of human nature is the problem of psychological heredity.
L. MALSON *Wolf Children*, 1972

HUMOUR

10 ... jokes are from their nature to be distinguished from the comic.... [We] locate the pleasure of jokes in the unconscious; no reason being found for making the same localization in the sense of the comic.... Jokes and the comic are distinguished first and foremost in their psychical localization; *the joke it may be said, is the contribution made to the comic from the realm of the unconscious.*
SIGMUND FREUD (1856–1939) *Jokes and their Relation to the Unconscious*

11 As one explores humour and thinks about it as a clinical tool, the conviction grows that humour is a vital component of living and of human affairs. Its powers as a liberating and constructive force are often acknowledged, but never fully exploited. It restores perspective on any human activity, institution or person whose image has become overblown or distorted. Strangely, though humour liberates us from the irrational, it helps us to be more rational.
JACOB LEVINE *Children's Humour*, 1980

12 The marvellous thing about a joke with a double meaning is that it can mean only one thing.
RONNIE BARKER *Sauce*, 1977

13 Humor is emotional chaos remembered in tranquility.
JAMES THURBER (1894–1961) *New York Post*, 29 February 1960

14 Whatever is funny is subversive, every joke is ultimately a custard pie.... A dirty joke is a sort of mental rebellion.
GEORGE ORWELL (1903–1950) *Horizon*, September 1941

15 He that jokes confesses.
ITALIAN PROVERB

16 The language of humour is power-less without the *speech* of humour. Jokes are *told*; somewhere beyond the text is a voice, telling, delivering, timing.
WALTER NASH *The Language of Humour*, 1985

1 A different taste in jokes is a great strain on the affections.
GEORGE ELIOT (1819–1880) *Daniel Deronda*

2 Look for the ridiculous in everything and you will find it.
JULES RENARD *Journal*, 1890

3 Humour brings insight and tolerance. Irony brings a deeper and less friendly understanding.
AGNES REPPLIER *In Pursuit of Laughter*, 1936

4 A Scot or an Irishman is funny to the English because he is almost exactly like himself, only slightly different. He talks English as his native tongue, only with an incorrect accent; what could possibly be funnier? A Scot is more funny than a Frenchman just as a monkey is more amusing than a dog; he is nearer the real thing.
RONALD KNOX (1888–1957) *Essays in Satire*

5 The bridegroom was most disagreeably surprised when the bride was introduced to him, and drew the broker on one side and whispered his remonstrances: 'Why have you brought me here?' he asked reproachfully. 'She's ugly and old, she squints and has bad teeth and bleary eyes...' – 'You needn't lower your voice', interrupted the broker, 'she's deaf as well.'
SIGMUND FREUD (1856–1939) *Jokes and their Relation to the Unconscious*

HYPNOSIS

6 Hypnosis exploits the fact that social intercourse involves layers of messages, attended to at various levels of awareness, that can influence experience.
B. VANDENBERG *Child Development*, 1998

7 The power to heal by Hypnotism is almost entirely the power of the patient to accept and believe the strengthening suggestions of health which by Hypnotism are forced upon the attention of the sub-conscious mind.
THE PSYCHIC RESEARCH COMPANY *A Course of Practical Psychic Instruction*, 1912

8 ... it seems likely that some at least of the claims made for the usefulness of hypnosis in helping recall stems from the hypnotist's capacity to induce the subject to imagine the context in which the incident occurred before attempting detailed recall.
ALAN BADDELEY *Human Memory*, 1990

9 The study of hypnosis is the study of Human Nature. So long as the world produces some to lead and some who are led, some who are strong and some who are weak, some who are dependent and some who are independent, Hypnotism will be a factor in human happiness.
MASTERS OF THE SCIENCE *The Perfect Course in Hypnotism, Mesmerism, Clairvoyance, Suggestion, Therapeutics, and the Sleep Cure*, 1901

10 Hypnosis is reminiscent of childhood. It does not necessarily recreate particular memories or experiences from the past, but rather re-evokes the childhood experience.
B. VANDENBERG *Child Development*, 1998

HYPOCHONDRIA

11 I have had an hospital these fourteen years within myself, and studied my own case with the most painful attention.
TOBIAS SMOLLETT (1721–1771) *The Expedition of Humphrey Clinker*

12 Nothing is more fatal to *Health* than an *over Care* of it.
BENJAMIN FRANKLIN (1706–1790) *Poor Richard's Almanack*

HYPOTHESES

13 A genuine empirical hypothesis can only describe or explain a class of phenomena identifiable on grounds that are independent of anything stated in the hypothesis itself.
B.R. TILGHMAN *But is It Art?*, 1994

1 We are forced to improvise, to create hypotheses where someday it may be possible simply to invoke established laws.
R.R. HOLT *Diagnostic Psychological Testing*, 1968

2 The intensity of conviction that a hypothesis is true has no bearing over whether it is true or not.
PETER MEDAWAR *Advice to a Young Scientist*, 1979

3 Hypothesis creation (in contrast to hypothesis testing) remains a tantalizing mystery – so much so that sober philosophers of science, like Karl Popper characterize science as consisting principally of the falsification of hypotheses no matter the source whence the hypothesis came.
J.S. BRUNER *Actual Minds, Possible Worlds*, 1986

4 It is a good morning exercise for a research scientist to discard a pet hypothesis every day before breakfast. It keeps him young.
KONRAD LORENZ *On Aggression*, 1963

5 The great tragedy of Science – the slaying of a beautiful hypothesis by an ugly fact.
T.H. HUXLEY (1825–1895) *Collected Essays*

6 There once was a man who said 'God
Must think it exceedingly odd
If he finds that this tree
Continues to be
When there's no one about in the Quad.'
RONALD KNOX (1888–1957) cit. B. Russell *History of Western Philosophy*, 1946

IDEAS

7 … an idea is no more an even relatively constant thing than is a feeling or emotion or volitional process. There exist only changing and transient ideational processes; there are no permanent ideas that return again and disappear again.
WILHELM WUNDT *An Introduction to Psychology*, 1912

8 What is an idea? It is an image that paints itself in my brain.
VOLTAIRE (1697–1778) in P. Gay *Philosophical Dictionary*, 1962

9 One can live in the shadow of an idea without grasping it.
ELIZABETH BOWEN (1897–1973) *The Heat of the Day*

10 It is indeed ideas that endure. But it is human beings who give them life.
A.R. LURIA in M. Cole, S. Cole *The Making of Mind*, 1979

11 Our ideas are only intellectual instruments which we use to break into phenomena; we must change them when they have served their purpose, as we change a blunt lancet that we have used long enough.
CLAUDE BERNARD (1813–1878) *An Introduction to the Study of Experimental Medicine*

12 It is desirable at times for ideas to possess a certain roughness, like drawings on heavy-grain paper. Thoughts having this quality are most likely to match the texture of actual experience.
HAROLD ROSENBERG *Discovering the Past*, 1973

IDENTITY

1 Identity is a unified, purposeful aspect of self ... it is also the term most invoked by those who struggle to create meaning and purpose when culturally significant, ideologically powerful social category systems clash with personal and collective group member experiences.
D.E.S. FRABLE *Annual Review of Psychology*, 1997

2 ... identity establishes *what* and *where* the person is in social terms.
C.P. STONE in A.M. Rose *Human Behavior and Social Processes*, 1962

3 Every individual's sense of identity is rooted largely in his or her place within various groups.
HOWARD GARDNER *Leading Minds*, 1996

4 When you notice a cat in profound
      meditation,
The reason, I tell you, is always the same:
His mind is engaged in a rapt
      contemplation
Of the thought, of thought, of the
      thought of his name:
His ineffable effable
Effanineffable
Deep and inscrutable singular Name.
T.S. ELIOT (1888–1965) 'The Naming of Cats'

5 The precursor of the mirror is the mother's face.
DONALD WINNICOTT *Playing and Reality*, 1971

IGNORANCE

6 ... I found myself saddled with so many doubts and errors that I seemed to have gained nothing in trying to educate myself unless it was to discover more and more fully how ignorant I was.
RENÉ DESCARTES (1596–1650) *Discourse on Method*

7 Ignorance gives one a large range of probabilities.
GEORGE ELIOT (1819–1880) *Daniel Deronda*

8 Our lives are universally shortened by ignorance.
HERBERT SPENCER (1820–1903) *Principles of Biology*

9 We hear it not seldom said that ignorance is the mother of admiration. No falser word was ever spoken, and hardly a more mischievous one.
R.C. TRENCH *The Study of Words*, 1853

10 ... ignorance is never better than knowledge.
ENRICO FERMI (1901–1954) cit. Laura Fermi *Atoms in the Family*, 1955

11 What should they know of England who only England know?
RUDYARD KIPLING (1865–1936) *The English Flag*

12 Ignorance is ignorance; no right to believe anything can be derived from it.
SIGMUND FREUD (1856–1939) *The Future of an Illusion*

13 Uncultivated minds are not full of wild flowers, like uncultivated fields. Villainous weeds grow in them, and they are full of toads.
LOGAN PEARSALL SMITH (1865–1946) *Afterthoughts*

14 Science, especially twentieth-century science, has provided us with a glimpse of something we never really knew before, the revelation of human ignorance.
LEWIS THOMAS *Late Night Thoughts*, 1983

15 Hatred of discussion and hatred of men are born of the same process.
SOCRATES (469–399 BC) *Phaedo*

16 The bookful blockhead, ignorantly
      read,
With loads of learned lumber in his
      head.
ALEXANDER POPE (1688–1744) *An Essay on Criticism*

ILLNESS

1 Illness is in part what the world has done to a victim, but in a larger part it is what a victim has done with his world and himself.
KARL MENNINGER (1893–1990) cit. Susan Sontag *Illness as Metaphor*, 1978

2 I was always myself even when I was ill but now I seem myself.
ALAN BENNETT *The Madness of King George*, 1995

3 In the case of illness, one's confinement, one's hopes and one's fears, what one hears, or believes, one's physician, *his* behavior, are all coalesced in a single picture or drama.
OLIVER SACKS *Awakenings*, 1973

4 We are all ill; but even a universal sickness implies an idea of health.
LIONEL TRILLING *The Liberal Imagination*, 1950

5 Diseases have a character of their own, but they also partake of our character; we have a character of our own, but we also partake of the world's character.
OLIVER SACKS *Awakenings*, 1973

6 How sickness enlarges the dimensions of a man's self to himself.
CHARLES LAMB (1775–1834) *Last Essays of Elia*

ILLUSIONS

7 The study of what are called illusions of the senses is however a very prominent and important part of the physiology of the senses; for just those cases in which external impressions evoke conceptions which are not in accordance with reality are particularly instructive for discovering the laws of those means and processes by which normal perceptions originate.
HERMANN HELMHOLTZ (1821–1894) *On the Relation of Optics to Painting*

8 Illusions are not false beliefs, though false beliefs may be caused by illusions. What may make a painting like a distant view through a window is not the fact that the two can be as indistinguishable as is a facsimile from the original; it is the similarity between the mental activities both can arouse, the search for meaning, the testing for consistency, expressed in the movement of the eye and, more important, in the movements of the mind.
E.H. GOMBRICH *Illusion in Nature and Art*, 1973

9 Nature rejoices in illusion. If a man destroys the power of illusion, either in himself or in others, she punishes him like the harshest tyrant.
JOHANN GOETHE (1749–1832) *Maxims and Reflections*

10 Experimental psychology was delivered from philosophy by illusions.
RICHARD GREGORY in B.M. Foss *New Horizons in Psychology*, 1966

11 Anyone who can handle a needle convincingly can make us see a thread which is not there.
E.H. GOMBRICH *Art and Illusion*, 1960

IMAGERY

12 Perhaps the most bothersome problem in talking about imagery phenomena is that it is hard to say just what is being talked about.
ROBERT SCHWARTZ in N. Block *Imagery*, 1982

13 A person imaging differs from a person hallucinating in that the former has a greater awareness that the image is the product of mental processes rather than a perception of reality.
M. MARTIN, R. WILLIAMS in P.J. Hampson *et al. Imagery*, 1990

1 According to our times and to our experience we represent the natural and the human world by a great set of images. To this set of images we apply, as a template, a system of hypotheses which seems to us coherent.
C.F.A. PANTIN *The Relation Between the Sciences*, 1968

2 When you are searching for a book you may generate a visual memory image ... as an aid to maintaining control of attention. Once the object is in view, however, its perceptual image may bear only a slight resemblance to the image you have used as a crutch for attention and memory.
G.A. MILLER, P.N. JOHNSON-LAIRD *Language and Perception*, 1976

3 ... all parties agree that much of image processing, whatever that is, is inaccessible to consciousness, that experimental data and computational and neurological feasibility are the proper constraints on imagery theories, and that introspective reports are psychological phenomena to be accounted for, not accurate descriptions of psychological mechanisms.
STEVEN PINKER *Visual Cognition: An Introduction*, 1986

4 With indefatigable perseverance man is constructing his life, giving a concrete and neatly-shaped image to that which is supposed to be unknown and which he alone, through his constructions, does constantly let be known. He creates the images of his world, he corrects them and he changes them in the course of years, of centuries.
NAUM GABO in K.S. Drier *et al. Three Lectures on Modern Art*, 1949

5 ... scientific men, as a class, have feeble powers of visual representation. There is no doubt whatever of the latter point, however it may be accounted for. My own conclusion is that an over-ready perception of sharp mental pictures is antagonistic to the acquirement of habits of highly generalized and abstract thought, especially when the steps of reasoning are carried on by words as symbols, and that if the faculty of seeing the pictures was ever possessed by men who think hard, it is very apt to be lost by disuse.
FRANCIS GALTON (1822–1911) *Enquiries into the Human Faculty and Its Development*

6 My eyes make pictures, when they are shut.
SAMUEL TAYLOR COLERIDGE (1772–1834) *A Day-Dream*

7 Pictures are a set of chosen images, a stream of pleasant thoughts passing through the mind. It is a luxury to have the walls of our rooms hung round with them, and no less so to have such a gallery in the mind.
WILLIAM HAZLITT (1778–1830) *Table Talk*

IMAGINATION

8 The moment there is imagination, there is myth.
CAMILLE PAGLIA *Sexual Personnae*, 1990

9 I think it is possible to subsume both the production of new ideas and subjective simulation under one category – that of bold imagination.... And imagination ... is needed not only for thinking up new ideas, but also for criticizing them.
KARL POPPER in H.A. Krebs, J.H. Shelley *The Creative Process in Science and Medicine*, 1975

10 All poets adore explosions, thunderstorms, tornadoes, conflagrations, ruins, scenes of spectacular carnage. The poetic imagination is not at all a desirable quality in a statesman.
W.H. AUDEN (1907–1973) *The Dyer's Hand*

11 You see things; and you say 'Why?' But I dream things that never were; and I say 'Why not?'
GEORGE BERNARD SHAW (1856–1950) *Back to Methusalah*

12 I am giddy, expectation whirls me round.
The imaginary relish is so sweet
That it enchants my sense.
WILLIAM SHAKESPEARE (1564–1616) *Troilus and Cressida*

110

1 Where there is no imagination there is no horror.
ARTHUR CONAN DOYLE (1859–1930) *A Study in Scarlet*

2 Sometimes we see a cloud that's dragonish;
A vapour sometimes like a bear or lion,
A tower'd citadel, a pendant rock,
A forked mountain, or blue promontory
With trees upon't.
WILLIAM SHAKESPEARE (1564–1616) *Anthony and Cleopatra*

3 Heard melodies are sweet, but those unheard
Are sweeter; therefore ye pipes, play on;
Not to the sensual ear, but, more endear'd,
Pipe to the spirit ditties of no tone.
JOHN KEATS (1795–1821) 'Ode on a Grecian Urn'

4 Imagination, which, in truth,
Is but another name for absolute power
And clearest insight, amplitude of mind,
And Reason in her most exalted mood.
WILLIAM WORDSWORTH (1770–1850) 'The Prelude'

5 What is now proved was once only imagin'd.
WILLIAM BLAKE (1757–1827) 'The Marriage of Heaven and Hell'

6 It is not too much to say that next after the passion to learn there is no quality so indispensable to the successful prosecution of science as imagination. Find me a people whose early medicine is not mixed up with magic and incantations and I will find you a people devoid of scientific ability.
C.S. PEIRCE (1839–1914) *Collected Papers, Vol. 2*

7 Imagination depends mainly upon memory, but there is a small percentage of creation of something out of nothing with it.
SAMUEL BUTLER (1835–1902) *The Notebooks of Samuel Butler*

8 There is nothing either good or bad, but thinking makes it so.
WILLIAM SHAKESPEARE (1564–1616) *Hamlet*

9 I too can feel claustrophobia, but not here. To me, this small, dark room, cluttered with apparatus and a tangle of wires, is a place of infinite possibilities and far horizons, full of pathways into the unknown.
K.J.W. CRAIK *The Nature of Psychology*, 1966

10 The function of the imagination is not to make strange things settled, so much as to make settled things strange.
G.K. CHESTERTON (1874–1936) *The Defendant*

11 Imagination is impossible without sensation, and conceptual thought is impossible without imagination.
ARISTOTLE (384–322 BC) *De Anima*

IMITATION

12 When people are free to do as they please, they usually imitate each other.
ERIC HOFFER *The Passionate State of Mind*, 1955

13 The truth is that the property of man to imitate what is before him is one of the strongest parts of his nature.
WALTER BAGEHOT (1826–1877) *Physics and Politics*

14 Imitation to the intelligent and earnest imitator is never slavish, never mere repetition; it is, on the contrary, *a means for further ends*, a method of absorbing what is present in others and of making it over in forms peculiar to one's own temper and valuable to one's own genius.
J.M. BALDWIN *The Individual and Society*, 1911

15 I soon found that no man was ever great by imitation.
SAMUEL JOHNSON (1709–1784) *Rasselas*

16 No living person is sunk so low as not to be imitated by somebody.
WILLIAM JAMES *Talks to Teachers and to Students*, 1899

INDIVIDUAL DIFFERENCES

1 Broadly speaking, human beings may be divided into three classes: those who are toiled to death, those who are worried to death, and those who are bored to death.
WINSTON CHURCHILL (1874–1965) *Painting as a Pastime*

2 I have no patience with the hypothesis occasionally expressed, and often implied, especially in tales written to teach children to be good, that babies are both pretty much alike and that the sole agencies creating differences between boy and boy, and man and man, are steady application and moral effort.
FRANCIS GALTON (1822–1911) *Heredity Genius*

3 It is easier to know man in general than to understand one man in particular.
DUC FRANÇOIS DE LA ROCHEFOUCALD (1613–1680) *Maxims*

4 ... I have always maintained that, excepting fools, men did not differ much in intellect, only in zeal and hard work; and I still think there is an eminently important difference.
CHARLES DARWIN (1809–1882) letter cit. R. Pearson (1914–1930) *The Life, Letters and Labours of Francis Galton*

5 Only if we give respect to this inner core of inheritance can we respect the important individual differences which distinguish infants as well as men.
ARNOLD GESELL *Infancy and Human Growth*, 1928

6 Spoken words are the signs of affections of the soul, and written words are the signs of spoken words. Just as all men have not the same writing, so all men have not the same speech sounds, but the affections of the soul which they signify are the same for all, as also are those things of which our experience are images.
ARISTOTLE (384–322 BC) *De Interpretatione*

7 Though I've belted you and flayed you,
By the livin' Gawd that made you,
You're a better man than I am, Gunga Din!
RUDYARD KIPLING (1865–1936) 'Gunga Din'

8 Nature made him and then broke the mould.
LUDOVICO ARIOSTO (1474–1533) *Orlando Furioso*

9 ... psychology must devote itself to the study of the individual and not merely the study of mind in general.
C.S. MYERS *Experimental Psychology*, 1911

10 Individuality, uniqueness, is not outside the competence of science. It may, in fact it must, be understood scientifically.
Th. DOBZHANSKY *American Psychologist*, 1967

11 Each of us is a unique genetic experiment, never to be repeated again.
ROBERT PLOMIN *Development, Genes and Psychology*, 1986

12 Variety's the very spice of life,
That gives it all its flavour.
WILIAM COWPER (1731–1800) 'The Task'

13 Before a just knowledge can be attained concerning any faculty of the human race, we must inquire into its distribution among all sorts and conditions of men on a large scale, and not among those persons who belong to a highly specialized literary class.
FRANCIS GALTON (1822–1911) *Nature*, 1887

14 One half of the world cannot understand the pleasures of the other.
JANE AUSTEN (1775–1817) *Emma*

15 Men are born equal but they are also born different.
ERICH FROMM *Escape from Freedom*, 1941

16 Whilst we maintain the unity of the human species, we at the same time repel the depressing assumption of superior and inferior races of men. There are nations more susceptible of cultivation than others – but none in themselves nobler than others. All are in like degree designed for freedom.
A. VON HUMBOLDT *Cosmos*, 1849

1 I'm much more able now to be concerned with individual differences. I would now argue on the basis of all I've learned in the last twenty-five years that various functions, common to all people, can be operated and combined in different sequences and assemblies of sequences so that what will happen to any person can be unique.
D.E. BROADBENT cit. D. Cohen *Psychologists on Psychology*, 1977

2 There is no such thing as a single human being, pure and simple, unmixed with other human beings. Each personality is a world in himself, a company of many.
JOAN RIVIERE in M. Klein *et al. New Directions in Psychoanalysis*, 1955

3 Whatever may be the causes of group differences that remain after test bias is eliminated, the practical applications of sound psychometrics can help to reinforce the democratic ideal of treating every person according to the person's *individual* characteristics, rather than according to his or her sex, race, social class, religion or natural origin.
A.R. JENSEN *Bias in Mental Testing*, 1980

4 The individual is an idea like other ideas.
HAROLD ROSENBERG *Discovering the Present*, 1973

5 Probably a crab would be filled with a sense of personal outrage it if could hear us class it without ado or apology as a crustacean, and thus dispose of it. 'I am no such thing,' it would say: 'I am MYSELF, MYSELF alone'.
WILLIAM JAMES *The Varieties of Religious Experience*, 1902

6 The shoe that fits one person pinches another; there is no recipe for living that suits all cases.
CARL JUNG (1875–1961) *Modern Man in Search of a Soul*

INFANCY

7 ... the baby, assailed by eyes, ears, nose, skin, and entrails at once feels that all is one great blooming, buzzing confusion.
WILLIAM JAMES *The Principles of Psychology*, 1890

8 The same acts which help the baby survive help the culture to survive in him.
ERIK ERIKSON in O. Fenichel *et al. The Psychoanalytic Study of the Child*, 1945

9 The nature of the infant is *not* just a new permutation – and – combination of elements contained in the natures of the parents. There is in the nature of the infant that which is utterly unknown in the natures of the parents.
D.H. LAWRENCE (1885–1930) *Psychoanalysis and the Unconscious*

10 Babies in their mothers' arms
Exercise their budding charms
On their fingers and their toes,
Striving ever to enclose
In the circle of their will
Objects disobedient still.
W.H. AUDEN (1907–1973) 'Shorts'

11 The baby creates the object, but the object was there waiting to be created.
DONALD WINNICOTT *Playing and Reality*, 1971

12 The young child's hunger for his mother's love and presence is as great as his hunger for food....
JOHN BOWLBY *Attachment and Loss: Vol. 2, Separation: Anxiety and Anger*, 1973

13 Here we have a baby. It is composed of a Bald Head and a Pair of Lungs.
EUGENE FIELD (1850–1895) *The Tribune Primer*

14 The reason why the infant in arms wants to perceive the presence of its mother is only because it already knows by experience that she satisfies all of its needs without delay.
SIGMUND FREUD (1856–1939) *Inhibitions, Symptoms and Anxiety*

1 I hate babies. They're so human –
they remind one of monkeys.
SAKI (1870–1916) *The Watched Pot*

2 Defenceless as babies are, they have
mothers at their command, families to
protect the mothers, societies to support
the structure of families, and traditions
to give a cultural continuity to systems
of tending and training.
ERIK ERIKSON *Insight and Responsibility*,
1966

3 It is well known to those who have
charge of young infants, that it is
difficult to feel sure when certain
movements about their mouths are
really expressive; that is when they
really smile. Hence I carefully watched
my own infants. One of them at the age
of forty-five days, and being at the time
in a happy frame of mind, smiled.... I
observed the same thing on the following day: but on the third day the child
was not quite well and there was no
trace of a smile, and this renders it
probable that the previous smiles were
real.
CHARLES DARWIN (1809–1882) *The Expression of the Emotions in Man and Animals*

4 There is no finer investment for any
community than putting milk into babies.
WINSTON CHURCHILL (1874–1965) BBC
radio broadcast, 1943

5 A baby is like a beast, it does not
think but you have to nurse it, do you
not, the way it wants. For the child still
in swaddling clothes cannot tell us if he
is hungry or thirsty, if he needs to make
water. Children's young insides are a
law unto themselves.
AESCHYLUS (525–456 BC) *Libation-Bearers*

6 In the beginning was simplicity.
RICHARD DAWKINS *The Selfish Gene*, 1976

INFERENCE

7 Where more is meant than meets the
ear.
JOHN MILTON (1608–1674) 'Il Penseroso'

8 Nixon, not long before he was
deposed, was quoted as saying at a
news conference, 'I am not a crook'. We
all saw immediately that Nixon
shouldn't have said what he said. He
wanted to assure everyone that he was
an honest man, but the wording he
used was to deny that he was a crook.
Why should he deny that?
H.H. CLARK in P.N. Johnson-Laird, P.C.
Wason *Readings in Cognitive Science*, 1977

9 'I see nobody on the road,' said Alice.
'I only wish *I* had such eyes,' the King
remarked in a fretful tone. 'To be able to
see nobody! And at that distance too!
Why, it's as much as *I* can do to see real
people, by this light!'
LEWIS CARROLL (1832–1898) *Alice Through
the Looking Glass*

10 'Is there any point to which you
would like to draw my attention?'
'To the curious incident of the dog in
the night-time.'
'The dog did nothing in the night-time.'
'That was the curious incident,'
remarked Sherlock Homes.
ARTHUR CONAN DOYLE (1859–1930) *The
Memoirs of Sherlock Holmes*

11 Judging a poem is like judging a
pudding or a machine. One demands
that it work. It is only because an
artifact works that we infer the
intention of an artificer.
W. WIMSATT, M. BEARDSLEY *The Verbal
Icon: Studies in the Meaning of Poetry*, 1954

INFORMATION PROCESSING

12 There is no such thing as
information processing, there are no
mental modules. There are no mental
states. There are neurochemcial and
neurophysiological changes, and there
are public and private discourses, not
all the symbols of which are verbal.
ROM HARRÉ *Social Being*, 1993

1   Judge: I have read your case Mr Smith and I am no wiser now than when I started.
Smith: Possibly not, my Lord, but far better informed.
F.E. SMITH (1872–1930) *Lord Birkenhead*

2   Perhaps the most fundamental concept of information theory is that of a continuum extending from extreme lawfulness, or redundancy, or regularity, on one hand, to extreme disorder, or unpredictability, or uncertainty, on the other. One end of this continuum is homogeneity, the other chaos. It seems fairly evident that those objects which are most pleasing to an observer lie somewhere between these two extremes. One does not stare for a long time at a blank canvas because it is too simple, nor at the detail of a gravel road, because it is too complex.
FRED ATTNEAVE *Journal of Aesthetics and Art Criticism*, 1959

3   ... emphasis began shifting from 'meaning' to 'information', from the *construction* of meaning to the *processing* of information. These are profoundly different matters.
J.S. BRUNER *Acts of Meaning*, 1990

4   The amount of information is exactly the same concept that we have talked about for years under the name of variance. The equations are different, but if we hold tight to the idea that anything that increases variance also increases the amount of information we cannot go far astray.
G.A. MILLER *Psychological Review*, 1956

5   Information is information, not matter or energy. No materialism which does not admit this can survive at the present day.
NORBERT WIENER *Cybernetics*, 1948

6   Well, to say the brain is a computer is correct but misleading. It's really a highly specialized information processing device – or rather, a whole lot of them. Viewing our brains as information-processing devices is not demeaning and does not negate human values. If anything, it tends to support them and may in the end help us to understand what from an information-processing point of view human values actually are, why they have selective value, and how they are knitted into the capacity for social mores and organisation with which our genes have endowed us.
DAVID MARR *Vision*, 1982

7   The value of the concepts of information theory in leading us into new areas of investigation is not lessened, however, if in the pursuit of these investigations we find it possible to abandon information measures in favor of others more informative.
FRED ATTNEAVE *Applications of Information Theory to Psychology*, 1959

INSIGHT

8   One morning in my sixth year, my Mother and I were alone in the morning room, when my Father came in and announced some fact to us.... The shock to me was as that of a thunderbolt, for what my Father had said *was not true...* there was the appalling discovery, never suspected before, that my Father was not as God, and did not know every-thing. The shock was not caused by any suspicion that he was not telling the truth, as it appeared to him, but by the awful proof that he was not, as I had supposed, omniscient.
EDMUND GOSSE (1849–1928) *Autobiography*

9   Eureka!
ARCHIMEDES (c. 287–212 BC) attrib.

10   Where there is no vision, the people perish.
Bible, Proverbs

11   The pleasure of a real scientific insight is like an orgasm.
CARL DJERASSI *Independent on Sunday*, 21 September 1997

12   Insight: the appearance of a complete solution with reference to the whole lay-out of the field.
WOLFGANG KÖHLER *The Mentality of Apes*, 1927

1 Discovery consists of seeing what everybody has seen and thinking what nobody has thought.
ALBERT SZENT-GYORGYI cit. I.G. Good *The Scientist Speculates*, 1962

2 Ignorant men of genius are constantly rediscovering 'laws' of art which the academics have mislaid or hidden.
EZRA POUND (1885–1972) *ABC of Reading*

3 Many of the grandest discoveries in science have consisted, not in bringing to light any new individual fact, but in seeing a likeness between things formerly regarded as wholly unlike.
ALEXANDER BAIN (1818–1903) *Education as Science*

4 Whereof one cannot speak, thereof one must be silent.
LUDWIG WITTGENSTEIN (1889–1951) *Tractatus Logico-Philosophicus*

5 And now the announcement of Watson and Crick about DNA. This is for me the real proof of the existence of God.
SALVADOR DALI cit. J.F.C. Crick *Of Molecules and Men*, 1966

6 These changes – the more rapid pulse, the deeper breathing, the increase of sugar in the blood, the secretion from the adrenal glands – were very diverse and seemed unrelated. Then, one wakeful night, after a considerable collection of these changes had been disclosed, the idea flashed through my mind that they could be nicely integrated if conceived as bodily preparations for supreme effort in flight or in fighting.
WALTER B. CANNON (1871–1945) *The Way of an Investigator*

INSTINCT

7 I don't believe in this nonsense about instinct. To me you can have a certain talent, but that talent springs from something in your brain. Instinct is such a silly word.
DAME NINETTE de VALOIS, interview on her 100th birthday, *The Independent*, 6 June 1998

8 All claims about a language instinct and other mental modules are claims about the commonalities among all normal people. They have virtually nothing to do with possible genetic differences between people.
STEVEN PINKER *The Language Instinct*, 1994

9 If Mozart, instead of playing the pianoforte at three years old with wonderfully little practice, had played a tune with no practice at all, he might truly have been said to have done so instinctively.
CHARLES DARWIN (1809–1882) *Origin of Species*

10 The mind will be always most ready and expedite at that which it is naturally most inclined.
DESIDERIUS ERASMUS (1466–1536) *The Praise of Folly*

11 Our civilisation is entirely based upon the suppression of instincts.
SIGMUND FREUD (1856–1939) *Modern Sexual Morality and Modern Nervousness*

12 A young dog has the instinct to hunt, but by no means always sticks to one unchanging method in its hunting. The dog learns to exploit new possibilities as every huntsman knows. In order to break a dog in properly, one starts off from the instincts it has already.... It is with this capital of instinctive behaviour that the training works, by suppressing some, accentuating others and forming new combinations.
KARL BUHLER *The Mental Development of the Child*, 1933

13 Some cognitive scientists have described language as a psychological faculty, a mental organ, a neural system, and a computational module. But I prefer the admittedly quaint term 'instinct'. It conveys the idea that people know how to talk in more or less the same sense that spiders know how to spin webs.
STEVEN PINKER *The Language Instinct*, 1994

1   As no man is born an artist, so no man is born an angler.
ISAAC WALTON (1593–1683) *The Compleat Angler*

INTELLECT

2   The voice of the intellect is a soft one, but it does not rest till it has gained a hearing.
SIGMUND FREUD (1856–1939) *The Future of an Illusion*

3   Intellectual strength and intellectual weakness are ill-named; they are, in fact, only the manifestation of good or poor functioning on the part of our physical organs.
DUC FRANÇOIS DE LA ROCHEFOUCAULD (1613–1680) *Maxims*

4   A good sort of man is this Darwin and well meaning, but with little intellect.
THOMAS CARLYLE (1795–1881) *The Times*, 1877

5   What is a high-brow? He is a man who has found something more interesting than women.
EDGAR WALLACE (1875–1932) *New York Times*, 24 January 1932

6   Everyone is agreed that intellectual capacity, whatever its precise nature, is in large part – if not wholly – inherited.
O.L. ZANGWILL *An Introduction to Modern Psychology*, 1950

7   Most men, bringing up sons, wish for them intellect;
But I by my intellect have had a life-time of failure.
I would only desire that my child should be simple and dull,
That with no ill-fortune and no troubles he may attain to highest office.
SU SHIH (1036–1101) 'The Washing of the Infant'

8   It is not enough to have a good mind. The main thing is to use it well.
RENÉ DESCARTES (1596–1650) *Discourse on Method*

9   I care not whether a man is Good or Evil: all that I care
Is whether he is a Wise Man or a Fool.
   Go put off Holiness
And put on Intellect.
WILLIAM BLAKE (1757–1827) 'Jerusalem'

10   We should take care not to make intellect our god; it has, of course, powerful muscles, but no personality.
ALBERT EINSTEIN (1879–1955) *Out of My later Life*

11   There are three intellectual pursuits, and so far as I am aware, only three, in which human beings have performed major feats before the age of puberty. They are music, mathematics and chess.
GEORGE STEINER *Extraterritorial*, 1972

12   If the intellect is unstable
It is overturned by the world
A weak man embraced by a whore.

If the mind becomes disciplined,
The world is a distinguished woman
Who rejects her lover's advances.
ABU AL-ALA AL-MA'ARRI (973–1057) *Birds Through a Ceiling of Alabaster*

13   Intellectual development is marked by increasing capacity to deal with several alternatives simultaneously, to tend to several sequences during the same period of time, and to allocate time and attention in a manner appropriate to these multiple demands.
J.S. BRUNER *Toward a Theory of Instruction*, 1986

INTELLIGENCE

14   To judge well, to comprehend well, to reason well. These are the essential activities of intelligence.
A. BINET, T. SIMON *The Intelligence of the Feeble-Minded*, 1916

15   ... the available evidence indicates that a high degree of intelligence is often accompanied by a temperamental aversion from continuous work, by a lack of persistence and perseverance.
REX KNIGHT *Intelligence and Intelligence Testing*, 1933

1 Spearman's g is not an ineluctable entity; it represents one mathematical solution among many equivalent alternatives. The chimerical nature of g is the rotten core of Jensen's edifice, and the entire hereditarian school.
STEPHEN J. GOULD *The Mismeasure of Man*, 1981

2 ... the whole course of development of a child's intellectual capabilities is largely laid down genetically, and even extreme environmental changes ... have little power to alter this development.
HANS EYSENCK *The Inequality of Man*, 1973

3 With about fifty intellectual factors already known, we may say there are about fifty ways of being intelligent.
J.P. GUILFORD *American Psychologist*, 1959

4 Ultimately, intelligence is not a kind of ability at all, certainly not in the same sense that reasoning, memory, verbal fluency, etc, are so regarded. Rather it is something that is inferred from the way these abilities are manifested under different conditions and circumstances.
D. WECHSLER *Manual for the Wechsler Intelligence Scale for Children*, 1974

5 Because intelligence is not the object-ively defined explanatory concept it is often assumed to be, it is more an obstacle than an aid to understanding abilities.
M.J.A. HOWE *Sense and Nonsense about Hothouse Children*, 1990

6 While the teacher tried to cultivate intelligence, and the psychologist tried to measure intelligence, nobody seemed to know precisely what intelligence was.
P.B. BALLARD *Mental Tests*, 1930

7 Intelligence is characterised by a natural incomprehension of life.
HENRI BERGSON (1859–1941) *Creative Evolution*

8 The prime author and mover of the universe is intelligence.
ST AUGUSTINE (354–430) *Confessions*

9 To play chess requires no intelligence at all.
JOSE RAUL CAPABLANCA cit. B. Schecter *Discovery*, December 1982

10 When new turns in behaviour cease to appear in the life of the individual its behaviour ceases to be intelligent.
G.E. COGHILL *Anatomy and the Problem of Behaviour*, 1929

11 If worms have the power of acquiring some notion, however rude, of the shape of an object and over their burrows, as seems to be the case, they deserve to be called intelligent; for they then act in nearly the same manner as would a man under similar circumstances.
CHARLES DARWIN (1809–1882) *The Formation of Vegetable Mould, Through the Action of Worms*

12 The causes of this difference of wits are in the passions, and the difference of passions proceedeth partly from the different constitution of the body, and partly from different education.
THOMAS HOBBES (1588–1679) *Leviathan*

13 Man is so intelligent that he feels impelled to invent theories to account for what happens in the world. Unfortunately, he is not quite intelligent enough, in most cases, to find correct explanations.
ALDOUS HUXLEY (1894–1963) *Texts and Pretexts*

14 The dullard's envy of brilliant men is always assuaged by the suspicion that they will come to a bad end.
MAX BEERBOHM (1872–1956) *Zuleika Dobson*

15 Intelligence is quickness to apprehend as distinct from ability, which is capacity to act wisely on the thing apprehended.
A.N. WHITEHEAD (1861–1947) *Dialogues*

16 Intelligence is as much an advantage to an animal as physical strength or any other natural gift, and therefore ... the most intelligent is sure to prevail in the battle of life. Similarly, among intelligent animals, the most social race is sure to prevail, other qualities being equal.
FRANCIS GALTON (1822–1911) *Heredity Genius*

1 It is difficult to imagine that the concept of intelligence, by one name or another, has not been around at least since *Homo sapiens* appeared on earth.
A.R. JENSEN *Bias in Mental Testing*, 1980

2 To me 'intelligence' seems to denote little more than the complex of performances which we happen to respect, but do not understand.
MARVIN MINSKY *Proceedings of the Institute of Radio Engineers*, 1961

3 Intelligence is that faculty of mind, by which order is perceived in a situation previously considered disordered.
HANEEF FATINI, R.W. YOUNG *Nature*, 1970

4 Most present day psychologists try to explain intelligence without any appeal to logical theory.
JEAN PIAGET *Logic and Psychology*, 1953

5 Intelligence ... is really a kind of taste: taste in ideas.
SUSAN SONTAG *Against Interpretation*, 1966

6 Why is there almost universal assent that some animals are more intelligent than others.
A.R. JENSEN *Bias in Mental Testing*, 1980

7 The intelligence required to survive socially is something of quite a different order to that needed to cope with the material world.
NICHOLAS HUMPHREY *The Inner Eye*, 1986

8 Intelligence arises, we believe, not merely from rapid, accurate storage and recovery of specific knowledge – an unfortunate misconception in both psychology and education – but rather from *the ability to apply or adapt a small set of powerful skills and procedures to any particular task at hand.*
R. de BEAUGRANDE, W. DRESSLER *Introduction to Text Linguistics*, 1981

9 Indeed, it has come about that much of the present utterances there [the USA] on the whole subject of human ability and 'intelligence' are painfully suggestive of Rip Van Winkle.
CHARLES SPEARMAN in *A History of Psychology in Autobiography, Vol. 1*, 1930

INTELLIGENCE (IQ) TESTS

10 As everybody knows, inventing intelligence tests has almost achieved the rank of a sport.
F.C. BARTLETT *The Mind at Work and Play*, 1951

11 Existing instruments [tests of intelligence] represent enormous improvements over what was available twenty years ago, but three fundamental defects remain. Just what they measure is not known, how far it is proper to add, subtract, multiply divide and compute ratios with the measures obtained is not known; just what the measures obtained signify concerning the intellect is not known.
E.L. THORNDIKE *The Measurement of Intelligence*, 1927

12 From the very first questionings I noticed that though Burt's tests certainly had their diagnostic merits, based on the number of successes and failures, it was much more interesting to try to find out the reasons for the failures. Thus I engaged my subjects in conversations patterned after psychiatric questioning with the aim of discovering something about the reasoning process underlying their right, but especially their wrong answers.
JEAN PIAGET cit. R.I. Evans *Jean Piaget: The Man and His Ideas*, 1973

13 Our aim is, when a child is put before us, to take the measurement of his intellectual powers, in order to establish whether he is normal or if he is retarded.
A. BINET, T. SIMON *Année Psychologique*, 1905

14 It is evident, therefore, that one of the most fundamental problems of psychology is that of investigating the laws of mental growth. When these laws are known, the door of the future will in a measure be opened; determination of the child's present status will enable us to forecast what manner of adult he will become.
L.S. TERMAN *The Intelligence of School Children*, 1921

1 Overall IQ is simply the average of scores on a heterogeneous set of tests.
N.J. MACKINTOSH *Journal of Biosocial Science*, 1996

2 IQ: If it is a social construct then we have an interesting problem, the heritability of a social construct.
RICHARD LEWONTIN *Independent on Sunday*, 21 September 1997

3 These tests [intelligence tests], which were developed on a purely pragmatic basis to predict school performance, seemed to us then, as now, to be a hopelessly atheoretical and opaque means of observing the structure of higher psychological functions.
A.R. LURIA *The Making of Mind*, 1979

4 The term IQ is bound to the myths that intelligence is unitary, fixed, and predetermined.
D.J. RESCHLY *American Psychologist*, 1981

5 The defect in the intelligence test is that high marks are gained by those who subsequently prove to be practically illiterate. So much time has been spent in studying the act of being tested that the candidate has rarely had time for anything else.
C. NORTHCOTE PARKINSON *Parkinson's Law*, 1962

6 Intelligence is what the tests test.
E.G. BORING *New Republic*, June 1923

7 It is a general rule that children of border-line intelligence improve little if at all in IQ as they get older, not withstanding their increased school experience and the extra attention they received in special classes.
L.S. TERMAN *The Intelligence of School Children*, 1921

8 What people correlate are test scores on say a hundred items ... but people differ in the amount of time they spend on a problem. Some will never leave a problem undone. Some will move on quite happily. The whole behaviour is entirely different and to regard their scores as identical just because they both got the same number right is wrong.
HANS EYSENCK cit. D. Cohen *Psychologists on Psychology*, 1977

9 Suppose you are a ghetto resident in the Roxbury section of Boston. To qualify for being a policeman, you have to take a three hour general intelligence test in which you must know the meaning of words like 'quell' or 'pyromaniac' or 'lexicon'. If you do not know enough of these games or cannot play analogy games with them then you do not qualify and must be satisfied with some job as being a janitor for which an intelligence test is not yet required by the Massachusetts Civil Service Commission.
D. McCLELLAND *American Psychologist*, 1973

10 The number of words an individual can define or his ability to memorise digits backwards may tell us little about his ability to produce new forms and restructure stereotyped situations.
J. GETZELS, P. JACKSON *Creativity and Intelligence*, 1962

11 It seems more than possible that the social hassles, the individual hurts to confidence, and vital decisions on education and job opportunities are based on an illusory Golden Egg of intelligence which has been created by the mystique of IQ tests.
RICHARD GREGORY *Mind in Science*, 1981

12 Just as many a man has been hanged on the evidence of his finger prints, so many an individual might safely be committed to an institution for the feeble-minded on the evidence of ten or a dozen intelligence tests which have been standardised according to age norms.
L.S. TERMAN *The Intelligence of Schoolchildren*, 1921

1 Whereas common observation insists on distinguishing between knowing and discovering, between the ability to remember and the ability to invent, between 'intelligent' and being 'creative', it is this distinction that seems largely to have been lost sight of in the rush to apply the intelligence test or some other derivative of it to everything from grouping children in kindergarten to choosing executives in business.
J. GETZELS, P. JACKSON *Creativity and Intelligence*, 1962

INTENTION

2 A man's intention is what he aims at or chooses; his motive is what determines the aim or choice.
G.E.M. ANSCOMBE *Intention*, 1957

3 One of the big differences between physical entities and human beings is that the behaviour of people has a meaning for the people themselves and is mainly intentional ... psychologists look for the causes of [people's] behaviour and neglect to a large extent that people can have reasons and meanings for their actions.
L. VAN LANGEEHOVE in J. Smith *et al. Rethinking Psychology*, 1995

4 The specific goals we set for our-selves are almost always subsidiary to our long range intentions. A good parent, a good neighbour, a good citizen, is not good because his specific goals are acceptable, but because his successive goals are ordered to a dependable and socially desirable set of values.
G.W. ALLPORT *Psychological Review*, 1947

5 The mind sins, not the body. If there is no intention, there is no blame.
LIVY (59 BC–17 AD) *History of Rome*

6 ... humankind is symbol-using. In this simple and almost banal observation lies the possibility for the extraordinary degree of elaboration and diversification we find in human social life. Intentional structures overlay the biological patterns.
ROM HARRÉ *Social Being*, 1993

INTERVIEWS

7 The psychological interview has developed today into what is known as ordeal by house party. The candidates spend a pleasant weekend under expert observation.... There is no need to describe this method in detail, but its results are all about us and are obviously deplorable.
C. NORTHCOTE PARKINSON *Parkinson's Law*, 1958

8 There are many reasons why interviewing is such an unsatisfactory method of selection, of which the halo effect is one. An applicant who is well turned out, pleasant and self-confident, without conceit, is likely to be thought to have the skills for the job whether he has or not.
STUART SUTHERLAND *Irrationality*, 1992

INTROSPECTION

9 We do not introspect; we internally reconstruct – at least in outline or in edited or dramatized or surmised version – overt intelligent performances.
W. LYONS *The Disappearance of Introspection*, 1986

10 Many psychologists ... thought by turning their attention to their own consciousness to be able to explain what happened when we were thinking. Or they sought to attain the same end by asking another person a question, by means of which certain processes of thought would be excited, and then by questioning the person about the introspection he had made. It is obvious ... that nothing can be discovered in such experiments.
WILHELM WUNDT *An Introduction to Psychology*, 1912

11 It may seem easy to watch the working of one's own mind, but it is not so simple as it seems.
E.S. WATERHOUSE *The ABC of Psychology*, 1927

1 The rules for introspection are of two kinds: general and specific.... Suppose, e.g., that you were trying to find out how small a difference you could distinguish in the smell of beeswax.... It would be a special rule that you should work only on dry days; for beeswax smells much stronger in wet than fine weather.... The general rules of experimental introspection are as follows: 1. Be impartial.... 2. Be attentive.... 3. Be comfortable.... 4. Be perfectly fresh....
E.B. TITCHENER *A Primer of Psychology*, 1914

2 Our perception of the external world is always mediated by sensations or impressions of some kind, and the external world is thus known only indirectly and problematically. With introspection, however, our knowledge is immediate and direct.
P.M. CHURCHLAND *Matter and Consciousness*, 1984

3 Without introspection to guide me, the task of deciphering the behaviour of my fellow men would be quite beyond my powers.
NICHOLAS HUMPHREY *Consciousness Regained*, 1983

INTUITION

4 When intuition is joined to exact research it speeds the progress of exact research.
PAUL KLEE (1879–1940) *Bauhaus Prospectus*, 1929

5 The explanation of intuition is the same as that of advertisement: tell a man a thousand times that Pears Soap is good for the complexion and eventually he will have an intuitive certainty of the fact.
SOMERSET MAUGHAM (1874–1965) *A Writer's Notebook*

6 ... this term [intuition] does not denote something contrary to *reason*, but something outside the province of reason.
CARL JUNG (1875–1961) *Psychological Types*

7 A characteristic of intuitions is that they are fleeting and, curiously, very easily forgotten, in spite of the fact that at the time they enter the field of consciousness they are very vivid and the subject does not think he can or will forget them.
R. ASSAGLIO *Psychosynthesis: A Manual of Principles and Techniques*, 1971

8 A lot of our understanding of people is intuitive: it does not depend on any conscious process of interpreting evidence. And we are often quite unable to say exactly what it is based on.
JONATHEN GLOVER *The Philosophy and Psychology of Personal Identity*, 1988

9 ... an incident occurred – on which she would employ her intuition in attempting to interpret what her mind had failed to understand.
PATRICK WHITE *Riders in the Chariot*, 1961

10 Under conditions of unstated functional relationships the naive theorist is tempted to make predictions on the basis of intuition, which is anthropomorphic subjectivism.
CLARK L. HULL *Principles of Behavior*, 1943

11 A woman's guess is much more accurate than a man's certainty.
RUDYARD KIPLING (1865–1936) *Plain Tales from the Hills*

12 ... it has been said that intuition is that strange instinct that tells a person he is right, whether he is or not.
STUART SUTHERLAND *Irrationality*, 1992

IRRATIONALITY

13 To the rational animal only is the irrational intolerable.
EPICTETUS (c. 55–135) *Discourses*

14 The irrational is not necessarily unreasonable.
LEWIS NAMIER (1888–1960) *Personalities and Powers*

1 Given the multiple causes of irrationality, the question arises of whether anything can be done to reduce it. The most general approach would be to try to persuade people to keep an open mind, to come to conclusions only after they have surveyed all the evidence and to realise that, when the occasion merits, it is a sign of strength not weakness to change one's mind.
STUART SUTHERLAND *Irrationality*, 1992

2 Irrationally held truths may be more harmful than reasoned errors.
T.H. HUXLEY (1825–1895) *Darwiniana*

IRRITATION

3 He spoke with a certain what-is-it in his voice, and I could see that, if not actually disgruntled, he was far from being gruntled.
P.G. WODEHOUSE (1881–1975) *The Code of the Woosters*

4 Nations, like individuals, often tend to dwell on causes of irritation and not on their blessings, for the latter are usually taken for granted.
B. SEEBOHM ROWNTREE, G.R. LAVERS *English Life and Leisure*, 1951

5 too many creatures
both insects and humans
estimate their own value
by the amount of minor irritations
they are able to cause
to greater personalities than themselves
don marquis (1887–1937) *archy's life of mehitabel*

6 ... irritability presents a problem of fundamental physiological importance. For if we could analyze the irritability of living substance to its essence then the nature of life itself would be fathomed.
MAX VERWORN *Irritability*, 1913

JARGON

7 It might well be objected that psychologists use terms like 'drive', 'need' and 'motive' in a technical sense and that, provided that they give their own rules for using the term, it does not matter much what term they choose. In my view it would be a profound mistake for psychologists to take such a cavalier attitude towards ordinary speech.
R.S. PETERS *The Concept of Motivation*, 1958

8 Of all classes of writers, poets are the most accurate in the use of ordinary words; scientists the least, even those research professors who are at pains to improvise a supplementary vocabulary of extraordinary ones.
ROBERT GRAVES (1895–1985) *On English Poetry*

9 If this young man expresses himself
in terms too deep for me,
Why, what a very singularly deep young
man this deep young man must be!
W.S. GILBERT (1836–1911) *Patience*

10 Special languages, like sexual techniques, are cover ups.
ADAM PHILLIPS *Terrors and Experts*, 1995

11 Human pride
Is skilful to invent most serious names
To hide its ignorance.
PERCY BYSSHE SHELLEY (1792–1922)
'Queen Mab'

12 A vile conceit in pompous words express'd
Is like a clown in regal purple dress'd.
ALEXANDER POPE (1688–1744) *An Essay on Criticism*

1 ... jargon is the anesthetic of scholarship.
C.J. LUMSDEN, E.O. WILSON *Genes, Mind, and Culture*, 1981

2 A sociologist or psychologist who will spend his time translating familiar facts into professionally approved language must surely have more academic conscience than curiosity about strange or obscure phenomena. We are often told that such exercises are necessary because the behavioral sciences are young. Not long ago chemistry was young too ... but did any chemist ever write an article to show how a recipe for fudge could be stated in proper chemical form, ie 'without any household words'?
SUSAN LANGER *Mind: An Essay on Human Feeling*, 1967

JEALOUSY

3 ... jealousy is always derivative: a passion born of another passion, like a reflection, or an echo.
F. GONZALEZ-CRUSSI *On the Nature of Things Erotic*, 1988

4   O beware, my lord, of jealousy
It is the green-ey'd monster which doth mock
     The meat it feeds on.
WILLIAM SHAKESPEARE (1564–1616) *Othello*

5 Whenever a friend succeeds, a little something in me dies.
GORE VIDAL *Sunday Times Magazine*, 16 September 1973

6 ... trifles light as air
Are to the jealous confirmations strong
As proofs of holy writ;
WILLIAM SHAKESPEARE (1564–1616) *Othello*

7 It is not love that is blind, but jealousy.
LAURENCE DURRELL (1912–1990) *Justine*

8 Love is as strong as death: jealousy is cruel as the grave.
Bible, Song of Solomon

9 ... jealousy never arises in a consciousness that is untroubled.
F. GONZALEZ-CRUSSI *On the Nature of Things Erotic*, 1988

10 Jealousy was plainly exhibited when I fondled a large doll, and when I weighed his infant sister, he being then 15½ months old. Seeing how strong a feeling of jealousy is in dogs, it would probably be exhibited by infants at any earlier age than just specified if they were tried in a fitting manner.
CHARLES DARWIN (1809–1882) *Mind*

JUDGEMENT

11 I do not content myself with consulting a single authority in any branch; I consult several; I compare their opinions, and I choose that which seems to me the soundest. But I recognise no infallible authority, even in special questions; consequently, whatever respect I may have for the honesty and sincerity of such or such an individual, I have no absolute faith in any person. Such a faith would be fatal to my reason, to my liberty, and even to the success of my undertakings: it would immediately transform me into a stupid slave, an instrument of the will and interests of others.
MICHAEL BAKUNIN (1814–1896) *God and the State*

12 All kinds of Mice love grain and cheese, and if they come to many cheeses together they taste all, but they eat the best. And therefore the Egyptians in the *Hieroglyphicks* do picture a mouse, to signifie sound judgement and good choice.
C. GESNER (1516–1565) *Historiae Animalium de Quadrupedibus Viviparis*

13 Everyone complains of his lack of memory, but nobody of his lack of judgement.
DUC FRANÇOIS DE LA ROCHEFOUCAULD (1613–1680) *Maxims*

14 People are unwilling to suspend judgement: they seek explanations.
STUART SUTHERLAND *Irrationality*, 1992

1 Next to knowing when to seize an opportunity, the most important thing in life is to know when to forego an advantage.
BENJAMIN DISRAELI (1804–1881) *The Informal Marriage*

2 There is so much good in the worst of us,
And so much bad in the best of us,
That it ill behoves any of us,
To find fault with the rest of us.
ANON.

KISSING

3 In a kiss, two spirits meet, mingle and become one; and as a result there arises in the mind a wonderful feeling of delight that awakens and binds together the love of them that kiss.
AILRED OF RIEVAULX (1109–1166) *Treatise on Spiritual Friendship*

4 Where do the noses go? I always wondered where the noses would go.
ERNEST HEMINGWAY (1899–1961) *For Whom the Bell Tolls*

5 Kissing don't last: cooking do!
GEORGE MEREDITH (1828–1909) *The Ordeal of Richard Feveral*

6 For poets that have had my luck
Seldom write while they can kiss
ALEX COMFORT *Haste to the Wedding*, 1962

KNOWLEDGE

7 Ah, it's a lovely thing, to know a thing or two.
MOLIÈRE (1622–1673) *Le Bourgeois Gentilhomme*

8 Knowing does not really imply making a copy of reality but rather, reacting to it and transforming it.
JEAN PIAGET *Biology and Knowledge*, 1971

9 Without knowledge we could not live, for our world would seem too disordered and we would lose the stable psychological framework that is indispensable to our survival.
HENRY PLOTKIN *The Nature of Knowledge*, 1994

1 If a little knowledge is dangerous, where is the man who has so much as to be out of danger.
T.H. HUXLEY (1825–1895) *Collected Essays*

2 Knowledge is little; to know the right context is much, to know the right spot is everything.
HUGO VON HOFMANNSTHAL *The Book of Friends*, 1922

3 A little knowledge is a dangerous thing;
Drink deep, or taste not the Pierian spring.
ALEXANDER POPE (1688–1744) 'An Essay on Criticism'

4 If I had read as much as other men, I should know no more than they.
THOMAS HOBBES (1588–1679) cit. John Aubrey *Brief Lives*

5 He that increaseth knowledge increaseth sorrow.
Bible, Ecclesiastes

6 Knowledge itself is power.
FRANCIS BACON (1561–1626) *Sacred Meditations*

7 Beauty is truth, truth beauty, – that is all
Ye know on earth, and all ye need to know.
JOHN KEATS (1795–1821) 'Ode on a Grecian Urn'

8 Knowledge is of two kinds. We know a subject ourselves, or we know where we can find information on it.
SAMUEL JOHNSON (1709–1784) cit. James Boswell *The Life of Samuel Johnson*

9 Knowledge is proud that he has learn'd so much;
Wisdom is humble that he knows no more.
WILLIAM COWPER (1731–1800) 'Winter Walk at Noon'

10 Knowledge as commonly understood is a special kind of adaptation.
HENRY PLOTKIN *The Nature of Knowledge*, 1994

11 Socrates said, our only knowledge was
'To know that nothing could be known'; a pleasant
Science enough, which levels to an ass
Each man of wisdom, future, past or present.
LORD BYRON (1788–1824) *Don Juan*

12 The doing of anything pre-supposes some knowledge: for every action is the employment of certain agencies which stand in the relation of *means* to our particular *end* or object of desire.
JAMES SULLY *The Teachers' Handbook of Psychology*, 1886

13 The advance of knowledge is an infinite progression towards a goal that forever recedes.
JAMES G. FRAZER (1854–1941) *The Golden Bough*

14 It is a familiar jibe that philosophers only say what everyone knows, in a language that nobody can understand. Now I think that it is true that the starting point of philosophy is what everyone knows, but it is a well-known fact that half of what everyone knows is true, and the other half is false.
A.J.P. KENNY *The Nature of Mind*, 1972

15 Knowledge is a sacred cow, and my problem will be how we can milk her while keeping clear of her horns.
A. SZENT-GYORGYI *Science*, 1964

16 There can be no doubt that all our knowledge begins with experience. For how should our faculty of knowledge be awakened into action did not objects affecting our senses partly of themselves produce representations, partly arouse the activity of our understanding to compare these representations, and, by combining them or separating them, work up the raw material of the sensible impressions into that knowledge of objects which is entitled experience? In the order of time, therefore, we have no knowledge antecedent to experience, and with experience all our knowledge begins.
IMMANUEL KANT (1724–1804) *Critique of Pure Reason*

1 Knowledge is power, they say. Knowledge is not only power, it is good fun.
NORMAN DOUGLAS (1868–1952) *An Almanac*

2 The unknown is not necessarily unknowable.
K. KAYE *The Mental and Social Life of Babies*, 1982

3 Knowledge is one. Its division into subjects is a concession to human weakness.
H.J. MACKINDER *Proceedings of the Royal Geographical Society*, 1887

4 Knowledge is not happiness, and science
But an exchange of ignorance for that Which is another kind of ignorance.
LORD BYRON (1788–1824) 'Manfred'

5 We come to know through processes of active interpretation and integration.
MARGARET DONALDSON *Human Minds*, 1992

6 To know something is to incorporate the thing known into ourselves ... the knower is changed by knowledge, and that change represents, even if very indirectly, the thing known.
HENRY PLOTKIN *The Nature of Knowledge*, 1994

7 The accumulation of collective knowledge in the natural sciences can be compared to the piling up of a cone-shaped heap of a loose material with a low stacking coefficient.
KONRAD LORENZ *The Natural Science of the Human Species*, 1996

LANGUAGE

8 Were a language ever completely grammatical it would be a perfect engine of conceptual expressions.... Unfortunately, or luckily, no language is tyrannically consistent. All grammars leak.
E. SAPIR *Language*, 1921

9 Language is, in effect, the vehicle for concepts and ideas that belong to everyone, and it reinforces individual thinking with a vast system of collective concepts.
JEAN PIAGET *Six Psychological Studies*, 1964

10 Linguistic analysis. A lot of chaps pointing out that we don't always mean what we say, even when we say what we mean.
TOM STOPPARD *Professional Foul*, 1978

11 Language helps form the limits of our reality. It is our means of ordering, classifying and manipulating the world.
D. SPENDER *Man Made Language*, 1985

12 Although there is representation, there is no symbolic system prior to language: no intersubjectivity; and no social system in the strict sense.
K. KAYE *The Mental and Social Life of Babies*, 1982

13 Whenever the literary German dives into a sentence that is the last you are going to see of him till he emerges on the other side of the Atlantic with the verb in his mouth.
MARK TWAIN (1835–1910) *A Connecticut Yankee in King Arthur's Court*

1 But what I have most at Heart is, that some Method should be thought on for *ascertaining* and *fixing* our language for ever, after such Alterations are made in it as shall be thought requisite. For I am of opinion, that it is better a Language should not be wholly perfect, than that it should be perpetually changing.
JONATHAN SWIFT (1667–1745) *A Proposal for Correcting, Improving and Ascertaining the English Tongue*

2 God designed Man for a sociable Creature, made him not only with an inclination, and under a necessity to have a fellowship with those of his own kind; but furnished him also with language, which was to be the great Instrument, and common Type of society.
JOHN LOCKE (1632–1704) *An Essay Concerning Human Understanding*

3 I have laboured to reform our language to grammatical purity, and to clear it from colloquial barbarisms, licentious idioms, and irregular combinations.
SAMUEL JOHNSON (1709–1784) *The Rambler*

4 There are Stone Age societies, but there is no such thing as a Stone Age language.
STEVEN PINKER *The Language Instinct*, 1994

5 A sentence is not easy to define.
ERNEST GOWERS *The Complete Plain Words*, 1954

6 The English-speaking world may be divided into 1. those who neither know nor care what a split infinitive is; 2. those who do not know, but care very much; 3. those who know and condemn; 4. those who know and approve; and 5. those who know and distinguish. Those who neither know nor care are the vast majority and are happy folk, to be envied by most of the minority class.
HENRY FOWLER (1858–1933) *Modern English Usage*

7 The limits of my language mean the limits of my world.
LUDWIG WITTGENSTEIN (1889–1951) *Tractatus Logico-Philosophicus*

8 I pray thee, understand a plain man in his plain meaning.
WILLIAM SHAKESPEARE (1564–1616) *The Merchant of Venice*

9 There is no such thing as good and bad (or correct and incorrect, grammatical and ungrammatical, right and wrong) in language.
ROBERT A. HALL *Leave Your Language Alone*, 1950

10 If the users of language were not trained to recognize certain ways of speaking as right (correct, grammatical) and others as wrong, human communication would be a more chancy, a less tightly organized affair than it is.
MAX BLACK *The Labyrinth of Language*, 1968

11 Children clearly learn a good deal about different objects, actions and relations before they ever begin to talk. They learn to identify objects that can move on their own and make other things move. They also identify objects that can be moved ... they identify possible recipients.... In fact, one can plausibly argue that children have already organised much of their knowledge about particular categories of objects, actions and relations before they start on language at all.
E. CLARK in P. Fletcher, M. Garman *Language Acquisition*, 1979

12 ... the problems raised by the organisation of language seem to me to be characteristic of almost all other cerebral activity.
K.S. LASHLEY cit. L.A. Jeffress *Cerebral Mechanisms in Behavior*, 1951

13 There are two theories about this [the origin of language]. One ... would make man by degrees to have invented it.... But the truer answer ... is that God gave man language ... because he could not be man, that is, a social being, without it.
R.C. TRENCH (1807–1886) *The Study of Words*

14 Language is beginning to submit to that uniquely satisfying kind of understanding we call science, but the news has been kept a secret.
STEVEN PINKER *The Language Instinct*, 1994

1 When my elders named some object, and accordingly moved towards something, I saw this and I grasped that the thing was called by the sound they uttered when they meant to point it out. Their intention was shown by their bodily movements, as it were the natural languages of all peoples.... Thus, as I heard words repeated in various sentences, I gradually learned to understand what objects they signified.
ST AUGUSTINE (354–430) *Confessions*

2 As men abound in copiousness of language, so they become more wise, or more mad than ordinary.
THOMAS HOBBES (1588–1679) *The Leviathan*

3 We are able to use the linguistic structures that we do largely because through our cognitive abilities we are enabled to do so, not because language itself exists for all merely to imitate.
R. CROMER in B. M. Foss *New Horizons in Psychology*, 1974

4 Man makes his own language, but he makes it as the bee makes its cells, as the bird its nest.
R.C. TRENCH (1807–1886) *The Study of Words*

5 Thanks to words, we have been able to rise above the brutes; and thanks to language we have often sunk to the level of demons.
ALDOUS HUXLEY (1894–1963) *Adonis and the Alphabet*

6 We cannot predict verbal behavior in terms of the stimuli in the speaker's environment, since we do not know what the current stimuli are until he responds.
NOAM CHOMSKY, review of Skinner's *Verbal Behavior*, *Language*, 1957

7 The very same sentence marked as deviant in the corpus of one researcher is likely to show up in the work of another trailing clouds of deep structure and transformations.
J.F. ROSENBERG in B. Gelder *Knowledge and Representation*, 1982

8 Instinctively we use language rightly; but to the intellect this use is a puzzle.
LUDWIG WITTGENSTEIN (1889–1951) *Wittgenstein's Lectures, 1930–1932*

9 Language is a specialised and conventional extension of cooperative action.
J.S. BRUNER *Journal of Child Language*, 1975

10 The capacity to form and to operate with abstract ideas and symbols is correlated in evolution, if not in physiology, with the capacity to use human language.
Th. DOBZHANSKY *The Biology of Ultimate Concern*, 1969

11 The faculty of language stands at the centre of our conception of mankind: speech makes us human and literacy makes us civilized.
DAVID OLSON *Harvard Educational Review*, 1977

12 It is obvious that most speech forms are regular, in the sense that the speaker who knows the constituents and the grammatical patterns can utter them without having heard them; moreover, the observer cannot hope to list them since the possibilities of combination are practically infinite.
L. BLOOMFIELD *Language*, 1931

13 Language marks out what is relevant, and experience is transformed by that which is made relevant.
BASIL BERNSTEIN *Journal of Child Psychology and Psychiatry*, 1961

14 How much evidence does a child have to have to acquire a language? Well – remarkably little. Very complicated structures are set in motion in very specific, highly articulated ways on the basis of very rudimentary evidence.
NOAM CHOMSKY in D. Cohen *Psychologists on Psychology*, 1977

1   Children can learn to speak their parents' language without an accent, but not vice versa. I suspect there is a gene that shuts off that learning mechanism when a child reaches sexual maturity. If there weren't, parents would learn their children's language, and language itself would not have developed.
M. MINSKY *The New Yorker*, 14 December 1981

LANGUAGE AND THOUGHT

2   The purpose of Newspeak was not only to provide a medium of expression for the world-view and mental habits proper to the devotees of Ingsoc, but to make all other modes of thought impossible.... This was done partly by the invention of new words, but chiefly by eliminating undesirable words.
GEORGE ORWELL (1889–1951) *Nineteen Eighty-Four*

3   Matter and expression are parts of one: style is a thinking out into language. This is what I have been laying down, and this is literature; not *things* but the verbal symbols of things: not on the other hand mere *words*; but thought expressed in language.
JOHN HENRY (CARDINAL) NEWMAN *The Idea of a University*, 1852

4   ... if we lose the words, may we not also lose the feelings and emotions they represent.
JOSE SARAMAGO *Financial Times*, 9/10 January 1999

5   A single word even may be a spark of inextinguishable thought.
PERCY BYSSHE SHELLEY (1792–1822) *A Defence of Poetry*

6   Language disguises the thought; so that from the external form of the clothes one cannot infer the form of the thought they clothe because the external form of the clothes is constructed with quite another object than to let the form of the body be recognised.
LUDWIG WITTGENSTEIN (1889–1951) *Tractatus Logico-Philosophicus*

7   Language *evokes* ideas: it does not represent them. Linguistic expression is thus *not* a natural map of consciousness or thought. It is a highly selective and conventionally schematic map. At the heart of language use is the tacit assumption that most of the message can be left unsaid, because of mutual understanding (and probably also, mutual impatience).
D. SLOBIN in E. Wanner, L. Gleitman, *Language Acquisition*, 1982

8   The structure of speech does not simply mirror the structure of thought; that is why words cannot be put on by thought like a ready made garment. Thought undergoes many changes as it turns into speech. It does not merely find expression in speech; it finds reality and form.
L.S. VYGOTSKY *Thought and Language*, 1962

9   At best, language can but be the outward fact of thought on the highest, most generalized level of symbolic activity.
E. SAPIR *Language*, 1949

10   What people think and feel, and how they report what they think and feel, is determined, to be sure, by their individual physiological state, by their personal history, and by what actually happens in the outside world. But it is also determined by a factor which is often overlooked, namely the pattern of linguistic habits which people have acquired as members of a particular society.
C. KLUCKHOHN, D. LEIGHTON *The Navaho*, 1946

11   Language is the dress of thought.
SAMUEL JOHNSON (1709–1784) *Lives of the English Poets*

1   Don't you see the whole aim of New-speak is to narrow the range of thought? In the end we shall make thought crime literally impossible, because there will be no words in which to express it.
GEORGE ORWELL (1903–1950) *Nineteen Eighty-Four*

2   Thus we may conclude that the mental development of the individual, and his way of forming concepts, depend to a high degree, on language. This makes us realize to what extent the same language means the same mentality. In this sense, thinking and language are linked together.
ALBERT EINSTEIN (1879–1955) *Ideas and Opinions*

3   The relation of thought to word is first of all not a thing, but a process; it is a proceeding from thought to word and, conversely, from word to thought … every thought moves, grows and develops, each fulfils a function and solves a given problem.
L.S. VYGOTSKY *Psychiatry*, 1939

4   We dissect nature along lines laid down by our native languages.... We cut nature up, organize it into concepts and ascribe significance as we do, largely because we are parties to an agreement to organise it in this way – an agreement that holds throughout our speech community and it is codified in the patterns of our language.
BENJAMIN L. WHORF in J.B. Carroll *Language, Thought and Reality*, 1956

5   All human thought comes into existence by grasping the meaning and mastering the use of language.
MICHAEL POLANYI *Knowing and Being*, 1971

LAUGHTER

6   … laughter may be bifunctional in its arousal-reducing properties: It serves to gain or maintain the companion's attention in situations that are experienced as too low in intimacy and to break the attention in situations that are experienced as too high in intimacy.
H.C. FOOT, A.J. CHAPMAN, J.R. SMITH *Journal of Personality and Social Psychology*, 1977

7   Laughter would be bereaved if snobbery died.
PETER USTINOV *The Observer*, 13 March 1977

8   Laughter is pleasant, but the exertion is too much for me.
THOMAS LOVE PEACOCK (1785–1866) *Nightmare Abbey*

9   Nothing is so impenetrable as laughter in a language you don't understand.
WILLIAM GOLDING (1911–1993) *An Egyptian Journal*

10   The funniest thing about comedy is that you never know why people laugh. I know *what* makes them laugh but trying to get your hands on the *why* of it is like trying to pick an eel out of a tub of water.
W.C. FIELDS (1880–1946) in R.J. Anobile *A Flask of Fields*, 1972

11   The sound is produced by a deep inspiration followed by short, interrupted, spasmodic contractions of the chest, and especially the diaphragm … the mouth is open more or less widely, with the corners drawn much backwards, as well as a little upwards; and the upper lip is somewhat raised.
CHARLES DARWIN (1809–1882) *The Expression of the Emotions in Man and Animals*

12   For mirth prolongeth life, and causeth health.
NICHOLAS UDALL (1505–1556) *Ralph Roister Doister*

1 Laugh and the world laughs with you;
Weep, and you weep alone;
ELLA WHEELER WILCOX (1850–1919) 'Solitude'

2 'Tis the loud laugh bespeaks the vacant mind.
JAMES JOYCE (1882–1941) *Ulysses*

LAZINESS

3 He who desires but acts not, breeds pestilence.
WILLIAM BLAKE (1757–1827) 'The Marriage of Heaven and Hell'

4 Iron rusts from disuse; stagnant water loses its purity and in cold weather becomes frozen; even so does inaction sap the vigour of the mind.
LEONARDO DA VINCI (1452–1519) *Notebooks of Leonardo Da Vinci*

5 We would all be idle if we could.
SAMUEL JOHNSON (1709–1784) cit. James Boswell *The Life of Samuel Johnson*

LEADERSHIP

6 The leader has most often started as one of the led. He has himself been hypnotised by an idea, whose apostle he has since become.
GUSTAVE LE BON *The Crowd: A Study of the Popular Mind*, 1896

7 [leader] ... a person who affects the thoughts, behaviors, and feelings of a significant number of individuals.
HOWARD GARDNER *Leading Minds*, 1996

8 The leader takes on the qualities which his adherents project on him.
KIMBALL YOUNG *Social Psychology*, 1945

9 A leader is a man who has the ability to get other people to do what they don't want to do and like it.
HARRY S. TRUMAN cit. B.L. Montgomery, *The Memoirs of Field Marshall Montgomery*, 1958

10 When the leader arrives, people are full of panic, uncertain what to do and defeatist about the future. When the authentic leader has spoken, they have been given back their courage.
WILLIAM REES-MOGG *The Times*, 28 January 1993

11 It is nonsense to talk of leadership in the abstract since no one can just lead without having a goal. Leadership is always *in* some sphere of interest and *toward* some objective goal seen by leader and follower.
P. PIGORS *Leadership or Domination*, 1935

12 ... most individuals will placidly accept whatever status they have attained ... after they reach a certain age, most of them lose their drive to struggle upwards.
RICHARD MORRIS *Evolution and Human Nature*, 1983

13 My own definition of leadership is this: The capacity and the will to rally men and women in a common purpose, and the character which inspires confidence.
B.L. MONTGOMERY (1887–1970) *The Memoirs of Field Marshall Montgomery*

14 A great leader must be an educator, bridging the gap between the vision and the familiar. But he must also be willing to walk alone to enable his society to follow the path he has selected.
HENRY KISSINGER *New York Times Book Review*, 1993

15 Leadership is definable by a manner of interacting with others....
H.H. JENNINGS *Leadership and Isolation*, 1943

16 ... viewed in relation to the individual, leadership is not an attribute of the personality but a quality of his role....
C.A. GIBB *Journal of Abnormal and Social Psychology*, 1947

17 ... the successful leader is the one who most keenly senses the wishes of a potential audience.
HOWARD GARDNER *Leading Minds*, 1996

1 All leadership takes place through communication of ideas to the minds of others.
C.H. COOLEY cit. D.A. Rustow *Philosophers and Kings*, 1970

2 While the advisors of a great leader should be as cold as ice, the leader himself should have fire, a spark of divine madness.
CONFUCIUS (c. 551–479 BC) *Analects*

3 What are the defining characteristics of a leader? At the top of the list, in my view, is the ability to inspire his own generation and generations to come, with a zest for living and a sense of high possibilities for his country and mankind in the future.
GEORGE W. BALL *New York Review of Books*, 1994

4 The final test of a leader is that he leaves behind him in other men the conviction and the will to carry on.
WALTER LIPPMANN *New York Herald Tribune*, 14 April 1945

5 And if the blind lead the blind, both shall fall into the ditch.
Bible, Matthew

6 The art of leadership is saying no, not yes. It is very easy to say yes.
TONY BLAIR *Mail on Sunday*, 2 October 1994

7 He that would govern others, first should be
The master of himself.
PHILIP MASSINGER (1583–1640) *The Bondsman*

8 How can the ability to lead depend on the ability to follow? You might as well say that the ability to float depends on the ability to sink.
L.J. PETER, R. HULL *The Peter Principle*, 1969

9 Political leadership is like being a teacher. It's about changing the language of others. I say it and go on saying it until I hear the man in the pub saying my words back to me.
JOHN HUME *The Independent*, 21 December 1996

10 One man who has a mind and knows it, can always beat ten men who havnt and dont.
GEORGE BERNARD SHAW (1856–1950) *The Apple Cart*

LEARNING

11 Social learning is inevitably moral.
J.J. GIBSON in J.G. Miller *Experiments in Social Process*, 1950

12 We think with our fingers and hands as well as with our brains, and we learn with our muscles as well as with our nervous system.
E.H. GARRET *General Psychology*, 1955

13 All man's learning, and indeed all his behavior, is *selective*. Man does not, in any useful sense of the words, ever absorb, or re-present, or mirror, or copy, a situation uniformly.
E.L. THORNDIKE *The Psychology of Learning*, 1913

14 Soon learnt, soon forgotten.
ANON.

15 ... a major difference between young and old learners is their ability to access and flexibly use competencies they posses.... It appears to be the ability to acquire an abstract principle ... that best discriminates between two groups of participants.
G. HALFORD *Learning and Individual Differences*, 1989

16 Learning without thinking is useless. Thinking without learning is dangerous.
CONFUCIUS (c. 551–479 BC) *Analects*

17 Observational learning is vital for both development and survival. Because mistakes can produce costly or even fatal consequences, the prospects for survival would be slim indeed if one could learn only by suffering the consequences of trial and error.
ALBERT BANDURA *Social Learning Theory*, 1977

1 The progress of learning is from indefinite to definite, not from sensation to perception. We do not learn to have percepts but to differentiate them.
J.J. GIBSON *The Perception of the Visual World*, 1950

2 ... when animals and children learn, not only does their behaviour change, but it changes usually for the better.
W. ROSS ASHBY *Design for a Brain*, 1952

3 It is likely that response to an infant's cries does more than reinforce crying. It reinforces active coping with the environment, reaching out to obtain feedback from people and objects.
L.J. YARROW *et al. Infant and Environment*, 1975

4 One of the fundamental properties of states is that they can be modified.
KARL PRIBRAM *Languages of the Brain*, 1971

5 ... the chick, when confronted by loneliness and confining walls responds by those acts which in similar situations in nature would be likely to free him. Some of these acts lead him to the successful act, and the resulting pleasure stamps it in. Absence of pleasure stamps all others out.
E.L. THORNDIKE *Animal Intelligence*, 1911

6 It appears ... as if the difference between sense and nonsense material were not nearly so great as one would be inclined *a priori* to imagine. At least I found in the case of learning by heart a few cantos from Byron's 'Don Juan' no greater range of distribution of the separate numerical measures than in the case of a series of nonsense syllables in the learning of which an approximately equal time had been spent.
HERMAN EBBINGHAUS *Memory*, 1885

7 ... there are no laws of learning that can be taught with confidence.
E.R. HILGARD *Theories of Learning*, 1948

8 For it is impossible for a man to begin to learn that which he thinks that he knows.
EPICTETUS (c. 55–135) *Discourses*

9 How does the individual organism manage to adjust itself better and better to its environment? How is it that we, or the amoeba, can learn to do anything? This latter problem is the most urgent, difficult and neglected question of the new genetic psychology.
JAMES MARK BALDWIN *Mental Development in the Child and Race*, 1895

10 Concentration of experimental work upon learning seems to stem almost exclusively from the anthropocentric orientation of American psychology.
FRANK BEACH *American Psychologist*, 1950

11 Learning in old age is writing on sand but learning in youth is engraving in stone.
ARABIAN PROVERB

12 Now since learning is nothing but imitation, the greatest ability, or aptness as a pupil, is still, as such, not equivalent to genius.
IMMANUEL KANT (1724–1804) *Critique of Pure Reason*

13 Learners must start from beliefs that are accepted or at least familiar.
ARISTOTLE (384–322 BC) *Nicomachean Ethics*

14 Much learning does not teach understanding.
HERACLITUS (c. 540–c. 475 BC) *Fragments*

15 There is a crude, naive psychological interpretation that the bait of pleasure and the whip of aversion provide the indispensable preconditions for the occurrence of any learning or conditioning.
KONRAD LORENZ *The Natural Science of the Human Species*, 1996

16 Could most examples of learning be illusory? Do our decisions and actions result from our discovering what is already in our brains?
MICHAEL GAZZANIGA *Nature's Mind*, 1992

17 It is of selective advantage to learn.
C.F.A. PANTIN *The Relation Between the Sciences*, 1968

1 One must learn by doing the thing; though you think you know it, you have no certainty until you try.
SOPHOCLES (c. 496–406 BC) *Trachinial*

2 The will to learn is an intrinsic motive, one that finds both its source and its reward in its own exercise.
J.S. BRUNER *Towards a Theory of Instruction*, 1966

LIFE

3 Life is a game boy. Life is a game that one plays according to the rules.
J.D. SALINGER *The Catcher in the Rye*, 1951

4 The great tragedy of life is not that men perish but that they cease to love.
SOMERSET MAUGHAM (1874–1965) *The Summing Up*

5 Life is a maze in which we take the wrong turning before we have learned to walk.
CYRIL CONNOLLY (1903–1974) *The Unquiet Grave*

6 To transcend the obvious – this is the basic problem of man.
G.A. KELLY in D. Bannister, F. Fransella *Inquiring Man*, 1971

7 No life is without its regrets or without its consolations.
ALAN BENNETT *The Madness of King George*, 1995

8 Crude classifications and false generalisations are the curse of all organised human life.
H.G. WELLS (1866–1946) *A Modern Utopia*

9 Life is a struggle for many and a puzzle for most.
CHARLES HANDY *The Empty Raincoat*, 1994

10 Never lose sight of the role your particular subject has within the great performance of the tragi-comedy of human life; keep in touch with life – not so much with practical life as with the ideal background of life, which is ever

so much more important, and, *keep life in touch with you.*
ERWIN SCHRÖDINGER *Science and Humanism*, 1951

11 There is no cure for birth and death save to enjoy the interval.
G. SANTAYANA (1863–1952) *Soliloquies in England*

12 It matters not how a man dies, but how he lives.
SAMUEL JOHNSON (1709–1784) cit. James Boswell *The Life of Samuel Johnson*

13 Life itself is essentially appropriation, injury, conquest of the strange and the weak, suppression, severity, obtrusion of its own forms, incorporation, and at the least, putting it mildest, exploitation.
FRIEDRICH NIETZSCHE (1844–1900) *Beyond Good and Evil*

14 In the long run we are all dead.
JOHN MAYNARD KEYNES (1883–1946) *A Tract on Monetary Reform*

15 Men will not be content to manufacture life: they will want to improve on it.
J.D. BERNAL *The World, the Flesh and the Devil*, 1969

16 Life is a sexually transmitted disease.
GRAFFITI

17 The essence of life is statistical improbability on a colossal scale.
RICHARD DAWKINS *The Blind Watchmaker*, 1986

18 Life is rather like a tin of sardines. We're all of us looking for the key.
ALAN BENNETT *Beyond the Fringe*, 1960

19 Life is a gamble of terrible odds – if it was a bet, you wouldn't take it.
TOM STOPPARD *Rosencrantz and Guildenstern are Dead*, 1967

20 The Answer to the Great Question Of ... Life, the Universe and Everything .. [is] Forty-Two.
DOUGLAS ADAMS *The Hitch Hiker's Guide to the Galaxy*, 1979

1 There's no need to worry –
Whatever you do, life is hell.
WENDY COPE 'Advice to Young Women', 1992

2 Life is the art of drawing sufficient
conclusions from insufficient premises.
SAMUEL BUTLER (1835–1902) *The Notebooks
of Samuel Butler*

3 Choose life. Choose mortgage
payments; choose washing machines;
choose cars; choose sitting on a couch
watching mind-numbing and spirit-
crushing game shows, stuffin' fuckin'
junk food in tae yir mouth.... Choose life.
IRVINE WELSH *Trainspotting*, 1996

4 life's too damn funny
it's one day sunny
the next day rain
life's too damn funny
for me to explain
don marquis (1878–1937) 'mehitabel sings a
song'

5 Life is a jest and all Things show it;
I thought so once, but now I know it.
JOHN GAY (1685–1732) proposed epitaph in
letter to Alexander Pope, October 1727

6 Life's but a walking shadow; a poor
     player,
That struts and frets his hour upon the
     stage,
And then is heard no more: it is a tale
Told by an idiot, full of sound and fury,
Signifying nothing.
WILLIAM SHAKESPEARE (1564–1616) *Macbeth*

7 What drives life is thus a little
electric current, kept up by the
sunshine. All the complexities of
intermediary metabolism are but the
lacework around this basic fact.
A. SZENT-GYORGYI *Introduction to
Submolecular Biology*, 1960

8 No man can have a peaceful life who
thinks too much about lengthening it.
SENECA (4 BC–65 AD) *Moral Epistles to
Lucilius*

9 What trifling coil do we poor mortals
     keep;
Wake, eat, and drink, evacuate, and
     sleep.
MATTHEW PRIOR (1664–1721) *Human Life*

10 Men are immortal till their work is
done.
DAVID LIVINGSTONE (1813–1873) letter from
Dr Livingstone to General Wynyard, 1862

11 To the psychotherapist an old man
who cannot bid farewell to life appears
as feeble and sickly as a young man
who is unable to embrace it.
CARL JUNG (1875–1961) *Modern Man in
Search of a Soul*

12 Life is a tragedy wherein we sit as
spectators for a while and then act out
our part in it.
JONATHAN SWIFT (1667–1645) *Thoughts on
Various Subjects*

13 Life is a great bundle of little
things.
OLIVER WENDELL HOLMES (1809–1894) *The
Professor at the Breakfast Table*

14 If I had to define life in a single
phrase, I should clearly express my
thought by throwing into relief the one
characteristic which, in my opinion,
sharply differentiates biological science.
I should say: life is certain.
CLAUDE BERNARD (1813–1878) *An
Introduction to the Study of Experimental
Medicine*

15 Life is one long process of getting
tired.
SAMUEL BUTLER (1835–1902) *The Notebooks
of Samuel Butler*

16 My baby has not lived in vain – this
life has been to him what it is to all of
us, education and development.
SAMUEL TAYLOR COLERIDGE (1772–1834)
letter to Thomas Poole, 6 April 1799

LIFE EVENTS

17 There are but three events in a
man's life: birth, life and death. He is
not conscious of being born, he dies in
pain, and he forgets to live.
JEAN DE LA BRUYERE *Characters*, 1688

1   ... negative life events, such as the death of a spouse, divorce or losing one's job, make people ill; the more negative in terms of intensity the duration and consequence of the event, the more severe is the illness.... Although the mechanism by which negative life-events influence health and illness is by no means clear, most studies have demonstrated a significant relationship between the two.
ADRIAN FURNHAM, STEPHEN BOCHNER *Culture Shock*, 1986

2   Every psychological event depends upon the state of the person and at the same time on the environment, although their relative importance is different in different cases.
KURT LEWIN *Principles of Topological Psychology*, 1936

3   When our first parents were driven out of Paradise, Adam is believed to have remarked to Eve: 'My dear, we live in an age of transition.'
W.R. INGE *Evening Standard*, 13 June 1928

4   Birth, and copulation, and death.
That's all the facts when you come to
    brass tacks:
Birth, and copulation, and death.
T.S. ELIOT (1888–1965) 'Sweeney Agonistes'

LIFE SPAN

5   The four stages of man are infancy, childhood, adolescence and obsolescence.
ART LINKLATER *A Child's Garden of Misinformation*, 1965

6   And surely we are all out of the computation of our age, and every man is some months older than he bethinks him; for we live more, have a being, and are subject to the actions of the elements, and the malice of diseases, in that other world, the truest Microcosm, the womb of our mother.
THOMAS BROWNE *Religio Medici*, 1642

7   Childhood often holds a truth with its feeble fingers, which the grasp of manhood cannot retain, which it is the pride of utmost age to recover.
JOHN RUSKIN (1819–1900) *Modern Painters*

8   Being thirty and forty, one is
    distracted by the Five lusts;
Between seventy and eighty, one is a
    prey to a hundred diseases.
But from fifty to sixty one is free from
    all ills.
Calm and still – the heart enjoys rest.
PO CHU-I (772–846) 'On Being Sixty'

9   The young have aspirations that never come to pass, the old have reminiscences of what never happened.
SAKI (1870–1916) *Reginald*

10   The certainties of one age are the problems of the next.
R.H. TAWNEY *Religion and the Rise of Capitalism*, 1926

11   When I was a child, I spake as a child, I understood as a child, I thought as a child: but when I became a man, I put away childish things.
Bible, Corinthians

12   A child becomes an adult when he realises that he has a right not only to be right but also to be wrong.
THOMAS SZASZ *The Second Sin*, 1973

13   Behold the child, by Nature's kindly
    law,
Pleased with a rattle, tickled with a
    straw:
Some livelier plaything gives his youth
    delight,
A little louder, but as empty quite:
Scarfs, garters, gold amuse his ripe
    stage,
And beads and prayer-books are the
    toys of age:
Pleased with this bauble still, as that
    before:
Till tired he sleeps, and Life's poor play
    is o'er.
ALEXANDER POPE (1688–1744) 'An Essay on Man'

1 Each generation criticizes the unconscious assumptions made by its parent. It may assent to them, but it brings them out in the open.
A.N. WHITEHEAD *Science and the Modern World*, 1925

2 'He no longer loves the person he loved ten years ago.' I quite believe it: she is not the same any more, nor is he. He was young and so was she; now she is quite different. Perhaps he would still love her as she used to be then.
BLAISE PASCAL (1623–1662) *Pensées*

3 To everything there is a season, and a time to every purpose under heaven: A time to be born and a time to die
Bible, Ecclesiastes

4 At thirty a man suspects himself a fool;
Knows it at forty, and reforms his plan;
At fifty chides his infamous delay,
Pushes his prudent purpose to resolve;
In all the magnanimity of thought
Resolves; and resolves; then dies the same.
EDWARD YOUNG (1683–1765) *Night Thoughts*

5 Youth is a blunder; Manhood a struggle; Old Age a regret.
BENJAMIN DISRAELI (1804–1881) *Coningsby*

6 Live as long as you may, the first twenty years are the longest half of your life.
ROBERT SOUTHEY (1774–1843) *The Doctor*

7 And so, from hour to hour, we ripe and ripe,
And then, from hour to hour, we rot and rot.
WILLIAM SHAKESPEARE (1564–1616) *As You Like It*

LIFE STYLE

8 Pick the right grandparents, don't eat or drink too much, be circumspect in all things, and take a two mile walk every morning before breakfast.
HARRY S. TRUMAN, said on his 80th birthday, 8 May 1964, attrib.

9 Teach him to live a life rather than avoid death; life is not breath but action.
JEAN-JACQUES ROUSSEAU (1712–1778) *Émile*

10 be a tabby tame if you want somebody s pussy and pet
the life i led was the life i liked
and there s pep in the old dame yet
don marquis (1878–1937) 'mehitabel dances with boreas'

LITERACY

11 To be literate it is not enough to know the words; one must learn how to participate in the discourse of some textual community.
DAVID OLSON *The World on Paper*, 1994

12 I have made this [letter] longer than usual, only because I have not had the time to make it shorter.
BLAISE PASCAL (1623–1662) *Lettres Provinciales*

13 And when we consider the first uses to which writing was put, it would seem quite clear that is was connected first and foremost with power: it was used for inventories, catalogues, censuses, laws, and instructions.
CLAUDE LÉVI-STRAUSS in G. Charbonnier *Conversations with Claude Lévi-Strauss*, 1973

14 ... who reads
Incessantly, and to his reading brings not
A spirit and judgement equal or superior
(And what he brings, what needs he elsewhere seek?)
Uncertain and unsettled still remains,
Deep versed in books and shallow in himself.
JOHN MILTON (1608–1674) *Paradise Regained*

15 What is written without effort is in general read without pleasure.
SAMUEL JOHNSON (1709–1784) *Miscellanies*

1 English orthography satisfies all the requirements of respectability under the law of conspicuous waste. It is archaic, cumbrous, and ineffective: its acquisition consumes much time and effort; failure to acquire it is easy of detection. Therefore it is the first and readiest test of reputability in learning and conformity to its ritual is indispensable to a blameless scholastic life.
THORSTEN VEBLEN *The Theory of the Leisure Class*, 1899

2 My spelling is Wobbly. It's good spelling but it Wobbles, and letters get in the wrong place.
A.A. MILNE (1882–1936) *Winnie-the-Pooh*

3 Those who write as they speak, even though they speak well, write badly.
COMTE DE BUFFON (1707–1778) *Discours sur le Style*

4 Written speech is a separate linguistic function differing from oral speech in both structure and mode of functioning.
L.S. VYGOTSKY *Thought and Language*, 1962

5 Knowledge is the foundation and source of good writing.
HORACE (65–8 BC) *Ars Poetica*

6 Composition is for the most part an effort of slow diligence and steady perseverance, to which the mind is dragged by necessity or resolution.
SAMUEL JOHNSON (1709–1784) *The Adventurer*

7 Why is it that man through his entire life as *Homo scribens* will continue to write with no improvement in his sense of craft and little improvement in his use of mind?
J.S. BRUNER *Towards a Theory of Instruction*, 1966

8 More writers fail from lack of character than from lack of intelligence. Technical solidity is not attained without at least some persistence.
EZRA POUND (1885–1972) *The ABC of Reading*

9 Readers may be divided into four classes: 1. Sponges, who absorb all they read and return it nearly in the same state.... 2. Sandglasses, who retain nothing and are content to get through a book for the sake of getting through the time. 3. Strain-bags, who retain merely the dregs of what they read. 4. Mogul diamonds, equally rare and valuable, who profit by what they read, and enable others to profit by it also.
SAMUEL TAYLOR COLERIDGE (1794–1819) *Notebooks*

10 ... the true significance of writing is that it was destined to revolutionize the transmission of human knowledge. By its means a man can immortalize his experience and transmit it directly to contemporaries living far off and to generations yet unknown. It is the first step to raising science above the limits of space and time.
V.G. CHILDE *Man Makes Himself*, 1956

11 Literacy, it was grasped, could ease the transition and assimilation of the working class and the poor to industrial and 'modern' social habits, if provided in carefully structured institutions.
H. GRAFF *Literacy and Social Development*, 1981

12 I keep asking the academics to do more work on what goes on when you're reading. It's the great dark area in literature .... I have this dilemma: do I hate this writer because of his evil or crabbed views of life, or do I admire him because he is clever with words, funny even when he's being foully rude or inhuman?
JOHN FOWLES *Writers Talking*, 1989

13 Achievement in handling the tools of reading and writing is obviously one of the most important axes of social differentiation in modern societies; and this differentiation extends on to more minute differences between professional specializations so that even members of the same socio-economic groups of literate specialists may hold little intellectual ground in common.
J. GOODY, I. WATT *The Consequences of Literacy*, 1962

LONELINESS

1 The dread of loneliness is greater than the fear of bondage, so we get married.
CYRIL CONNOLLY (1903–1974) *The Unquiet Grave*

2 What is hell?
Hell is oneself
Hell is alone.
T.S. ELIOT (1888–1965) *The Cocktail Party*

3 Voluntary loneliness, isolation from others, is the readiest safeguard against the unhappiness that may arise out of human relations.
SIGMUND FREUD (1856–1939) *Civilisation and its Discontents*

4 Alone, alone, all, all, alone,
Alone on a wide wide sea!
And never a saint took pity on
My soul in agony.
SAMUEL TAYLOR COLERIDGE (1772–1834) 'The Ancient Mariner'

LOSS

5 Tis better to have loved and lost
Than never to have loved at all.
ALFRED, LORD TENNYSON (1809–1892) 'In Memoriam'

6 ... two mournful friends and companions of almost all true love: separation and loss.
MIKHAIL SHOLOKOV (1905–1984) *Harvest on the Don*

7 When I am dead, my dearest
Sing no sad songs for me.
CHRISTINA ROSSETTI (1830–1894) 'The First Day'

8   Now conscience wakes despair
That slumber'd, wakes the better memory
Of what he was, what is, and what must be.
JOHN MILTON (1608–1674) *Paradise Lost*

9 It is of no avail to weep for the loss of a loved one, which is why we weep.
SOLON (c. 638–c. 559 BC) cit. Diogenes Laertius *Lives and Opinions of Eminent Philosophers*

10 She lived unknown, and few could know
When Lucy ceased to be;
But she is in her grave, and, oh,
The difference to me!
WILLIAM WORDSWORTH (1770–1850) 'She Dwelt Among the Untrodden Ways'

11 Cold in the earth, and fifteen wild Decembers
From those brown hills have melted into spring
Faithful indeed is the spirit that remembers
After such years of change and suffering.
EMILY BRONTË (1818–1848) 'Remembrance'

12 Break, break, break,
At the foot of thy crags, O Sea!
But the tender grace of a day that is dead
Will never come back to me.
ALFRED, LORD TENNYSON (1808–1892) 'In Memoriam'

13 Woman much missed, how you call to me, call to me,
Saying that now you are not as you were
When you had changed from the one who was all to me,
But as at first, when our day was fair.
THOMAS HARDY (1840–1928) 'The Voice'

14 Whither is it fled the visionary gleam?
Where is it now, the glory and the dream?
WILLIAM WORDSWORTH (1770–1850) 'Intimations of Immortality'

LOVE

1 Love is not an emotion. Emotions come and go in a matter of seconds or minutes. Parental love or romantic love is not so transitory, and clearly different from momentary emotions.
PAUL EKMAN, ed., Charles Darwin *The Expression of the Emotions in Man and Animals, 3rd edn*, 1997

2 Love, used in a romantic or passionate context, is merely a license for indulgence of our own needs and fantasies, a prop for our weakness and an accessory for our shaky egos. True love is, above all, an emanation of reason; a rational apprehension of another human being and a logical assessment of his or her particular needs, virtues and failings in the light of reality.
JILL TWEEDIE *In the Name of Love*, 1979

3 Knowest thou not that as the almond tree beareth most fruit when he is old, so love have greatest faith when it groweth in age.
JOHN LYLY (1554–1600) *Eupheus, His England*

4 Loving is not just a matter of affectionate contact. Loving has to gather to itself the instinctual urges which have a biological backing to them, and the relationship that develops between an infant and a mother (or a father or someone else) carries with it destructive ideas. It is not possible to love freely and fully without having ideas that are destructive.
DONALD WINNICOTT *The Family and Individual Development*, 1965

5 Love conquers all things – except poverty and toothache.
MAE WEST (1892–1980) attrib.

6 Dogs love their friends and bite their enemies, quite unlike people who are incapable of pure love and always have to mix love and hate in their object relations.
SIGMUND FREUD (1856–1939) *The Diary of Sigmund Freud 1929–1939*

7 Love is, above all, the gift of oneself.
JEAN ANOUILH (1910–1987) *Ardele*

8 What is love, except thinking you're in it?
DAVID LODGE *Therapy*, 1995

9 Of all man's inborn dispositions there is none more heroic than the love in him.
LAURENS VAN DER POST (1906–1996) *The Lost World of the Kalahari*

10 ... rather than say that love can colour our reasonings, we may say that the right brain hemisphere affects the left one, and that sex hormones can act upon the cell assemblies that do the thinking.
M. BUNGE *Neuroscience*, 1977

11 Love comforteth like sunshine after rain.
WILLIAM SHAKESPEARE (1564–1616) *Venus and Adonis*

12 Most people experience love, without noticing that there is anything remarkable about it.
BORIS PASTERNAK (1890–1960) *Doctor Zhivago*

13 What will survive of us is love.
PHILIP LARKIN (1922–1985) 'An Arundel Tomb'

14 A man who falls in love tends to lose some or all of the sentiments that he has in common with his fellows and that bind him to them in a common social life.
J.C. FLUGEL *British Journal of Medical Psychology*, 1927

15 Familiar acts are beautiful through love.
PERCY BYSSHE SHELLEY (1792–1822) 'Prometheus Unbound'

16 It falleth out in love as it doth in vines, for the young vines bring the most wine, but the old the best: so tender love maketh great show of blossoms, but tried love bringeth forth sweetest juice.
JOHN LYLY (1554–1600) *Eupheus, His England*

1 For a crowd is not company, and faces are but a gallery of pictures: and talk but a tinkling cymbal, where there is no love.
FRANCIS BACON (1561–1626) *Essays*

2 Love raises man, not only above himself, but also above the bounds of his mortality and earthliness, up to divinity itself, and in the very act of raising him it destroys him.
CARL JUNG (1875–1961) *Psychology of the Unconscious*

3 When a healthy three-year-old child says 'I love you' there is meaning in it like that between men and women who love and are in love.
DONALD WINNICOTT *The Child, the Family and the Outside World*, 1964

4 Love is like any other luxury. You have no right to it unless you can afford it.
ANTHONY TROLLOPE (1815–1882) *The Way We Live Now*

5 The affirmation of one's own life, happiness, growth, freedom is rooted in one's capacity to love, i.e., in care, respect, responsibility, and knowledge. If an individual is able to love productively, he loves himself too; if he can love only others, he cannot love at all.
ERICH FROMM *The Art of Loving*, 1957

6 Love is like the measles: we all have to go through it.
JEROME K. JEROME (1859–1927) *Idle Thoughts of an Idle Fellow*

7 And now good-morrow to our waking souls,
Which watch not one another out of fear;
For love all love of other sights controls,
And makes one little room an everywhere.
JOHN DONNE (1571–1631) 'The Good-Morrow'

8 I call 'crystallisation' that action of the mind that discovers fresh perfections in its beloved at every turn of events.
STENDHAL (1783–1842) *De l'amour*

9 When it comes, will it come without warning
Just as I'm picking my nose?
Will it knock on the door in the morning
Or tread in the bus on my toes?
Will it come like a change in the weather?
Will its greeting be courteous or rough?
Will it alter my life altogether?
O tell me the truth about love.
W.H. AUDEN (1907–1973) 'Twelve Songs'

10 There can be no peace of mind in love, since the advantage one has secured is never anything but a fresh starting-point for further desires.
MARCEL PROUST (1871–1922) *Remembrance of Things Past*

11 Love is a kind of warfare.
OVID (43 BC–17 AD) *Ars Amatoria*

12 Absence sharpens love, presence strengthens it.
THOMAS FULLER (1608–1661) *Gnomologia*

13 Love is a universal migraine,
A bright stain on the vision
Blotting out reason.
ROBERT GRAVES (1895–1985) 'Symptoms of Love'

14 Love makes up for the lack of long memories by a sort of magic. All other affections need a past: love creates a past which envelopes us, as if by enchantment.
BENJAMIN CONSTANT (1767–1834) *Adolphe*

M

MANAGEMENT

1 The encroachment of psychologists into the field of scientific management was of doubtful wisdom, and today it has been rendered obsolete by the mushrooming of management consultants and work study engineers.
L.S. HEARNSHAW *A Short History of British Psychology 1840–1940*, 1964

2 ... many management groups have come to the conclusion that different groups require different types of leadership.
F.E. FIEDLER *Discovery*, April 1965

3 Time spent on any item on the agenda will be in inverse proportion to the sum involved.
C. NORTHCOTE PARKINSON *Parkinson's Law*, 1958

4 Hell hath no fury like a bureaucrat scorned.
MILTON FRIEDMAN in B. Redhead, K. McLeish *Pieces of Hate*, 1982

5 The manager sat in his office,
Smoked a Corona cigar,
Said; 'Victor's a decent fellow but
He's too mousey to go far.'
W.H. AUDEN (1907–1973) 'Victor'

6 Human beings of today are attacked by so called managerial diseases...; they succumb to barbarism because they have no time for cultural interests. And all this is unnecessary because they could agree to take things more quietly but in practice it is just as impossible for them as it is for the argus pheasant to grow shorter wing feathers.
KONRAD LORENZ *On Aggression*, 1963

7 Day by day your estimation clocks up
Who deserves a smile and who a frown,
And girls you have to tell to pull their socks up
Are those whose pants you'd most like to pull down.
PHILIP LARKIN (1922–1985) 'Administration'

8 A committee is a cul-de-sac down which ideas are lured and then quietly strangled.
BARNETT COCKS *New Scientist*, 8 November 1973

MANNERS

9 What I understand by manners, then, is a culture's buzz of implication. I mean the whole evanescent context which is made up of half-uttered or un-uttered or unutterable expressions of value.
LIONEL TRILLING *The Liberal Imagination*, 1950

10 To Americans, English manners are far more frightening than none at all.
RANDALL JARRELL (1914–1965) *Pictures from an Institution*

11 I have always gone by the belief that if you try to make sure not to step on anybody's toes, you will have no space left to walk.
RUDOLPH ARNHEIM *Parables of Sun Light*, 1989

12 The [Phoenix] park is full of statues, mainly to British generals, and the IRA spent a good deal of their time in the twenties and thirties trying to blow them up – a harmless enough occupation and a bit like them sentencing me to death one time in my absence: I sent a polite note back saying they could shoot me in my absence also.
BRENDAN BEHAN (1923–1964) *Brendan Behan's Other Island*

13 Manners must adorn knowledge, and smooth its way through the world.
LORD CHESTERFIELD, PHILIP STANHOPE (1694–1773) *Letters to His Son*

1 Polite behaviour is ritual performed for the sake of other people, and for the sake of our relationship with other people.
MARGARET VISSER *The Rituals of Dinner*, 1991

2 The late Gilbert Harding once observed that the best manners in marriage are to be seen in the icy politeness that accompanies a marital row. 'If it isn't too much trouble, would you be so kind as to pass me the newspaper?' instead of 'Throw over the paper.' Maybe the best way to make up quarrels would be to revert to normal speech again. But for some occasions normal speech is unthinkable.
MARGHANITA LASKI *Words*, 1975

3 The proper way to leave a room
Is not to plunge it into gloom;
Just make a joke before you go,
And then escape before they know.
GELETT BURGESS (1866–1951) *The Burgess Nonsense Book*

4 Perfect behaviour is born of complete indifference.
CESARE PAVESE (1908–1950) *This Business of Living: Diaries 1935–50*

MARRIAGE

5 One doesn't have to get anywhere in marriage. It's not a public conveyance.
IRIS MURDOCH *A Severed Head*, 1961

6 I was ever of the opinion, that the honest man who married and brought up a large family, did more service than he who continued single and only talked of population.
OLIVER GOLDSMITH (1728–1774) *The Vicar of Wakefield*

7 Whoso findeth a wife findeth a good thing.
Bible, Proverbs

8 Marriage is the waste-paper basket of the emotions.
SYDNEY WEBB (1859–1947) cit. B. Russell *Autobiography*, 1967

9 In the hour of sorrow or sickness, a wife is a man's greatest blessing.
EURIPIDES (484–406 BC) *Antigone*

10 Wives are young men's mistresses, companions for middle age, and old men's nurses.
FRANCIS BACON (1561–1626) *Essays*

11 Hogamous, higamous
Man is polygamous
Higamous, hogamous
Woman monogamous.
WILLIAM JAMES (1842–1910) *Oxford Book of Marriage*

12 'Tis melancholy and a fearful sign
Of human frailty, folly also crime
That love and marriage rarely can
     combine.
LORD BYRON (1788–1824) *Don Juan*

13 When a merry maiden marries
Sorrow goes and pleasure tarries
Ev'ry sound becomes a song
All is right and nothing's wrong
W.S. GILBERT (1836–1911) *The Gondoliers*

14 A large proportion of mankind, like pigeons and partridges, on reaching maturity, having passed through a period of playfulness or promiscuity, establish what they hope and expect will be a permanent and fertile mating relationship. This we call marriage.
C.D. DARLINGTON *Genetics and Man*, 1964

15 Matrimony is a reversed fever, it starts with heat and ends with cold.
GERMAN PROVERB

16 When any two young people take it into their heads to marry, they are pretty sure by perseverance to carry their point, be they ever so poor, or ever so imprudent, or ever so little likely to be necessary to each other's ultimate comfort.
JANE AUSTEN (1775–1817) *Persuasion*

17 A married couple are well suited when both partners feel the need for a quarrel at the same time.
JEAN ROSTAND *Le Mariage*, 1927

1 Call it a good marriage –
For no one ever questioned
Her warmth, his masculinity,
Their interlocking views;
Except one stray graphologist
Who frowned in speculation
At her h's and her s's,
His p's and w's.
ROBERT GRAVES (1895–1985) 'Call It a Good Marriage'

2 Good marriages do exist, but not delectable ones.
DUC FRANÇOIS DE LA ROUCHEFOUCALD (1613–1680) *Maxims*

3 The fundamental trouble with marriage is that it shakes a man's confidence in himself, and so diminishes his general competence and effectiveness. His habit of mind becomes that of a commander who has lost a decisive and calamitous battle. He never quite trusts himself thereafter.
H.L. MENCKEN (1880–1956) *Prejudices: Second Series*

4 The particular charm of marriage is the duologue, the permanent conversation between two people who talk over everything and everyone till death breaks the record. It is this back-chat which, in the long run, makes a reciprocal equality more intoxicating than any form of servitude or domination.
CYRIL CONNOLLY (1903–1974) *The Unquiet Grave*

5 Accordingly we conclude that the appropriate age for marriage is about the eighteenth year for girls and for men the thirty-seventh plus or minus.
ARISTOTLE (384–322 BC) *Politics*

6 Wen you're a married man, Samivel, you'll understand a good many things as you don't understand now; but vether it's worth while goin' through so much to learn so little, as the charity boy said when he got to the end of the alphabet, is a matter of taste. *I* rather think it isn't.
CHARLES DICKENS (1812–1870) *Pickwick Papers*

7 How marriage ruins a man. It's as demoralizing as cigarettes, and far more expensive.
OSCAR WILDE (1854–1900) *Lady Windemere's Fan*

8 A husband is a man who two minutes after his head touches the pillow is snoring like an overloaded omnibus
OGDEN NASH (1902–1971) *The Trouble with Women is Men*

MATHEMATICS AND PSYCHOLOGY

9 ... while twentieth-century social scientists have tried desperately to become more quantitative in the belief that this would make them more mathematical, twentieth century mathematicians have become increasingly nonquantitative.
NIGEL HOWARD *Paradoxes of Rationality*, 1971

10 The first man who noted the analogy between a group of seven fishes and a group of seven days made a notable advance in the history of thought. He was the first man who entertained a concept belonging to the science of *pure* mathematics.
A.N. WHITEHEAD *Science and the Modern World*, 1926

11 What reputation academic psychology has with the educated layman depends almost entirely on the researchers of the line of distinguished men, who following Fechner have attempted to apply the precision which accompanies mathematical thinking alone to psychological problems. Thanks to them, we may determine as much about an individual's intellect in an hour and that probably more accurately, than a teacher's subjective estimate furnishes in a year.
J.F. BROWN *Psychometrika*, 1936

1 The result of a mathematical development should be continuously checked against one's own intuition about what constitutes reasonable biological behavior.
HARVEY J. GOLD *Mathematical Modeling of Biological Systems*, 1977

2 Young psychologists who share one or more of my disabilities may take comfort in the fact that, after all, I have done useful experiments without mechanical ability or training and have investigated quantitative relations with very meagre knowledge of mathematics.
E.L. THORNDIKE in *A History of Psychology in Autobiography, Vol. 3*, 1936

3 It would be a pity if Wundt had taken Psychology from her mother Philosophy and married her to Science only to have her desert to a paramour Mathematics.
E.B. WILSON *Psychometrika*, 1939

4 As far as the laws of mathematics refer to reality, they are not certain: and as far as they are certain, they do not refer to reality.
ALBERT EINSTEIN (1879–1955) *Sidelights on Relativity*

5 The idea that mathematics is the science of quantity is a nineteenth-century notion, and social scientists who pursue it are immersing themselves in dead ideas.
NIGEL HOWARD *Paradoxes of Rationality*, 1971

6 The application of mathematics has so far helped little towards making psychology a systematized science.
J.F. BROWN *Psychometrika*, 1936

MATING

7 In the males of all healthy animals the periodic stimulus to reproduction finds expression in more or less striking eccentric codes of conduct.
W.P. PYCRAFT *The Courtship of Animals*, 1914

8 A million million spermatozoa,
All of them alive:
Out of their cataclysm but one poor Noah
Dare hope to survive.

And among that billion minus one
Might have chanced to be
Shakespeare, another Newton, a new Donne –
But the One was Me.
ALDOUS HUXLEY (1894–1963) 'Fifth Philosopher's Song'

MEANING

9 'Then you should say what you mean,' the March Hare went on.
'I do,' Alice hastily replied; 'at least – at least I mean what I say – that's the same thing you know.'
LEWIS CARROLL (1832–1898) *Alice's Adventures in Wonderland*

10 If we hope to live not just from moment to moment, but in true consciousness of our existence, then our greatest need and most difficult achievement is to find meaning in our lives.
BRUNO BETTELHEIM *The Uses of Enchantment*, 1978

11 For while species develop in an extraordinarily chancey way from the bottom of the tree upward, human lives, even when haphazard, 'reek with purpose'.
J.S. BRUNER *In Search of Mind*, 1983

12 We struggle – and it can be a long hard struggle – to make sense.
MARGARET DONALDSON *Human Minds*, 1992

13 The belief that words have a meaning of their own account is a relic of primitive word magic, and it is still a part of the air we breathe in nearly every discussion.
C.K. OGDEN, I.A. RICHARDS *The Meaning of Meaning*, 1930

1 'When *I* use a word,' Humpty Dumpty said in a rather scornful tone, 'it means just what I choose it to mean – neither more nor less.'
LEWIS CARROLL (1832–1898) *Alice Through the Looking Glass*

MEASUREMENT

2 It is much easier to make measurements than to know exactly what you are measuring.
J.W.N. SULLIVAN (1886–1937) in R.L. Weber *More Random Walks in Science*, 1982

3 Make explicit to everyone (pupils, parents, public and professionals of all kinds) that a person's abilities, activities and attitudes cannot be measured. The public especially, misperceive that hard data exist, and that test scores constitute these data. The public does not realise how quickly the point is reached where we do not know how to discriminate validly among people but where data mislead us to think we do. This is what is meant by the myth of measurability.
R.W. TYLER, S.H. WHITE *Testing, Teaching and Learning*, 1979

4 Measurement began our might.
W.B. YEATS (1865–1939) 'Under Ben Bulben'

5 Measurement in the physical sciences is now a fairly straightforward matter. In the social and behavioral sciences however the situation is fundamentally different. There is controversy not only about how concepts should be measured and the precision of these measurements, but there is considerable controversy over the meaning of the constructs themselves.
B.F. GREEN *American Psychologist*, 1981

6 If we have a sense of what is worth measuring, we shall measure better.
J.S. BRUNER, *Towards a Theory of Instruction*, 1966

7 Psychologists have shown a perfectly amazing ingenuity and fertility in adapting or inventing simple tasks to aid them in their attempts to study the effects upon behaviour of unusual conditions. The results are ... almost invariably disappointing.
F.C. BARTLETT *The Problem of Noise*, 1934

MEGALOMANIA

8 What an artist dies with me!
NERO (37–68 AD) cit. Suetonius *Life of Nero*

9 We have become a grandmother.
MARGARET THATCHER, BBC TV interview cit. *The Times*, 3 March 1989

MEMORY

10 Every attempt to produce coherent memories amounts to falsification. No human memory is so arranged as to recollect everything in continuous sequence. Letters and diaries often turn out to be bad assistants.
ANNA AKHMATOVA (1888–1966) cit. Isaiah Berlin *Personal Impressions*, 1980

11 Much of what is remembered is reconstructed from stored fragments.
J.A. FODOR *The Language of Thought*, 1975

12 Phenomenal memory may now be relegated to computers and to the occasional variety-show act, but in former times it was of vital importance to the public figure. It is difficult nowadays, in an era of plentiful supplies of pens, paper and print-outs, to appreciate the absolute importance of human memory, when orators spoke perforce without notes.
MICHAEL BILLIG *Arguing and Thinking*, 1987

1 Scores of eyewitness and facial identification studies indicate that people's reliability is quite variable, depending on the specific circumstances of observing, recalling, and reporting ... because crimes against people are often rapid, unexpected, confusing, and involve real, changeable people, perhaps the variable levels of eyewitness accuracy are not surprising.... To make matters worse, eyewitness memory seems especially vulnerable to the way questions are asked.
S.T. FISKE, S.E. TAYLOR *Social Cognition*, 1991

2 There are no chance memories. Out of the incalculable number of impressions which meet an individual, he chooses to remember only those which he feels, however darkly, to have a bearing on his situation.
ALFRED ADLER (1870–1937) in H.R. Ausbacher, R.R. Ausbacher *The Individual Psychology of Alfred Adler*, 1956

3 ... over confidence in the accuracy of autobiographical memories is due to the fact that many 'events' could have happened as remembered because such events are consistent with the theme or gist of one's life ... they are truthful but inaccurate recollections. This gist tends to remain fairly stable over time because it is derived from a relatively stable sense of self.
C.R. BARCLAY in M.M. Gruneberg *et al. Practical Aspects of Memory*, 1988

4 The reminiscence comes
Of sunless dry geraniums
And dust in crevices,
Smells of chestnuts in the streets,
And female smells in shuttered rooms,
And cigarettes in corridors
And cocktail smells in bars.
T.S. ELIOT (1881–1965) 'Rhapsody on a Windy Night'

5 ... the phenomena of memory and of heredity have a common source.
E. HERING *On Memory as a Universal Function of Organised Matter*, 1870

6 Sometimes things come into my head when I'm leeching or poulticing, or such, as I could never think on when I was sitting still.
GEORGE ELIOT (1819–1880) *Silas Marner*

7 For the young child, to think means to recall; but for the adolescent, to recall means to think.
L.S. VYGOTSKY *Mind in Society*, 1978

8 The biological (if not the aesthetic) value of remembering is not that it allows one to reminisce about the past but that it permits one to calculate coldly about the unknown future.
COLIN BLAKEMORE *Listener*, 2 December 1976

9 Remembering is not the re-excitation of innumerable fixed, lifeless, and fragmentary traces. It is an imaginative reconstruction, or construction, built out of the relation of our attitude towards a whole mass of past experience.
F.C. BARTLETT *Remembering*, 1932

10 In my old age I find no pleasure save in the memories which I have of the past.
GIOVANNI CASANOVA (1725–1798) *Memoirs*

11 Those who cannot remember the past are condemned to repeat it.
GEORGE SANTAYANA (1863–1952) *The Life of Reason*

12 In plucking the fruit of memory one runs the risk of spoiling its bloom.
JOSEPH CONRAD (1857–1924) *Heart of Darkness*

13 When we listen to a person speaking or read a page of print, much of what we think we see or hear is supplied from our memory. We overlook misprints, imagining the right letters, though we see the wrong ones.
WILLIAM JAMES *Talks to Teachers*, 1899

14 Memories are not shackles ... they are garlands.
ALAN BENNETT *Forty Years On*, 1969

1   If only I could recollect it! Such
A day of days! I let it come and go
As traceless as a thaw of bygone snow.
It seemed to mean so little, meant so
    much!
CHRISTINA ROSSETTI (1830–1894) 'The First
Day'

2   Many a man fails to become a
thinker for the sole reason that his
memory is too good.
FRIEDRICH NIETZSCHE (1844–1900) *Maxims*

3   A great memory does not make a
philosopher, any more than a dictionary
can be called a grammar.
JOHN HENRY (CARDINAL) NEWMAN (1801–
1890) *Knowledge in Relation to Culture*

4   Memory, of all the powers of the
mind, is the most delicate and frail.
BEN JONSON (1573–1637) *Explorata:
Memoria*

5   Memory, the warder of the brain.
WILLIAM SHAKESPEARE (1564–1616)
Macbeth

6   Memory [is] like a purse, – if it be
overfull that it cannot shut, all will drop
out.
THOMAS FULLER (1608–1661) *The Holy and
Profane State*

7   The music in my heart I bore
Long after it was heard no more.
WILLIAM WORDSWORTH (1770–1850) 'The
Solitary Reaper'

8   My verbal memory is like flypaper.
That is both good and bad because
one's mind becomes filled with
irrelevant as well as useful things.
SUSAN LANGER *New York Times, Book
Review*, 26 May 1968

9   ... what is essentially new about my
theory is the thesis that memory is
present not once but several times over....
SIGMUND FREUD (1856–1939) letter to W.
Fliess, 1896, *The Complete Letters of Sigmund
Freud to Wilhelm Fliess*, 1985

10   Imagine ... that our minds contain
a block of wax, which in this or that
individual may be larger or smaller, and
composed of wax that is comparatively
pure or muddy, and harder in some,
softer in others, and sometimes of the
right consistency ... whenever we wish
to remember something we hear or
conceive in our own minds, we hold this
wax under the perceptions or ideas and
imprint them on it as we might stamp
the impression of a seal ring. Whatever
is so imprinted we remember and know
so long as the image remains; whatever
is rubbed out or has not succeeded in
leaving an impression we have forgotten
and do not know.
PLATO (427–347 BC) *Theaetus*

11   In memory everything seems to
happen to music.
TENNESSEE WILLIAMS (1911–1983) *The
Glass Menagerie*

12   The memory of most men is an
abandoned cemetery where lie, unsung
and unhonoured, the dead whom they
have ceased to cherish. Any lasting grief
is reproof to their forgetfulness.
MARGUERITE YOURCENAR (1903–1987)
Memoirs of Hadrian

13   Footfalls echo in the memory
Down the passage which we did not take
Towards the door we never opened.
T.S. ELIOT (1888–1965) 'Burnt Norton'

14   We are able to find everything in
our memory, which is like a dispensary
or chemical laboratory in which chance
steers our hand sometimes to a sooth-
ing drug sometimes to a dangerous
poison.
MARCEL PROUST (1871–1922) *Remembrance
of Things Past*

15   Human memory is a marvellous
but fallacious instrument ... the
memories which lie within us are not
carved in stone; not only do they tend to
become erased as the years go by, but
often they change, or even increase by
incorporating extraneous features.
PRIMO LEVI (1919–1987) *The Drowned and
the Saved*

16   Our memories are card indexes
consulted and then returned in disorder
by authorities whom we do not control.
CYRIL CONNOLLY (1903–1974) *The Unquiet
Grave*

1 ... the most essential characteristic of mind is memory, using this word in its broadest sense to include every influence of past experience on present reactions....
BERTRAND RUSSELL (1872–1970) *Portraits from Memory and Other Essays*

2 There seems something more speakingly incomprehensible in the powers, the failures, the inequalities of memory, than in any other of our intelligencies. The memory is sometimes so retentive, so serviceable, so obedient – at others, so bewildered and so weak – and at others again, so tyrannic and beyond control.
JANE AUSTEN (1775–1817) *Persuasion*

3 The development of memory with age is the history of gradual organisations closely dependent on the structuring activities of the intelligence.
JEAN PIAGET *Memory and Intelligence*, 1968

4 Memory is the diary we all carry about with us.
OSCAR WILDE (1854–1900) *The Importance of Being Earnest*

5 Do not be impressed by all that is presumably known about the psychology of memory. Less is known that you might think.
D.A. NORMAN *Perspectives on Cognitive Science*, 1981

6 ... nothing once formed in the mind could ever perish, that everything survives in some way other, and is capable under certain conditions of being brought to light again....
SIGMUND FREUD (1856–1939) *Civilisation and its Discontents*

MEN AND WOMEN

7 But most men regard their life as a poem that women threaten. They may not have two spondees to rub together but they still want to pen their saga untrammelled by life-threatening activities like trailing round Sainsbury's, emptying the dishwasher or going to the nativity play.
ALAN BENNETT *Writing Home*, 1994

8 Take my word for it, the silliest women can manage a clever man; but it takes a very clever woman to manage a fool.
RUDYARD KIPLING (1865–1936) *Plain Tales from the Hills*

9 From my experience of life I believe my personal motto should be 'Beware of any man bringing flowers'.
MURIEL SPARK *Curriculum Vitae*, 1992

10 'Tis strange what a man may do, and a woman yet think him an angel.
WILLIAM MAKEPEACE THACKERY (1811–1863) *The History of Henry Esmond*

11 Women have served all these centuries as looking-glasses possessing the magic and delicious power of reflecting the figure of man at twice its natural size.
VIRGINIA WOOLF (1854–1900) *A Room of One's Own*

12 A woman can become a man's friend only in the following stages – first an acquaintance, next a mistress, and only then a friend.
ANTON CHEKHOV (1860–1904) *Uncle Vanya*

13 It's not the men in my life that counts – it's the life in my men.
MAE WEST (1892–1980) attrib.

14 Always suspect any job men willingly vacate for women.
JILL TWEEDIE *Its Only Me*, 1980

15 I should like to know what is the proper function of women, if it is not to make reasons for husbands to stay at home, and still stronger reasons for bachelors to go out.
GEORGE ELIOT (1819–1880) *Mill on the Floss*, 1860

16 The female of the species is more deadly than the male.
RUDYARD KIPLING (1865–1936) 'The Female of the Species'

MENTAL DISORDERS

1 It has been argued that mental illness is a consequence of a labelling process which induces people to take on a sick role. If this were so, any study of psychiatric disorders would merely constitute an analysis of how society perceives and responds to various forms of behaviour ... there is little evidence to suggest that labelling processes are sufficiently powerful to constitute a major influence in producing chronic disorder.
MICHAEL RUTTER, NICOLA MADGE *Cycles of Disadvantage*, 1976

2 The mind like a sick body can be healed and changed by medicine.
LUCRETIUS (96–55 BC) *On the Nature of Things*

3 Hysterical patients suffer from reminiscences. Their symptoms are the remnants and the memory of certain (traumatic) experiences.
SIGMUND FREUD (1856–1939) *The Origin and Development of Psychoanalysis*

4 For the mental patient's family and society, mental illness is a 'problem'; for the patient himself it is a 'solution'.
THOMAS SZASZ *The Second Sin*, 1974

5 Oh, let me not be mad, not mad, sweet Heaven!
Keep me in temper; I would not be mad!–
WILLIAM SHAKESPEARE (1564–1616) *King Lear*

6 The classification of the constituents of chaos, nothing less here is essayed.
HERMAN MELVILLE (1819–1891) *Moby Dick*

7 There is little that cannot be remedied later, there is much that can be prevented from happening at all.
ERIK ERIKSON in M.J.E. Senn *Symposium on Healthy Personality*, 1950

8 One of the symptoms of approaching nervous breakdown is the belief that one's work is terribly important.
BERTRAND RUSSELL (1872–1970) *Autobiography*

9 I am here but not all there.
ALAN BENNETT *The Madness of King George*, 1995

10 O, what a noble mind is here o'erthrown.
WILLIAM SHAKESPEARE (1564–1616) *Hamlet*

11 Madness need not be all breakdown. It may also be break-through.
R.D. LAING *The Politics of Experience*, 1967

12 Poets do not go mad; but chess players do. Mathematicians go mad, and cashiers; but creative artists very seldom.
G.K. CHESTERTON (1874–1936) *Orthodoxy*

13 The body's delicate; the tempest in my mind doth from my senses take all feeling else save what beats there.
WILLIAM SHAKESPEARE (1564–1616) *King Lear*

14 Men are so inevitably mad that not to be mad would be to give a mad twist to madness.
BLAISE PASCAL (1623–1662) *Pensées*

15 I cannot help myself at all for he [the demon] uses my limbs and organs, my neck, my tongue, and my lungs......
JACOB SPRENGER *Malleus Maleficarum*, 1489

16 I think for my part one half of the nation is mad – and the other not very sound.
TOBIAS SMOLLET (1721–1771) *The Adventures of Sir Launcelot Greaves*

17 My means are sane, my motive and my object mad.
HERMAN MELVILLE (1819–1891) *Moby Dick*

18 The first step towards madness is to think oneself wise.
FERNANDO DE ROJAS (1499–1502) *La Celestina*

19 Man is certainly stark mad; he cannot make a flea, and yet he will be making gods by dozens.
MICHEL DE MONTAIGNE (1533–1592) *Essays*

1 Madness in great ones must not unwatch'd go.
WILLIAM SHAKESPEARE (1564–1616) *Hamlet*

2 The gods have made thee mad.
HOMER (8th cent. BC) *Odyssey*

3 We are all born mad. Some remain so.
SAMUEL BECKETT (1906–1989) *Waiting for Godot*

4 today after 15 years of therapeutic tears
and an awful lot of ratepayers' shillings
down the hospital meter
sad Aunt Madge
no longer tucks up the furniture
before kissing it goodnight
and admits
that her affair with Mussolini
clearly was not right
particularly in the light
of her recently announced engagement
to the late pope.
ROGER McGOUGH 'Sad Aunt Madge', 1967

5 Richard Napier used three plain words to describe men and women who were patently insane: mad, lunatic and distracted. To these he added a fourth, more ambiguous term, light-headed.... The distinctive feature of the behaviour of madmen and lunatics was their propensity to rage and threaten violence. People who were distracted were also often violent, but their distinctive action was idle talk – raving, seemingly incomprehensible speech. Those light-headed patients who were plainly insane instead of just giddy were also characterized by a tendency toward idle talk and frantic babble, but they were seldom given to violence.
MICHAEL MACDONALD *Mystical Bedlam*, 1981

6 Insanity is a kind of innocence.
GRAHAM GREENE (1904–1991) *The Quiet American*

7 What have I done ... I here proclaim was madness,
If Hamlet from himself be ta'en away...
And when he's not himself does wrong...
Then Hamlet does it not; Hamlet denies it,
Who does it then? His madness.
WILLIAM SHAKESPEARE (1564–1616) *Hamlet*

8 Sanity is a madness put to good uses; waking life is a dream controlled.
GEORGE SANTAYANA (1863–1952)
Interpretations of Poetry and Religion

9 When a lot of remedies are suggested for a disease, that means it can't be cured.
ANTON CHEKHOV (1860–1904) *The Cherry Orchard*

10 Insanity left him when he needed it most.
ROGER McGOUGH 'Tramp, Tramp, Tramp', 1986

11 Schizophrenia cannot be understood without understanding despair.
R.D. LAING *The Divided Self*, 1959

12 The madman is not the man who has lost his reason. The madman is the man who has lost everything except his reason.
G.K. CHESTERTON (1874–1936) *Orthodoxy*

13 A paranoid is a person in full possession of all the facts.
WILLIAM BURROUGHS cit. *Independent on Sunday*, 21 September 1997

MENTAL SET

14 When the only tool you have is a hammer, it is tempting to treat everything as if it were a nail.
ABRAHAM H. MASLOW *Towards a Psychology of Being*, 1962

15 Definition of scientific phenomena should be based on the phenomena as we see them. We have no business to base our definition on ideas of what we think phenomena *ought* to be like.
C.F.A. PANTIN *The Relation Between the Sciences*, 1968

METAPHOR

1 What history teaches is that progress is retarded when scholars fail to distinguish between the metaphor and the fact that the metaphor is intended to represent.... Of course, the modern psychologist may very well ignore these lessons of history.
DANIEL ROBINSON *An Intellectual History of Psychology*, 1981

2 Yesterday's daring metaphors are today's cliches.
ARTHUR KOESTLER *The Act of Creation*, 1964

3 Our ordinary conceptual system, in terms of which we both think and act, is fundamentally metaphorical in nature.
G. LAKOFF, M. JOHNSON *Metaphors We Live By*, 1980

4 I hate to hunt down a tired metaphor.
LORD BYRON (1788–1824) *Don Juan*

5 Location in space is one of the two fundamental metaphors in language, used for thousands of meanings. The other is force, agency and causation.... Space and force pervade language.
STEVEN PINKER *How the Mind Works*, 1997

6 But the greatest thing by far is to be a master of metaphor. It is the one thing that cannot be learned from others.
ARISTOTLE (384–322 BC) *Poetics*

7 A remarkably intelligent little girl of four years, but who had never in her own family been used to the common phrases which sometimes pass for humour, happened to hear a gentleman say, as he looked out of the window one rainy morning, 'It rains cats and dogs today'. The child, with a surprised but believing countenance, immediately went to look out of the window to see the phenomenon.
MARIA EDGEWORTH and R.L. EDGEWORTH *Essays on Practical Education*, 1822

8 Strangely, with progressive loss of its virility as a figure of speech, a metaphor becomes not less but more like literal truth. What vanishes is not its veracity but its vivacity. Metaphors, like new styles of representations, become more literal as their novelty wanes.
NORMAN GOODMAN *Language of Art*, 1976

9 In understanding a theorist's or practitioner's point of view on a given practical problem, it is important to understand the metaphor from which the individual is working, because the individual's point of view is likely to be shaped by the metaphor.
R.J. STERNBERG *Metaphors of Mind*, 1990

METHODS

10 [Most] people prefer to carry out the kinds of experiments that allow the scientist to feel that he is in full control of the situation rather than surrendering himself to the situation, as one must in studying human beings as they actually live.
MARGARET MEAD *Blackberry Winter*, 1972

11 The comparative psychologist must try to ask questions of his animals and to understand their answers. When Pfungst demonstrated that the horses of Elberfeld, who were showing marvellous linguistic and mathematical ability, were merely reacting to movements of the trainer's head, Mr Krall, their owner, met the criticism in the most direct manner. He asked the horses whether they could see such small movements and in answer they spelled out an emphatic 'no'. Unfortunately, we cannot all be so sure that our questions are understood or obtain such clear answers.
K.S. LASHLEY *Quarterly Review of Biology*, 1949

12 Galloping empiricism, which is our present occupational disease, dashes forth like a headless horseman. It has no rational objective; uses no rational methods other than mathematical; reaches no rational conclusion.
G.W. ALLPORT *American Psychologist*, 1966

1 Reaction times are only a shadow of the mental work they record.
ROGER BROWN, RICHARD J. HERRNSTEIN in N. Block *Imagery*, 1982

2 Such is the method [learning nonsense syllables] and such the main conclusions of this remarkable series of investigations, remarkable, it is perhaps needless to observe, more for their method than for their results.
JOSEPH JACOBS *Mind*, 1885

3 Traditional scientific method has always been at the very *best* 20-20 hindsight. It's good for seeing where you've been.
ROBERT M. PIRSIG *Zen and the Art of Motorcycle Maintenance*, 1974

4 You know my method, it is founded upon the observance of trifles.
ARTHUR CONAN DOYLE (1859–1930) *The Adventures of Sherlock Holmes*

5 We have three principal means: observation of nature, reflection, and experiment. Observation gathers the facts, reflection combines them, experiment verifies the result of the combination. It is essential that the observation of nature be assiduous, that reflection be profound, and that experimentation be exact. Rarely does one see these abilities in combination.
DENIS DIDEROT (1713–1784) *Pensées sur l'interprétation de la nature*

6 Foolproof methods, however desirable for all, are essential only for fools.
A.S. PARKES *Off-Beat Biologist*, 1985

7 The scientific method, as far as it is a method, is nothing more than doing one's damndest with one's mind, no holds barred.
P.W. BRIDGEMAN *Reflections of a Physicist*, 1980

MIDDLE AGE

8 The long, dull, monotonous years of middle-aged prosperity or middle-aged adversity are excellent campaigning weather for the Devil.
C.S. LEWIS (1898–1963) *The Screwtape Letters*

9 Every man over forty is a scoundrel.
GEORGE BERNARD SHAW (1856–1950) *Man and Superman*

10 It sometimes happens, that a woman is handsomer at twenty-nine than she was ten years before; and, generally speaking if there had been neither ill health nor anxiety, it is a time of life at which scarcely any charm is lost.
JANE AUSTEN (1775–1817) *Persuasion*

11 The girl in the tea shop
Is not so beautiful as she was.
The August has worn against her.
She does not get up the stairs so
    eagerly;
Yes, she also will turn middle-aged,
EZRA POUND (1885–1972) 'The Tea Shop'

12 The effective, moving, vitalizing work of the world is done between the ages of twenty-five and forty – these fifteen golden years of plenty, the anabolic or constructive period, in which there is always a balance in the mental bank and the credit is still good.
WILLIAM OSLER (1849–1919) cit. H. Cushing *Life of Sir William Osler*, 1925

13 Of all the barbarous middle ages,
    that
Which is most barbarous is the middle
    age
Of man: it is – I really scarce know
    what;
But when we hover between fool and
    sage.
LORD BYRON (1788–1824) *Don Juan*

14 One of the pleasures of middle age is to *find out* that one WAS right, and that one was much righter than one knew at say 17 or 23.
EZRA POUND (1885–1972) *ABC of Reading*

MIND

1 'Mind' ... is as useless an explanatory concept to today's scientific psychologist as the mythical element 'phlogiston' that chemists once believed caused all fires.
JAMES V. McCONNELL *Esquire*, 1968

2 Mind, for anything perception can compass, goes therefore in our spatial world more ghostly than a ghost. Invisible, intangible, it is a thing not even of outline; it is not a 'thing'.
CHARLES SHERRINGTON *Man on His Nature*, 1940

3 'Mind' is understood to mean simply the sum total of mental processes experienced by the individual during his lifetime. Ideas, feelings, impulses etc, are mental processes; the whole number of ideas, feelings, impulses etc, experienced by me during my life constitutes my 'mind'.
E.B. TITCHENER *An Outline of Psychology*, 1899

4 No neurone, no mind.
R.J.A. BARRY *Brain and Mind: Or the Nervous System of Man*, 1928

5 The mind is its own place, and in
　itself
Can make a heaven of hell, a hell of
　heaven.
JOHN MILTON (1608–1674) *Paradise Lost*

6 That's the classical mind at work, runs fine inside but looks dingy on the surface.
ROBERT M. PIRSIG *Zen and the Art of Motorcycle Maintenance*, 1974

7 The mind is not like a sheet of white paper which receives just what is written upon it, nor like a mirror which simply reflects more or less every object, but by it is connoted a plastic power of ministering to a complex process of organisation in which what is suitable to development is assimilated, what is unsuitable is rejected.
HENRY MAUDSLEY (1835–1918) *Physiology and Pathology of the Mind*

8 Mental states are biological phenomena. Consciousness, intentionality, subjectivity and mental causation are all part of our biological life history, along with growth, reproduction, the secretion of bile and digestion.
JOHN SEARLE *Minds, Brain and Science*, 1984

9 Minds are like parachutes. They only function when open.
JAMES DEWAR (1842–1923) attrib.

10 No attributes of 'energy' seem findable in the processes of mind.
CHARLES SHERRINGTON *Man on His Nature*, 1940

11 Mind is a complex organization, held together by interaction of processes and by the time scales of memory, centered about the body image.
K.S. LASHLEY *Proceedings of the Association for Research in Nervous Mental Diseases*, 1958

12 The first observation I make at this point is that there is a great difference between the mind and the body, inasmuch as the body is by its very nature always divisible, while the mind is utterly indivisible.
RENÉ DESCARTES (1596–1650) *Meditations on First Philosophy*

13 Only one thing in life is of actual interest for us – our psychical experience. Its mechanism, however, has been, and remains, wrapped in deep mystery. All human resources – art, religion, literature, philosophy, historical science – all these unite to cast a beam of light into this mysterious darkness.
IVAN PAVLOV *Lectures on Conditioned Reflexes*, 1928

14 Biology cannot go far in its subject without being met by mind.
CHARLES SHERRINGTON *Man on His Nature*, 1940

1 Mind is a moving scene, which we are perpetually copying. We spend a great deal of time in rendering it faithfully: but the original exists as a complete whole, for the mind does not proceed step by step, like expression. The brush takes time to represent what the artist's eye sees in an instant.
DENIS DIDEROT (1713–1784) *Letter on the Deaf and Dumb*

2 'Mind' refers not to an object but to mental activity and since mental activities occur throughout much of the animal kingdom (depending on how we define 'mental'), one can say that mind occurs whenever organisms are found that can be shown to have mental processes.
E. MAYR *The Growth of Biological Thought*, 1982

3 Bishop Berkeley destroyed this world in one volume octavo: and nothing remained, after his time, but mind: which experienced a similar fate from the hand of Mr Hume in 1739.
SYDNEY SMITH (1771–1845) *Sketches of Moral Philosophy*

4 The function of mind is to draw a plan of action in order to predict what results will occur when nature is acted upon in this way or that.
JOHN DEWEY (1859–1952) *Lectures in China, 1919–1920*

5 The existence of a mind absolutely independent of conditions of life is unthinkable.
F. BOAS *The Mind of Primitive Man*, 1911

6 For of the soul the body form doth take;
For soul is form, and doth the body make.
EDMUND SPENSER (1552–1599) 'A Hymn in Honour of Beauty'

7 ... the notion of any *relation* between mind and body is absurd – because mental activity and living bodily activity are identical.
C.S. MYERS *In the Realm of Mind*, 1937

8 Mens sana in corpore sano is a foolish saying. The sound body is a product of the sound mind.
GEORGE BERNARD SHAW (1856–1950) *Man and Superman*

9 The human body is the best picture of the human soul.
LUDWIG WITTGENSTEIN *Philosophical Investigations*, 1953

10 Man is to himself the most wonderful object in nature; for he cannot conceive what the body is, less what the mind is, and least of all how a body should be united to a mind.
BLAISE PASCAL (1623–1662) *Pensées*

MORALITY

11 Moralities legitimize and rationalize relations within and between groups. The moral ideology of a group ... sets the bounds of legitimate action; it establishes codes of practice.... Identity is immutably tied to moralities which are evolved through the contingencies of intergroup conflict.
H. WEINREICH-HASTE, D. LOCKE *Morality in the Making*, 1983

12 There is, I am aware, a disposition to believe that a person who sees in a moral obligation a transcendental fact, an objective reality belonging to the province of 'things in themselves', is likely to be more obedient to it than one who believes it to be entirely subjective, having its seat in human consciousness only.
JOHN STUART MILL (1806–1873) *Utilitarianism*

13 The defenders of traditional morality are seldom people with warm hearts, as may be seen from the love of militarism displayed by Church dignitaries.
BERTRAND RUSSELL (1872–1970) *What I Believe*

1 In fact, aren't the people one thinks
of as immoral
Just the people who we say have no
moral sense?
I've never noticed that immorality
Was accompanied by a sense of sin.
T.S. ELIOT (1888–1965) *The Cocktail Party*

2 The ethical progress of society
depends, not on imitating the cosmic
process, still less in running away from
it, but in combating it.
T.H. HUXLEY (1825–1895) *Evolution and
Ethics*

3 Morality is the custom of one's
country and the current feeling of one's
peers. Cannibalism is moral in a
cannibal country.
SAMUEL BUTLER (1835–1902) *The Notebooks
of Samuel Butler*

4 My father, to whom I owe so much,
never told me the difference between
right and wrong; now, I think that's why
I remain so greatly in his debt.
JOHN MORTIMER *Clinging to the Wreckage*,
1982

5 … feeling, not logic, sustains the
superego.
JEROME KAGAN *The Nature of the Child*,
1984

6 I like the English. They have the
most rigid code of immorality in the
world.
MALCOLM BRADBURY *Eating People is
Wrong*, 1959

7 It is easier to fight for one's
principles than to live up to them.
ALFRED ADLER cit. P. Bottome *Alfred Adler*,
1939

8 More people are flattered into virtue
than bullied out of vice.
R.S. SURTEES (1805–1864) *The Analysis of
the Hunting Field*

9 The people who are regarded as
moral luminaries are those who forego
ordinary pleasures themselves and find
compensation in interfering with the
pleasures of others.
BERTRAND RUSSELL (1872–1970)
Autobiography

10 Morality which is based on ideas or
on an ideal, is an unmitigated evil.
D.H. LAWRENCE (1885–1930) *Fantasia of the
Unconscious*

11 Half, at least, of all morality is
negative and consists in keeping out of
mischief.
ALDOUS HUXLEY (1894–1963) *The Doors of
Perception*

12 What is moral is what you feel good
after, and what is immoral is what you
feel bad after.
ERNEST HEMINGWAY (1899–1961) *Death in
the Afternoon*

13 The highest possible stage in moral
culture is when we recognize that we
ought to control our thoughts.
CHARLES DARWIN (1809–1882) *Descent of
Man*

14 Moral indignation is jealousy with a
halo.
H.G. WELLS (1866–1946) *The Wife of Sir Isaac
Harmon*

15 The world is full of injustice, and
those who profit by injustice are in a
position to administer rewards and
punishments. The rewards go to those
who invent ingenious justifications for
inequality, the punishments go to those
who try to remedy it.
BERTRAND RUSSELL (1872–1970) *The Harm
that Good Men Do*

16 The ends cannot justify the means,
for the simple and obvious reason that
the means employed determine the
nature of the ends produced.
ALDOUS HUXLEY (1894–1963) *Ends and
Means*

17 But Christes lore, and his apostles
twelve,
He taught, but first he folwed it himselve.
GEOFFREY CHAUCER (1340–1400)
Canterbury Tales

18 The last temptation is the greatest
treason:
To do the right thing for the wrong
reason.
T.S. ELIOT (1888–1965) *Murder in the
Cathedral*

1 Everything's got a moral, if you can only find it.
LEWIS CARROLL (1832–1898) *Alice's Adventures in Wonderland*

2 Pickering: Have you no morals, man?
Doolittle: Can't afford them, Governor.
GEORGE BERNARD SHAW (1856–1950) *Pygmalion*

3 When a man is old enough to do wrong he should be old enough to do right also.
OSCAR WILDE (1854–1900) *A Woman of No Importance*

4 Thus at last man comes to feel, through acquired and perhaps inherited habit, that it is best for him to obey his more persistent impulses. The imperious word ought seems merely to imply the consciousness of the existence of a rule of conduct, however it may have originated.
CHARLES DARWIN (1809–1882) *Descent of Man*

5 I and the public know
What all schoolchildren learn,
Those to whom evil is done
Do evil in return.
W.H. AUDEN (1907–1973) 'September 1, 1939'

6 The right moment to begin the requisite moral training is the moment of birth, because then it can be begun without disappointing expectations.
BERTRAND RUSSELL (1872–1970) *On Education, Especially in Early Childhood*

MOTHERS

7 Mothers create a sense of trust in their children by that kind of administration which in its quality combines sensitive care of the baby's individual needs and a firm sense of personal trustworthiness within the trusted framework of their culture's life style.
ERIK ERIKSON *Childhood and Society*, 1950

8 The dance of development is impoverished indeed, if the mother is not available to be the primary partner. With no mother, there is often no one to hug back when you hug. Your coos and smiles are unreturned.
MARTIN SELIGMAN *Helplessness*, 1975

9 Few misfortunes can befall a boy which bring worse consequences than to have a really affectionate mother.
SOMERSET MAUGHAM (1874–1965) *A Writer's Notebook*

10 When I dressed up in a surplice and hood, and preached her [my mother] a sermon, she entered into the game; and she has treasured a notebook containing numerous sermons which I wrote, or rather commenced, at the age of seven, and from which I once rashly computed my own IQ.
CYRIL BURT in *A History of Psychology in Autobiography, Vol. 4*, 1952

11 It is unquestionable, that the hopes of human society and the hopes of the Church of God are to be found in the character, in the views, and in the conduct of mothers.
E.N. KIRK *The Mother's Magazine*, 1844

12 Who ran to help me when I fell,
And would some pretty story tell,
Or kiss the place to make it well?
My Mother.
ANN TAYLOR (1782–1866) 'My Mother'

13 There was never a great man who had not a great mother.
OLIVE SCHREINER (1855–1920) *The Story of an African Farm*

14 The lullaby is the spell whereby the mother attempts to transform herself back from an ogre to a saint.
JAMES FENTON *Independent on Sunday*, 11 March 1990

15 God could not be everywhere and therefore he made mothers.
JEWISH PROVERB

16 Who but the infant's mother troubles to know and feel the infant's needs?
DONALD WINNICOTT *The Family and Individual Development*, 1965

1 The best predictors of the child's competence at 24–30 months and 42–48 months turn out to be measures of mother's control and disciplinary techniques, not mother's IQ or educational level, parental occupations, or family income.
SANDRA SCARR *American Psychologist*, 1981

2 ... all women are the mothers of great men – it isn't their fault if life disappoints them later.
BORIS PASTERNAK (1890–1960) *Doctor Zhivago*

3 Women know
The way to rear up children (to be just)
They know a simple, merry, tender
   knack
Of tying sashes, fitting baby-shoes,
And stringing pretty words that make
   no sense,
And kissing full sense into empty words,
ELIZABETH BARRETT BROWNING (1806–1861) 'Aurora Leigh'

4 After the mother has succeeded in connecting the child with herself, her next task is to spread his interest towards his father ... the older children of the family, to friends, relatives.... She must give the child his first experience of a trustworthy fellow being and then ... spread this trust and friendship until it includes the whole of our human society.
ALFRED ADLER in H.R. Ausbacher, R.R. Ausbacher *The Individual Psychology of Alfred Adler*, 1956

5 Mothers love their children more than fathers, because parenthood costs the mother more trouble.
ARISTOTLE (384–322 BC) *Nicomachean Ethics*

6 Summoned from a dream of your
   summoning
by your cry, I steal out of bed and leave
my doting husband deaf to the world.
We meet, couple, and cling, in the dim
   light –
your soft mouth tugs and fills and
   empties me.
JILL HOFFMAN 'Rendezvous' *Mink Coat*, 1973

MOTIVATION

7 There are at least five sets of goals which we call basic needs. These are, briefly, physiological safety, love, esteem and self-actualization. In addition we are motivated by the desire to achieve or maintain the various conditions upon which these basic satisfactions rest and by certain more intellectual desires. These basic goals are related to one another, being arranged in a hierarchy of prepotency.... Thus man is a perpetually wanting animal.
ABRAHAM H. MASLOW *Psychological Review*, 1943

8 Motives may explain actions to us; but that is not to say that they determine, in the sense of causing, actions.
G.E.M. ANSCOMBE *Intention*, 1957

9 [There is a] very old and still prevalent superstition inherent in the word 'drive', that the organism is driven and guided to certain external goals, such as money or murder, by a mysterious force or homunculus who sits somewhere inside, preferably in the heart or brain.
H.W. NISSEN *Nebraska Symposium on Motivation*, 1954

10 But *all* behavior is motivated. Without motivation there is *no activity*.
ELIZABETH DUFFY *Journal of General Psychology*, 1941

11 Something important is left out when we make drives the operating forces in animal and human behavior.
R.H. WHITE *Psychological Review*, 1959

12 We call something a goal not because it is a natural terminating point of movements but because movements persist towards it and vary in accordance with perceived changes in it and conditions that lead to it. This adaptiveness or relevant variation in relation to change is also part of what we call intelligence.
R.S. PETERS *The Concept of Motivation*, 1958

1 ... things dictate to a child what he must do: a door demands to be opened and closed, a staircase to be run up, a bell to be rung. In short things have an inherent motivating force in respect to a young child's actions and determine the child's behaviour.
L.S. VYGOTSKY in J.S. Bruner, K. Sylva *Play*, 1976

2 In general, a drive has direction as well as intensity; it is selective as well as activating.
R.W. WOODWORTH *Dynamics of Behavior*, 1958

3 Capacity is its own motivation.
H.W. NISSEN *Nebraska Symposium on Motivation*, 1954

4 The inclination to engage in a particular activity is as important as the ability to carry out that activity.
R.T. KELLOGG *The Psychology of Writing*, 1994

5 The new psychology intuitively disposed of instincts and painlessly disposed of hedonism. But having completed this St-Bartholomew-type massacre, behavioristic motivation theory was left with an aching void.
HARRY F. HARLOW *Psychological Review*, 1953

6 ... close reflection suggests that there is an intimate relation between the preferred modes of behavior of the individual and the psychological motivations of his conduct, contact with others, likes and dislikes, and attitudes towards life.
KURT GOLDSTEIN *Human Nature in the Light of Psychopathology*, 1940

7 All progress is based upon a universal innate desire on the part of every organism to live beyond its income.
SAMUEL BUTLER (1835–1902) *Note Books*

8 Motivation is always contemporary.
G.W. ALLPORT *Personality: A Psychological Perspective*, 1937

9 Sir, there are two passions which have a powerful influence in the affairs of men. These are *ambition* and *avarice*: the love of power and the love of money. Separately, each of these has great force in prompting men of action; but when united in view of the same object, they have in many minds the most violent effects.
BENJAMIN FRANKLIN (1706–1790), speech in the Constitutional Convention, 3 June 1789

10 ... an attempt at explanation by rape rather than honest wooing still characterises the psychology of motivation.
LESLIE HENDERSON *British Journal of Psychology*, 1972

11   I have no spur
To prick the sides of my intent, but only
Vaulting ambition, which o'erleaps itself
And falls on the other.
WILLIAM SHAKESPEARE (1564–1616) *Macbeth*

12 I was taught to fear God, the police, and what people will think. As a result, I usually do what I have to do with no great struggle.
B.F. SKINNER in *A History of Psychology in Autobiography, Vol. 5*, 1967

13 In interpreting the behaviour of animals, experimenters use categories of descriptions which are really only applicable to human beings. For instance we often speak of an animal 'wanting' something.... When, however, we apply this sort of concept to animals we do so by tacitly withdrawing some of the conditions for using the word.
R.S. PETERS *The Concept of Motivation*, 1958

14 Lives of great men all remind us
We can make our lives sublime,
And, departing, leave behind us
Footprints on the sands of time.
HENRY W. LONGFELLOW (1807–1882) 'A Psalm of Life'

15 *Fame* is the spur that the clear
    spirit doth raise
(That last infirmity of the Noble mind)
To scorn delights, and live laborious
    dayes:
JOHN MILTON (1608–1674) 'Lycidas'

1 The motive for my first investigations of animal intelligence was chiefly to satisfy requirements for courses and degrees.
E.L THORNDIKE in *A History of Psychology in Autobiography, Vol. 3*, 1930

2 Three passions, simple but overwhelmingly strong, have governed my life: the longing for love, the search for knowledge, and unbearable pity for the suffering of mankind.
BERTRAND RUSSELL (1872–1970)
Autobiography

3 Intellectual competence, beginning with symbolization and language, is inextricably entwined with motivational and adjustment characteristics.
SANDRA SCARR *American Psychologist*, 1981

4 Now he had recognised himself as a dead man it became important to stay alive as long as possible.
GEORGE ORWELL (1903–1959) *Nineteen Eighty-Four*

5 Nothing will ever be attempted, if all possible objections must first be overcome.
SAMUEL JOHNSON (1709–1784) *Rasselas*

6 While behavior is almost always motivated, it is also almost always biologically, culturally and situationally determined as well.
ABRAHAM H. MASLOW *A Theory of Human Motivations*, 1943

7 A child of the new generation
Refused to learn multiplication
He said 'Don't conclude
That I'm stupid or rude:
I am simply without motivation'.
J.H. HILDEBRAND *Perspectives in Biology and Medicine*, 1970

8 What I have most wanted to do all my life is to make a contribution to knowledge. If you feel you are doing this it is much more fun than running things, or being a military commander, a departmental chairman, a participant in the brotherhood of workers, a mountain climber, or even an actor. And it seems to me that you can contribute to knowledge without being very bright (which I am not) but merely by being stubborn about it.
J.J. GIBSON in *A History of Psychology in Autobiography, Vol. 5*, 1967

9 One should distinguish between giving prizes, which adds to the sum total of human unhappiness, and giving awards, which enable someone to complete a useful piece of work that would not otherwise be undertaken.
STUART SUTHERLAND *Irrationality*, 1992

10 Where there is no desire, there will be no industry.
JOHN LOCKE (1632–1704) *Some Thoughts Concerning Education*

11 A man's most open actions have a secret side to them.
JOSEPH CONRAD (1857–1924) *Under Western Eyes*

MUSIC

12 Music seems to act as a 'tonic', freshening the worker who has become bored by the monotony of a repetitive task.
REX KNIGHT in C.S. Myers *Industrial Psychology*, 1929

13 Extraordinary how potent cheap music is.
NOEL COWARD (1899–1973) *Private Lives*

14 If music be the food of love, play on;
Give me excess of it, that, surfeiting,
The appetite may sicken, and so die.
WILLIAM SHAKESPEARE (1564–1616)
Twelfth Night

15 Music, when soft voices die,
Vibrates in the memory.
PERCY BYSSHE SHELLEY (1792–1822) 'To —:
Music, When Soft Voices Die'

1 Music, though supremely capable of whipping up militant enthusiasm, is fortunately quite unable to specify what the hearers are expected to be enthusiastic about. So the most feudalistic old aristocrat can appreciate the inspiring beauty of the Marseillaise, even though the text of the song suggests that his impure blood should be used as fertilizer.
KONRAD LORENZ *On Aggression* 1963

2 Although it may not be possible to account for a faculty like musical talent in terms of ordinary Natural Selection, it is impossible to ignore the fact that response to music has often been of survival-value both in war and in peace.
J. ARTHUR THOMSON *Man in the Light of Evolution*, 1926

3 A man that hath no music in himself,
Nor is not mov'd with concord of sweet sounds,
Is fit for treasons, stratagems, and spoils;
The motions of his spirit are dull as night,
And his affections dark as Erebus:
Let no such man be trusted.
WILLIAM SHAKESPEARE (1564–1616) *The Merchant of Venice*

4 Sweetest melodies
Are those by distance made more sweet.
WILLIAM WORDSWORTH (1770–1850) 'Personal Talk'

5 Music has charms to soothe the savage breast.
WILLIAM CONGREVE (1670–1729) *The Mourning Bride*

6 This music crept by me upon the waters,
Allaying both their fury, and my passion,
With its sweet air.
WILLIAM SHAKESPEARE (1564–1616) *The Tempest*

MYTHS

7 Primitive man is clearly capable of positive thought ... but it is his myth-creating capacity which plays the vital part in his life.... I believe that these two ways of thinking have always existed in man, and they go on existing, but the importance they are given is not the same here and there.
CLAUDE LÉVI-STRAUSS *Realites*, 1965

8 Science must begin with myths, and with the criticism of myths.
KARL POPPER in C.A. Mace *British Philosophy in the Mid-Century*, 1957

9 ... the fundamental consanguinity of our species is apparent not only in our bodies and our genes but in our myths, dreams, psychoses, and cultural artefacts.
ANTHONY STEVENS *Private Myths*, 1995

10 A myth is a private dream, a dream is a private myth.
JOSEPH CAMPBELL *The Masks of God, Vol. 1: Primitive Mythology*, 1959

11 A myth is, of course, not a fairy story. It is the presentation of facts belonging to one category in the idioms appropriate to another. To explode a myth is accordingly not to deny the facts but to re-allocate them.
GILBERT RYLE *The Concept of Mind*, 1949

12 We can keep from a child all knowledge of earlier myths, but we cannot take from him the need for mythology.
CARL JUNG (1875–1961) *Symbols of Transformation*

13 ... since the purpose of myth is to provide a logical model capable of over-coming a contradiction (an impossible achievement if, as it happens, the contradiction is real), a theoretically infinite number of [versions] will be generated, each slightly different from the others.
CLAUDE LÉVI-STRAUSS *Structural Anthropology*, 1973

N

NATURE AND NURTURE

1 This sudden switch from a belief in Nurture, in the form of social conditioning, to Nature, in the form of genetics and brain physiology, is the great intellectual event ... of the late twentieth century.
TOM WOLFE *Independent on Sunday*, 2 February 1997

2 We no longer need the term [instinct] in psychology.... As a corollary from this we draw the conclusions that there is no such thing as an inheritance of *capacity, talent, temperament, mental constitution* and *characteristics*.
J.B. WATSON *Behaviorism*, 1924

3 Man has no nature, what he has is history.
J. ORTEGA Y GASSET (1883–1955) in R. Klibansky, J.H. Paton *Philosophy and History*, 1936

4 There can be no behavior purely dependent upon innate endowment and none purely dependent upon past training.
E.C. TOLMAN *Purposive Behavior in Man and Animals*, 1932

5 Man proposes, but God disposes.
THOMAS a KEMPIS (c. 1380–1471) *The Imitation of Christ*

6 When you spoke of a nature gifted or not gifted in any respect, did you mean to say that one man will acquire a thing easily, another with difficulty; a little learning will lead the one to discover a great deal; whereas the other, after

much study and application, no sooner learns than he forgets; ... would not these be the sort of differences which distinguish the man gifted by nature from the one who is ungifted?
PLATO (429–347 BC) *The Republic*

7 For we brought nothing into this world and it is certain we carry nothing out.
Bible, Timothy

8 It is a matter of shame and regret that only an amateurish beginning has been made by psychologists in applying modern genetic methods to fundamental study in the nature–nurture area.
C.P. STONE *Psychological Review* 1947

9 ... the effects of experience are conditioned by the genotype.
JERRY HIRSCH *Science*, 1963

10 Environmental determinism remains the frame of reference within which many social scientists and many men of letters still do their feeling and their thinking. Theirs, surely, is an inexcusable one-sidedness: for the science of genetics has been with us for a long lifetime and the unscientific study of innate human differences is as old as literature. At no period and in no place would any dramatist or story teller in his right mind have dreamed of clothing the character, say, of Falstaff, in the physique of Hotspur, the temperament of Mr. Pickwick in the body of Uriah Heep.
ALDOUS HUXLEY (1894–1963) *Literature and Science*

11 If innate only means possible, or even likely in certain environments then everything we do is innate and the word has no meaning.
STEPHEN J. GOULD *The Mismeasure of Man*, 1981

12 Nature is usually wrong.
JAMES McNEILL WHISTLER (1834–1903) *Ten O'Clock*

13 Without a drop of English blood I was born an Englishman.
PETER USTINOV *Quotable Ustinov*, 1995

1 ... nature prevails enormously over nurture when the differences of nurture do not exceed what is commonly to be found among persons of the same rank of society and in the same country.
FRANCIS GALTON (1822–1911) *Enquiries into the Human Faculty and Its Development*

2 A good theory of the environment can only be one in which experience is guided by genotypes that both push and restrain experiences.
SANDRA SCARR, K. McCARTNEY *Child Development*, 1983

3 Can you, Socrates, tell me, is human excellence something teachable? Or, if not teachable, is it something to be acquired by training? Or, if it cannot be acquired by training or by learning, does it accrue to men at birth or in some other way?
PLATO (429–347 BC) *Meno*

4 Men are more like the times they live in than they are like their fathers.
ALI IBN-ABI-TALIB (7th cent.) *Sentences*

5 Predestined by their heredity, human beings are postdestined by their environment. A mildly bad predestination may be offset by a more than averagely good postdestination, but even the best of postdestinations has never as yet shown itself capable of nullifying the effects of a very bad predestination.
ALDOUS HUXLEY (1894–1956) *Literature and Science*

6 Past excesses, oversimplifications, and a history of sociological perversions discourage use of the terms 'innate' and 'learned'.
B.B. BECK *Animal Tool Behavior*, 1980

7 He is a barbarian, and thinks that the customs of his tribe and island are the laws of nature.
GEORGE BERNARD SHAW (1856–1950) *Caesar and Cleopatra*

8 For a particular mental ability, realisation of genetic potential depends upon the presence of certain environmental influences. Beyond some threshold level of favourable environmental influences, however, further increases do not make for appreciable movements in ability. An analogy is the effect of diet on physical stature.
A.R. JENSEN *Harvard Educational Review*, 1969

9 Nature gets credit which should in truth be reserved for ourselves: the rose for its scent, the nightingale for his song; the sun for his radiance.... Nature is a dull affair, soundless, senseless, colourless; merely the hurrying of material, endlessly, meaninglessly.
A.N. WHITEHEAD *Science and the Modern World*, 1926

10 I was a modest, good-humoured boy. It is Oxford that has made me insufferable.
MAX BEERBOHM (1872–1956) *More*

11 Babies imbibe along with the alien milk of the foster mother, morals different from those of their parents
JOHN COMENIUS (1592–1670) *The School of Infancy*

12 Every luxury was lavished on you – atheism, breast-feeding, circumcision.
JOE ORTON (1933–1967) *Loot*

NEEDS

13 When a condition arises for which action on the part of the organism is a prerequisite to optimum probability of survival of either the individual or the species, a state of need is said to exist.
CLARK L. HULL *Principles of Behavior*, 1943

14 O, reason not the need: our basest
    beggars
Are in the poorest things superfluous:
Allow not nature more than nature
    needs,
Man's life as cheap as beast's.
WILLIAM SHAKESPEARE (1564–1616) *King Lear*

15 Mankind shares one universal characteristic: when a need occurs there is activity which seeks to satisfy the need.
JOHN DEWEY (1859–1952) *Lectures in China, 1919-1920*

1 Needs do not really enter in the control of behavior, except in the long run through the mediation of natural selection.
JAMES OLDS *Nebraska Symposium on Motivation*, 1954

2 It is not good to have all one needs.
BLAISE PASCAL (1623–1662) *Pensées*

3 The mosquito knows full well, small
as he is
he's a beast of prey
But after all
he only takes his bellyful,
he doesn't put my blood in the bank.
D.H. LAWRENCE (1885–1930) 'Mosquito'

4 Animals may almost be regarded as aggregates of needs. The function of the effector apparatus is to mediate the satiation of these needs. They arise through progressive changes within the organism or through the injurious impact of the external environment.
CLARK L. HULL *Principles of Behavior*, 1943

5 One need succeeds another.
H A. MURRAY *Explorations in Personality*, 1938

NEGOTIATION

6 Not only must the negotiator avoid displaying irritation when confronted by stupidity, dishonesty, brutality or conceit of those with whom it is his unpleasant duty to negotiate, but he must eschew all personal animosities, all personal predilections, all enthusiasms, prejudices, vanities, exaggerations, dramatizations, and moral indignations.
HAROLD NICOLSON *Diplomacy*, 1969

7 (let's go said he
not too far said she
what's too far said he
where you are said she)
e.e. cummings (1894–1962) 'may I feel said he'

NEUROSIS

8 The artist has also an introverted disposition and has not far to go to become neurotic. He is one who is urged on by instinctive needs that are too clamorous; he longs to attain honour, power, riches, fame, and love of women; but he lacks the means of achieving these gratifications. So, like any other with unsatisfied longing, he turns away from reality, and transfers all his interest, and all his Libido too, onto the creation of his wishes in the life of phantasy, from which the way might readily lead to neurosis.
SIGMUND FREUD (1856–1939) *Introductory Lectures on Psychoanalysis*

9 Absence of psychoneurotic illness may be health, but it is not life.
DONALD WINNICOTT *Playing and Reality*, 1971

10 Doubt is to certainty as neurosis is to psychosis. The neurotic is in doubt and has fears about persons and things; the psychotic has convictions and makes claims about them. In short the neurotic has problems, the psychotic has solutions.
THOMAS SZASZ *The Second Sin*, 1974

11 The life plan of the neurotic demands categorically that if he fails, it should be through someone else's fault and that he should be freed from personal responsibility.
ALFRED ADLER in H.R. Ausbacher, R.R. Ausbacher *The Individual Psychology of Alfred Adler*, 1956

12 I have found love of the mother and jealousy of the father in my own case too, and now believe it to be a general phenomenon of early childhood, even if it does not always occur so early as in children who have been made hysterics.
SIGMUND FREUD, letter to W. Fliess, 15 October 1887, *The Complete Letters of Sigmund Freud to Wilhelm Fliess*, 1985

1 The symptoms of a neurosis are not simply the effects of long past causes, whether 'infantile sexuality' or the infantile urge to power; they are also attempts at a new synthesis of life – unsuccessful attempts, let it be added in the same breath, yet attempts nevertheless, with a core of value and meaning.
CARL JUNG (1875–1961) *Two Essays on Analytical Psychology*

2 A neurosis is a secret you don't know you're keeping.
KENNETH TYNAN (1927–1980) in Kathleen Tynan *Life of Kenneth Tynan*, 1987

3 Neurosis seems to be a human privilege.
SIGMUND FREUD (1856–1939) *Moses and Monotheism*

4 Psychoneurotic disorder in the father or mother provides a complication for the growing child, but psychosis in a parent presents the child with more subtle threats to healthy development.
DONALD WINNICOTT *The Family and Individual Development*, 1965

5 Every neurotic has an inferiority complex and is also low in activity.
ALFRED ADLER in H.R. Ausbacher, R.R. Ausbacher *The Individual Psychology of Alfred Adler*, 1956

6 Everything we think of as great has come to us from neurotics. It is they and they alone who found religions and create great works of art. The world will never realise how much it owes to them and what they have suffered in order to bestow their gifts on it.
MARCEL PROUST (1871–1922) *Remembrance of Things Past*

7 Neurosis operates at the level of articulate, semantically conventional, or only moderately disordered communication. Psychosis transcends grammar.
GEORGE STEINER *Extraterritorial*, 1972

8 The true believer is in a high degree protected against the danger of certain neurotic afflictions; by accepting the universal neurosis he is spared the task of forming a personal neurosis.
SIGMUND FREUD (1856–1939) *The Future of an Illusion*

9 A mistake which is commonly made about neurotics is to suppose that they are interesting. It is not interesting to be always unhappy, engrossed with oneself, malignant and ungrateful, and not quite in touch with reality.
CYRIL CONNOLLY (1903–1974) *The Unquiet Grave*

NOISE

10 Noise is any sound which is treated as a nuisance.
F.C. BARTLETT *The Problem of Noise*, 1934

11 It will be generally admitted that Beethoven's Fifth Symphony is the most sublime noise that has ever penetrated into the ear of man.
E.M. FORSTER (1879–1970) *Howards End*

12 I have been enjoying the rare luxury of the freedom of silence.
ZING-YANG KUO *The Dynamics of Behavior Development*, 1967

13 Of all the animals, Man is the one that has carried noise-making to the highest pitch of development.
A. LLOYD JAMES *Our Spoken Language*, 1938

NORMS

14 The Aristotelian 'mean' signifies equilibrium in the exercise of one's own passions, the passions balanced by the discriminating virtue of prudence. But one who harbors passions to an average degree and possesses an average prudence is a poor sample of humanity.
UMBERTO ECO *Misreadings*, 1961

1 ... the intensive study of the average behavior of a species ... generally leads the ... psychologist to ignore the more interesting differences between individuals from whom 'the average individual' is abstracted. The average individual is, in fact, a man-made fiction.
R.C. TRYON in F.A. Moss *Comparative Psychology*, 1934

2 It is not informative to study variations of behaviour unless we know beforehand the norm from which the variants depart.
PETER MEDAWAR *The Art of the Soluble*, 1967

3 The circumference of an average English head is twenty-two inches.
E. STACKPOOL O'DELL *Phrenology: Its Truthfulness and Usefulness*, 1892

4 Every normal person, in fact, is only normal on the average.
SIGMUND FREUD (1856–1939) cit. J. Sandler *On Freud's Analysis Terminable and Interminable*, 1987

NOSTALGIA

5 People were poorer, and had not the comforts, amusements or knowledge we have today, but they were happier.
FLORA THOMPSON (1876–1947) *Lark Rise to Candleford*

6 They spend their time mostly looking forward to the past.
JOHN OSBORNE (1929–1994) *Look Back in Anger*

7 Almost all pathos includes a reference to the lapse of time.
A.N. WHITEHEAD (1861–1947) *Symbolism*

8 That is the land of lost content
I see it shining plain,
The happy highways where I went
And cannot come again.
A.E. HOUSEMAN (1859–1936) *A Shropshire Lad*

9 Do we want to return to the womb?
    Not at all.
No one really desires the impossible.
W.H. AUDEN (1907–1973) 'Shorts'

OBEDIENCE

10 Obedience is the psychological mechanism that links individual action to political purpose. It is the dispositional cement that binds men to systems of authority.
STANLEY MILGRAM *Obedience to Authority*, 1974

11 All the good of which humanity is capable is comprised in obedience.
JOHN STUART MILL (1806–1873) *On Liberty*

12 He that most courteously commandeth, to him men most obey.
GEOFFREY CHAUCER (1340–1400) *The Tale of Melibus*

13 I am forever astonished that when lecturing on the obedience experiments in colleges across the country, I faced young men who were aghast at the behavior of the experimental subjects and proclaimed that they would never behave in such a way, but who, in a matter of months, were brought into the military and performed without compunction actions that made shocking the victim seem pallid.
STANLEY MILGRAM *Obedience to Authority*, 1974

OBJECTIVITY/ SUBJECTIVITY

1 Even in our nation's most advanced centres for psychological assessment, the measurement of intelligence (or personality, memory, or other psychological functions) is not, even today, a totally objective, completely science based activity. Rather than being totally objective, assessment involves a subjective component.
J.D. MATARAZZO *American Psychologist*, 1990

2 There is every reason to believe that the relative backwardness of the behavioral sciences is due not so much to their inherent complexity as to the difficulty of maintaining a consistent and vigorous objectivism.
CLARK L. HULL *Principles of Behavior*, 1943

3 We are part of history ourselves, and we cannot avoid the consequences of being unable to think impartially.
J.B.S. HALDANE *Heredity and Politics*, 1938

4 After all, the ultimate goal of all research is not objectivity but truth.
HELENE DEUTSCH *The Psychology of Women*, 1944

5 Only objective knowledge is criticizable; subjective knowledge becomes criticizable only when it becomes objective. And it becomes objective when we *say* what we think; and even more so when we *write* it, or *print* it.
KARL POPPER *Objective Knowledge* 1972

6 If a man become a judge of these grave questions ... he will commit a sin more grievous than most breaches of the Decalogue, unless he avoid a lazy reliance on the information that is gathered by prejudice and filtered through passion, unless he go back to the prime sources of knowledge – the facts of Nature.
T.H. HUXLEY (1825–1895) *Methods and Results*

7 Always, century by century, item after item is transferred from the object's side of the account to the subject's. And now in some extreme form of Behaviourism, the subject himself is discounted as merely subjective; we only think that we think.
C.S. LEWIS (1898–1963) *The Discarded Image*

8 The peculiarity of subjective states is that they can be perceived only by the one person directly experiencing them – the subject.
H.S. JENNINGS *Behavior of Lower Organisms*, 1906

9 To observations which ourselves we make,
We grow more partial for th'observer's sake.
ALEXANDER POPE (1688–1744) 'Moral Essays'

10 The fact that the myths of subjectivism and objectivism have stood for so long in Western culture indicates that each serves some important function.
G. LAKOFF, M. JOHNSON *Metaphors We Live By*, 1980

OBSERVATION

11 Aristotle maintained that women have fewer teeth than men; although he was twice married, it never occurred to him to verify this statement by examining his wives' mouths.
BERTRAND RUSSELL (1872–1970) *The Impact of Science on Society*

12 You see, but you do not observe.
ARTHUR CONAN DOYLE (1859–1930) *The Adventures of Sherlock Holmes*

13 Scientific observation is never performed just by looking.
ROM HARRÉ in J. Miller *States of Mind*, 1983

14 In high tragedy as in low journalism there is no room for the dispassionate observations, the marshalled data and logical thinking of science.
ALDOUS HUXLEY (1894–1963) *Literature and Science*

1 To see what is in front of one's nose needs a constant struggle.
GEORGE ORWELL (1903–1950) *Collected Essays*

2 All my experience is that observation in real-life situations may be mistaken and, if you impose some explanation on it, your first theoretical guess is almost always wrong or it's wrong fifty per cent of the time.
D.E. BROADBENT cit. D. Cohen *Psychologists on Psychology*, 1977

3 To observe is to alter; to define and to understand, even in the most neutral, abstract fashion, is to incorporate the evidence within a particular matrix of human choices, images, and symbolic reflexes.
GEORGE STEINER *Extraterritorial*, 1972

4 I am a camera with its shutter open, quite passive, recording, not thinking.
CHRISTOPHER ISHERWOOD (1904–1986) *Goodbye to Berlin*

5 Perhaps I should have learned nothing from the first chance opportunity of seeing two ants mating, if I had been less familiar with the ways of these small insects.
R.A.F. de REAMUR (1683–1757) *Histoires des Fourmis*

6 For whether in the laboratory or outside of it nothing is ever observed except in a setting of past experience and present interests.
F.C. BARTLETT *The Mind at Work and Play*, 1951

OBSESSION

7 Obsessions are the result of slow accumulating growth, seeded early in life when the mind is at its most receptive.
GEORGE LASSALLE *The Fish in my Life*, 1989

8 My problem is that I have been persecuted by an integer [the magic number 7]. For seven years this number has followed me around, has intruded in my most private data, and has assaulted me from the pages of our most public journals.
GEORGE MILLER *Psychological Review*, 1956

9 As I was going up the stair
I met a man who wasn't there
He wasn't there again today
I wish that man would go away.
ANON.

10 From a very early age, perhaps between the age of five or six, I knew that when I grew up I should be a writer. Between the ages of about seventeen and twenty-four I tried to abandon this idea, but I did so without the consciousness that I was outraging my true nature and that sooner or later I should have to settle down and write books.
GEORGE ORWELL (1903–1950) *Why I Write*

OCCUPATION

11 Overemphasis on activity as an end instead of upon *intelligent* activity, leads to identification of freedom with immediate execution of impulses and desires.
JOHN DEWEY (1859–1952) *Experience and Education*

12 Her small tubby person exuded energy and indignation…. Denied the need to work by her husband's income, she pursued occupation.
PENELOPE LIVELY *The Road to Lichfield*, 1977

13 Everyone has time if he likes. Business runs after nobody: people cling to it of their own free will and think that to be busy is a proof of happiness.
SENECA (4 BC–65 AD) *Moral Epistles to Lucilius*

OLD AGE

1 When old age is evil, youth can learn no good.
PROVERB

2 Growing old is no more than a bad habit which a busy man has no time to form.
ANDRÉ MAUROIS (1885–1967) *The Art of Living*

3 I must reluctantly observe that two causes, the abbreviation of time, and the failure of hope, will always tinge with a browner shade, the evening of life.
EDWARD GIBBON (1737–1796) *The Autobiography*

4 Only the old are innocent.... Original sin is the property of the young. The old grow beyond corruption very quickly.
MALCOLM BRADBURY *Stepping Westward*, 1965

5 No one is so old as to think he cannot live one more year.
CICERO (106–43 BC) *De Senectute*

6 Old people are more interesting than young. One of the particular points of interest is to observe how after fifty they revert to the habits, mannerisms and opinions of their parents, however wild they were in youth.
EVELYN WAUGH (1903–1966) letter to Nancy Mitford, 29 October 1963, M. Amory ed. *The Letters of Evelyn Waugh*, 1980

7 It is important to realise that the fact that old people become slow and suffer from memory failures does not mean that they are contentedly insensitive to their mistakes.
PATRICK RABBITT *New Scientist*, 1981

8 Last scene of all,
That ends this strange eventful history,
Is second childishness, and mere oblivion,
Sans teeth, sans eyes, sans taste, sans everything.
WILLIAM SHAKESPEARE (1564–1616) *As You Like It*

9 I grow old ... I grow old ...
I shall wear the bottom of my trousers rolled.
T.S. ELIOT (1888–1965) 'The Love Song of J. Alfred Prufrock'

10 Older people have absorbed these attitudes which they once held as young people, and lead their lives in ways which confirm the stereotyped images, and perpetuate the myths of ageism from generation to generation.
S. SCRUTTON in D. McEwan *Age, The Unrecognised Discrimination*, 1990

11 Few people know how to be old.
DUC FRANÇOIS DE LA ROCHEFOUCAULD (1613–1680) *Maxims*

12 Seventy years have I lived,
Seventy years man and boy,
And never have I danced for joy.
W.B. YEATS (1865–1939) 'Imitated from the Japanese'

13 Old age, though despised, is coveted by all men.
PROVERB

14 The tragedy of old age is not that one is old, but that one is young.
OSCAR WILDE (1854–1900) *The Picture of Dorian Gray*

15 Let me disclose to you the gifts reserved for age
To set a crown upon your lifetime's effort.
First, the cold friction of expiring sense
Without enchantment, offering no promise
But bitter tastelessness of shadow fruit
As body and soul begin to fall asunder.
T.S. ELIOT (1888–1965) 'Little Gidding'

16 Old age begins at forty-six years according to the common opinion.
CICERO (106–53 BC) *De Senectute*

17 Old age has the last word: the purely naturalistic look at life, however enthusiastically it may begin, is sure to end in sadness.
WILLIAM JAMES *Varieties of Religious Experience*, 1902

1   Certainly old age has a great sense of calm and freedom; when the passions relax their hold, then, as Sophocles says, you have escaped from the control not of one master, but of many.
PLATO (429–347 BC) *The Republic*

2   When does it happen? When did I turn into this? The sagging cistern lagged with an overcoat of flesh that gets thicker and thicker every year. The skin sags, the veins break down, more and more galleries are sealed off. And you never notice. There is no pain. No warning shots. No bells ring back at base to indicate that another section of the front line has collapsed.
ALAN BENNETT *Getting On*, 1971

3   The best way to attain old age is to have old parents.
J.Z. YOUNG *An Introduction to the Study of Man*, 1970

4   How horrid it was being young, and how nice it is being old and not have to mind what people think.
GWEN RAVERAT (1885–1957) *Period Piece*

5   Every man desires to live long; but no man would be old.
JONATHAN SWIFT (1667–1745) *Thoughts on Various Subjects*

6   As I grow older and older,
And totter towards the tomb,
I find that I care less and less.
Who goes to bed with whom.
DOROTHY L. SAYERS (1893–1957) *That's Why I Never Read Modern Novels*

7   Old age lacks the heavy banquet, the loaded table and the oft-filled cup; therefore it also lacks drunkenness, indigestion and lack of sleep.
CICERO (106–53 BC) *De Senectute*

8   Old age is the most unexpected of all the things that happen to a man.
LEON TROTSKY (1874–1940) *Diary in Exile*

9   Some old people on reaching a certain age go on living out of habit – a bad habit too.
W.N.P. BARBELLION *The Journal of a Disappointed Man*, 1919

10   Old age plants more crumbles in the mind than in the face.
MICHEL DE MONTAIGNE (1533–1592) *Essays*

11   What is the worst of woes that wait on age?
What stamps the wrinkle deeper on the brow?
To view each loved one blotted from life's page,
And be alone on earth, as I am now.
LORD BYRON (1788–1824) 'Childe Harold'

12   An aged man is but a paltry thing,
A tattered coat upon a stick.
W.B. YEATS (1865–1939) 'Sailing to Byzantium'

13   Perhaps being old is having lighted rooms
Inside your head, and people in them, acting.
People you know, yet can't quite name.
PHILIP LARKIN (1922–1985) 'The Old Fools'

14   Old men like to give good advice in order to console themselves for no longer being able to set bad examples.
DUC FRANÇOIS DE LA ROCHEFOUCAULD (1613–1680) *Maxims*

15   People expect old men to die,
They do not really mourn old men
Old men are different. People look
At them with eyes that wonder when...
People watch with unshocked eyes;
But the old men know when an old man dies.
OGDEN NASH (1902–1971) *Collected Verse*, 1929

16   It's a joy to be old
Kids through school,
The dog dead and the car sold.
ROGER McGOUGH 'A Joy to be Old', 1986

17   Much did I rage when young,
Being by the world oppressed.
But now with flattering tongue,
It speeds the parting guest.
W.B. YEATS (1865–1939) 'Sailing to Byzantium'

18   There are no old men any more. *Playboy* and *Penthouse* have between them made an ideal of eternal adolescence, sunburnt and saunaed, with the grey drained out of it.
PETER USTINOV *Dear Me*, 1977

OPTIMISM

1 ... optimism helps us to succeed in social competition, where bluffing is the routine, and also keeps us pursuing important strategies and relationships even at times when they are not paying off.
R.M. NESSE, G.C. WILLIAMS *Evolution and Healing*, 1995

2 If the children and youth of a nation are afforded opportunity to develop their capacities to the fullest, if they are given the knowledge to understand the world and the wisdom to change it, then the prospects for the future are bright.
URIE BRONFENBRENNER *Two Worlds of Childhood*, 1970

3 ... but all shall be well and all shall be well and all manner of thing shall be well.
JULIAN OF NORWICH (c. 1343–1416) *Revelations of Divine Love*

4 Change itself does not necessarily produce ideologies of optimism and pessimism. It is possible to view change with a sense of optimism: history is leading progressively towards betterment. On the other hand, change can produce bewilderment: the past is disappearing and the familiar social landmarks of one generation are being rejected by the next.
MICHAEL BILLIG *Talking of the Royal Family*, 1992

5 The optimist proclaims that we live in the best of all possible worlds; and the pessimist fears that this is true.
JAMES B. CABELL *The Silver Stallion*, 1926

6 In the best of possible worlds ... all is for the best.
VOLTAIRE (1697–1778) *Candide*

7 an optimist is a guy
that has never had
much experience
don marquis (1878–1937) 'certain maxims of archy'

8 The place where optimism most flourishes is in the lunatic asylum.
HAVELOCK ELLIS (1859–1939) *The Dance of Life*

9 What human beings have that machines do not have is superb optimism.
JACOB BRONOWSKI *The Origins of Knowledge and Imagination*, 1978

ORIGINALITY

10 A society made up of individuals who were all capable of original thought would probably be unendurable. The pressure of ideas would simply drive it frantic.
H.L. MENCKEN (1880–1956) *Minority Report: Notebooks*

11 There are no new truths, but only truths that have not been recognized by those who have perceived them without noticing.
MARY McCARTHY (1912–1989) *On the Contrary*

12 Original thoughts can be understood only in virtue of the unoriginal elements they contain.
STANISLAV ANDRESKI *Social Sciences as Sorcery*, 1972

P

PAIN

1 ... the power of pain (as in torture) is that it obliterates our connection with the personal-cultural world and wipes out the meaningful context that gives direction to our hopes and strivings.
J.S. BRUNER *Acts of Meaning*, 1990

2 Pain hardens and great pain hardens greatly, whatever the comforters say, and suffering does not ennoble.
A.S. BYATT *The Virgin in the Garden*, 1978

3 It is by poultices, not by words, that pain is ended, although pain is by words both eased and diminished.
PETRARCH (1304–1374) *Letter to Guido Sette*, 1359

4 Nothing begins, and nothing ends,
That is not paid with moan;
For we are born in other's pain
And perish in our own.
FRANCIS THOMPSON (1859–1907) 'Daisy'

5 When two pains occur together, but not in the same place, the more violent obscures the other.
HIPPOCRATES (c. 460–377 BC) *Aphorisms*

6 It is almost a definition of a gentleman to say that he is one who never inflicts pain.
JOHN HENRY (CARDINAL) NEWMAN (1801–1890) *The Idea of a University*

7 There was a faith healer of Deal
Who said, 'Although pain isn't real
If I sit on a pin
And it punctures my skin
I dislike what I fancy I feel'.
ANON.

8 Beyond a certain pitch of suffering, men are overcome by a kind of ghastly indifference.
VICTOR HUGO (1802–1885) *Les Misérables*

9 Pain is the necessary contrast to pleasure; it ushers us into existence or consciousness; it alone is capable of exciting the organs into activity; it is the compassion and the guardian of human life.
CHARLES BELL (1774–1842) *The Hand, Its Mechanisms and Vital Endowments as Evincing Design*

PARAPSYCHOLOGY

10 It has been said and with justice that the greatest disappointment for an advocate of telepathy would be to have it explained.
K.S. LASHLEY, letter to R.E. McConnell, 3 October 1951 cit. G.A. Kimble *et al. Portraits of Pioneers in Psychology*, 1991

11 Napier's world abounded with natural and supernatural perils that struck down men and women invisibly and indiscriminately, and nothing was more obscure than the etiology of mental disorders. The magical and scientific beliefs of his age complemented one another ... witchcraft beliefs assuaged the anxieties of unfortunate people by enabling them to relieve their guilt and punish their enemies; scientific theories enabled physicians and magistrates to discredit the baseless accusations of malicious hysterics.
MICHAEL MACDONALD *Mystical Bedlam*, 1981

12 The phenomena are there, lying broadcast over the surface of history. No matter where you open its pages, you will find things recorded under the name of divinations, inspirations, demoniacal possessions, apparitions, trances, ecstasies, miraculous healings and production of disease, and occult powers possessed by peculiar individuals over persons and things in their neighbourhood.
WILLIAM JAMES *The Will to Believe*, 1897

1 The strangeness of paranormal events ... derives from the fact that they present an implicit challenge to scientific declarations about the world and, moreover, undermine common-sense knowledge of what sorts of things are possible.
R. WOOFITT *Telling Tales of the Unexpected*, 1992

2 Many scientists do not accept the reality of these [paranormal] phenomena – because of an *a priori* rejection of the possibility of psi phenomena.... The psychology of human scientists is such that committed to a generally successful and wide-ranging theory of how things work narrows their perception so data that do not fit into the paradigmatic view are overlooked or considered inherently invalid.
C.T. TART in R.E. Ornstein *The Nature of Human Consciousness*, 1973

3 The work of some psychologists on extrasensory perception and pre-cognition may be a present-day example of a discovery before its time. Most scientists have difficulty in accepting the conclusions of these workers despite apparently irrefutable evidence, because the conclusions cannot be reconciled with present knowledge of the physical world.
W.B. BEVERIDGE *The Art of Scientific Investigation*, 1957

4 The question of whether or not the operation of psi shows any relation to known physical law is not a matter of interpretation. It has been brought into experimental focus and is now only a question of the facts themselves.
J.B. RHINE, G. PRATT *Parapsychology: Frontier Study of the Mind*, 1962

5 Psychical research, whether one calls it 'parapsychology', 'Psi', 'the study of the paranormal', or 'ESP research', is far more than it appears to be on first glance. In the most profound sense, it is the study of the basic nature of man.
LAWRENCE LeSHAN *Toward a General Theory of the Paranormal*, 1973

6 It is probably true that most scientists do not find the evidence for parapsychological phenomena very convincing. In spite of human variety there are close similarities between many of us. The reporting of common experiences, especially between relatives, is not really strange or unexpected. People are easily influenced to think alike, even when they are far apart.
J.Z. YOUNG *An Introduction to the Study of Man*, 1970

7 We're dealing with testable [ESP and psychic] claims. We choose what we hope is an interesting issue, but we try to do proper science with it. It all comes down to stats in the end.
RICHARD WISEMAN cit. O. Burkeman *The Guardian Higher Education*, 12 May 1998

8 Meanwhile, can we, or need we, measure psychic being? Many students have felt that its most realistic index lies in the sensitivity of the individual, his awareness of the forces surrounding him. They feel that the secret of 'intuition' lies in the ability to perceive that which is too fine for the average perception.
IDA ROLF *Systematics*, 1963

PARENTS AND CHILDREN

9 To be a good parent you have to believe in the species – somehow.
BENJAMIN SPOCK cit. E. Erikson *Group Processes*, 1956

10 Parentage is a very important profession, but no test of fitness for it is ever imposed in the interest of the children.
GEORGE BERNARD SHAW (1856–1950) *Everybody's Political What's What?*

11 Parents, especially mothers, are much-maligned people.
JOHN BOWLBY *A Secure Base: Clinical Applications of Attachment Theory*, 1988

1 ... many behaviour patterns which are regarded as typically sexual, such as kissing and caressing, are in origin actually actions of parental care.
I. EIBL-EIBESFELDT *Love and Hate*, 1971

2 In considering the difficulties of parents, it is always valuable to remind ourselves that parents are not necessarily fully mature just because they have achieved marriage and the establishment of a family.
DONALD WINNICOTT *The Family and Individual Development*, 1965

3 Individual differences exist in the sensitivity of parents to the needs of their offspring, but the evidence indicates that parental 'folk wisdom' results in more than social management by trial and error – the species survives.
W.W. HARTUP *American Psychologist*, 1979

4 Oh, what a tangled web do parents weave
When they think their children are naive.
OGDEN NASH (1902–1971) 'Baby, What Makes the Sky Blue'

5 They fuck you up, your mum and dad
They may not mean to, but they do.
They fill you with the faults they had
And add some extra, just for you.
PHILIP LARKIN (1922–1985) 'This Be the Verse'

6 The joys of parents are secret, and so are their griefs and fears.
FRANCIS BACON (1561–1626) *Essays*

7 Parents – especially step parents – are sometimes a bit of a disappointment to their children. They don't fufill the promise of their early years.
ANTHONY POWELL *A Buyer's Market*, 1952

8 Children always assume the sexual lives of their parents come to a grinding halt at their conception.
ALAN BENNETT *Getting On*, 1972

9 The art of being a parent consists in sleeping when the baby isn't looking.
PROVERB

10 The value of marriage is not that adults produce children but that children produce adults.
PETER de VRIES *The Tunnel of Love*, 1954

11 Most parents have some basic philosophy of child-rearing, and most hold certain principles and values which they consider important and which they hope to implant in their children; but it is also clear that their actual handling of practical day-to-day issues is often tempered by expediency and the necessity of coping somehow in an environment or situation not chosen by themselves.
J. NEWSOME, E. NEWSOME *Four Year Olds in an Urban Community*, 1968

12 One of the most obvious facts about grown-ups to a child, is that they have forgotten what it is like to be a child.
RANDALL JARRELL (1914–1965) cit. C. Stead *The Man Who Loved Children*, 1965

13 Parents must not only have certain ways of guiding by prohibition and permission; they must also be able to represent to the child a deep, and almost somatic conviction that there is a meaning to what they are doing.
ERIK ERIKSON *Childhood and Society*, 1950

14 Children unavoidably treat their parents as though they were experts on life.
ADAM PHILLIPS *Terrors and Experts*, 1995

15 Children need more of their parents than to be loved; they need something that carries over when they are hated and even hateful.
DONALD WINNICOTT *The Family and Individual Development*, 1965

16 One can love a child, perhaps, more deeply than one can love another adult, but it is rash to assume that the child feels any love in return.
GEORGE ORWELL (1903–1950) *Such, Such Were the Joys*

17 Children aren't happy with nothing to ignore,
And that's what parents were created for.
OGDEN NASH (1902–1971) 'The Parent'

1 Our virtues and vices couple with one another, and get children that resemble both their parents.
GEORGE SAVILE, MARQUESS OF HALIFAX (1633–1695) *Moral Thoughts and Reflections*

2 Parents learn a lot from their children about coping with life.
MURIEL SPARK *The Comforters*, 1957

3 The predominant effect of parent behavior upon the preschool child is to raise or lower his willingness and ability to behave actively towards his environment.
ALFRED BALDWIN *Child Development*, 1948

4 Children begin by loving their parents; after a time they judge them: rarely, if ever, do they forgive them.
OSCAR WILDE (1854–1900) *A Woman of No Importance*

5 It is a terrible thing, and yet it is true, that sometimes there is no hope for the children till the parents have died.
DONALD WINNICOTT *The Family and Individual Development*, 1965

6 Genetic and cultural factors are intertwined also in the parent–child relationships. Although this matter has been quite insufficiently studied from the point of view of genetics, it is highly probable that the focussing of the emotional attachments of the mother on her child or children is rooted in the genes.
Th. DOBZHANSKY *The Biology of Ultimate Concern*, 1969

PASSION

7 A man who has not passed through the inferno of his passions has never overcome them.
CARL JUNG (1875–1961) *Memories, Dreams and Reflections*

8 The ruling passion, be it what it will, The ruling passion conquers reason still.
ALEXANDER POPE (1688–1744) 'To a Lady'

9 Passions destroy more prejudices than philosophy does.
DENIS DIDEROT (1713–1784) *Discourses*

10 Death is the only pure, beautiful conclusion of a great passion.
D.H. LAWRENCE (1885–1930) *Fantasia of the Unconscious*

11 All passions that allow themselves to be savoured and digested are only mediocre.
MICHEL DE MONTAIGNE (1533–1592) *Essays*

12 There is a passion for hunting something deeply implanted in the human breast.
CHARLES DICKENS (1812–1870) *Oliver Twist*

13 To hide a passion is inconceivable: not because the human subject is too weak, but because passion is in its essence made to be seen.
ROLAND BARTHES (1915–1980) *A Lover's Discourse*

14 Expression is to passion what language is to thought.
CHARLES BELL (1774–1842) *Essays on the Anatomy and Philosophy of Expression*

PATIENCE

15 Beware the fury of a patient man.
JOHN DRYDEN (1631–1700) *Absalom and Achitophel*

16 Patience, the beggar's virtue.
PHILIP MASSINGER (1583–1640) *A New Way to Pay Old Debts*

17 Patience, n. A minor form of despair disguised as a virtue.
AMBROSE BIERCE (1842–1914) *Devil's Dictionary*

PERCEPTION

1 ... perception is a functional affair based on action, experience, and probability. The thing perceived is an inseparable part of the function of perceiving, which in turn includes all aspects of the total process of living.
W.H. ITTLESON, F.P. KILPATRICK *Scientific American*, 1951

2 Many of the properties of the world as we perceive it are due to our own behaviour.
MICHAEL MORGAN *Molyneux's Question*, 1977

3 ... it is interesting to think about which representations the different artists concentrate on and sometimes disrupt. The pointillists, for example, are tampering primarily with the image; the rest of the scheme is left intact, and the picture has a conventional appearance otherwise. Picasso, on the other hand, clearly disrupts most at the 3-D model level. The three-dimensions in his figures are not realistic. An example of someone who operates primarily at the surface representation stage is a little harder – Cezanne perhaps?
DAVID MARR *Vision*, 1982

4 We perceive so that we may act.
P.H. WIEGERSMA, A. VAN DER VELDE *Journal of Child Psychology and Psychiatry* , 1983

5 Not that there is any natural or necessary connection between the sensation we perceive by the turn of the eyes and greater or lesser distance. But ... there has grown a habitual or customary connection between these two sorts of ideas so that the mind no sooner perceives the sensation ... but it withal perceives the different idea of distance.
BISHOP GEORGE BERKELEY (1685–1753) *An Essay Towards a New Theory of Vision*

6 ... the average human infant discriminates depth as soon as it can crawl. By the time that locomotion is adequate, which is the time when depth discrimination is necessary for survival, the infant can discriminate depth.
R.D. WALK, E.J. GIBSON *Psychological Monographs*, 1961

7 The primary imagination I hold to be the living Power and Prime Agent of all human Perception.
SAMUEL TAYLOR COLERIDGE (1772–1834) *Boigraphia Literaria*

8 The more he looked inside the more Piglet wasn't there.
A.A. MILNE (1882–1956) *The House at Pooh Corner*

9 [The] perception of an object does not depend on a series of ... perceptions of its forms or perspectives, but depends on the invariant features of the forms or perspectives over time. Object-perception does not depend on form-perception but on invariant-detection. And these invariants are 'formless', that is to say, they are not themselves forms.
J.J. GIBSON *Leonardo*, 1973

10 How can we know the dancer from the dance?
W.B. YEATS (1865–1939) 'Among School Children'

11 The perception of Form is entirely a matter of experience. We *see* nothing but flat colours; and it is only by a series of experiments that we find out that a stain of black or grey indicates the dark side of a solid substance, or that a feint line indicates that the object in which it appears is far away.
JOHN RUSKIN (1819–1900) *The Elements of Drawing*

12 For it is a certain maxim, no man sees what things are, that knows not what they ought to be.
JONATHEN RICHARDSON *The Works of Jonathen Richardson*, 1792

13 [The bad habits of painters] even affect their organs, so that their eyes see the objects of nature coloured as they are used to painting them.
ROGER DE PILES *Dialogue sur le coloris*, 1673

1 The art of seeing nature is a thing almost as much to be acquired as the art of reading the Egyptian hieroglyphs.
JOHN CONSTABLE (1776–1837) cit. C. Leslie *Memoires of the Life of John Constable*, 1843

2 Eyes are of no use without light, and visual perception inevitably involves geometry
M. BERRY in R.L. Gregory *et al. The Artful Eye*, 1995

3 Science is nothing but perception.
PLATO (429–347 BC) *Theoctetus*

4 If the doors of perception were closed everything would appear to man as it is, infinite.
For man has closed himself up, till he sees all things thro' narrow chinks of his cavern.
WILLIAM BLAKE (1757–1827) 'The Marriage of Heaven and Hell'

5 Why does the eye see a thing more clearly in dreams than the imagination when awake?
LEONARDO DA VINCI (1452–1519) *Notebooks of Leonardo Da Vinci*

6 I now assume that perception does not depend on sensory impressions at all, but instead on the pickup of stimulus information.
J.J. GIBSON in *A History of Psychology in Autobiography, Vol. 5*, 1967

PERSONALITY

7 Personality is the more or less stable and enduring organization of a person's character, temperament, intellect, and physique, which determines his unique adjustment to the environment.
HANS EYSENCK *The Structure of Human Personality*, 1953

8 I think that most people believe that their true personalities, as they construe them, are immediately apparent to others. They seem to feel that there is no need to make an effort to appear the way they think they really are. However, when it is really important to them that another person should be aware of their virtuous personality traits, they may not take any chances [but use] regulation that strengthens the link between personality and expressiveness.
BELLA de PAULO in K.H. Craik *et al. Fifty Years of Personality Psychology*, 1993

9 ... the ways in which [the clinician's] personality may affect his practice ... undoubtedly represents one of the major uncontrolled sources of variation in psychological interpretation, and an extremely subtle one as well.
L.H. LEVY *Psychological Interpretation*, 1963

10 Why is it that in our times, when Western culture is sadly disorganized, our personalities are not correspondingly disorganized?
G.W. ALLPORT *Personality: A Psychological Perspective*, 1937

11 The two goals of personality psychology, to understand both dispositions and dynamics, have long had separate histories driven by different conceptions and commitments, more in competition than in the service of building a cumulative coherent science of personality.
W. MISCHEL, Y. SHODA *Annual Review of Psychology*, 1998

12 ... the general set of the tide runs inexorably round the room [at cocktail parties]. People who matter, people who are literally 'in the swim', keep to the channel where the tide runs strongly.... Those who appear to be glued to the walls, usually deep in conversation with people they meet every week, are nobodies. Those who jam themselves into the corners of the room are the timid and feeble. Those who drift to the centre are the eccentric and merely silly.
C. NORTHCOTE PARKINSON *Parkinson's Law*, 1958

13 The phrase 'nature and nurture' is a convenient jingle of words, for it separates under two distinct heads the innumerable elements of which personality is composed.
FRANCIS GALTON (1822–1911) *The Human Faculty*

1 'I, me' ... are terms enormously complex. This is the idea of personality; that is to say, the reunion of presentations, the remembrance of all past impressions, the imagination of future phenomena.
P. JANET (1859–1947) *The Mental State of Hystericals*

2 ... the history of the organism *is* the organism....
H A. MURRAY *Explorations in Personality*, 1938

3 I am asking you to consider a rather simple, naive and disturbing hypothesis, a conception which points not to the solitary grandeur and rugged independence of personality, as we like to conceive it, but to personality as a node or region of relative concentration in a field of vast and complex inter-penetrating forces, in which none of us is completely individualized anymore than he is completely washed out in a sink of impersonality.
GARDNER MURPHY *Historical Introduction to Modern Psychology*, 1949

4 No brain, no personality.
H A. MURRAY *Dialectica*, 1951

5 I divide the world into two classes: those who divide the world into two classes and those who do not.
ANON.

6 The terrorist and the policeman both come from the same basket.
JOSEPH CONRAD (1857–1924) *The Secret Agent*

7 Our culture, increasingly based on the conquest of nature and the control of man, is in decline. Emerging through the ruins is the new person, highly aware, self-directing, an explorer of inner, perhaps more than outer space, scornful of the conformity of institutions and the dogma of authority.
CARL ROGERS *American Psychologist*, 1974

8 Personality is social, but it is more. It is a drop of the cosmos, and its surface tensions bespeak only a fragile and indefinite barrier that marks a region of relative structuring, relative independence. This structuring and independence can exist only because they are relative, that is, because of the confluence of the self and the nonself.
GARDNER MURPHY *Personality*, 1947

9 The man who orders his life in terms of many special and inflexible convictions about temporary matters makes himself the victim of circumstances. Each little prior conviction that is not open to review is a hostage he gives to fortune: it determines whether the events of tomorrow will bring happiness or misery.
G.A. KELLY *The Psychology of Personal Constructs*, 1955

10 Personality study is an integral part of experimental psychology, simply because the subject of an experiment is a person. This ineluctable truth is finally dawning on many experimentalists.
HANS EYSENCK *The Structure of Human Personality*, 1953

11 All charming people have something to conceal, usually their total dependence on the appreciation of others.
CYRIL CONNOLLY (1903–1974) *Enemies of Promise*

12 I have never understood why Personality should place such heavy emphases on theories originating in the study of atypical groups. The study of pathology frequently provides illuminating information, but it seems to me more sensible to regard pathology as a deviation from general patterns on the basis of the exceptional.
G.A. MENDELSOHN in K.H. Craik *et al. Fifty Years of Personality Psychology*, 1993

13 A man's personality reflects others' image and recognition of him.
KIMBALL YOUNG *Social Psychology*, 1945

14 Crude conceptions apart, Personality, like Intelligence, is a term which probably causes much less trouble to the informed – or even the uninformed – layman than to the psychologist.
BORIS SEMENOFF *Personality Assessment*, 1966

1 A personality is a full congress of orators and pressure-groups, of children, demagogues, communists, isolationists, war-mongers, mugwumps, grafters, leg-rollers, lobbyists, Caesars and Christs, Machiavels and Judases, Tories and Promethean revolutionists.
H.A. MURRAY *Journal of Abnormal and Social Psychology*, 1940

2 The most positive men are the most credulous.
ALEXANDER POPE (1688–1744) 'Thoughts on Various Subjects'

3 My ambition was to give a psychological definition of the field of personality as I saw it.... I wanted to fashion an experimental science, so far as appropriate, but chiefly I wanted an 'image of man' that would allow us to test in full whatever democratic and human potentialities he might possess.
G.W. ALLPORT in *A History of Psychology in Autobiography, Vol . 5*, 1967

4 ... personality is actualized not only through [man] being drawn to other men but through his being drawn, as an artist, to patterns of colour and tone or, as scientist, to schemata in time and space.
GARDNER MURPHY *Personality*, 1947

5 Man's main task in life is to give *birth* to himself, to become what he potentially is. The most important product of his effort is his own personality.
ERICH FROMM *Man for Himself*, 1947

6 Personality is an unbroken series of successful gestures.
F. SCOTT FITZGERALD (1896–1940) *The Great Gatsby*

7 Personality psychology would seem to be paying an exorbitant price in potential knowledge for the security afforded by preserving norms of con-venience and methodological orthodoxy. Must these important unanswered questions be left to literature and psychiatry.
R. CARLSON *Psychological Bulletin*, 1971

8 ... what the psychologist has to study are the interactions between a 'personality' and an environment – the behaviour of a dynamic mind in a dynamic field of which it forms a part.
CYRIL BURT *British Journal of Educational Psychology*, 1945

9 Personality is the original personal property.
N.O. BROWN *Love's Body*, 1967

10 ... I must also observe that the classification of types according to extraversion and introversion is by no means to be regarded as the only possible method. Any other psychological criterion could equally well be employed, although, in my view, no other possesses so great a practical significance.
CARL JUNG (1875–1961) *Contributions to Analytical Psychology*

11 There are only two kinds of men: the righteous who think they are sinners and the sinners who think they are righteous.
BLAISE PASCAL (1623–1662) *Pensées*

12 Sow a thought and you may reap an act; sow an act and you reap a habit; sow a habit and you reap a personality, sow a personality and you reap a destiny.
BUDDIST PROVERB

13 A sensitive person is one who, because he has corns himself, always treads on other people's toes.
OSCAR WILDE (1854–1900) *The Remarkable Rocket*

14 Extroverts of equal intelligence as introverts will tend to give more answers to suggestions because they are less afraid of making fools of themselves. The introverts tend to censor themselves. They have as many ideas but they tend to keep the bad ones to themselves.
HANS EYSENCK cit. D. Cohen *Psychologists on Psychology*, 1977

15 It is a matter of common experience that in our normal selves our personality is ever changing according to our environment.
C.S. MYERS *In the Realm of Mind*, 1937

1 There are only two qualities in this world: efficiency and inefficiency; and only two sorts of people: the efficient and the inefficient.
GEORGE BERNARD SHAW (1856–1950) *John Bull's Other Island*

2 The educated man tries to repress the inferior one in himself, without realising that by this he forces the latter to become a revolutionary.
CARL JUNG (1875–1961) *Psychology and Religion*

3 Thus grave and morose men seldom prove fast friends; they are too captious and censorious, and will not bear with one another's infirmities.
DESIDERIUS ERASMUS (1466–1536) *The Praise of Folly*

4 The choleric drinks, the melancholic eats, the phlegmatic sleeps.
PROVERB

5 Mice too have personality. Suppose you ask the question 'Is the activity of the mouse affected by alcoholic fumes?' It sounds a reasonable question but is meaningless unless you specify what kind of mouse.
HANS EYSENCK cit. D. Cohen *Psychologists on Psychology*, 1977

6 A patronizing disposition always has its meaner side.
GEORGE ELIOT (1819–1880) *Adam Bede*

PHRENOLOGY

7 ... it seems to me that most scientists have not sufficiently recognized the great truth of which Phrenology is an adumbration. Whoever calmly considers the question, cannot long resist the conviction that different parts of the cerebrum must, in some way or other, subserve different kinds of mental action.
HERBERT SPENCER *The Principles of Psychology*, 1896

8 Among neuroscientists, phrenology now has a higher reputation than Freudian psychiatry, since phrenology was in a certain crude way a precursor of electroencephalography. Freudian psychiatrists are now regarded as old crocks with sham medical degrees, as ears with wire hairs sprouting out of them that people with more money than sense can hire to talk into.
TOM WOLFE *Independent on Sunday*, 2 February 1997

9 Phrenology is just as infallible as any other science, and no more.
E. STACKPOOL O'DELL *Phrenology: Its Truthfulness and Usefulness*, 1892

10 Phrenology is not dead, nor does it give any sign of decay, but manifests a vigorous and a hardihood that pretend a long life. Its nomenclature has permeated the languages of all civilised nations, and its principles are more believed in and practised now than they ever were at any former date.
NICHOLAS MORGAN *The Skull and Brain: Their Indications of Character and Anatomical Relations*, 1875

PLANNING

11 We have a plan when we know, or at least know in outline, which calculations, computations, or constructions we have to perform in order to obtain the unknown. The way from understanding the problem to conceiving a plan may be long and tortuous.
G. POLYA *How to Solve It*, 1945

12 Any complete description of behavior should be adequate to serve as a set of instructions, that is, it should have the characteristics of a plan that could guide the action described.... *A Plan is any hierachical process in the organism that can control the order in which a sequence of operations is to be performed.*
G.A. MILLER, E. GALANTER, K.H. PRIBRAM *Plans and the Structure of Behavior*, 1960

1 Perfection of planning is a symptom of decay. During a period of exciting discovery or progress there is no time to plan.
C. NORTHCOTE PARKINSON *Parkinson's Law*, 1958

2 May I ask whether these pleasing attentions proceed from the impulse of the moment, or are the result of previous study.
JANE AUSTEN (1775–1817) *Pride and Prejudice*

3 The best laid schemes o' mice and men
Gang aft a-gley.
An lea'e us nought but grief an' pain
For promised joy.
ROBERT BURNS (1759–1796) 'To a Mouse'

4 In aiming at a new construction, *we must clearly conceive what is aimed at*; we must have the means of judging whether or not our tentatives are successful.
ALEXANDER BAIN *Education as Science*, 1880

PLAY

5 The child uses play to make up for defects, sufferings, and frustrations.
ERIK ERIKSON *Genetic Psychology Monographs*, 1940

6 Imaginative play can be viewed as a major resource by which children can cope immediately with the cognitive, affective, and social demands of growing up.
JEROME SINGER, paper at a meeting of the American Psychological Association, 1977

7 Play ... appears in children while they are learning to make use of words and to put thoughts together. This play probably obeys one of the instincts which compel children to practise their capacities. In doing so they come across pleasurable effects, which arise from a repetition of what is similar, a rediscovery of what is familiar, ... which are to be explained as unsuspected economies in psychical expenditure.
SIGMUND FREUD (1856–1939) *Jokes and their Relation to the Unconscious*

8 It should be noted that children at play are not playing about: their games should be seen as their most serious-minded activity.
MICHEL MONTAIGNE (1533–1592) *Essays*

9 ... for a series of years, play is the absorbing aim of existence, indeed life is virtually controlled thereby, and for some good reason must exist.
ALICE RAVENHILL *Some Characteristics and Requirements of Childhood*, 1908

10 The essential attribute of play is a rule which has become an affect.
L.S. VYGOTSKY *Soviet Psychology*, 1967

11 Behavior is called playful only if it seems useless in the eyes of an observer.
H. SCHLOSBERG *Psychological Review*, 1947

12 The animals do not play because they are young, but they have their youth because they must play.
KARL GROOS *The Play of Animals*, 1898

13 [Play is] the outward expression of subjective stimulation.
J. MONOD *Chance and Necessity*, 1970

14 Play is finite creativity in the major dimension of illusion.
E. FINK *Yale French Studies*, 1968

15 We may consider play as an experimental dialogue with the environment.
I. EIBL-EIBESFELDT *Ethology: The Biology of Behavior*, 1970

16 Play expresses the essence of the youthful.
F.J.J. BUYTENDIJK cit. Robert Fagen, *Animal Play Behavior*, 1981

1 Another drawback of the free play situation is that it often drifts from true constructive activity into *ad hoc* creative play. By *ad hoc* creative play I mean that the child assigns meanings to things on the spur of the moment for the purposes of the game, like putting down a block and calling it a car.... This kind of play is often entertaining, but it does not develop the child's observational skills or his ability to analyze the problem and determine the elements and combinations of the elements that are best suited for the constructive task.
A.R. LURIA *The Making of Mind*, 1979

2 Play is essentially wish fulfilment.
L.S. VYGOTSKY *Soviet Psychology*, 1966

3 The poet has it, that man is never more human than when he plays.
ERIK ERIKSON *Play and Development*, 1972

4 Almost as soon as the child has learned to preserve his equilibrium in ordinary walking, he proceeds to complicate the problem by trying to walk on curbstones, in a rut, on a beam, on a balustrade or narrow wall.
KARL GROOS *The Play of Man*, 1901

PLEASURE

5 ... pleasure belongs to that category of events which cannot be brought about by direct intention, but on the contrary, as a mere side-effect or by-product. Therefore the more one strives for pleasure, the less one is able to attain it.
VIKTOR FRANKL *American Journal of Psychotherapy*, 1960

6 We are so made, that we can only derive intense enjoyment from a contrast, and only very little from a state of things.
SIGMUND FREUD (1856–1939) *Civilisation and its Discontents*

7 Pleasure's a sin, and sometimes sin's a pleasure.
LORD BYRON (1788–1824) *Don Juan*

8 Believe me, my young friend, there is *nothing* – absolutely nothing – half so much worth doing as simply messing about in boats.
KENNETH GRAHAME (1859–1932) *Wind in the Willows*

9 If merely 'feeling good' could decide, drunkenness would be the supremely valid human experience.
WILLIAM JAMES *The Varieties of Religious Experience*, 1902

10 A cigarette is the perfect type of pleasure. It is exquisite, and leaves one unsatisfied. What more can one want?
OSCAR WILDE (1854–1900) *The Picture of Dorian Gray*

POPULATION

11 The investigation and understanding of the psychology and even the psychiatry of rapidly expanding populations may well be of paramount importance in the near future.
H. FLOREY *Proceedings of the Royal Society London, B* 1964

12 Any species that does not control its fertility must rely on famine, parasites and predators to control its population.
CLAUDE MASSET cit. A. Burguière *et al. A History of the Family*, 1996

13 Population, when unchecked, increases in a geometrical ratio. Subsistence increases only in an arithmetic ratio.
THOMAS MALTHUS (1766–1834) *An Essay on the Principle of Population*

14 So it is reasonable to hope and, indeed, to expect that co-operative behaviour in the future will enable even an enlarged population to maintain itself with the aid of the multitude of new tools now at our disposal.
J.Z. YOUNG *An Introduction to the Study of Man*, 1970

1 We want better reasons for having children than not knowing how to prevent them.
DORA RUSSELL *Hypatia*, 1925

POVERTY

2 Poverty curtails freedom of choice. The freedom to eat as you wish, to go where and when you like, to seek the leisure pursuits or political activities which others expect; all are denied to those without resources ... poverty is most comprehensively understood as a condition of partial citizenship.
PETER GOLDING *Excluding the Poor*, 1986

3 Under the term poor I shall include all those persons whose incomes are insufficient for the satisfaction of their wants – a want being ... contra-distinguished from a mere desire by a positive physical pain, instead of a mental uneasiness accompanying it. The large and comparatively unknown body of people included in this definition I shall contemplate in two distinct classes, viz., the *honest* and the *dishonest* poor ... according as they *will* work, they *can't* work, and they *won't* work.
HENRY MAYHEW *Morning Chronicle*, October 1849

4 Quiescent public acceptance of poverty as a fact of social life depends upon how it is defined, far more than upon its severity.
MURRAY EDLEMAN *Political Language*, 1977

5 There is no touchstone, except the treatment of childhood, which reveals the true character of a social philosophy more clearly than the spirit in which it regards the misfortunes of those of its members who fall by the way.
R.H. TAWNEY *Religion and the Rise of Capitalism*, 1926

6 There are many kinds of poverty
My mother knows them well,
She sits and counts them in a tenement
A mile or so from hell.
BRIAN PATTEN 'Song of the Grateful Chair', 1979

7 And the mistake of the best men through generation after generation, has been that great one of thinking to help the poor by almsgiving, and by preaching patience or hope, and by every other means, emollient or consolatory, except the one thing that God orders for them, justice.
JOHN RUSKIN (1819–1900) *Unto This Last*

8 One advocates the prevention of excessive child-bearing among the poorest classes not on the ground that they are the 'worst stocks', but in order to put a stop to the tragedy of fine children doomed to inadequate lives solely on account of parental poverty.
MICHAEL FIELDING *Parenthood: Design or Accident?*, 1928

9 It's a question of priorities, I
    suppose,
Give them the money and it goes on
    booze.
Why can't the poor be seen to be poor?
Then we could praise the Lord, and give
    them shoes.
ROGER McGOUGH 'A Fair Day's Fiddle', 1986

10 Poverty is no disgrace to a man, but it is profoundly inconvenient.
SYDNEY SMITH (1771–1845) *Wit and Wisdom of Sydney Smith*

11 It is not so much that the slums create the dullards, but rather that the duller stocks gravitate automatically to the slums.
KARL PEARSON *Philosophical Transactions*, 1904

12 Children of the poor know but few pleasures.
CHARLES DICKENS (1812–1870) *The Old Curiosity Shop*

13 If the misery of our poor be caused not by the laws of nature, but by our institutions, great is our sin.
CHARLES DARWIN (1809–1882) *Journal of Researches*

14 Extreme grinding poverty does produce helplessness, and it is a rare individual who can maintain a sense of mastery in the face of it.
MARTIN SELIGMAN *Helplessness*, 1975

1 It is easy enough to say that poverty is no crime. No; if it were men wouldn't be ashamed of it. It is a blunder, though, and is punished as such. A poor man is despised the whole world over.
JEROME K. JEROME (1859–1927) *Idle Thoughts of an Idle Fellow*

2 Some folks for certain have thought
     it was shocking,
When Famine appeals and when Poverty
     groans,
That life should be valued at less than a
     stocking,
And breaking of frames led to breaking
     of bone.
LORD BYRON (1788–1824) 'An Ode to the Framers of the Frame Bill'

3 The greatest of evils and the worst of crimes is poverty.
GEORGE BERNARD SHAW (1856–1950) *Major Barbara*

4 Without self pity she (my mother) spoke of the early days and early hopes and of the slow acceptance of reality – the toil, the grind, the struggle, the poverty of it all, and of the even more barren lives of those about her; of how, in time, it stifled human qualities – kindliness, sensitivity, intelligence, and left no way out – 'the too much sacrifice' that 'turns the heart to stone'.... 'But go on!' she said 'Whatever you do, go on learning, and some time, somewhere, the chance will surely come.'
ROBERT ROBERTS *A Ragged Schooling*, 1976

5 Plenty has made me poor.
OVID (43 BC–17 AD) *Metamorphoses*

6 I've never been poor, only broke. Being poor is a frame of mind. Being broke is only a temporary situation.
MICHAEL TODD *Newsweek*, 31 March 1958

7 I saw Sir Edward Elgar at the Garrick the other day. I said I was working hard. He at once said, 'Ah, you work because it pleases you; we poor men work because we have to.' He seldom talks to me without mentioning his poverty and my riches....
ARNOLD BENNETT (1867–1931) *Diary*, 10 May 1924

POWER

8 What we believe to be love of progress is really, in nine cases out of ten, a love of power, an enjoyment of the feeling that by our fiat we can make things different.... It is this temperament which makes Western nations 'progressive'.
BERTRAND RUSSELL (1872–1970) *Selected Papers*

9 I began to see clearly in every psychological phenomenon the striving for superiority. It runs parallel to physical growth and is an intrinsic necessity of life itself. It lies at the root of life's problems and is manifested in the way in which we meet these problems.
ALFRED ADLER in C. Murchinson *Psychoanalysis of 1930*, 1930

10 A tomb now suffices him for whom the whole world was not sufficient.
ANON., epitaph for Alexander the Great

11 Chimpanzees, ... are quite blatant about their 'baser' motives. Their 'interest' in power is not greater than that of humanity; it is just more obvious.
FRANS de WAAL *Chimpanzee Politics: Power and Sex and Apes*, 1982

12 I don't mind how much my ministers talk, so long as they do what I say.
MARGARET THATCHER *The Observer*, 27 January 1980

13 In the Country of the Blind the One-eyed Man is King.
H.G. WELLS (1866–1946) *The Country of the Blind*

14 Justice is that which is in the interests of the stronger party.
PLATO (429–347 BC) *The Republic*

15 Who controls the past controls the future.
GEORGE ORWELL (1903–1950) *Nineteen Eighty-Four*

1 I do not envy you your hat, your
  shoe,
Why should you envy me my small
  estate?
It's fearfully illogical in you
To fight with economic force and fate.
Moreover, I have got the upper hand,
And mean to keep it. Do you
  understand?
HILAIRE BELLOC (1870–1953) 'The Justice of
the Peace'

2 People who have power respond
simply. They have no minds but their
own.
IVY COMPTON-BURNETT (1884–1969) *The
Mighty and their Fall*

3 ... the hierarchy is a *cohesive* factor,
which puts limits on competition and
conflict. Child care, playing, sex and
cooperation depend on the resultant
stability. But underneath the surface
the situation is constantly in a state of
flux. The balance of power is tested
daily and if it proves too weak, it is
challenged and a new balance
established. Consequently chimpanzee
politics are also constructive.
FRANS de WAAL *Chimpanzee Politics: Power
and Sex and Apes*, 1982

4 The fundamental concept in social
science is Power, in the same sense in
which Energy is the fundamental
concept in physics.
BERTRAND RUSSELL (1872–1970) *Power: A
New Social Analysis*

5 What interests me politically, as a
person and as a writer, are those truths
possessed by those without power to
which those with power are more or less
blind.
JOHN BERGER cit. N. Gray *Writers Talking*,
1989

PRACTICE

6 ... practice is a particular type of
repetition without repetition....
NICHOLAI BERNSTEIN *The Co-ordination and
Regulation of Movements*, 1967

7 No art is at the first finding out so
perfect as industry may after make it.
RICHARD HOOKER (1554–1600)
Ecclesiastical Polity

8 If you wish to be a good writer, write.
EPICTETUS (c. 55–135) *Discourses*

9 O what a tangled web we weave
When first we practise to deceive!
But when we've practised quite a while
How vastly we improve our style.
J.R. POPE 'A Word of Encouragement', 1996

10 The more a man writes, the more
he can write.
WILLIAM HAZLITT (1778–1830) *Lectures on
Dramatic Life*

11 I never practice; I always play.
WANDA LANDOWSKA *Time*, 1 December 1952

PRECOCITY

12 Prodigies are generally born into
families that recognize and value the
talent when it emerges, they are
schooled by master teachers, and their
talent area is culturally valued and also
accessible to children
A. ROBINSON, P.R. CLINKENBEARD *Annual
Review of Psychology*, 1998

13 My cousins the Rossettis were
horrible monsters of precocity. Let me
set down here with what malignity I
viewed their proficiency in Latin and
Greek at ages incredibly small. Thus, I
believe, my cousin Olive wrote a Greek
play at the age of something like five.
FORD MADDOX FORD *Ancient Lights*, 1911

14 Endeavouring to make children
prematurely wise is a useless labour.
Suppose they have more knowledge at
five or six years old than other children,
what use can be made of it? It will be
lost before it is wanted, and the waste of
so much time and labour of the teacher
can never be repaid. Too much is
expected from precocity, and too little
performed.
SAMUEL JOHNSON (1709–1784) cit. James
Boswell *The Life of Samuel Johnson*

1 At the age of eleven, I began Euclid, with my brother as my tutor.... I had not imagined that there was anything so delicious in the world. After I had learned the fifth proposition, my brother told me that it was generally considered difficult, but I had found no difficulty whatever. This was the first time it had dawned upon me that I might have some intelligence.
BERTRAND RUSSELL *Autobiography*, 1967

2 Whom the gods wish to destroy they first call promising.
CYRIL CONNOLLY (1903–1974) *Enemies of Promise*

3 Contrary to what sometimes happens in music, miracle children do not exist in painting. What might be taken for a precocious genius is *the genius of childhood*. When the child grows up it will disappear without trace.... As for me, I didn't have this genius. I outgrew the period of that marvellous vision very rapidly. At that boy's age I was making drawings that were completely academic. Their precision, their exactitude frightens me. My father was a professor of drawing, and it was probably he who pushed me prematurely in that direction.
PABLO PICASSO cit. G. Brasscii *Picasso and Company*, 1966

PREJUDICE

4 Let it appear in a criminal trial that the accused is a Sunday-school superintendent, and the jury says guilty almost automatically.
H.L. MENCKEN (1880–1956) *Minority Report*

5 I don't like principles ... I prefer prejudices.
OSCAR WILDE (1954–1900) *An Ideal Husband*

6 He had but one eye, and the popular prejudice runs in favour of two.
CHARLES DICKENS (1812–1870) *Nicholas Nickleby*

7 Bigotry may be roughly defined as the anger of men who have no opinions.
G.K. CHESTERTON (1874–1936) *Heretics*

8 It seems reasonable to assume that as long as anxiety and insecurity persist as a root of intolerance, the effort to dispel stereotyped thinking or feelings of ethnic hostility by rational propaganda is at best a half-measure.
BRUNO BETTELHEIM, M. JANOWITZ *Scientific American*, 1950

9 Four legs good, two legs bad.
GEORGE ORWELL (1903–1950) *Animal Farm*

10 When people feel deeply, impartiality is bias.
LORD REITH *Into the Wind*, 1945

11 We should therefore claim, in the name of intolerance, the right not to tolerate the intolerant.
KARL POPPER *The Open Society and Its Enemies*, 1945

12 Without the aid of prejudice and custom, I should not be able to find my way across the room.
WILLIAM HAZLITT (1778–1830) *On Prejudice*

13 Intolerance of groups is often, strangely enough, exhibited more strongly against small differences than against fundamental ones.
SIGMUND FREUD (1856–1939) *Moses and Monotheism*

14 No tree takes so deep a root as a prejudice.
AMERICAN PROVERB

15 Open-mindedness is the antithesis of prejudice, pride and selfishness; it means accepting all truth even when this means that one's own ideas and preconceptions must be altered or abandoned, or even when this requires that one forego some personal advantage.
JOHN DEWEY (1859–1952) *Lectures in China, 1919–1920*

16 Surprising though how people still
Swallow all this
Prejudiced stuff – not us of course,
Oh no, not us.
VERNON SCANNELL 'Popular Mythologies', 1982

1 Prejudice, n. A vagrant opinion without visible means of support.
AMBROSE BIERCE (1842–1914) *Devil's Dictionary*

2 Knowledge humanizes mankind, and reason inclines to mildness; but prejudices eradicate every tender disposition.
CHARLES MONTESQUIEU (1689–1755) *Spirit of Laws*

PROBLEM SOLVING

3 I have yet to see any problem, however complicated, which, when you looked at it in the right way, did not become still more complicated.
P. ANDERSON *New Scientist*, 25 September 1969

4 … the ability to solve any problem, although involving intelligence, is not identical with it.
REX KNIGHT *Intelligence and Intelligence Tests*, 1933

5 We learn from failure much more than success. We often discover what *will* do, by finding out what will *not*.
SAMUEL SMILES (1812–1904) *Self-Help*

6 We tend to overlook the fact that problems only exist in relation to a background of expectations that are usually taken for granted.
K. HUNDEIDE in J.V. Wertsch *Culture, Communication and Cognition*, 1985

7 The situation is one for an open mind.
W.H.R. RIVERS *Social Organisation*, 1924

8 'Excellent' I cried.
'Elementary', said he.
ARTHUR CONAN DOYLE (1859–1930) *The Memoirs of Sherlock Holmes*

9 We have first raised a dust and then complain we cannot see.
BISHOP GEORGE BERKELEY (1685–1753) *A Treatise Concerning the Principles of Human Knowledge*

10 Why have psychologists paid so little attention to the nature of the problem or of the question? Or to what precedes the problem; doubt, uneasiness, wonder?
MARY HENLE *American Psychologist*, 1975

11 Mighty rivers can easily be leaped at their source.
PUBLILIUS SYRUS (1st cent. BC) *Moral Sayings*

12 Father Brown laid down his cigar and said carefully, 'It isn't that they can't see the solution. It is that they can't see the problem.'
G.K. CHESTERTON (1874–1936) *The Scandal of Father Brown*

PROCRASTINATION

13 procrastination is the
art of keeping
up with yesterday
don marquis (1878–1937) 'certain maxims of archy'

14 Defer not till tomorrow to be wise,
To-morrow's sun to thee may never rise.
WILLIAM CONGREVE (1670–1729) letter to Cobham

15 Procrastination is the thief of time.
EDWARD YOUNG (1742–1746) *Night Thoughts*

16 Whilst we deliberate how to begin a thing, it grows too late to begin it.
QUINTILIAN (35–100) *Institutio Oratoria*

17 Give me chastity and continency, but do not give it yet.
ST AUGUSTINE (354–430) *Confessions*

PROGRESS

18 … any scientist of any age who wants to make important discoveries must study important problems.
PETER MEDAWAR *Advice to a Young Scientist*, 1979

1 Technological progress turns man into a superman under sentence of quantification and depersonalisation.
ARMELLE GAUFFENIC *Impact of Science on Society*, 1983

2 The simple faith in progress is not a conviction belonging to strength, but one belonging to acquiescence and hence to weakness.
NORBERT WIENER *The Human Use of Human Beings*, 1954

3 The art of progress is to preserve order amid change, and to preserve change amid order.
A. N. WHITEHEAD (1861–1947) *Process and Reality*

4 Progress in science often yields a simplification of what previously seemed to be a complex and confusing phenomenon.
R.Q. BELL *American Psychologist*, 1979

PROPAGANDA

5 That branch of the art of lying which consists in very nearly deceiving your friends without quite deceiving your enemies.
F.M. CORNFORD (1874–1943) *Microcosmographia Academica*

6 I run the *Daily Express* purely for propaganda and for no other purpose.
LORD BEAVERBROOK (1879–1964) evidence to the Royal Commission on the Press, 1948

7 The successful propagandist does not behave when on the platform in a relaxed, informal, and 'familial' style; on the contrary he has 'presence' and dramatizes himself and his message by a certain amount of showmanship. Schizophrenics and hysterics have often been successful in the past as religious leaders, probably because their intense conviction or dramatic self-presentation courted authority with their audiences.
MICHAEL ARGYLE *The Psychology of Interpersonal Behaviour*, 1969

8 Promise, large promise, is the soul of an advertisement.
SAMUEL JOHNSON (1709–1784) *The Idler*

9 Through clever and constant application of propaganda, people can be made to see paradise as hell, and also the other way round to consider the most wretched sort of life as paradise.
ADOLF HITLER (1889–1945) *Mein Kampf*

PSYCHIATRY

10 The general science of psychiatry seems to me to cover much the same field as that which is studied by social psychology, because scientific psychiatry has to be defined as the study of interpersonal relations.
HARRY STACK SULLIVAN *The Interpersonal Theory of Psychiatry*, 1953

11 Neurotics build castles in the air. Psychotics live in them. And psychiatrists take the rent.
ANON.

12 If the nineteenth century was the age of the editorial chair, ours is the century of the psychiatrist's couch.
MARSHALL McLUHAN *Understanding Media*, 1964

13 The trump card of a new science of the brain has often enough been played, unsuccessfully in the history of the discipline [psychiatry], and the claims of brain scientists to understand consciousness and its terrors have been shown to be shallow, indeed deluded.
ROY PORTER *The Greatest Benefit to Mankind*, 1997

14 Sir Roderick Glossop ... is always called a nerve specialist, because it sounds better, but everybody knows he's really a sort of janitor to the looney-bin.
P.G. WODEHOUSE (1881–1975) *The Inimitable Jeeves*

15 The demise of Freudianism can be summed up in a single word: lithium.
TOM WOLFE *Sunday Independent*, 2 February 1997

1 The new definition of psychiatry is the care of the id by the odd.
ANON.

2 A psychiatrist is a man who goes to the Folies-Bergere and looks at the audience.
MERVYN STOCKWOOD cit. *The Observer*, 15 October 1961

PSYCHOANALYSIS

3 ... by shifting the emphasis from an actual world of sadness, misery, and cruelty to an internal stage on which actors performed invented dramas for an invisible audience of their own creations, Freud began a trend away from the real world that ... is at the root of the present-day sterility of psychoanalysis and psychiatry throughout the world.
J.M. MASSON *Freud: The Assault on Truth*, 1984

4 Whatever the ultimate importance may prove to be of specific psycho-analytic concepts and assumptions, no sentient person could defend the theory in any existing form as even crudely simulating a comprehensive and fully adequate theory of behavior.
GARDNER LINDZEY *American Psychologist*, 1967

5 Psychoanalysis unhesitatingly ascribes the primacy in mental life to the affective process, and it reveals an unexpected amount of affective disturb-ance and blinding of the intellect in normal no less than sick people.
SIGMUND FREUD (1856–1939) *The Claim of Psychoanalysis to Scientific Interest*

6 The influence of psychoanalysis has been so overwhelming that one can hardly find a modern piece of art criticism that does not include an explicit or implicit reference to the idea of psychoanalysis or its method of approach.
H. KREITLER, S. KREITLER *Psychology of the Arts*, 1972

7 It is integral to the practice of psychoanalysis that the analyst has to fall into the trap of being treated like a parent – an authority of sorts – and then refuse to be one.
ADAM PHILLIPS *Terrors and Experts*, 1995

8 When Freud wants to describe goings-on of which it is appropriate to say a man is acting, that he has a *reason* for what he does, and so on, he talks about the Ego: when on the other hand he wants to say that a person suffers something, or is made or driven to do something he speaks of the Id. The concept of the Ego makes explicit the sorts of things that are presupposed in having a reason for acting.
R.S. PETERS *The Concept of Motivation*, 1958

9 I should now like to call attention to a recent movement in psychology, a movement which, in spite of all its faults, I am inclined to see as one of the most important which has ever taken place in the history of science. This movement ... is connected especially with the name of Freud....
W.H.R. RIVERS *Psychology and Ethnology*, 1926

10 Freudian psychoanalysis changed the self-image of the Western mind.
ROY PORTER *The Greatest Benefit to Mankind*, 1997

11 If the outside public forgets its com-mon sense, then, lacking the constraints this provides, the public is liable to allow its extended analytical sensitivity to go wild and be debased ... the public may be open to seduction by a technical discourse, such as psychoanalysis, which purports to give a general account of human nature, and which seems to contain a ready answer to most questions about human difficulties.
B.A. FARRELL *The Standing of Psychoanalysis*, 1981

12 In the theory of psychoanalysis we have no hesitation in assuming that the course taken by mental events is automatically regulated by the pleasure principle.
SIGMUND FREUD (1856–1939) *Beyond the Pleasure Principle*

1 The picture [The Full Monty] goes even further in refuting Freud's theory about penis envy, establishing that nowadays, at least, it's a male problem, and that women find men's private parts more comic than enviable.
PHILIP FRENCH *The Observer*, 31 August 1997

2 Psychoanalysis cannot enable the patient to know what he wants, but only to risk finding out.
ADAM PHILLIPS *Terrors and Experts*, 1995

3 Where *id* was, there *ego* shall be.
SIGMUND FREUD (1856–1939) *New Introductory Lectures on Psychoanalysis*

4 Though initially unaware of the fact, even resistant to it, the psychoanalytic movement was, fundamentally, an exploration of language habits, of the verbal gestures of consciousness; the raw material of the psychoanalytic process is inevitably linguistic.
GEORGE STEINER *Extraterritorial*, 1972

5 Psychoanalysis is essentially a translational language, one possible bridge to a more personal, less compliant idiom.
ADAM PHILLIPS *On Kissing, Tickling and Being Bored*, 1993

6 Psychoanalysis is confession without absolution.
G.K. CHESTERTON (1874–1936) attrib.

7 Perhaps psychoanalysis could only come about in a Vienna of stiff collars and whalebone corsets. If Freud had worn a kilt in the prescribed Highland manner he might have had a different attitude to genitals.
ANTHONY BURGESS *The Observer*, 24 August 1996

8 Psychoanalysis does not permit itself to be ranged with other conceptions: it refuses to be put on an equal basis with them.
ANNA FREUD in C. Murchison *A Handbook of Child Psychology*, 1931

9 Fortunately analysis is not the only way to resolve inner conflicts. Life itself still remains a very effective therapist.
KAREN HORNEY *Our Inner Conflicts*, 1945

10 Most psychoanalytic theory now is a contemporary version of the etiquette book; improving our internal manners, advising us on our best sexual behaviours (usually called maturity, or mental health, or a decentred self).
ADAM PHILLIPS *Terrors and Experts*, 1995

11 I regard psychoanalysis as a completely ephemeral mythology. To me it is the Jewish vengeance on Christian science and nothing is more charged with primitive animism than psychoanalysis.
GEORGE STEINER *The God Shaped Hole*, Channel 4 TV, 27 May 1992

12 Freud's views become intelligible only if one realises that they have been directly transferred from phenomena in sick people to the normal.... From this erroneous method originates the conflict between 'mind' and 'drives' and that peculiar form of 'unconscious' that appears during analysis.
KURT GOLDSTEIN *The Organism*, 1938

13 Considered in its entirety, psychoanalysis won't do. It is an end product, moreover, like a dinosaur or a zeppelin; no better theory can ever be erected on its ruins, which will remain for ever one of the saddest and strangest of all landmarks in the history of twentieth century thought.
PETER MEDAWAR *The Hope of Progress*, 1972

14 Psychoanalysis was created to enable man to accept the problematic nature of life without being defeated by it, or giving in to escapism.
BRUNO BETTELHEIM *The Uses of Enchantment*, 1978

15 Writings that seek to apply the findings of psycho-analysis to topics in the field of the mental sciences have the inevitable defect of offering too little to readers of both classes.
SIGMUND FREUD (1856–1939) *Totem and Taboo*

16 The only pathological states which fail to react favourably to analysis are those based on a defence prompted by the patient's dread of the strength of his instincts.
ANNA FREUD *The Ego and the Mechanisms of Defence*, 1954

1 The psychoanalytic movement has about spent itself, after a career of popular and unscientific propaganda, notably in the United States.
J.M. BALDWIN in *A History of Psychology in Autobiography, Vol. 1*, 1930

2 Psychoanalysis does not measure. But this turns out to be much less of a difference (from other sciences) when we know that in modern physics what can be measured is the statistical probability of action of a great many units. The single electron is as flighty and unpredictable as the compulsive neurotic in Freud's office.
JAQUES BARZUN *Harper's Magazine*, June 1949

PSYCHOLOGISTS

3 The role of specialists and experts has several drawbacks. They tend to grow rather crazy and attach a quasi-religious importance to their specialised conclusions; and the sanest of them makes mistakes which no one, except a fellow specialist, is equipped to challenge.
KENNETH CLARK *Moments of Vision*, 1981

4 He [William Wundt] isn't a genius, he is a professor – a being whose duty is to know everything, and have his own opinion about everything connected with his [subject].
WILLIAM JAMES (1842–1910) in H. James *The Letters of William James*

5 In spite of the shortcomings of his system Spearman was a great pioneer in British psychology – remarkable for his singleness of purpose, the immense synthetic power and range of his mind, the originality of his vision, and his capacity to inspire a varied and devoted following.
L.S. HEARNSHAW *A Short History of British Psychology 1840–1940*, 1964

6 I divide my career into two periods: the small and insignificant period before my meeting with Vygotsky and the more important and essential one after the meeting.
A.R. LURIA cit. K. Levitin *One is Not Born a Personality*, 1982

7 The outstanding feature of my personality seems to me however, to have been the conflict between my *need for power and achievement* and my *need for approval and affection*.
E.G. BORING in *A History of Psychology in Autobiography, Vol. 4*, 1952

8 Psychologists seem to be constantly embroiled in disputes that are aimed at defining what psychology should be about.
DAVID COHEN *Psychologists on Psychology*, 1977

9 I had a breakdown – sleepless nights for a week – a typical Angst ... for three weeks I went to sleep only with the light turned on. This in a way was one of my best experiences in my university course. It taught me to watch my step and in a way prepared me to accept a large part of Freud, when I first began to get really acquainted with him around 1910.
J.B. WATSON in *A History of Psychology in Autobiography, Vol. 3*, 1936

10 I came to New York, bringing in a basket my two most educated chickens, from whom I expected in due time to breed, and so test the influence of acquired mental traits upon inherited capacity, a foolish project in view of the slow breeding rate of fowls. I also expected to test the permanence of their learning over a long interval, but never did, the first of a regrettable list of enterprises left incomplete.
E.L. THORNDIKE in *A History of Psychology in Autobiography, Vol. 3*, 1936

11 Excellent work can surely be done by men with widely different notions of what psychology is and should be, the best work of all perhaps being done by men such as Galton, who gave little or no thought to what it is or should be.
E.L. THORNDIKE in *A History of Psychology in Autobiography, Vol. 3*, 1936

1 I would rise at six, study until breakfast, go to classes, laboratories and libraries with no more than fifteen minutes unscheduled during the day, study until exactly nine o' clock at night and go to bed. I saw no movies or plays, seldom went to concerts, had scarcely any dates and read nothing but physiology and psychology.
B.F. SKINNER *Particulars of My Life*, 1976

2 ... I gave in when Jerome S. Bruner, like Edward VIII before Stanley Baldwin, pleaded for the right of the social psychologists to marry for love.
CYRIL BURT in *A History of Psychology in Autobiography, Vol. 4*, 1952

3 He (Gibson) asked the critically important question. How does one obtain constant perceptions in everyday life on the basis of continually changing sensations.... His problem was that he had a much oversimplified explanation of how this should be done.
DAVID MARR *Vision*, 1982

4 Melanie Klein was the stuff of which myths are made.
PHYLLIS GROSSKURTH *Melanie Klein*, 1986

5 A psychologist who thinks his work is done, that all that is now needed is the application of a final scheme to new instances, is dead. Psychology will go on and leave him lamenting. Like the reactions it studies, psychology is living and orientated forward: there can be no end to its achievements.
F.C. BARTLETT in *A History of Psychology in Autobiography, Vol. 3*, 1936

6 Rarely have I been sure of the quality of my work. I have needed repeated approbation and often mistrusted its validity.
E.G. BORING in *A History of Psychology in Autobiography, Vol. 4*, 1952

7 Between biology and the analysis of knowledge I needed something other than philosophy ... a need that could be satisfied only by psychology.
JEAN PIAGET in E.G. Boring *A History of Psychology in Autobiography, Vol. 4*, 1952

8 But if a psychologist, however self-consciously scientific, is in need of personal insight – if his marriage has collapsed or his children hate him – he does not turn to the professional journals in search of it – he goes to Donne or Chekhov, Freud or Laing.
L. HUDSON in L. Michaels, C. Ricks *The State of the Language*, 1980

9 I think there is something religious in the way he [Skinner] writes though, of course, not believing in God. But there is the idea that there is a moral law which in his case gets converted into the law of science.
D. McCLELLAND cit. D. Cohen *Psychologists on Psychology*, 1977

10 It is no exaggeration to say that Vygotsky was a genius.
A.R. LURIA *The Making of Mind*, 1979

11 I can say in a nutshell what I think about Chomsky and Piaget; neither has good arguments, but there is almost certainly something to what each one says.
HILARY PUTNAM in M. Piatelli-Palmarini *Language and Learning*, 1980

12 St Augustine was the first real psychologist for he was the first to see the basic fact about human nature, namely that the Natural Man hates nature, and the only act which can really satisfy him is the *acte gratuite*.
W.H. AUDEN (1907–1973) in C.C. Abbott *Poets at Work*, 1948

13 Ebbinghouse conducted a series of experiments in which he set pupils to learn certain nonsense syllables. These were speedily forgotten.
E.S. WATERHOUSE *The ABC of Psychology*, 1927

14 The psychologist, as such, is not concerned with man but with mind.
ERIC GILL (1882–1940) *The Necessity of Belief*

1 So to someone attracted today to psychological or epistemological enquiry, one may say: Read Piaget. Remember that he is usually vague and often wrong and that there are still-uncharted dimensions of structural and procedural complexity within the mind that he seemingly has little inkling of. But yes – read Piaget.
MARGARET BODEN *Piaget*, 1979

2 I would assume that by being a linguist I am automatically a psychologist.
NOAM CHOMSKY cit. D. Cohen *Psychologists on Psychology*, 1977

3 Havelock Ellis was far too rational to be a complete rationalist.
D. MACCARTHY *The New Statesman*, 22 July 1939

4 I began my career in the first years of the great Russian revolution. This single, momentous event decisively influenced my life and that of everyone I knew.
A.R. LURIA *The Making of Mind*, 1979

5 I feel I strayed into achievement motivation accidentally. I wanted to raise some money for research. There was a cocktail party and someone said he had some money for research in the Navy.
D. McCLELLAND cit. D. Cohen *Psychologists on Psychology*, 1977

6 Chomsky ... speaks very quickly and in long sentences that sometimes become too involved, so that he has to scrap them and start again. His written, revised work, is very precise but it is curious to note that a man who has changed our attitude to how we analyse language should get himself embedded in his own sentences.
DAVID COHEN *Psychologists on Psychology*, 1977

7 Skinner misses this point with his usual instructive thoroughness....
MARY MIDGLEY *Heart and Mind*, 1981

8 When Vygotsky got up to deliver his speech, he had no printed text from which to read, not even notes. Yet he spoke fluently, never seeming to stop and search his memory for the next idea. Even if the content of his speech had been pedestrian, his performance would have been notable for the persuasiveness of his style. But his speech was by no means pedestrian.... Although he failed to convince everyone of the correctness of his views, it was clear that this man from a small provincial town in western Russia was an intellectual force who would have to be listened to.
A.R.LURIA in M. Cole, S. Cole *The Making of Mind*, 1979

9 Nothing was beneath his [S.S. Stevens] contempt or above his suspicion.
J.S. BRUNER *In Search of Mind*, 1983

10 Cyril Burt was my professor ... he was probably the most intelligent person I ever met – very knowledgeable.
HANS EYSENCK cit. D. Cohen *Psychologists on Psychology*, 1977

11 Like the great language mystics, who extend from Nicholas of Cusa to Jakob Boehme, Chomsky often seems to conjure up the radiant picture of that single tongue spoken by Adam and his sons but forever lost and pulverised at Babel.
GEORGE STEINER *Extraterritorial*, 1972

12 In situations of every kind and description, from the delving into the profundities of science to leading the amenities of society, everywhere alike Wundt stood out as the Master. Bizarrely enough, however, the very matter upon which I was least inclined to admire him without stint was just his psychology.
CHARLES SPEARMAN in *A History of Psychology in Autobiography*, Vol. 1, 1930

13 The more I write, the more antagonism I seem to provoke.
W. McDOUGALL in *A History of Psychology in Autobiography*, Vol. 1, 1930

14 A snapper up of unconsidered trifles.
WILLIAM SHAKESPEARE (1564–1616) *The Winter's Tale*

PSYCHOLOGY

1 It is still open to question whether psychology is a natural science, or whether it can be regarded as a science at all.
IVAN PAVLOV *Conditioned Reflexes*, 1927

2 I am not fond of the word psychological. There is no such thing as psychological.
R.D. LAING *The Divided Self*, 1959

3 Social psychology has not yet acquired any valid claim to unintelligibility, and it is still malleable enough to benefit from the attention and the questions of educated men and women.
D.W. HARDING *Social Psychology and Individual Values*, 1952

4 Psychology: the science that tells you what you already know in words you don't understand.
ANON.

5 Only the understanding of human nature by every human being can be the proper goal for the science of human nature.
ALFRED ADLER *Understanding Human Nature*, 1927

6 I use the term 'psychology' for the science which deals with mental phenomena, conscious and unconscious. I am fully aware that, from the point of view of the psychologist, I am begging the whole question as it interests him by my use of the word 'mental'.... The definition of psychology I wish to exclude is ... the science of the behaviour of living things.
W.H.R. RIVERS *Psychology and Ethnology*, 1926

7 Common human experience alone is not a material with which we can build a science of psychology.
WOLFGANG KOHLER *Dynamics in Psychology*, 1942

8 To know psychology, therefore is no guarantee that we shall manage our minds rightly.
WILLIAM GLOVER *Know Your Own Mind*, 1918

9 Is there any royal, best road into psychology? I cannot think there is. Even when it is treated scientifically, and I am sorry to imply that I think this is the only way in which it can be treated, psychology is a very wide subject, in which there is room for the exploitation of the most varied interests.
F.C. BARTLETT in *A History of Psychology in Autobiography, Vol. 3*, 1936

10 Up to now the 'behavioral sciences' including psychology, have not provided us with a picture of man capable of creating or living in a democracy.
G.W. ALLPORT *Becoming*, 1955

11 Betterment of the human condition is one of the distinctive promises of psychology.
PAUL MUSSEN, NANCY EISENBERG *Roots of Caring, Sharing and Helping*, 1977

12 Magicians pull rabbits out of hats. Psychologists pull habits out of rats!
ANON.

13 The world of psychology contains looks and tones and feelings; it is the world of dark and light, of noise and silence, of rough and smooth; its space is sometimes large and sometimes small, as everyone knows who in adult life has gone back to his childhood's home; its time is sometimes short and sometimes long, it has no invariables. It contains all the thoughts, emotions, memories, imaginations, volitions that you naturally ascribe to mind.
E.B. TITCHENER *A Beginner's Psychology*, 1916

14 We insist that our students become well versed in experimental design. We drill them in objective and quantitative methods. We do everything we can to make them into first rate experimentalists. And then we give them so narrow a view of the field of behavior that they are satisfied to work on the same kinds of problems and to employ the same methods that have been used for the past quarter of a century.
FRANK BEACH *American Psychologist*, 1950

1 If we are ever to have a compre-hensive theoretical psychology, we must attack the problems whose solution offers hope of insight into human behavior, and it is my belief that if we face our problems honestly and without regard to, or fear of, difficulty, the theoretical psychology of the future will catch up with and eventually even surpass, common sense.
HARRY F. HARLOW *Psychological Review*, 1953

2 ... medicine has nothing to learn from psychology nor psychology from medicine.
WILLIAM McDOUGALL *British Medical Journal*, 1939

3 This is no science, it is only the hope of a science.
WILLIAM JAMES *Psychology, Briefer Course*, 1890

4 Every academic discipline tends towards insularity.
JOHN BOWLBY in K.J. Connolly, J.S. Bruner *The Growth of Competence*, 1974

5 [Psychology] carries on its practical work ... with instruments of strange and wonderful name: chronographs, algometers, stroboscopes, pseudoptics, hand-dynamometers, aesthesiometric compasses and plethysmographs.
WILLIAM GLOVER *Know Your Own Mind*, 1918

6 Psychology is not a young science; it is merely a difficult one.
J.C. MARSHALL, D.M. FRYER in M.M. Gruneberg, P. Morris *Aspects of Memory*, 1978

7 Psychology is not primarily concerned in determining the *average* threshold, the *average* memory, the *average* imagery, the *average* emotionality, the *average* conduct of an unorganised mass of individuals under given conditions. Its primary interests lie in the study of the *individual* and in the study of *differences* between individuals.
C.S. MYERS *In the Realm of Mind*, 1937

8 Are we building a general science of behaviour or merely a science of rat learning?
FRANK BEACH *American Psychologist*, 1950

9 Would there be any truth in saying that psychology was created by the sophists to sow distrust between man and his world?
RUDOLPH ARNHEIM *Parables of Sun Light*, 1989

10 Psychology must not only strive to become a useful basis for the other mental sciences, but it must also turn again and again to the historical sciences, in order to obtain an under-standing for the more highly developed mental processes.
WILHELM WUNDT *An Introduction to Psychology*, 1912

11 Psychology is a science, but science is only exactified common sense.
E.S. WATERHOUSE *The ABC of Psychology*, 1927

12 There is no psychology; there is only biography and autobiography.
THOMAS SZASZ *The Second Sin*, 1974

13 The separation of psychology from the premises of biology is purely artificial, because the human psyche lives in indissoluble union with the body.
CARL JUNG (1875–1961) *Factors Determining Human Behavior*

14 Popular psychology is a mass of cant, of slush and of superstition worthy of the most flourishing days of the medicine man.
JOHN DEWEY (1859–1952) *The Public and its Problems*

15 In the future I see open fields for far more important researches. Psychology will be securely based on the foundation already well laid by Mr. Herbert Spencer, that of the necessary acquirement of each mental power and capacity by gradation.
CHARLES DARWIN (1809–1882) *Origin of Species*

16 Metaphysical dreaming has a vital part to play in the progress of psychology.
L.S. HEARNSHAW *The Shaping of Modern Psychology*, 1987

1 Complete systems and schemes of psychological explanation are the biggest stumbling-block in psychology.
F.C. BARTLETT in *A History of Psychology in Autobiography, Vol. 3*, 1936

2 But psychology is more difficult than physics – at least psychologists often find it easier to get themselves into a mess in their field than physicists do in theirs.
S.S. STEVENS *Psychological Bulletin*, 1939

3 The discipline's health is suspect: ... it has failed to produce a coherent body of scientific law; and its fruits, unmistakably, have about them an air of triviality.
L. HUDSON *The Cult of Fact*, 1972

4 Psychology deals with the organisation of information, not with its representation in organic tissue.
U. NEISSER *Cognitive Psychology*, 1967

5 With good fortune psychology may hope eventually to achieve that degree of implausibility – and fertility – that now characterizes the longer established sciences.
D.O. HEBB *Textbook of Psychology*, 1958

6 The person conceived hierarchically and developmentally, is the unifying concept that psychology requires for the detailed research upon which its progress depends.
L.S. HEARNSHAW *The Shaping of Modern Psychology*, 1987

7 There are certain dogmatic elements in association and empiricist psychology which mark it as extremely hostile to the spirit of the sciences.
NOAM CHOMSKY cit. D. Cohen *Psychologists on Psychology*, 1977

8 Psychology, both in theory and practice, is much more difficult than physics.
NICHOLAS HUMPHREY *Consciousness Regained*, 1983

9 There is a tendency to define psychology in what strikes me as a curious, and basically unscientific way, as having to do only with behaviour or only with processing of information or only with certain low-level types of interaction with the environment ... and to exclude from psychology the study of what I call competence.
NOAM CHOMSKY cit. D. Cohen *Psychologists on Psychology*, 1977

10 The history of modern psychology is a record, not of scientific advance, but of intellectual retreat.
R.B. JOYNSON *Bulletin of the British Psychological Society*, 1970

PSYCHOSOMATICS

11 Psychosomatic illnesses have always existed, because psychogenesis – the conversion of stress or psychological problems into physical symptoms – is one of nature's basic mechanisms in mobilizing the body to cope with mental distress.
EDWARD SHORTER *From Paralysis to Fatigue*, 1992

12 I find my spirits and my health affect each other reciprocally – that is to say, everything that decomposes my mind produces a correspondent disorder in my body; and my bodily complaints are remarkably mitigated by those conditions that dissipate the clouds of mental chagrin.
TOBIAS SMOLLET (1721–1771) *The Expedition of Humphrey Clinker*

13 'Tis very certain the desire of life prolongs it.
LORD BYRON (1788–1824) *Don Juan*

14 Her pure and eloquent blood
Spoke in her cheeks, and so distinctly wrought,
That one might almost say, her body thought.
JOHN DONNE (1571–1631) 'Second Anniversary'

15 But besides real diseases we are subject to many that are only imaginary for which physicians have invented imaginary cures.
JONATHEN SWIFT (1667–1745) *Gulliver's Travels*

1   It has been demonstrated that settling matters of conscience inspires a state of mind in the patient that facilitates the physician's task.
GABRIEL GARCÍA MÁRQUEZ *The General in His Labyrinth*, 1989

PUNISHMENT

2   This is the first of punishments, that no guilty man is acquitted if judged by himself.
JUVENAL (c. 60–130) *Satires*

3   Anyone who has been to an English public school will always feel comparatively at home in prison. It is the people brought up in the gay intimacy of the slums ... who find prison so soul destroying.
EVELYN WAUGH (1903–1966) *Decline and Fall*

4   To crush, to annihilate a man utterly, to inflict on him the most terrible punishment so that the most ferocious murderer would shudder at it beforehand, one need only give him work of an absolutely, completely useless and irrational character.
FEODOR DOSTOYEVSKY (1821–1881) *The House of the Dead*

5   My object all sublime
I shall achieve in time
To let the punishment fit the crime –
The punishment fit the crime.
W.S. GILBERT (1836–1911) *The Mikado*

6   He that spareth his rod hateth his son.
Bible, Proverbs

7   All punishment is mischief: all punishment in itself is evil.
JEREMY BENTHAM (1748–1832) *Principles of Morals and Legislation*

8   To prevent the future commission of faults ought always to be the object of punishment; it should, therefore be inflicted with judgement, with composure, with affection, and with promptness.
MRS J. BAKEWELL *The Mother's Practical Guide*, 1845

QUALITATIVE PSYCHOLOGY

9   Discourse analysis ... is a functionally oriented approach to the analysis of talk and text. As it has been carried out up to now it has been overwhelmingly qualitative. However, quantification *per se*, is not frowned upon for theoretical reasons; rather, it is the sorts of 'operationalizations' that typically underpin quantification in psychology, and the sorts of theoretical concerns they mask, that are rejected.
D. EDWARDS, J. POTTER *Discursive Psychology*, 1992

10   We shall apply the term *qualitative* to correspondence that is based only on the qualities of the corresponding elements.... *Numerical* correspondence, on the other hand, will be that in which each element is considered as a unit, irrespective of the qualities, e.g., *n* blue counters corresponding to *n* red counters, whatever their distribution
JEAN PIAGET *The Child's Conception of Number*, 1941

11   Words should be weighed and not counted.
YIDDISH PROVERB

R

REASON

1 All our knowledge begins with the senses, proceeds then to the understanding, and ends in reason. There is nothing higher than reason.
IMMANUEL KANT (1724–1804) *Critique of Pure Reason*

2 Psychology has been celebrating the role of 'emotional factors' and 'unconscious drives' in behavior for so long now that man's capacity for rational coping with his world has come to seem like some residual capacity that shows its head only when the irrational lets up.
J.S. BRUNER, J.J. GOODNOW, G.A. AUSTIN *A Study of Thinking*, 1956

3 How quick come the reasons for approving what we like!
JANE AUSTEN (1775–1817) *Persuasion*

4 On human Actions reason though you can,
It may be Reason, but it is not Man.
ALEXANDER POPE (1688–1744) 'Moral Essays'

5 ... there is an appealing romantic charm about the idea of freedom to respond to 'reality' in a variety of styles, reflecting different, but perhaps equally valid, modes of thoughts and feelings. We are all 'relativists' nowadays and belief in 'universal laws of reason' or absolutes of any sort is likely to be regarded as dogmatic.
MAX BLACK *The Labyrinth of Language*, 1968

6 Reason is God's crowning gift to man.
SOPHOCLES (496–406 BC) *Antigone*

7 The reasonable man adapts himself to the world: the unreasonable one persists in trying to adapt the world to himself. Therefore all progress depends on the unreasonable man.
GEORGE BERNARD SHAW (1856–1950) *Maxims for Revolutionists*

8 Those who will not reason
Perish in the act:
Those who will not act
Perish for that reason.
W.H. AUDEN (1907–1973) 'Shorts'

9 Reason ... is never aware of its hidden assumptions
L.L. WHYTE *The Unconscious Before Freud*, 1962

10 A useful habit for scientists to develop is that of not trusting ideas based on reason only.... Practically all reasoning is influenced by feelings, prejudice and past experience, albeit often subconsciously.
W.B. BEVERIDGE *The Art of Scientific Investigation*, 1957

11 I can stand brute force, but brute reason is quite unbearable. There is something unfair about its use. It is hitting below the intellect.
OSCAR WILDE (1854–1900) *An Ideal Husband*

12 There are two futures, the future of desire and the future of fate, and man's reason has never learnt to separate them.
J.D. BERNAL *The World, the Flesh and the Devil*, 1969

13 Callum: Is God everywhere?
Mother: Yes, dear.
Callum: Is he in this room?
Mother: Yes, he is.
Callum: Is he in my mug?
Mother: (growing uneasy) Er – yes.
Callum: (clapping his hands over his mug) Got him!
(Callum was four years old at the time of the conversation)
MARGARET DONALDSON *Human Minds*, 1992

1 All processes of reasoning, however abstract, are participated in and influenced by feeling.
WILFRED TROTTER *The Collected Papers of Wilfred Trotter FRS*, 1941

2 If we fall into the error of believing that vitally important questions are to be decided by reasoning, the only hope of salvation lies in formal logic, which demonstrates in the clearest manner that reasoning itself testifies to its own ultimate subordination to sentiment. It is like a Pope who should declare *ex cathedra* and call upon all the faithful to implicitly believe on pain of damnation by the power of the keys that he was *not* the supreme authority.
C.S. PIERCE (1839–1914) *Collected Papers, Vol. 1*

REDUCTIONISM

3 Whether we use the language of stimuli and responses, the language of cell assembly and reverberating circuits or some new language still to be invented, it is part of the faith of the materialists that physical science can ultimately be extended to include all the phenomena of human behavior and experience.
R.B. MACLEOD *The Persistent Problems of Psychology*, 1975

4 The autonomy of personal experience and its laws cannot in principle be explained in terms of chemical and physical laws or of neuro-physiological structure, however complex.
KONRAD LORENZ *Beyond the Mirror*, 1977

5 Our meddling intellect
Mis-shapes the beauteous forms of things:–
We murder to dissect.
WILLIAM WORDSWORTH (1770–1850) 'The Tables Turned'

6 I would say that reductionism today is a mask for nihilism.
VIKTOR FRANKL *Beyond Reductionism* 1969

7 Psychologists are attempting to express facts more and more in terms of the complete organism rather than in specific parts (brain etc.) or isolated functions.
J.R. KANTOR *Psychological Bulletin*, 1922

8 The often too materialistically-minded biologist is so fearful of meeting a certain bogy, the 'psyche', that he hastens to analyse every case of behavior into its component reflexes without venturing first to observe it as a whole.
E.B. HOLT *The Freudian Wish*, 1915

9 Some say that everything that is called a psychical law is nothing but a psychological reflex of physical combinations, which is made up of sensations joined to certain central cerebral processes.... It is contradicted by the fact of consciousness itself, which cannot possibly be derived from any physical qualities of material molecules or atoms.
WILHELM WUNDT *An Introduction of Psychology*, 1912

10 As an expression of personal opinion, I would say that reductionism is lousy philosophy, but a good recipe for making a quick (scientific) buck by discovering some useful practical information, but is bad again as a method for making major advances in human comprehension, such as those of Darwin, Freud, Einstein or the quantum physicists.
C.H. WADDINGTON *Tools for Thought*, 1977

11 I believe that the acceptance of an oversimplified mechanistic theory of life has narrowed considerably the front of progress in biological sciences.
RENÉ J. DUBOS *The Dreams of Reason*, 1961

REINFORCEMENT

12 There is no such whetstone, to sharpen a good wit and encourage a will to learning, as is praise.
ROGER ASCHAM (1515–1568) *Scholemaster*

1 Be sparing in praise, and more so in blame.
WILLIAM LANGLAND (1330–1400) *Piers Plowman*

2 I could not have predicted that among the reinforcers which explain my scientific behavior the opinions of others would not rank high, but that seems to be the case.
B.F. SKINNER in *A History of Psychology in Autobiography, Vol. 5*, 1967

3 For, beat a child, if he daunce not well, and cherish him though he learne not well, ye shall have him unwilling to go to daunce, and glad to go to his booke.
ROGER ASCHAM (1515–1568) *Scholemaster*

REJECTION

4 Heav'n has no rage, like love to
  hatred turn'd,
Nor Hell a fury, like a woman scorned.
WILLIAM CONGREVE (1670–1729) *The Mourning Bride*

5 Some say this city has ten million
  souls,
Some are living in mansions, some are
  living in holes:
Yet there's no place for us, my dear, yet
  there's no place for us.
W.H. AUDEN (1907–1973) 'Refugee Blues'

6 Silence is the most perfect expression of scorn.
GEORGE BERNARD SHAW (1856–1950) *Back to Methuselah*

7 My infant mind even was bitter with those who insisted on regarding me as a normal child and not a prodigy. Since then I have struggled with this canker for many a day, and as success fails to arrive it becomes more gnawing.
W.N.P. BARBELLION *The Journal of a Disappointed Man*, 1919

RELATIONSHIPS

8 The science of personal relations is not assisted by the fact that only a few psychologists are concerned to discover valid personal ways in which person, and relations between persons, can be studied by persons.
R.D. LAING *Self and Others*, 1980

9 When people who are tolerably fortunate in their outward lot do not find in life sufficient enjoyment to make it valuable to them, the cause generally is, caring for nobody but themselves. To those who have neither public nor private affections, the excitements of life are much curtailed....
JOHN STUART MILL (1806–1873) *Utilitarianism*

10 If you believe in me, I'll believe in you.
LEWIS CARROLL (1832–1898) *Alice Through the Looking Glass*

11 We seek the company of others for the same general reason that we seek the company of things, because we strive to relate ourselves meaningfully to the surroundings.
S.E. ASCH *Social Psychology*, 1952

12 He makes no friend who never made a foe.
ALFRED, LORD TENNYSON (1808–1892) *Idylls of the King*

13 Scratch a lover, and find a foe.
DOROTHY PARKER (1893–1967) 'Ballade of a Great Weariness'

14 Scientists see nature reflected in the mirror of social relationships.
RICHARD LEWONTIN *Independent on Sunday*, 21 September 1997

15 ... you are always under an obligation to anyone you've helped once.
PENELOPE FITZGERALD *The Gate of Angels*, 1990

16 Everything we say and do with one another includes an element of confirming, extending, contradicting or changing the rules of a relationship.
KEITH OATLEY *Selves in Relation*, 1984

1 It takes two men to make one brother.
ISRAEL ZANGWILL (1864–1926) *The Principle of Nationalities*

2 No man is an *Iland*, intire of it selfe; every man is a peece of the *Continent*, a part of the maine.
JOHN DONNE (1573–1631) *Devotions Upon Emergent Occasions*

RELIGION

3 The highest flights of charity, devotion, trust, patience, bravery, to which the wings of human nature have spread themselves have been flown for religious ideals.
WILLIAM JAMES *Varieties of Religious Experience*, 1902

4 The brain should not be abused by having forced upon it any religious or political mystique that stunts the reason, or any form of crude rationalism that stunts the religious sense.
WILLIAM SARGANT *Battle for the Mind*, 1957

5 ... all new religion begins in dissent, that is, in a refusal to believe what those in power would have us believe – what they command and oblige us ... to believe. But in essence it is an eternal biological or evolutionary mechanism, not something that was needed once, merely to meet the chance of an earlier society, when religious belief was a great metaphor, and would-be conforming matrix, for many things beside religion.
JOHN FOWLES *A Maggot*, 1985

6 Many people think they have religion when they are troubled with dyspepsia.
ROBERT G. INGERSOLL (1833–1899) *Liberty of Man, Woman and Child*

7 I think all the great religions of the world – Buddhism, Hinduism, Christianity, Islam and Communism – both untrue and harmful. It is evident as a matter of logic that, since they disagree, not more than one of them can be true. With very few exceptions, the religion which a man accepts is that of the community in which he lives, which makes it obvious that the influence of the environment is what has led him to accept the religion in question.
BERTRAND RUSSELL (1872–1970) *Why I Am Not a Christian*

8 Science without religion is lame, religion without science is blind.
ALBERT EINSTEIN (1879–1955) *Out of My Later Years*

9 In the long run nothing can withstand reason and experience, and the contradiction religion offers to both is only too palpable.
SIGMUND FREUD (1856–1939) *The Future of an Illusion*

10 Religion and natural science are fighting a joint battle in an incessant, never relaxing crusade against scepticism and against dogmatism, against disbelief and against superstition, and the rallying cry in this crusade has always been, and will always be: '*On to God!*'.
MAX PLANCK (1858–1947) *Scientific Autobiography and Other Papers*

11 There is a profound human instinct to seek something personal behind the processes of nature; and people are led both by intellectual and by emotional paths to the contemplation of religious questions.
C. HINSHELWOOD *The Vision of Nature*, 1961

12 If we ask Western man what is good and what is evil, what is worth striving for and what has to be rejected, we shall find time and time again that his answers reflect the ethical norms of Christianity even when he has long since lost touch with Christian images and parables.
W. HEISENBERG *Physics and Beyond*, 1971

13 The antireligious views of many scientists can be explained because the demands of science are so exacting that there is no time for them to consider philosophical and religious questions deeply.
JOHN ECCLES *The Human Psyche*, 1980

1 The most poignant problem of modern life is probably man's feeling that life has lost significance.... The search for significance, the formulation of new meanings for the words of God and Man, may be the most worthwhile pursuit in the age of alienation.
RENÉ J. DUBOS *So Human an Animal*, 1968

2 Religion is ... morality touched by emotion.
MATTHEW ARNOLD (1822–1888) *Literature and Dogma*

3 Religion, in fact, for the great majority of our own race *means* immortality, and nothing else.
WILLIAM JAMES *The Varieties of Religious Experience*, 1902

4 Know then thyself, presume not God to scan,
The proper study of Mankind is Man.
ALEXANDER POPE (1688–1744) 'Essay on Man'

5 I'm afraid there's many a bespectacled sod
Prefers the British Museum to God.
W.H. AUDEN (1907–1973) 'Shorts'

REMORSE

6 Of all means to regeneration Remorse is surely the most wasteful. It cuts away healthy tissue with the poisoned. It is a knife that probes far deeper than the evil.
E.M. FORSTER (1879–1970) *Howards End*

7 I would far rather feel remorse than know how to define it.
THOMAS à KEMPIS (1380–1471) *The Imitation of Christ*

REPRESSION

8 If society is in danger, it is not because of man's aggressiveness but because of the repression of personal aggressiveness in individuals.
DONALD WINNICOTT *Aggression in Relation to Emotional Development*, 1958

9 The power which makes it difficult or impossible for women, and to a lesser degree for men as well, to enjoy undisguised obscenity is termed by us 'repression'.... It is our belief that civilization and higher education have a large influence in the development of repression, and we suppose that, under such conditions, the psychological organization undergoes an alteration (that can also emerge as an inherited disposition) as a result of which what was formerly felt as agreeable now seems unacceptable and is rejected with all possible psychical force.
SIGMUND FREUD (1856–1939) *Jokes and their Relation to the Unconscious*

10 Taboos on racial discussion do not prevent the development of awareness or feeling, but they do allow for the persistence of confusion, conflict and inaccuracies.
MARY GOODMAN *Race Awareness in Young Children*, 1952

REPUTATION

11 A man who does not lose his reputation over certain things has none to lose.
G.E. LESSING (1729–1781) *Emilia Galotti*

12 It is reputation rather than personality that reflects a person's 'social stimulus value'.
D.B. BROMLEY *Reputation, Image and Impression Management*, 1993

13 A man's *fame*, good or bad, and his *honor* or dishonor, are names for one of his social selves.
WILLIAM JAMES *Principles of Psychology*, 1890

1 Until you've lost your reputation, you never realize what a burden it was or what freedom really is.
MARGARET MITCHELL *Gone with the Wind*, 1936

2 Who steals my purse steals trash;
'tis something, nothing;
'Twas mine, 'tis his, and has been slave to thousands;
But he that filches from me my good name
Robs me of that which not enriches him,
And makes me poor indeed.
WILLIAM SHAKESPEARE (1564–1616) *Othello*

3 If you want people to think well of you, do not speak well of yourself.
BLAISE PASCAL *Pensées*, 1670

4 In a world of competition people are taken at their face value. Everything depends on reputation – 'face' as they say out East. Lose that and you lose everything.
EVELYN WAUGH (1903–1966) *The Loved One*

5 Reputation is an idle and most false imposition; oft got without merit, and lost without deserving.
WILLIAM SHAKESPEARE (1564–1616) *Othello*

6 A man had rather have a hundred lies told of him, than one truth which he does not wish should be told.
SAMUEL JOHNSON (1709–1784) cit. James Boswell *The Life of Samuel Johnson*

7 Reputation, reputation, reputation! O! I have lost my reputation. I have lost the immortal part of myself and what remains is bestial.
WILLIAM SHAKESPEARE (1564–1616) *Othello*

RESEARCH

8 In research the front line is almost always in a fog.
FRANCIS CRICK *What Mad Pursuit*, 1988

9 What good is freedom to research without free time to do it in.
BERTOLT BRECHT *Life of Galileo*, 1958

10 It is an old maxim of mine that when you have excluded the impossible, whatever remains, however improbable, must be the truth.
ARTHUR CONAN DOYLE (1859–1930) *The Adventures of Sherlock Holmes*

11 Attempts to justify psychological research in terms of its social utility at present lead inexorably to bathos. There is little we have produced in the last fifty years that is, in any sense of that complex word, 'relevant'.
L. HUDSON *The Cult of Fact*, 1972

12 ... my work needs to be supplemented and corrected by the observations of others.
ERNST H. WEBER (1795–1878) *The Sense of Touch*

13 We can see a short distance ahead, but we can see plenty that needs to be done.
ALAN TURING *Mind*, 1950

14 If you steal from one author, it's plagiarism; if you steal from many, its research.
WILSON MIZNER cit. A. Johnston *The Legendary Mizners*, 1953

15 We often discover what *will* do by finding out what will not do; and probably he who never made a mistake never made a discovery.
SAMUEL SMILES (1812–1904) *Self-Help*

16 We shall not cease from exploration
And the end of our exploring
Will be to arrive where we started
And know the place for the first time.
T.S. ELIOT (1888–1965) 'Little Gidding'

17 To probe a hole we first use a straight stick to see how far it takes us. To probe the visible world we use the assumption that things are simple until they prove to be otherwise.
E.H. GOMBRICH *Art and Illusion*, 1960

18 He travels the fastest who travels alone.
RUDYARD KIPLING (1865–1936) *Story of the Gadsbys*

1 Care and diligence bring luck.
THOMAS FULLER (1608–1661) *Gnomologia*

2 I'll publish right or wrong:
LORD BYRON (1788–1824) *Don Juan*

3 They are yet the wisest who transcribe whole discourses from others, and then reprint them as their own. By doing so they make a cheap and easy seizure to themselves of that reputation which cost the first author so much time and trouble to procure.
DESIDERIUS ERASMUS (1466–1536) *The Praise of Folly*

4 I hated to serve as a subject. I didn't like the stuffy, artificial instructions given to subjects. I was always uncomfortable and acted unnaturally. With animals I was at home. I felt that, in studying them, I was keeping close to biology with my feet on the ground.
J.B. WATSON in *A History of Psychology in Autobiography, Vol. 3*, 1936

5 It is always the novice who exaggerates.
C.S. LEWIS (1898–1963) *The Screwtape Letters*

6 ... there is no real recipe for this type of research [vision] ... any more than there is a straightforward procedure for discovering things in any other branch of science. Indeed, part of the fun is that we never really know where the next key is going to come from – a piece of daily experience, the report of a neurological deficit, a theorem about three-dimensional geometry, a psychophysical finding in hyperacuity, a neurophysiological observation, or a careful analysis of a representational problem.
DAVID MARR *Vision*, 1982

7 The most important contribution that can be made to a field is indirect, in making possible and encouraging work by others.
R.B. AMMONS in G.S. Seward, J.P. Seward *Current Psychological Issues*, 1960

8 Lost in a gloom of uninspired research.
WILLIAM WORDSWORTH (1770–1850) 'The Excursion'

9 Attempt the end, and never stand to doubt;
Nothing's so hard but search will find it out.
ROBERT HERRICK (1591–1674) *Hesperides*

10 Destroy his fib or sophistry – in vain!
The creature's at his dirty work again.
ALEXANDER POPE (1688–1744) 'Epistle to Dr Arbuthnot'

11 Timidity in dealing with ideas is contrary to the spirit of the scientific method, and the thinker who is afraid of looking like a fool has tied one hand behind his back before entering the ring.
D.O. HEBB *Proceedings of the Royal Society, 1964–65*

12 Nothing is so difficult but that it may be found out by seeking.
TERENCE (185–159 BC) *Heauton Timorumenos*

13 In the long run, all practical results depend on basic research.
P. HANDLER *Biology and the Future of Man*, 1970

14 Nothing so stimulates research as the presence of students.
LEWIS THOMAS *The Youngest Science*, 1983

15 Plagiarize
Let no one else's work evade your eyes,
Remember why the good Lord made your eyes,
So don't shade your eyes,
But plagiarize, plagiarize, plagiarize –
Only be sure always to call it please –
'research'.
TOM LEHRER *Too Many Songs by Tom Lehrer*, 1981

16 An advantage of working with flies ... is the low cost of surgical instruments.
V.G. DETHIER *To Know a Fly*, 1962

17 Some ne'er advance a Judgement of their own,
But catch the spreading notion of the Town;
They reason and conclude by precedent,
And own stale nonsense which they ne'er invent.
ALEXANDER POPE (1688–1744) 'An Essay on Criticism'

REST

1 Absence of occupation is not rest,
A mind quite vacant is a mind
  distress'd.
WILLIAM COWPER (1731–1800) 'Retirement'

2 I have the feeling that once I am at
home again I shall need to sleep three
weeks on end to get rested from the rest
I have had.
THOMAS MANN (1875–1955) *The Magic
Mountain*

3 Rest, with nothing else, results in
rust. It corrodes the mechanisms of the
brain.
WILDER PENFIELD *The Second Career*, 1963

RETIREMENT

4 In fantasy, I have thought perhaps
that my most important contribution
when I reach retirement age would be to
have my frontal lobes removed and see
what I could do without them.
K.S. LASHLEY in L.A. Jeffress *Cerebral
Mechanisms in Behavior*, 1951

REVENGE

5 I think in the final analysis *gratitude
and revenge are the most important
factors governing our actions in everyday
life*; upon them also chiefly depend our
peace of mind, our feelings of security
or insecurity, of fulfillment or
frustration, in short, the extent to which
we can make a success of life.
HANS SEYLE *The Stress of Life*, 1956

6 Indeed, revenge is always the
pleasure of a paltry, feeble, tiny mind.
JUVENAL (c. 60–130) *Satires*

7 To refrain from imitation is the best
revenge.
MARCUS AURELIUS (121–180) *Meditations*

REWARD

8 The reward of a thing well done is to
have done it.
RALPH WALDO EMERSON (1803–1882)
Essays: Second Series

9 Praise youth and it will prosper.
ANON.

10 With the catching end the
pleasures of the chase.
ABRAHAM LINCOLN, speech, 27 January
1838

11 And if the means be just, the
  conduct true,
Applause, in spite of trivial faults, is
  due.
ALEXANDER POPE (1688–1744) 'An Essay on
Criticism'

ROLES

12 Everyone is always and everywhere,
more or less consistently, playing a
role.... It is in these roles that we know
each other; it is in these roles that we
know ourselves.
R.E. PARK *Survey*, 1926

13 Roles have a magiclike power to
alter how a person is treated, how she
acts, what she does, and thereby even
what she thinks and feels.
URIE BRONFENBRENNER *The Ecology of
Human Development*, 1979

14 I'm very good at integral and
  differential calculus,
I know the scientific names of beings
  animalculous.
In short, in matters vegetable, animal
  and mineral,
I am the very model of a modern Major
  General.
W.S. GILBERT (1836–1911) *The Pirates of
Penzance*

1 ... self-presentation and impression management are not trivial party games. They are fundamental processes, rooted in our history as group-living animals. They are archaic, powerful, compulsive tendencies that are closely tied to our chances for survival and reproductive success.
R. HOGAN, W.H. JONES. J.M. CHEEK in B.R. Schlenker *The Self and Social Life*, 1985

2 ... roles are never in reality defined with such a degree of precision that no room is left for interpretation.
R. BOUDON *The Logic of Social Action*, 1981

3 I have two or three, perhaps four friends, but I am forced to be a different man with each of them.
EUGENE DELACROIX (1798–1863) *Journal*

4 If you're anxious for to shine in the high aesthetic line, as a man of culture rare,
You must get up all the germs of the transcendental terms, and plant them everywhere.
W.S. GILBERT (1836–1911) *Patience*

RULES

5 No rule is so general, which admits not some exception.
ROBERT BURTON (1577–1640) *The Anatomy of Melancholy*

6 The golden rule is that there are no golden rules.
GEORGE BERNARD SHAW (1856–1950) *Man and Superman*

7 School Rules
1. I must punctual
2. I must not steal
3. I must respect for others
    a. not to fight
    b. not to gossip
    c. no to swear
4. I must not damage school properties
5. I must keep the school compass clean
6. I must not smoke and chew during duty hours
8. I must not gamble in the school grounds
9. I must not enter other classrooms
10. No sexual relationships with children/teachers
11. I must abide by the church philosophy
12. I must bring me lunch every day.
Togban School Rules, Papua New Guinea, 1982

8 Continuing our analogy between social structure and games, I want to propose that all social situations are rule-governed.
ROM HARRÉ in A.J. Chapman, D.M. Jones *Models of Man*, 1980

9 ... rules are developed gradually, as cultural products, as ways of handling certain situations; they can be changed, but changes are slow.
MICHAEL ARGYLE *The Structure of Social Action*, 1980

S

SATISFACTION

1 If intrinsic job satisfaction or identification with the work is to be aroused and maximised, then the job itself must provide sufficient variety, sufficient complexity, sufficient challenge and sufficient skill to engage the abilities of the worker.
D. KATZ *Behavioral Science*, 1964

2 The book of my enemy has been remaindered
And I am pleased.
In vast quantities it has been remaindered.
Like a van-load of counterfeit that has been seized
And sits in piles in a police warehouse,
My enemy's much-prized effort sits in piles
In the kind of bookshop where remaindering occurs.
CLIVE JAMES 'The Book of My Enemy Has Been Remaindered', 1987

3 I have not got a single enemy I would not want.
NORMAN TEBBIT cit. *The Independent*, 16 February 1991

4 After that, sex is a bit of an anticlimax.
MICK FITZGERALD, comment after winning the Grand National, 1996

SCIENCE AND PSYCHOLOGY

5 This is the task of natural science: to show that the wonderful is not incomprehensible, to show how it can be comprehended, but not to destroy wonder.
H.A. SIMON *The Sciences of the Artificial*, 1969

6 Classification and description are the lowest stage of science. They sink into the background the moment questions of genesis are formulated, and remain important, only so far as they facilitate our answering these.
WILLIAM JAMES *Psychological Review*, 1894

7 There may only be one language of science but there are many dialects.
J.R. NAPIER *Hands*, 1990

8 Science has run the world into difficulties and the world is looking to us as psychologists for another dose of science to run us out of them.
F.C. BARTLETT *Proceedings of the 12th International Congress of Psychology, Edinburgh*, 1950

9 Natural science cannot answer all questions.
ISAIAH BERLIN *The Sense of Reality*, 1966

10 Alas! The scientific conscience has got into the debasing company of money, obligation and selfish respects.
GEORGE ELIOT (1819–1880) *Middlemarch*

11 We have genuflected before the god of science only to find that it has given us the atomic bomb, producing fears and anxieties that science can never mitigate.
MARTIN LUTHER KING (1929–1968) *Strength Through Love*

12 At a certain stage in the development of every science a degree of vagueness is what best consists with fertility.
WILLIAM JAMES *Principles of Psychology*, 1890

1 A scientist must at once be a dog with his nose to the ground, and a god using the purest form of reason.
J.B.S. HALDANE cit. K.R. Dronamrajn *Haldane's Daedalus Revisited*, 1995

2 Science is a way of life which can only flourish when men are free to have faith.
NORBERT WIENER *The Human Use of Human Beings*, 1954

3 There is no quicker way for a scientist to bring discredit upon himself and upon his profession than roundly to declare – particularly when no declaration of any kind is called for – that science knows or soon will know the answers to all questions worth asking, and that questions which do not admit a scientific answer are in some way non-questions or 'pseudoquestions' that only simpletons ask and only the gullible profess to be able to answer.
PETER MEDAWAR *Advice to a Young Scientist*, 1979

4 Every man is, in his own particular way, a scientist [whose] ultimate aim is to predict and control.
G.A. KELLY *The Psychology of Personal Constructs*, 1955

5 Science is nothing else than the search to discover unity in the wild variety of nature – or more exactly, in the variety of our experience. Poetry, painting, the arts are the same search, in Coleridge's phrase, for unity in variety. Each in its own way looks for likeness under the variety of human experience.
JACOB BRONOWSKI *Science and Human Values*, 1961

6 Just because one can't easily achieve replicability, it doesn't mean to say that one should rule out whole areas of science as soft.
ROBERT HINDE cit. J. Miller *States of Mind*, 1983

7 In Ethnology, as in other sciences, nothing is too insignificant to receive attention. Indeed it is a matter of common experience among scientific men that apparently trivial objects or operations have an interest and importance that are by no means commensurate with the estimation in which they are ordinarily held.
A.C. HADDON in C.F. Jayne *String Figures and How to Make Them*, 1906

8 Science may be defined as a device for investigating, ordering and communicating the more public of human experiences.
ALDOUS HUXLEY (1894–1963) *Literature and Science*

9 Progress in science depends as much on creative observations and intuitive interpretation as on verification.
E.A. TINBERGEN, N. TINBERGEN *Zeitschrift fur Tierpsychologie*, 1972

10 I think we must get accustomed to the idea that ... science ... is a system of guesses or anticipations which in principle cannot be justified, but with which we work as long as they stand up to tests.
KARL POPPER *The Logic of Scientific Discovery*, 1935

11 It is the customary fate of new truths to begin as heresies and to end as superstitions.
T.H. HUXLEY (1825–1895) *Science and Culture*

12 Science is practised amid folklore and ideology, and it is foolishly romantic to imagine that the scientist conducts his professional affairs on a high plateau of reason untainted by the miasmous exhalations of ordinary life.
JONATHEN BARNES *London Review of Books*, February 1984

13 Science ... commits suicide when it adopts a creed.
T.H. HUXLEY (1825–1895) *Darwiniana*

14 Science is the great antidote to the poison of enthusiasm and superstition.
ADAM SMITH (1723–1790) *The Wealth of Nations*

15 Man cannot live by contemplative receptivity and artistic creation alone. As well as every word proceeding from the mouth of God, he needs science and technology.
ALDOUS HUXLEY (1894–1963) *Literature and Science*

1   To thee
Science appears but, what in truth she
   is,
Not as our glory and our absolute boast,
But as a succedaneum, and a prop
To our infirmity.
WILLIAM WORDSWORTH (1770–1850) 'The
Prelude'

2   The practice of astronomy, physics,
chemistry or biology normally fails to
evoke the controversies over
fundamentals that today seem endemic
among, say, psychologists or
sociologists.
THOMAS KUHN *The Structure of Scientific
Revolutions*, 1962

SELF

3   Know thyself.
ANON., inscription on the Delphic Oracle

4   People will sometimes go to considerable lengths to escape the unpleasant
consequences of self-awareness,
including engaging in masochistic
behavior, suicide, and other maladaptive
behavior patterns. In general, self-aware
people are likely to be more honest, more
helpful, more industrious and less
punitive than others.
S.T. FISKE, S.E. TAYLOR *Social Cognition*,
1991

5   I celebrate myself, and sing myself
And what I assume you shall assume
For every atom belonging to me
As good as belongs to you.
WALT WHITMAN (1819–1892) 'Song of Myself'

6   A marked change occurs when the
child develops consciousness of his ego,
a fact which is registered by his
referring to himself as 'I'. This change
normally takes place between the third
and fifth year, but it may begin earlier.
CARL JUNG (1875–1961) *The Development of
Personality*

7   ... identity establishes *what* and
where the person is in social terms.
GREGORY STONE in A.M. Rose *Human
Behavior and Social Processes*, 1962

8   Adults recalling their childhood say
they observe their past self much as
they observe a child on a playground, as
somehow both separate and living from
a wholly different perspective.
SUSAN ENGEL *The Stories Children Tell*, 1995

9   The current narcissism engendered
by the idea of just 'being oneself'
involves the belief that psychological
characteristics and sexual proclivities
are entirely *conscious* choices made by
the individual, and not the functions of
the unconscious or instinctual life as
well.
R.D. ROSEN *Psychobabble*, 1978

10   ... the individual's self-imaging and
his interpretation of his own experience
cannot be divorced from the concept of
self that is characteristic of his society.
A.I. HALLOWELL *Culture and Experience*,
1955

11   We can go back directly a few
moments in our experience and then we
are dependent upon memory images for
the rest. So that the 'I' in memory is the
spokesman of the self of the second, or
minute, or a day ago. As given, it is a
'me' which was the 'I' at the earlier time.
G.H. MEAD *Mind, Self and Society*, 1934

12   And our bodies themselves, are
they simply ours, or are they *us*?
WILLIAM JAMES *Principles of Psychology*,
1890

13   The 'self' ... is the central concept
of a theory, which the persons who hold
it use to impose order upon their
thoughts, feelings and actions.
ROM HARRÉ in K. Yardley, T. Honess *Self
and Identity*, 1987

14   A person is not a static thing. If
there are some constant things about us
... we are also changing entities with
both a history and a possible future. For
this reason alone there can be no
complete story about what has to be
known for adequate self-knowledge.
Indeed it might be said that a central
fact about self-knowledge is that there
is no thing to be known.
D. HAMLYN in T. Mischel *The Self:
Psychological and Philosophical Issues*, 1977

1 Just as different people entertain various beliefs about the nature of the universe, they likewise differ in their ideas about the nature of the self.
A.I. HALLOWELL *Culture and Experience*, 1955

2 ... what have you in common with the child of five whose photograph your mother keeps on the mantlepiece? Nothing, except that you happen to be the same person.
GEORGE ORWELL (1903–1950) *The Lion and the Unicorn*

3 I am a part of all that I have met.
ALFRED, LORD TENNYSON (1808–1892) *Ulysses*

4 Self-knowledge does not involve any form of inference or perception or labelling. It is nothing more or less than the ability to articulate the contents and objects of our emotions, motives, beliefs, etc.
JOHN GREENWOOD *Relations and Representations*, 1991

5 A man's *social self* is the recognition he gets from his mates.
WILLIAM JAMES *Principles of Psychology*, 1890

6 The self ... has come to have two distinct meanings. On the one hand it is defined as the person's attitudes and feelings about himself and on the other hand it is regarded as a group of psychological processes which govern behavior and adjustment.
C.S. HALL, G. LINDZEY *Theories of Personality*, 1957

7 One builds one's identity out of claims which, if denied, give one the right to feel righteously indignant.
ERVING GOFFMAN *Interaction Ritual*, 1967

8 ... self-deception is problematic ... how can I be at the same time deceiver and deceived?... Self deception presents the disturbing appearance of being both widespread and impossible.
JONATHEN GLOVER *The Philosophy and Psychology of Personal Identity*, 1988

9 ... every 'age' constructs its own concepts of the subject, its own myths of self. For our own life time it is clear that any description of the subject which ignores Freud's lifework ... would to some extent be very partial.
PETER de BOLLA *The Discourse of the Sublime*, 1989

10 It is not, in my judgement, the personality type that makes the difference, but the self. To the self I ascribe motivation and style, the choice of meaning, and the making of meaning, in work, career, and life course.
F. BARRON in R.J. Sternberg *The Nature of Creativity*, 1988

11 ... even though I know I am constantly changing – all molecules are changing, everything in one is being turned over substantially – there is nevertheless my identity, my consciousness of being essentially the same that I was 20 years ago.
P. WEISS in A. Koestler, J. Smithies *Beyond Reductionism*, 1969

12 The concept 'self' taken with all its connotations has become vastly far-reaching and intricate. Yet it would seem to have at its core an element relatively simple – the awareness or consciousness of each of us, prominent in certain of our motor acts, relates the self to the act.
CHARLES SHERRINGTON *Man on His Nature*, 1940

13 This above all – to thine own self be true.
WILLIAM SHAKESPEARE (1564–1616) *Hamlet*

14 He who conquers others is strong. He who conquers himself is mighty.
LAO-TZE (6th cent. BC) *Tao Te Ching*

15 It can never be the case that there is a 'self' independent of one's cultural-historical existence.
J.S. BRUNER *Actual Minds, Possible Worlds*, 1986

1 I believe that my genetic coding is not responsible for my uniqueness as an experiencing being.... Nor do my postnatal experiences and education provide a satisfactory explanation of the self that I experience. It is a necessary but not sufficient condition.... We go through life living with this mysterious experience of ourselves as experiencing beings. I believe that we have to accept what I call a personalist philosophy – that central to our experience existence is our personal uniqueness.
JOHN ECCLES *The Understanding of the Brain*, 1977

2 The baby new to earth and sky,
What time his tender palm is prest
Against the circle of the breast,
Has never thought that 'this is I.'

But as he grows he gathers much,
And learns the use of 'I', and 'me',
And finds 'I am not what I see,
And other than the things I touch.'
ALFRED, LORD TENNYSON (1809–1892) 'In Memoriam'

3 The self is the highest controlling and directing power.
C.S. MYERS *In the Realm of Mind*, 1937

4 Clinical evidence strongly indicates that the self is a stereotype of memories centering about the body image.
KARL S. LASHLEY *Proceedings of the Association for Research in Nervous and Mental Disease*, 1958

5 ... perceptual-cognitive processes, while physiological, are also personal – it is not a world that one perceives or constructs but *one's own* world – and they lead to, are linked to, a perceptual self, with a will, an orientation, and a style of its own.
OLIVER SACKS *An Anthropologist on Mars*, 1995

6 It is often by a trivial, even an accidental decision, that we direct our activities into a certain channel, and then determine which of our potential expressions of our individuality become manifest.... Every decision is like a murder, and our march forward is over the stillborn bodies of all our possible selves that we'll never be.
RENÉ J. DUBOS *Louis Pasteur*, 1950

7 ... the one and only thing of paramount interest to us in ourselves is, that we feel and think and perceive.
ERWIN SCHRÖDINGER *What is Life*, 1944

8 People often say that this or that person has not yet found himself. But the self is not something one finds, it is something one creates.
THOMAS SZASZ *The Second Sin*, 1973

9 If I am not for myself, who will be for me? If I am for myself only, what am I? If not now – when?
The Talmud

10 Self consciousness appears to be almost strictly a human attribute.
ROGER SPERRY *Neuropsychologia*, 1979

11 Ful wys is he that can him-selven knowe.
GEOFFREY CHAUCER (1340–1400) *Canterbury Tales*

12 It is therefore Death alone that can suddenly make man to know himself. He tells the proud and insolent that they are but abjects.... He takes account of the rich, and proves him a beggar.... He holds a glass before the eyes of the most beautiful, and makes them see therin their deformity and rotteness, and they acknowledge it.
WALTER RALEIGH (1552–1618) *History of the World*

13 Man's destiny turns on his knowledge of himself and of his total environment.
PHILIP HANDLER *Biology and the Future of Man*, 1970

SELF-ESTEEM

14 Nobody holds a good opinion of a man who has a low opinion of himself.
ANTHONY TROLLOPE (1815–1882) *Orley Farm*

1 I am the only person in the world I should like to know thoroughly.
OSCAR WILDE (1854–1900) *Lady Windemere's Fan*

2 Each of us in his own person feels that a high-hearted indifference to life would expiate all his shortcomings.
WILLIAM JAMES *Varieties of Religious Experience*, 1902

3 Only the person who has faith in himself is able to be faithful to others.
ERICH FROMM *The Art of Loving*, 1957

4 He was like a cock who thought the sun had risen to hear him crow.
GEORGE ELIOT (1819–1880) *Adam Bede*

5 Anything you can do, I can do better, I can do anything better than you.
IRVING BERLIN (1888–1989) 'Anything You Can Do'

6 a good many
failures are happy
because they don't
realize it many a
cockroach believes
himself as beautiful
as a butterfly
have a heart o have
a heart and
let them dream on
don marquis (1878–1937) 'archygrams'

7 One complication about self-esteem is that some people develop an exaggerated self-regard in compensation for basic feelings of inferiority. In these cases it is difficult to decide whether they 'really' have high or low self-esteem.
MICHAEL ARGYLE *The Psychology of Interpersonal Behaviour*, 1969

8 Oft times nothing profits more
Than self esteem, grounded on just and right
Well manag'd.
JOHN MILTON (1608–1674) *Paradise Lost*

9 Self-respect and popular esteem are active needs. If a man is deprived of them he becomes anxious, tense, and restless.
ROBERT THOMSON *The Psychology of Thinking*, 1959

10 I cannot love anyone if I hate myself. That is the reason why we feel so extremely uncomfortable in the presence of people who are noted for their special virtuousness, for they radiate an atmosphere of the torture to which they subject themselves.
CARL JUNG (1875–1961) *Psychological Reflections*

11 The very purpose of existence is to reconcile the glowing opinion we have of ourselves with the appalling things that other people think about us.
QUENTIN CRISP *How to Become a Virgin*, 1981

12 A sense of worth, mastery, or self-esteem cannot be bestowed. It can only be earned. If it is given away, it ceases to be worth having, and it ceases to contribute to individual dignity.
MARTIN SELIGMAN *Helplessness*, 1975

13 Some valuing those of their own
side or mind,
Still make themselves the measure of
mankind;
Fondly we think we honour merit
then,
When we but praise ourselves in other
men.
ALEXANDER POPE (1688–1744) 'An Essay on Criticism'

14 He that overvalues himself will undervalue others, and he that undervalues others will oppress them.
SAMUEL JOHNSON (1709–1784) *Sermons*

SELF-IMAGE

15 Our greatest illusion is to believe that we are what we think ourselves to be.
H.F. AMIEL (1821–1888) *Journal*

16 Only the shallow know themselves.
OSCAR WILDE (1854–1900) *The Chameleon*

1 We are all worms. But I do believe that I am a glow-worm.
WINSTON CHURCHILL (1874–1965) cit.
V. Bonham-Carter *Winston Churchill as I Knew Him*, 1965

2 Amnesia is not knowing who one is and wanting desperately to find out. Euphoria is not knowing who one is and not caring. Ecstasy is knowing exactly who one is – and still not caring.
TIM ROBBINS *Another Roadside Attraction*, 1972

3 We confess our faults in the plural, and deny them in the singular.
RICHARD FULKE GREVILLE (1554–1628) *Maxims, Characters and Reflections*

4 And indeed there will be time
To wonder, 'Do I dare?' and ' Do I dare?'
Time to turn back and descend the
    stair,
With a bald spot in the middle of my
    hair
(They will say: 'How his hair is growing
    thin!')
T.S. ELIOT (1888–1965) 'The Love Song of J. Alfred Prufrock'

5 I am His Highness' dog at Kew,
Pray tell me, sir, whose dog are you?
ALEXANDER POPE (1688–1744) 'Epigram'

6 We, living now, are always to ourselves young men and women.
GERTRUDE STEIN (1874–1946) *The Making of Americans*

7 I'm fat, but I'm thin inside. Has it ever struck you that there's a thin man inside every fat man, just as they say there's a statue inside every block of stone?
GEORGE ORWELL (1903–1959) *Coming Up for Air*

8 I am a creature of a prosperous age.
J.J. GIBSON in *A History of Psychology in Autobiography, Vol. 5*, 1967

9 He that is giddy thinks the world turns round.
WILLIAM SHAKESPEARE (1564–1616) *Taming of the Shrew*

SELFISHNESS

10 We are born selfish.
RICHARD DAWKINS *The Selfish Gene*, 1976

11 True selfishness, if obedient to the other constraints of mammalian biology, is the key to a more nearly perfect society.
E.O. WILSON *On Human Nature*, 1978

12 All sensible people are selfish.
RALPH WALDO EMERSON (1803–1832) *The Conduct of Life*

13 Selfishness is one of the qualities apt to inspire love.
NATHANIEL HAWTHORNE (1837–1840) *American Notebooks*

SENSATION

14 Only I who have performed the movement, can know how it feels.
D. BEST *Expression in Movement and the Arts*, 1974

15 ... sounds and smells are there to be sensed by all, the pain I feel exists only in so far as I feel it.
B. RUNDLE *Perception, Sensation, and Verification*, 1972

16 Some say the senses receive the species of things, and deliver them to the common sense, and the common sense delivers them over to the fancy, and the fancy to the memory, and the memory to the judgement.
THOMAS HOBBES (1588–1679) *Leviathan*

17 I keep my countenance,
I remain self-possessed
Except when a street piano,
mechanical and tired
Reiterates some worn-out common song
With the smell of hyacinths across the
    garden
Recalling things that other people have
    desired.
T.S. ELIOT (1888–1965) 'Portrait of a Lady'

1 The entire history of sensation is a commentary on our inability to tell whether two sensations received apart are exactly alike. What appeals to our attention far more than the absolute quality or quantity of a given sensation is its ratio to whatever other sensations we may have at the same time.
WILLIAM JAMES *Principles of Psychology*, 1890

2 The cat in gloves catches no mice.
PROVERB

3 ... we are not in the habit of observing our sensations accurately, except as they are useful in enabling us to recognize external objects. On the contrary, we are wont to disregard all those parts of the sensations that are of no importance so far as external objects are concerned.
HERMANN HELMHOLTZ *Treatise on Physiological Optics*, 1866

4 The discriminative faculty of idiots is curiously low; they hardly distinguish between heat and cold, and their sense of pain is so obtuse that some of the more idiotic seem hardly to know what it is. In their dull lives, such pain as can be excited in them may literally be accepted as a welcome surprise.
FRANCIS GALTON (1822–1911) *Enquiries into the Human Faculty and Its Development*,

5 The popular notion of the five senses has been corrected by modern physiology, which has added three more: the kinaesthetic sense, the static sense and the visceral sensations. While the five original senses communicate the exterior world to our brain, the three others provide a cerebral registration of what is going on in our own body.
CHARLOTTE WOLFF *The Psychology of Gesture*, 1945

6 The dancer experiences certain kinesthetic sensations as she moves, and these constitute the aesthetic meaning of the dance.
D. BEST *Expression in Movement and the Arts*, 1974

7 As the sense of smell is so intimately connected with that of taste, it is not surprising that an excessively bad odour should excite retching or vomiting in some persons.
CHARLES DARWIN (1809–1882) *The Expression of the Emotions in Man and Animals*

8 I counted two-and-twenty stenches, All well defined, and several stinks.
SAMUEL TAYLOR COLERIDGE (1772–1834) 'Cologne'

9 [Sight], most of all senses, makes us know and brings to light many differences between things.
ARISTOTLE (384–322 BC) *Metaphysics*

10 Human sense organs can receive *only* news of difference, and the differences must be coded into events in *time* (i.e., into *changes*) in order to be perceptible. Ordinary static differences that remain constant for more than a few seconds become perceptible only by scanning.
GREGORY BATESON *Mind and Nature*, 1979

11 I test my bath before I sit, And I'm always moved to wonderment That what chills the fingers not a bit Is so frigid upon the fundament.
OGDEN NASH (1902–1971) 'Samson Agonistes'

SENTIMENTALITY

12 Sentimentality is a superstructure covering brutality.
CARL JUNG (1875–1961) *Reflections*

13 Sentimentality is the emotional promiscuity of those who have no sentiment.
NORMAN MAILER *Cannibals and Christmas*, 1966

14 Hatred of humanity and love of animals make a very bad combination.
KONRAD LORENZ *Man Meets Dog*, 1954

SEPARATION

1 Absence from whom we love is worse than death.
WILLIAM COWPER (1731–1800) 'Hope Like the Short-Lived Ray'

2 A liability to experience separation anxiety and grief are the ineluctable results of a love relationship, of caring for someone.
JOHN BOWLBY *Attachment and Loss, Vol. 2: Separation: Anxiety and Anger*, 1973

3 Parting is all we know of heaven,
And all we need of hell.
EMILY DICKENSON (1830–1883) 'My Life Closed Twice before it Closed'

4 In every parting there is an image of death.
GEORGE ELIOT (1819–1880) *Scenes of Clerical Life*

5 It was because the place was just the same
That made your absence seem a savage force.
ELIZABETH JENNINGS 'Absence', 1962

6 He first deceased; she for a little tried
To live without him, liked it not, and died.
HENRY WOTTON (1568–1630) 'Death of Sir Albertus Moreton's Wife'

SEX

7 Continental people have sex life; the English have hotwater bottles.
GEORGE MIKES *How to be an Alien*, 1946

8 All this fuss about sleeping together. For physical pleasure I'd sooner go to my dentist any day.
EVELYN WAUGH (1903–1966) *Vile Bodies*

9 What is it men in women do require?
The lineaments of gratified desire.
What is it women do in men require?
The lineaments of gratified desire.
WILLIAM BLAKE (1757–1827) 'Epigram'

10 It doesn't matter what you do in the bedroom so long as you don't do it in the streets and frighten the horses.
MRS PATRICK CAMPBELL cit. D. Fielding *The Duchess of Jermyn Street*, 1964

11 What men call gallantry and the gods adultery
Is much more usual where the climate's sultry.
LORD BYRON (1788–1824) *Don Juan*

12 The educability of a young person as a rule comes to an end when sexual desire breaks out in its final strength.
SIGMUND FREUD (1856–1939) *A General Introduction to Psychoanalysis*

13 … Freud's concept of sexuality is thoroughly elastic, and so vague that it can be made to include almost anything.
CARL JUNG (1875–1961) *Modern Man in Search of a Soul*

14 An impersonal and scientific knowledge of the structure of our bodies is the surest safeguard against prurient curiosity and lascivious gloating.
MARIE STOPES *Married Love*, 1918

15 Down, wanton, down! Have you no shame
That at the whisper of Love's name,
Or Beauty's presto! up you raise
Your angry head and stand at gaze?
ROBERT GRAVES (1895–1985) 'Down, Wanton, Down'

16 Our great social institutions, our schools and colleges, our clubs, our armies and our churches, are all concerned in some degree or other to keep sex at a distance.
J.C. FLUGEL *British Journal of Medical Psychology*, 1927

17 Sexual needs are not capable of uniting men in the same way as are the demands of self-preservation. Sexual satisfaction is essentially the private affair of each individual.
SIGMUND FREUD (1856–1939) *Totem and Taboo*

1 Our most important sex organ is our brain.
JOAN SMITH *Independent on Sunday*, 30 November, 1997

2 Sexual intercourse began
In nineteen sixty-three
(Which was rather late for me) –
Between the end of the *Chatterly* ban
And the Beatles' first LP.
PHILIP LARKIN (1922–1985) 'Annus Mirabilis'

3 The political system is a breeding system. When we apply the word 'lust' to both power and sex, we are nearer to the truth than we imagine.
LIONEL TIGER, ROBIN FOX *The Imperial Animal*, 1971

4 'But lets unclip your minds
And let tumble free
The mad, mangled crocodile of love.'

So they did,
There among the woodbines and the guinness stains,
And later he caught a bus and she a train
An all there was between them then was rain.
BRIAN PATTEN 'Party Piece', 1967

5 It has been found that in early childhood there are signs of bodily activity to which only an ancient prejudice could deny the name of sexual, and which are linked to psychical phenomena that we come across later in adult erotic life – such as fixation to particular objects, jealousy and so on.
SIGMUND FREUD (1856–1939) *An Outline of Psycho-Analysis*

6 When a man has married a wife, he finds out whether
Her knees and elbow are only glewed together.
WILLIAM BLAKE (1757–1827) 'Proverbs'

7 The turtle lives twixt plated decks
Which practically conceal its sex.
I think it clever of the turtle
In such a fix to be so fertile.
OGDEN NASH (1902–1971) 'The Turtle'

8 It amazes me that organs that piss
Can give human beings such perfect bliss.
IRVING LAYTON *The Whole Bloody Bird*, 1969

9 The pleasure is momentary, the position ridiculous and the expense damnable
LORD CHESTERFIELD, PHILIP STANHOUSE (1694–1773) *Letters to His Son*

10 Broad vistas open up for us when we bear in mind the fact that man's sexual instinct is not at all primarily meant to serve purposes of reproduction but is intended to furnish certain forms of gratification.
SIGMUND FREUD (1856–1939) *Modern Sexual Morality and Modern Nervousness*

11 Nine adulteries, 12 liaisons, 64 fornications and something approaching a rape
Rest nightly upon the soul of our delicate friend Florialis,
And yet the man is so quiet and reserved in his demeanour
That he passes for bloodless and sexless.
Bastadides, on the contrary, who both talks and writes of nothing save copulation,
Has become the father of twins,
But he accomplished this feat at some cost;
He had to be four times cuckold.
EZRA POUND (1885–1972) 'The Temperaments'

12 It may be that all roads lead to sex, but some of the short cuts are ugly.
K.J.W. CRAIK *The Nature of Psychology*, 1966

13 Traditionally, sex has been a very private, secretive activity. Herein perhaps lies its powerful force for uniting people in a strong bond. As we make sex less secretive, we may rob it of its power to hold men and women together.
THOMAS SZASZ *The Second Sin*, 1974

14 It takes all sorts to make a sex.
SAKI (1870–1916) *The Square Egg*

1 But how shall I ever forget the strange, inexplicable rapture of my first experience? What marvellous thing was this that suddenly transformed a mere water tap into a pillar of fire – and water into an elixir of life?
ERIC GILL (1882–1940) *Autobiography*

SEX DIFFERENCES

2 We have more than a 'sneaking suspicion' that the female of the species is not only more deadly but also more intelligent than the male.
D. WECHSLER *The Measurement of Adult Intelligence*, 1939

3 Arabs of means rode none but she-camels, since they ... were patient and would endure to march long after they were worn out, indeed they tottered with exhaustion and fell in their tracks and died: whereas the coarser males grew angry, flung themselves down when tired, and from sheer rage would die there unnecessarily.
T.E. LAWRENCE (1888–1935) *The Seven Pillars of Wisdom*

4 There is more difference within the sexes than between them.
IVY COMPTON-BURNETT (1884–1969) *Mother and Son*

5 Men have had every advantage of us in telling their own story. Education has been theirs in so much higher a degree; the pen has been in their hands.
JANE AUSTEN (1775–1817) *Persuasion*

6 If all men are born free, how is it that women are born slaves?
MARY ASTELL (1668–1731) *Some Reflections on Marriage*

7 A man can brave opinion, a woman must submit to it.
GERMAINE de STAËL (1766–1817) *Delphine*

8 It is hard for a woman to define her feelings in language which is chiefly made by men to express theirs.
THOMAS HARDY (1840–1928) *Far from the Madding Crowd*

9 Wherever a culture offers a choice between activities that are a matter of impersonal manipulation or control and ones of personal relationships and caring, it is men who seem drawn towards the first, women towards the second.
L. HUDSON *Bodies of Knowledge*, 1982

10 A man's presence suggests what he is capable of doing to you or for you.... By contrast, a woman's presence expresses her own attitude to herself, and defines what can and cannot be done to her.
JOHN BERGER *Ways of Seeing*, 1973

11 As vivacity is the gift of women, gravity is that of men.
JOSEPH ADDISON (1672–1719) *The Spectator*, November 1712

12 'Why didn't we think of clothes
   before?'
Asked Adam
Removing Eve's.

'Why did we ever think of clothes?'
Asked Eve,
Laundering Adam's.
D.J. ENRIGHT 'Paradise Illustrated', 1981

13 Women deprived of the company of men pine, men deprived of the company of women become stupid.
ANTON CHEKHOV (1860–1904) *Notebooks, 1892–1904*

14 In the sex-war thoughtlessness is the weapon of the male, vindictiveness of the female.
CYRIL CONNOLLY (1903–1974) *The Unquiet Grave*

SEXISM

15 Man shall be trained for war, and woman for the recreation of the warrior; all else is folly.
FRIEDRICH NIETZSCHE (1844–1900) *Thus Spoke Zarathustra*

1 If God considered woman a fit helpmeet for man, he must have had a very poor opinion of man.
SAMUEL BUTLER (1835–1902) *The Note Books of Samuel Butler*

2 Man for the field and woman for the hearth;
Man for the sword and for the needle she;
Man with the head and woman with the heart;
Man to command and woman to obey:
All else confusion.
ALFRED, LORD TENNYSON (1808–1892) *The Princess*

3 Men have broad and large chests, and small narrow hips, and more understanding than women who have but small and narrow breasts, and broad hips, to the end they should remain at home, sit still, keep house, and bear and bring up children.
MARTIN LUTHER (1483–1546) cit. W. Hazlitt *Table Talk*, 1821

4 Fickle and changeable also is woman.
VIRGIL (70–19 BC) *Aeneid*

5 Years ago, manhood was an opportunity for achievement, and now its a problem to be overcome.
GARRISON KEILLOR *The Book of Guys*, 1994

6 Social scientists have claimed that dominated groups tended to be marked out as conspicuously deviant, while the dominant majority disappears into the 'naturalness' of the social landscape. In particular, maleness is taken for granted, while femaleness becomes conspicuous.... Male interests will be treated as 'obviously interesting' and not specially male, while female interests will be marginalised.
MICHAEL BILLIG *Talking of the Royal Family*, 1992

7 Men, some to business, some to pleasure take;
But every woman is at heart a rake.
ALEXANDER POPE (1688–1744) 'Moral Essays'

8 I expect that Woman will be the last thing civilised by Man.
GEORGE MEREDITH (1828–1909) *The Ordeal of Richard Feveral*

9 All psychologists who have studied the intelligence of women ... recognize today that they represent the most inferior forms of human evolution and that they are closer to children and savages than to an adult civilized man. They excel in fickleness, inconstancy, absence of thought and logic, and the incapacity to reason.
GUSTAVE LE BON *Revue d'anthropologie*, 1879

10 The sum total of food converted into thought by women can never equal the sum total of food converted into thought by men. It follows, therefore that *men will always think more than women.*
MISS M.A. HARDAKER *The Popular Science Monthly*, 1882

11 I think ... that the undubitable fact of woman's intellectual inferiority is to be traced to the mental restraints placed upon her in order to repress her sexual instincts.
SIGMUND FREUD (1856–1939) *Modern Sexual Morality and Modern Nervousness*

12 The thought could not be avoided that the best place for a feminist was in another person's lab.
JAMES D. WATSON *The Double Helix*, 1968

13 Man is the hunter: woman is his game:
The sleek and shining creatures of the chase,
We hunt them for the beauty of their skins;
They love us for it, and we ride them down.
ALFRED, LORD TENNYSON (1809–1892) *The Princess*

14 Every woman should marry – and no man.
BENJAMIN DISRAELI (1804–1881) *Lothair*

15 A woman never forgets her sex. She would rather talk with a man than an angel, any day.
OLIVER WENDELL HOLMES (1809–1894) *The Poet at the Breakfast Table*

1 Do not forget that in taking you to wife your husband had paid you the highest compliment he can command.... And in doing so he has made many sacrifices.... He rightly hopes that you will more than make up to him for all the losses; and it is your primary task to see that this expectation shall not be disappointed.
WILLIAM McDOUGALL *Character and Conduct of Life*, 1932

SHAME

2 The capacity to feel shame is built into human beings, and it has a civilising effect in adapting a child to his family and culture.
F. ENGLISH *Transactional Analysis Journal*, 1975

3 Cultures change over time. Our culture has become more shame-driven as we have turned toward personal freedom, and beyond it to narcissism. The self, now the object and the subject, is more likely to experience shame. And we have simultaneously rid ourselves of the religious institutions that are capable of absorbing shame, so many of us lack mechanisms for securing forgiveness.
MICHAEL LEWIS *Shame*, 1992

4 Doubt is the brother of shame.
ERIK ERIKSON *Childhood and Society*, 1950

5 I never wonder to see men wicked, but I often wonder to see them not ashamed.
JONATHEN SWIFT (1667–1745) *Thoughts on Various Subjects*

6 The only shame is to have none.
BLAISE PASCAL (1623–1662) *Pensées*

7 Shame operates most strongly in our early years.
SAMUEL JOHNSON (1709–1784) *Notes upon Shakespeare*

8 Shame is like an atomic particle: we often know where it is only by the trace it leaves, by the effects it causes.
MICHAEL LEWIS *Shame*, 1992

SKILL

9 ... a skilful performance is achieved by the observance of a set of rules which are not known as such to the person following them.
MICHAEL POLYANI *Personal Knowledge*, 1958

10 The skilled person is the one who can predict accurately on the fewest possible initial events.
H. KAY *Occupational Psychology*, 1957

11 When I make the stroke [at tennis] I do not as a matter of fact, produce something absolutely new, and I never repeat something old.
F.C. BARTLETT *Remembering*, 1932

12 Skill implies spatial precision.
J.A. SCOTT KELSO *Human Motor Behavior*, 1982

13 'You are old', said the youth, 'one
   would hardly suppose
That your eye was as steady as ever;
Yet you balanced an eel on the end of
   your nose –
What made you so awfully clever?'
LEWIS CARROLL (1832–1898) *Alice's Adventures in Wonderland*

14 ... try to glue the eyes on the ball until the very moment it hits the bat. This cannot always be achieved in practice but try. However, when it is a case of trying to make a catch there is no exception whatever to the rule – watch the ball all the way.
DON BRADMAN *The Art of Cricket*, 1958

15 Children are given Mozart because of the small *quantity* of notes: grown-ups avoid Mozart because of the great *quality* of the notes.
ARTHUR SCHNABEL *My Life and Music*, 1961

16 His hand had to reconnect with his intention before they re-entered the maze together.
PATRICK WHITE (1912–1990) *The Vivisector*

17 The entire output of our thinking machine consists of nothing but patterns of motor coordination.
ROGER SPERRY *American Scientist*, 1952

1 When you are just beginning to learn a skill, one of the first things you will notice is that you eliminate, as it were, some of your degrees of freedom – put more simply, you keep a good part of your body fairly rigid ... acquiring a skill is essentially trying to find ways of controlling the degrees of freedom and exploiting the forces made available by the context.
M.T. TURVEY, M.L. FITCH, B. TULLER in J.A. Scott Kelso *Human Motor Behavior*, 1982

2 The centipede was happy quite
Until a toad in fun
Said, 'Pray which leg goes after which?'
That worked her mind to such a pitch,
She lay distracted in a ditch
Considering how to run.
MRS EDWARD CRASTER *Pinafore Poems*, 1871

3 The life so short, the craft so long to learn. Th'assay so hard, so sharp the conquering.
GEOFFREY CHAUCER (1340–1400) *The Parlement of Foules*

4 We had a man who worked in our garden and he was the best man with the scythe I ever knew – nor do I believe there could be a better. The way he walked through it was literally 'heavenly'. He was that rare scyther who hardly bends his back at all, so that he never tired. We used to do the field in the day – I did about the ¼ acre and he did the acre.
ERIC GILL (1882–1940) *Adelphi*, December 1940

5 The same man cannot well be skilled in everything: each has his special excellence.
EURIPIDES (484–406 BC) *Rhesus*

6 Men of quality are in the wrong to undervalue, as they often do, the practise of a fair and quick hand in writing: for it is no immaterial accomplishment.
QUINTILIAN (35–100) *Instituto Oratoria*

7 If, therefore, one can describe the kinds of neural circuitry and organizational principles that enable animals to make rapid but functionally appropriate modifications of ongoing patterns of movement, one has begun to describe the physical basis of intelligence.
F.C. BARTLETT *Thinking*, 1958

8 How we come to achieve control of our movements we can none of us remember; nor do we have any direct knowledge of how we now do it.
MARGARET DONALDSON *Human Minds*, 1992

9 Skills vary with the man. We must tread a straight path and strive by that which is born in us.
PINDAR (518–438 BC) *Odes*

SLEEP

10 Sleep, that knits up the ravell'd
    sleave of care,
The death of each day's life, sore
    labour's bath,
Balm of hurt minds, great nature's
    second course,
Chief nourisher in life's feast.
WILLIAM SHAKESPEARE (1564–1616) *Macbeth*

11 Sleep rests the body.... Dreaming, however, rests the mind.
WILLIAM T. POWERS *Behavior: The Control of Perception*, 1974

12 There ain't no way to find out why a snorer can't hear himself snore.
MARK TWAIN (1835–1910) *Tom Sawyer Abroad*

13 It is alleged by a friend of my family that I used to suffer from insomnia at the age of four; and that when she asked me how I managed to occupy my time at night I answered: 'I lie awake and think about my past'.
RONALD KNOX (1809–1882) *Literary Distractions*

14 It is said that the effect of eating too much lettuce is 'soporific'.
BEATRIX POTTER (1866–1943) *The Tales of Beatrix Potter*

1 Oh sleep! it is a gentle thing,
Beloved from pole to pole.
SAMUEL TAYLOR COLERIDGE (1772–1834)
'The Ancient Mariner'

2 ... sleep is that golden chain that ties health and our bodies together.
THOMAS DEKKER (1570–1641) *The Gull's Hornbook*

3 I believe in sleep: the time spent in sleep (the time when we are out of trouble) is not charged to our account but is handed back to us later in life to use as we please.
CYRIL CONNOLLY (1903–1974) *Encounter*

4 There is weariness even in too much sleep.
HOMER (8th cent. BC) *Odyssey*

5 I haven't been to sleep for over a year. That's why I go to bed early. One needs more rest if one doesn't sleep.
EVELYN WAUGH (1903–1966) *Decline and Fall*

6 The most powerful soporific is sleep itself.
MARCEL PROUST (1871–1922) *Remembrance of Things Past*

7 Sleep comes to the perplexed – if the perplexed are only weary enough.
GEORGE ELIOT (1819–1880) *Adam Bede*

SLIPS OF ACTION, TONGUE AND PEN

8 What I find ... both in grosser disturbances of speech and in those more subtle ones which can still be subsumed under the heading 'slips of the tongue', is that it is not the influence of the 'contact effects of sounds' but the influence of thoughts that lie outside the intended speech which determines the occurrence of the slip and provides an adequate explanation of the mistake.
SIGMUND FREUD (1856–1939) *The Psychopathology of Everyday Life*

9 You have hissed all my mystery lectures and you have tasted the worm.
WILLIAM SPOONER (1844–1930) attrib. in W. Hayter *Spooner: A Biography*, 1979

10 In the course of normal speaking the inhibitory function of the will is continuously directed to bringing the course of ideas and the articulatory movements into harmony with each other. If the expressive movement which follows the idea is retarded through mechanical causes, as is the case in writing ... such anticipations make their appearance with particular ease.
WILHELM WUNDT *Folk Psychology*, 1900

11 ... there is nothing to prevent our treating misprints as 'writing mistakes' on the compositor's part, and our regarding them as being in a very great measure [psychologically] motivated.
SIGMUND FREUD (1856–1939) *The Psychopathology of Everyday Life*

12 Illiterate him, I say, quite from your memory.
RICHARD BRINSLEY SHERIDAN (1751–1816) *The Rivals*

13 Slips of the tongue are not without their parallels. They correspond to the slips which often occur in other human activities and which are known by the somewhat foolish name of 'oversights'.
R. MERINGER, C. MAYER *Versprechen und Verlesen*, 1895

14 ... falling, stumbling and slipping need not always be interpreted as purely accidental miscarriages of motor actions. The double meanings that language attaches to these expressions are enough to indicate the kind of phantasies involved, which can be represented by such losses of bodily equilibrium.... We can also count as bungled actions cases of giving a beggar a gold coin instead of a copper or small silver coin.... They are sacrificial acts designed to appease fate, to avert harm, and so on.
SIGMUND FREUD (1856–1939) *The Psychopathology of Everyday Life*

15 An aspersion upon my parts of speech!
RICHARD BRINSLEY SHERIDAN (1751–1816) *The Rivals*

1   ... 'the Freudian slip', no less than the disguised plots and fantasies of the dream world, under the penetrating lights of psychoanalysis, can be shown to have a direct bearing on the remnants of childhood traumas.
DANIEL ROBINSON *An Intellectual History of Psychology*, 1981

2   The cat popped on its drawers.
WILLIAM SPOONER (1844–1930) attrib. in W. Hayter *Spooner: A Biography*, 1979

3   The craftsman who makes a false stroke with his chisel or hammer, or the billiard player who misses his stroke, show examples of behaviours strictly comparable with slips of the tongue or pen ... both kinds of occurrence are due to a failure of highly complex and delicately balanced adjustment between controlling and controlled processes.
W.H.R. RIVERS *Psychology and Ethnology*, 1926

4   If I reprehend anything in this world it is the use of my oracular tongue, and a nice derangement of epitaphs.
RICHARD BRINSLEY SHERIDAN (1751–1816) *The Rivals*

SOCIAL CLASS

5   Social status is a relative rather than an absolute concept.... Economic inequality and social inequality are not synonymous, nor is objective inequality the same as perceived inequality. An individual's satisfaction with his lot in life will depend in part on what he has been led to expect and with whom he compares himself.
MICHAEL RUTTER, NICOLA MADGE *Cycles of Disadvantage*, 1976

6   ... class happens when some men, as a result of common experiences (inherited or shared), feel and articulate the identity of their interests as between themselves, and as against other men whose interests are different from (and usually opposed to) theirs.
E.P. THOMPSON *The Making of the English Working Class*, 1963

7   ... the new cultural meaning of literacy marked a discontinuity. It drove a wedge through the working class. It came for the first time to be a mark distinguishing the respectable from the non-respectable poor, the washed and the unwashed.
T. LAQUEUR *Oxford Review of Education*, 1976

8   When everyone is somebodee.
Then no one's anybody.
W.S. GILBERT (1836–1911) *The Gondoliers*

9   The pedigree of honey
Does not concern the bee;
A clover, any time, to him
Is aristocracy.
EMILY DICKENSON (1830–1883) *Poems*

10   Dear me, I never knew the lower classes had such white skins.
LORD CURZON (1895–1925) in K. Rose *Superior Person*, 1969

11   No writer before the middle of the 19th century wrote about the working classes other than as grotesques or as pastoral decoration. Then when they were given the vote certain writers began to suck up to them.
EVELYN WAUGH (1903–1966) *The Paris Review*

12   Titles distinguish the mediocre, embarrass the superior, and are disgraced by the inferior.
GEORGE BERNARD SHAW (1856–1950) *Man and Superman*

13   O let us love our occupations,
Bless the squire and his relations,
Live upon our daily rations,
And always know our proper stations.
CHARLES DICKENS (1812–1870) *The Chimes*

14   Were it not for imagination, Sir, a man would be as happy in the arms of a chambermaid as of a Duchess.
SAMUEL JOHNSON (1709–1784) cit. James Boswell *The Life of Samuel Johnson*

15   Her occasional pretty and picturesque use of dialect words – those terrible marks of the beast to the truly genteel.
THOMAS HARDY (1840–1928) *The Mayor of Casterbridge*

1 How beastly the bourgeois is
Especially the male of the species.
D.H. LAWRENCE (1885–1930) 'How Beastly
the Bourgeois Is'

2 Guests' dogs are charged for at the
rate of either 1s., or 1s. 6d. each day,
according to the size and social
standing of the dog.
ANON., tariff of a Torquay Guest House, *New
Statesman*, 27 April 1946

3 One has often wondered whether
upon the whole earth there is anything
so unintelligent, so unapt to perceive
how the world is really going as an
ordinary young Englishman of our
upper class.
MATTHEW ARNOLD (1822–1888) *Culture and
Anarchy*

4 'If you're aristocratic', said Nietzsche,
'It's thumbs up, you're OK. Pleased to
    mietzche.
If you're working-class bones,
It's thumbs down and up yours!
If you don't know your place, then I'll
    tietzche.'
GERRY HAMILL *Oxford Book of Comic Verse*,
1994

5 Through tatter'd clothes small vices
    do appear;
Robes and furr'd gowns hide all. Plate
    sin with gold,
And the strong lance of Justice hurtless
    breaks;
Arm it in rags, a pigmy's straw doth
    pierce it.
WILLIAM SHAKESPEARE (1564–1616) *King
Lear*

6 I'm a class warrior. I've stopped
banging on about it these days, but I do
believe that class is a cancer in this
country, and I saw it waste so many
incredible intelligences that I grew up
with.
MICHAEL CAINE, interview, *The Guardian*, 8
February 1997

7 I come from the city of Boston
The home of the bean and the cod
Where the Lowells talk to the Cabots
And the Cabots talk only to God.
SAMUEL C. BUSHNELL (1852–1930) 'Boston'

8 It's the same the whole world over
It's the poor wot gets the blame.
It's the rich what gets the gravy
Ain't it all a bleedin' shame?
ANON.

9 The English have no respect for their
language, and will not teach their children to speak it. It is impossible for an
Englishman to open his mouth without
making some other Englishman despise
him.
GEORGE BERNARD SHAW (1856–1950)
Preface, *Pygmalion*

10 Really, if the lower orders don't set
us a good example, what on earth is the
use of them?
OSCAR WILDE (1854–1900) *The Importance of
Being Earnest*

SOCIAL INTERACTIONS

11 … in most human interaction,
'realities' are the results of prolonged
intricate processes of construction and
negotiation deeply embedded in the
culture.
J.S. BRUNER *Acts of Meaning*, 1990

12 It is difficult to separate the sexual
talk of preadolescents from their
aggressive talk and behaviour, because
the sexual imagery is frequently
aggressive. This aggression characterizes
much of preadolescent interaction, and
requires acclimatization by adults, who
must realize that it does not necessarily
indicate dislike.
G.A. FINE in H. Foot, A.J. Chapman, J.R.
Smith *Friendship and Social Relations in
Children*, 1980

1 Every person lives in a world of social encounters, involving him either in face-to-face or mediated contact with other participants. In each of these contacts, he tends to act out what is sometimes called a *line*.... Regardless of whether a person intends to take a line, he will find that he has done so in effect. The other participants will assume that he has more or less willfully taken a stand.
ERVING GOFFMAN *Interaction Ritual*, 1967

2 Usually, from our first meeting with a person, we get some main impression, of like or dislike, reality or artificiality, or some single vivid something that we cannot pin down in more than a tentative vague phrase.
TED HUGHES *Poetry in the Making*, 1967

3 There are some additional qualifications necessary in the practical part of business ... such as, an absolute command of your temper, so as not to be provoked to passion upon any account, patience, to hear frivolous, impertinent, and unreasonable applications, with address enough to refuse, without offending; or by your manner of granting, to double the obligation; dexterity enough to conceal a truth, without telling a lie; sagacity enough to read other people's countenance; and serenity enough not to let them discover anything by yours – a seeming frankness, with a real reserve. These are the rudiments of a politician; the world must be your grammar.
LORD CHESTERFIELD, PHILIP STANHOPE (1694–1773) *Letters to His Son*

4 'If everyone minded their own business,' said the Duchess in a hoarse growl, 'the world would go round a deal faster than it does!'
LEWIS CARROLL (1832–1898) *Alice's Adventures in Wonderland*

5 Most of us are generally united by our doubts and divided by our convictions.
PETER USTINOV *Quotable Ustinov*, 1995

6 Whenever students of the human scene have considered the dealings individuals have with one another, the issue of calculation has arisen.
ERVING GOFFMAN *Strategic Interaction*, 1969

7 If all the good people were clever,
And all clever people were good,
The world would be nicer than ever
We thought that it possibly could.

But somehow, 'tis seldom or never
The two hit it off as they should;
The good are so harsh to the clever,
And the clever so rude to the good.
ELIZABETH WORDSWORTH (1840–1932) 'Good and Clever'

SOCIALISATION

8 Socialization sensitizes the child to various orderings of society as they are made substantive in the various roles he is expected to play. In a sense then socialization is a process for making people safe.
BASIL BERNSTEIN in P.P. Giglioli *Language and Social Context*, 1970

9 Social adaptation requires skills in both seeking help (dependency) and giving it (nurturance), being passive and being sociable; ... being intimate and being self-reliant.
W.W. HARTUP in H. McGurk *Issues in Childhood Social Development*, 1978

10 The individual creates his social space and is in turn formed by it. On the one hand, his range of experiences and behavior are controlled by his social space, and on the other, everything he learns causes it to expand and become more differentiated.... In the evolution of an individual's social space we have a measure of his educational development.
M. FORTES in J. Middleton *From Child to Adult*, 1970

1   I believe it is precisely the 'private' worlds of desire, aspiration and conscience that must be studied if we are to succeed in the task of social engineering.
G.W. ALLPORT *Psychological Review*, 1947

2   Any man's death diminishes me, because I am involved in Mankind.
JOHN DONNE (1571–1631) *Devotions Upon Emergent Occasions*

3   It's right and legitimate that we should consider as 'good' the manners which parents taught us, that we should hold sacred the social norms and rites handed down to us by cultural tradition. What we must guard against, with all the power of rational responsibility, is our natural inclination to regard social norms and rites of other cultures as inferior.
KONRAD LORENZ *Transactions of the Royal Society London*, 1966

SOCIETY

4   The positive development of a society in the absence of creative, independent thinking, critical individuals is as inconceivable as the development of an individual in the absence of the stimulus of the community.
ALBERT EINSTEIN (1879–1955) cit. Einstein Museum, Bern

5   Commitment moves us from the mirror trap of the self absorbed with the self to the freedom of a community of shared values.
MICHAEL LEWIS *Shame*, 1992

6   Insignificant people are a necessary relief in society. Such characters are extremely agreeable, and even favourites, if they appear satisfied with the part they have to perform.
WILLIAM HAZLITT (1778–1830) *Characteristics*

7   If the capacity for abstract behavior were really the highest attribute of human nature, why, one may ask, are human beings not able to build up a social organization that will guarantee human existence at least to some degree? How is it possible that human ingenuity should be used essentially for the purpose of destruction.
KURT GOLDSTEIN *Human Nature in the Light of Psychopathology*, 1940

8   [Psychology] ... the only alternative to an arbitrary and class view of society.
JOHN DEWEY *Science*, 1900

9   What life have you if you have not life together?
There is no life that is not community.
T.S. ELIOT (1888–1965) Choruses from 'The Rock'

10   The greatest happiness of the greatest number is the foundation of morals and legislation.
JEREMY BENTHAM (1748–1832) *The Commonplace Book*

11   The worst enemy of life, freedom and the common decencies is total anarchy; their second worst enemy is total efficiency.
ALDOUS HUXLEY (1894–1973) *Adonis and the Alphabet*

12   The child's behavior is molded in every respect by his social situation ... his morale, his religion, and his political values are determined by his being a part of, and reacting to, the society in which he lives.
KURT LEWIN *American Journal of Sociology*, 1939

13   There is no such thing as society. There are individual men and women and there are families.
MARGARET THATCHER *Woman's Own*, 31 October 1987

14   Never speak disrespectfully of society. Only people who can't get into it do that.
OSCAR WILDE (1854–1900) *In Conversation*

SOCIOBIOLOGY

1   I think that a minor revolution has taken place in the way we think about social relationships. 'Genteel' ideas of vaguely benevolent mutual cooperation are replaced by an expectation of stark, ruthless, opportunistic mutual exploitation. This revolution is popularly associated with the name 'sociobiology'.
RICHARD DAWKINS *The Extended Phenotype*, 1982

2   When a person ... increases the fitness of another at the expense of his own fitness, he can be said to have performed an act of *altruism*.... In contrast, a person who raises his own fitness by lowering that of others is engaged in *selfishness*.... Finally, a person who gains nothing or even reduces his own fitness in order to diminish that of another has committed an act of *spite*.
E.O. WILSON *Sociobiology: The New Synthesis*, 1975

3   [Sociobiology] predicts that we shall continue to reproduce, consume resources, and destroy each other with abandon because we are programmed to care only about ourselves and our relatives. So far there is little evidence to show sociobiology is wrong.
P.L. VAN DEN BERGHE *Sociobiology and Human Nature*, 1978

4   ... if the strong were always fighting, the weak would inherit, if not the earth, at least the wives of the strong.
S. GENOVES *Perspectives in Biology and Medicine*, 1976

SOLITUDE

5   Learning, thinking, innovation, and maintaining contact with one's own inner world are all facilitated by solitude.
ANTHONY STORR *Solitude*, 1989

6   For solitude sometimes is best society,
And short retirement urges sweet return.
JOHN MILTON (1608–1674) *Paradise Lost*

7   Solitude is the profoundest fact of the human condition. Man is the only being who knows when he is alone.
OCTAVIO PAZ *The Labyrinth of Solitude*, 1962

8   Whosoever is delighted in solitude is either a wild beast or a god.
FRANCIS BACON (1561–1626) *Essays*

9   In solitude
What happiness? Who can enjoy alone,
Or all enjoying, what contentment find?
JOHN MILTON (1608–1674) *Paradise Lost*

SOMATOTYPES

10   Great men are but life-sized. Most of them, indeed, are rather short.
MAX BEERBOHM (1872–1956) *And Even Now*

11   Give me a doctor, partridge plump,
Short in the leg and broad in the rump.
An endomorph with gentle hands
Who'll never make absurd demands
That I abandon all my vices,
Nor pull a long face in a crisis,
But with a twinkle in his eye,
Will tell me that I have to die.
W.H. AUDEN (1907–1973) 'Shorts'

12   Yond' Cassius has a lean and hungry look;
He thinks too much: such men are dangerous.
WILLIAM SHAKESPEARE (1564–1616) *Julius Caesar*

13   Fading is the taper waist
Shapeless grows the shapely limb,
And although securely laced,
Spreading is the figure trim!
Stouter than I used to be
Still more corpulent grow I –
There will be too much of me
In the coming bye and bye.
W.S. GILBERT (1836–1911) *Patience*

SPECULATION

1 ... without metapsychological speculation and theorizing – I had almost say phantasying – we shall not get another step forward.
SIGMUND FREUD (1856–1939) cit. J. Sandler
Analysis Terminable and Interminable, 1987

2 Bold ideas, unjustified anticipation, and speculative thought, are our only means for interpreting nature; ... our only instrument for grasping her. And we must hazard them to win our prize.
KARL POPPER *The Logic of Scientific Discovery*, 1959

3 What might have been is an abstraction
Remaining a perceptual possibility
Only in a world of speculation.
T.S. ELIOT (1888–1965) 'Burnt Norton'

SPEECH

4 Speech is civilisation itself.
THOMAS MANN (1875–1955) *The Magic Mountain*

5 [Speech] would surely never have been ours if our lips had been required to perform the onerous and difficult task of procuring nourishment for our bodies. But our hands took over that task, releasing our mouths for the service of speech.
GREGORY OF NYSSA (c. 330–c. 395) *Treatise on the Creation of Man*

6 The general use of Speech, is to transferre our Mentall Discourse, into Verbal; or the Trayne of our Thoughts, into a Trayne of Words; and that for two commodities; whereof one is, the Registering of the Consequences of our Thoughts; which being apt to slip out of our memory, and put us to a new labour, may again be recalled, by such words as they were marked by.
THOMAS HOBBES (1588–1679) *Leviathan*

7 Watch your own speech and notice how it is guided by your less conscious purposes.
GEORGE ELIOT (1819–1880) *Mill on the Floss*

8 In general, children do not create their own speech; they master the existing speech of surrounding adults.
L.S. VYGOTSKY *Thinking and Speech*, 1934

9 Thought and expression ... are simultaneously constituted.... The spoken word is a genuine gesture, and it contains its necessary meaning in the same way as the gesture contains its. This is what makes communication possible.
M. MERLEAU-PONTY *Phenomenology of Perception*, 1962

10 Speech sounds cannot be understood, delimited, classified and explained except in the light of tasks which they perform in language.
R. JAKOBSON *Sound and Meaning*, 1978

11 The popular explanation of 'correct' and 'incorrect' speech reduces the matter to one of knowledge versus ignorance. There is such a thing as correct English. An ignorant person does not know the correct forms; therefore he cannot help using incorrect ones ... these notions do not correspond to the facts. There is no fixed standard of 'correct' English.
L. BLOOMFIELD in D. Hymes *Language, Culture and Society*, 1964

12 Some people speak well but do not write well. It is because the place and the audience stimulate them and get more out of them than they could manage without such stimulus.
BLAISE PASCAL (1623–1662) *Pensées*

13 The importance of babbling as a basis for human speech probably cannot be overestimated. To the onlooker, the babbling baby is obviously having fun, but at the same time he is learning to use his lips, tongue and breathing in different combinations. He is gaining control of these until in time he will be able to produce whatever sound he pleases. He is developing *the motor skill of vocalisation.*
CATHY HAYES *The Ape in Our House*, 1952

1 Speech is the greatest interest and most distinct achievement of man.
NORBERT WIENER *The Human Use of Human Beings*, 1950

SPORT

2 The traditional assumption that competitive sport builds character is still with us today in spite of overwhelming contrary evidence.
D.S. BUTT *Psychology of Sport*, 1976

3 Footeball ... causeth fighting, brawling, contention, quarrel picking, murder, homicide and great effusion of blood, as daily experience teacheth.
PHILIP STUBBES *Anatomie of Abuses*, 1583

4 I am always amazed when I hear people saying that sport creates goodwill between the nations, and that if only the common peoples of the world could meet one another at football or cricket they would have no inclination to meet on the battlefield. Even if one didn't know from concrete examples (the 1936 Olympic Games, for instance) that international sporting contests lead to orgies of hate, one could deduce it from general principles.
GEORGE ORWELL (1903–1950) *Tribune*, 1945

5 The most important function of sport lies in furnishing a healthy safety valve for that most indispensable and, at the same time, most dangerous form of aggression ... collective militant enthusiasm.
KONRAD LORENZ *On Aggression* 1963

STATISTICS

6 According to the famous *mot*, statistics is the science according to which if one man eats two chickens daily and another man eats none, then each has eaten one chicken.
UMBERTO ECO *Misreadings*, 1961

7 Repertory grid technique has the advantage of quantifying in precise and statistically sophisticated form the response of the subject while allowing him to deal with the vital and meaningful material in terms of his personal life.
DON BANNISTER in B.M. Foss *New Horizons in Psychology*, 1966

8 Whenever you can, count.
FRANCIS GALTON (1822–1911) cit. D.J. Kelves *In the Name of Eugenics*, 1986

9 As the chemist finds his new compounds in the rubbish of the retort, so the statistical enquirer finds his truths in the debris of investigation.
JOSEPH JACOBS *Mind*, 1885

10 Very, very, very few
People die at ninety-two.
I suppose that I shall be
Safer still at ninety-three.
W.R. ESPY *Another Almanac of Words*, 1981

11 ... there is no place for statistics in a strictly nomethetic, or ... systematic discipline.
EGON BRUNSWICK *Psychological Review*, 1943

12 Like dreams, statistics are a form of fulfilment.
JEAN BANDRILLARD *Cool Memories*, 1990

13 Statistics never prove anything.
ERNST SCHUMACHER *Small is Beautiful*, 1973

14 Nor has Bartlett held any truck with quantification. His writings are free of statistics. Statistical methods he regards as scientific make-shifts.
L.S. HEARNSHAW *A Short History of British Psychology 1840–1940*, 1964

15 The idea that statistics deal with nothing but measurable characteristics is a widespread but mistaken fallacy.
CHARLOTTE BANKS, CYRIL BURT in C.A. Mace, P. Vernon *Current Trends in British Psychology*, 1953

16 Chance is a name for our ignorance.
LESLIE STEPHEN (1832–1904) *English Thought in the 18th Century*

1 The mean is often nearer to one extreme than the other, or seems to be nearer because of our natural tendencies.
ARISTOTLE (384–322 BC) *Ethics*

2 There are three kinds of lies – lies, damned lies and statistics.
MARK TWAIN (1835–1910) *Autobiography*

3 Statistical Fellows –
A prying, spying, inquisitive clan,
Who have gone upon much of the self-
     same plan,
Jotting the labouring classes' riches;
And after poking in pot and pan,
And routing garments in want of stitches,
Have ascertained that a working man
Wears a pair and a quarter of average
     breeches.
THOMAS HOOD (1799–1845) *Playful Poems*

4 The object of factor analysis is to discover the mental faculties.
L.L. THURSTONE *Vectors of the Mind*, 1939

STEREOTYPES

5 The selection and use of stereotypes seems to depend on the needs of the person applying them. It also appears that the minority that shows the greater difference from the majority in physical characteristics, such as skin color, is used for projecting anxieties associated with dirt and sex desires, while the minority that is more like the majority in appearance becomes a symbol for anxieties concerning over-powering control.
BRUNO BETTELHEIM, M. JANOWITZ
Scientific American, 1950

6 But – oh! ye lords of ladies
     intellectual
Inform us truly have they not hen-
     pecked you all?
LORD BYRON (1788–1824) *Don Juan*

7 A statesman is an easy man,
He tells his lies by rote;
A journalist makes up his lies
And takes you by the throat;
So stay at home and drink your beer
And let the neighbours vote.
W.B. YEATS (1865–1939) 'The Old Stone Cross'

8 Give a man a reputation as an early riser and that man can sleep to noon.
MARK TWAIN (1835–1910) attrib.

9 Never trust a woman who wears mauve, whatever her age may be, or a woman over thirty-five who is fond of pink ribbons. It always means they have a history.
OSCAR WILDE (1854–1900) *The Picture of Dorian Gray*

10 did you ever
notice that when
a politician
does get an idea
he usually
gets it all wrong
don marquis (1878–1937) 'archygrams'

11 To the man in the street who I'm
     sorry to say
Is a keen observer of life,
The word *intellectual* suggests right
     away
A man who's untrue to his wife.
W.H. AUDEN (1907–1973) 'Shorts'

12 Our society distributes itself into Barbarians, Philistines, and Populace: and America is just as ourselves, with the Barbarians quite left out, and the Populace nearly.
MATTHEW ARNOLD *Culture and Anarchy*, 1869

13 a politician
is an arse upon
which everyone has sat
except a man
e.e. cummings (1894–1962) *Complete Poems*, 1981

14 You cannot hope
to bribe or twist
thank God, the
British journalist

But, seeing what
the man will do
unbribed, there's
no occasion to.
HUMBERT WOLFE (1886–1940) 'The Uncelestial City'

230

STIMULUS AND RESPONSE

1 Behaviorally, stimuli that reinforce are called rewarding and those that punish aversive. Although reward and aversion describe the impact a stimulus has on behavior, they do not address why we approach some stimuli and not others.
K. NADER, A. BECHARA, D van de KOOY
Annual Review of Psychology, 1997

2 The impressions which ... a terrifying object makes on the gland causes fear in certain men, and yet in other men can excite courage and confidence ... all brains are not constituted in the same manner.
RENÉ DESCARTES (1596–1650) *Les Passions*

3 ... the Pavlovian conditioned reflex is not to be interpreted too highly as being the attachment of a response to a stimulus simply because it happens at about the same time.... The whole situation is far more complicated than Pavlov or Watson thought.
D.E. BROADBENT *Behaviour*, 1964

4 The psychologist must not stand in awe of the stimulus.
F.C. BARTLETT *Remembering*, 1932

5 I still feel that 'response' is one of the most slippery and unanalyzed of our current concepts. We all gaily use the term to mean anything from a secretion of 10 drops of saliva to entering a given alley, to running an entire maze. For the slope of a Skinner box curve, to achieving a PhD, or to the symbolic act of hostility against one's father by attacking some authority figure.... The 'stimulus' as we use it today seems to be just as slippery a term as that of response.
E.C. TOLMAN cit. S. Koch *Psychology: A Study of a Science, Vol. 2*, 1959

6 It may be desirable to think of the stimuli used in any experiment as having positions in an 'information space' made up of all the dimensions discriminable by the sense organs.
D.E. BROADBENT *Perception and Communication*, 1958

STORIES

7 [Children] repeat stories in the same way that they practice newly learnt games or skills. With each telling they not only can repeat the pleasure or pain of the experience, they repeat the pleasure of telling about the experience, and they gain increased ownership or mastery over both the experience and the telling of it.
SUSAN ENGEL *The Stories Children Tell*, 1995

8 Narrative deals with the vicissitudes of human intentions. And since there are myriad intentions and endless ways for them to run into trouble ... there should be endless kinds of stories. But, surprisingly, this seems not to be the case.
J.S. BRUNER *Actual Minds, Possible Worlds*, 1986

9 ... human beings think, perceive, imagine, and make moral choices according to narrative structures. Present two or three pictures, or descriptive phrases, to a person and he or she will connect them to form a story, an account that related the picture or meanings of the phrases in some patterned way.
T. SARBIN *Narrative Psychology: the Storied Nature of Human Conduct*, 1986

10 The therapist knows only what you tell him about your life, past and present, so that the raw materials of therapy are predominantly stories, not behavior. As you change the way you see yourself, the stories are transformed. Thus the goal of therapy in this view is not simply to behave differently or to feel differently but to tell a different story about yourself than the one you used to tell.
SUSAN ENGEL *The Stories Children Tell*, 1995

11 The function of the story is to find an internal state that mitigates or at least makes comprehensible a deviation from a canonical cultural pattern
J.S. BRUNER *Acts of Meaning*, 1990

STRATEGIES

1 Be nice to people on your way up because you'll meet 'em on your way down.
WILSON MIZNER cit. A. Johnston *The Legendary Mizners*, 1953

2 Don't hit at all if it is honorably possible to avoid hitting; but *never* hit soft.
THEODORE ROOSEVELT (1858–1919) cit. J.B. Bishop *Theodore Roosevelt and his Times*

3 Why so dull and mute, young
    sinner?
Prithee, why so mute?
Will, when speaking well can't win her,
Saying nothing do't?
JOHN SUCKLING (1609–1642) 'Song'

4 Everyday
I think about dying.
About disease, starvation,
violence, terrorism, war,
the end of the world

It helps
keep my mind off things.
ROGER McGOUGH 'Survivor', 1979

STRESS

5 Stress is essentially the rate of all the wear and tear caused by life ... although we cannot avoid stress as long as we live, we can learn a great deal about how to keep its damaging side effects to a minimum.
HANS SEYLE *The Stress of Life*, 1956

6 The capacity of the nervous and endocrine systems to respond to stress may perhaps be one of the major selective factors in human evolution today.
J.Z. YOUNG *An Introduction to the Study of Man*, 1970

7 ... a mill seemed to be working inside my head. I could not banish obsessing ideas; at times I could hardly read a book, and found it painful even to look at a printed page.... It was as though I had tried to make a steam-engine perform more work than it was constructed for, by tampering with its safety valve and thereby straining its mechanism.
FRANCIS GALTON (1822–1911) *Memories of My Life*

8 In headaches and in worry
Vaguely life leaks away
And Time will have his fancy
Tomorrow or today.
W.H. AUDEN (1907–1973) 'As I Walked Out One Evening'

9 An ever increasing proportion of the human population dies from the so-called wear-and-tear diseases, or degenerative diseases, which are primarily due to stress.
HANS SEYLE *The Stress of Life*, 1956

SUICIDE

10 There is no suicide for which all society is not responsible.
CYRIL CONNOLLY (1903–1974) *The Unquiet Grave*

11 ... the trend to self-destruction is present to a certain degree in very many more human beings than those in whom it is carried out; self injuries are as a rule a compromise between their instinct and the forces that are still working against it, and even where suicide actually results, the inclination to suicide will have been present for a long time before in lesser strength or in the form of an unconscious and suppressed trend.
SIGMUND FREUD (1856–1939) *The Psychopathology of Everyday Life*

12 It is against the law to commit suicide in this man's town ... although what the law can do to a guy who commits suicide I am never able to figure out.
DAMON RUNYON *Guys and Dolls*, 1932

1 Many men would take the death-sentence without a whimper to escape the life-sentence which fate carries in her other hand.
T.E. LAWRENCE (1888–1935) *The Mint*

2 Razors pain you;
Rivers are damp;
Acids stain you;
And drugs cause cramp;
Guns aren't lawful;
Nooses give;
Gas smells awful;
You might as well live.
DOROTHY PARKER (1893–1967) 'Enough Rope'

3 Against self-slaughter
There is a prohibition so divine
That cravens my weak hand.
WILLIAM SHAKESPEARE (1564–1616) *Cymbeline*

4 Amid the miseries of our life on earth, suicide is God's best gift to man.
PLINY THE ELDER (23–79 AD) *Natural History*

5 There are many who dare not kill themselves for fear of what the neighbours might say.
CYRIL CONNOLLY (1903–1974) *The Unquiet Grave*

6 If you must commit suicide ... always contrive to do it as decorously as possible; the decencies, whether of life or of death, should never be lost sight of.
GEORGE BORROW (1803–1881) *Lavengro*

SUPERSTITION

7 ...for a living being lacking insight into the relation between causes and effects, it must be extremely useful to cling to a behaviour pattern which has many times proved to achieve its aim, and to have done so without danger. If one does not know which details of the whole performance are essential for its success as well as its safety, it is best to cling to them all with slavish exactitude.
KONRAD LORENZ *On Aggression*, 1963

SYMBOLS

8 A genuine symbol is a symbol that has a general meaning.
C.S. PEIRCE (1839–1914) *Collected Papers, Vol. 2*

9 ... current experimental psychology, because of its willingness to sacrifice significant problems to excessive methodological rigor, has almost completely neglected the study of expressive symbolism in spite of its centrality in almost all areas of cognitive behavior of everyday life in poetic language, in myth, in religious symbolism, etc.
HEINZ WERNER *On Expressive Language*, 1955

10 For the benefit of the Freudians one ought to collect instances where sex is not the final target of the symbol but is itself used as a symbol for an ulterior meaning. Hegel quotes from Herodotus to the effect that Sesostris used to erect a phallic column in every country he had conquered. If the people put up little resistance, he also had a vagina engraved on the monument.
RUDOLPH ARNHEIM *Parables of Sun Light*, 1989

11 Sometimes a cigar is just a cigar.
SIGMUND FREUD (1856–1939) cit. *Los Angeles Times*, 4 July 1982

12 Ontogenetically speaking, it seems that symbols are in the world first, and only later in the head.
EDWIN HUTCHINS *Cognition in the Wild*, 1996

SYNAESTHESIA

1 In the field of sound and music, it has been found that some people have constant images of colours or sometimes of lines, occurring when they hear certain notes or tones.... Some composers themselves seem to have had colour tonality associations. Thus Beethoven describes B minor as 'black', Scriabin connected C with 'red', G and D with 'yellow', and so on through the series to F sharp, which was 'purple'.
C.W. VALENTINE *The Experimental Psychology of Beauty*, 1962

2 ... all around him hung a deafening odour of aftershave.
JOHN MORTIMER *Rumpole and the Angel of Death*, 1995

3 With a name like yours, you might be any shape, almost.
LEWIS CARROLL (1832–1898) *Alice Through the Looking Glass*

4 love is more thicker than forget
more thinner than recall
more seldom than a wave is wet
more frequent than to fail
e.e. cummings (1894–1962) 'love is more thicker than forget'

5 A very well known living pianist has said that his synaesthesia is so vivid that he sees the colours aroused by the music the whole of the time he is playing at concerts and guides his interpretation according to whether it is blue, green, brown, etc.
P.E. VERNON *Psyche*, 1929/30

6 ... the colour of elephants' breath.
POSIE SIMMONS, interview, *The Independent*, 21 December 1996

7 Many people regard large, thick, angular, upward directed and distinct forms as corresponding to loudness in music, while they see small, thin, angular, and straightlined forms as equivalent to fast music. Similar observations have been made with regard to sounds in language: small, light and pointed forms ... are characterized best by names with blunted and hollow vowels.... Few people can overcome the urge to couple a round-curved form with the name 'Maluma', and a sharp-angled line drawing with the name 'Takete'.
H. KREITLER, S. KREITLER *Psychology of the Arts*, 1972

T

TALK

1 Understanding the other's way of talking is a giant leap across the communication gap between women and men, and a giant step towards opening lines of communication.
DEBORAH TANNEN *You Just Don't Understand*, 1992

2 Conversation is much more of a roughly prescribed ritual than most people think. Once someone speaks to you, you are in a relatively determined context and you are not free to say just what you please.
J.R. FIRTH in D. Hymes *Language Culture and Society*, 1964

3 No, Sir; we had *talk* enough, but no *conversation*; there was nothing *discussed*.
SAMUEL JOHNSON (1709–1784) cit. James Boswell *The Life of Samuel Johnson*

4 The opposite of talking isn't listening. The opposite of talking is waiting.
FRAN LEBOWITZ *Social Studies*, 1981

5 Nature has given man one tongue, but two ears, that we may hear twice as much as we speak.
EPICTETUS (c. 55–135) *Fragments VI*

6 Curtsey while you're thinking what to say. It saves time.
LEWIS CARROLL (1832–1898) *Alice Through the Looking Glass*

7 Strange the difference of men's Talk!
SAMUEL PEPYS (1633–1703) *Diary*

8 I don't want to talk grammar, I want to talk like a lady.
GEORGE BERNARD SHAW (1856–1950) *Pygmalion*, 1912

9 He knew the precise psychological moment to say nothing.
OSCAR WILDE (1854–1900) *The Picture of Dorian Gray*

10 For more than forty years I've been talking prose without knowing it.
MOLIÈRE (1622–1673) *Le Bourgeois Gentilhomme*

11 Many people can talk sense with concepts but cannot talk sense about them; they know by practice how to operate with concepts, anyhow inside their chosen fields, but they cannot state the logical regulations governing their use. They are like people who know their way around their own parish, but cannot construct or read a map of it, much less of the region, or continent in which their parish lies.
GILBERT RYLE *The Concept of Mind*, 1949

12 Be silent always, when you doubt your sense;
And speak, tho' sure, with seeming diffidence.
ALEXANDER POPE (1688–1744) 'An Essay on Criticism'

13 There is growing evidence that people modify their speech to at least some groups of older people, and some suggestion that styles can be unwarranted and demeaning.
N. COUPLAND, J. COUPLAND, H. GILES *Language, Society and the Elderly*, 1991

14 One may look upon social communication as ... based on efforts to equalize knowledge and mutual influence. Yet every new conversational move presupposes asymmetry of knowledge.... Dialogue thrives on this tension between exploiting asymmetries and returning to states of equilibrium.
P. LINELL, T. LUCKMAN in I. Markova, K. Foppa *Asymmetries in Dialogue*, 1991

15 Sir, you have but two topics, yourself and me. I am sick of both.
SAMUEL JOHNSON (1709–1784) cit. James Boswell *The Life of Samuel Johnson*

1 whenever i have nothing
particular to say
i find myself
always plunging into cosmic
philosophy
or something
don marquis (1878–1937) 'unjust'

2 Now because the subculture or culture, through its forms of integration,
generates a restricted code, it does not
mean that the resultant speech and
meaning system is linguistically or
culturally deprived, that the children
have nothing to offer to the school, that
their imaginings are not significant....
There is nothing, but nothing, in the
dialect as such which prevents a child
from internalizing and learning to use
universalistic meanings.
BASIL BERNSTEIN in D. Rubenstein, C.
Stoneman *Education for Democracy*, 1970

3 We usually only want to know
something so that we can talk about it;
in other words, we would never travel by
sea if it meant never talking about it,
and for the sheer pleasure of seeing
things we could never hope to describe to
others.
BLAISE PASCAL (1623–1662) *Pensées*

4 The meaning doesn't matter if it's
only idle chatter.
W.S. GILBERT (1836–1911) *Patience*

5 ... dialogue can take place only if
some basic commonalities of
perspectives are established between
participants.
I. MARKOVA, K. FOPPA *Asymmetries in
Dialogue*, 1991

6 I gotta use words when I talk to you
But if you understand or if you don't
That's nothing to me and nothing to you
We all gotta to do what we gotta do.
T.S. ELIOT (1888–1965) 'Sweeney Agonistes'

7 That his [Oscar Wilde's] talk was
mostly a monologue was not his own
fault. His manners were very good: he
was careful to give his guests or his
fellow guests many a conversational
opening; but seldom did anyone
respond with more than a few words.

Nobody was willing to interrupt the
music of so magnificent a virtuoso.
MAX BEERBOHM (1872–1956) *A Peep into the
Past*

TEACHING

8 Any subject can be effectively taught
in intellectually honest form to any
child at any stage in development.
J.S. BRUNER *The Process of Education*, 1960

9 No man ever got a word of sense out
of a schoolmaster. You may, at a pinch,
take their word about equilateral hexa-
gons but life, life's a closed book to them.
JOHN MORTIMER *A Voyage Round my
Father*, 1971

10 Certainly the average teacher
speaks too much.
MARGARET McMILLAN *Early Childhood*, 1900

11 The teacher or lecturer is a danger.
He very seldom recognises his nature or
his position. The lecturer is a man who
must talk for an hour.
EZRA POUND (1885–1972) *The ABC of Reading*

12 Even while they teach, men learn.
SENECA (4 BC–65 AD) *Moral Epistles*

13 And when he occupies a college,
Truth is replaced by Useful Knowledge;
He pays particular
Attention to Commercial Thought,
Public Relations, Hygiene, Sport,
In his curricula.
W.H. AUDEN (1907–1973) 'Under Which Lyre'

14 The condition in the average school
is a matter of widespread concern.
Modern children simply do not learn
arithmetic quickly or well. Nor is the
result simply incompetence. The very
subjects in which modern techniques are
weakest are those in which failure is
most conspicuous and in the wake of an
ever-growing incompetence come the
anxieties, uncertainties, and
aggressions, which in their turn present
other problems in the school.
B.F. SKINNER *Science and Human Behavior*,
1953

1 ... the tendency, already noticeable in primary school education, of teaching as much as possible by arousing and stimulating exploratory interest rather than by regimented instruction, is not only biologically sound but yields promising results.
N. TINBERGEN *Proceedings of the Royal Society London, B*, 1972

2   That we but teach
Bloody instructions, which, being taught, return,
To plague the inventor.
WILLIAM SHAKESPEARE (1564–1616) *Macbeth*

3 Like so many ageing college people, Pnin had long ceased to notice the existence of students on the campus.
VLADIMIR NABOKOV (1899–1977) *Pnin*, 1957

4 What does it matter to me if they can write
A description of a dog, or if they can't?
What is the point? To both of us, it is all my aunt!
And yet I'm supposed to care, with all my might.
I do not, and will not; they won't and they don't, and that's all!
D.H. LAWRENCE (1885–1930) 'Last Lesson of the Afternoon'

5 But it is only among humans that the adult *introduces* the novel, inducts the young into new, challenging, and frightening situations – sometimes in a highly ritualistic way, as with the *rites de passage.*
J.S. BRUNER *American Psychologist*, 1972

6 The first law of teaching then is: Be interesting.
E.S. WATERHOUSE *The ABC of Psychology*, 1927

7 Lectures were once useful; but now, when all can read, and books are so numerous, lectures are unnecessary.
SAMUEL JOHNSON (1709–1784) cit. James Boswell *The Life of Samuel Johnson*

8 But where's the man, who counsel can bestow,
Still pleased to teach, and yet not proud to know?
Unbiass'd, or by favour or by spite;
Not dully prepossess'd, nor blindly right?
ALEXANDER POPE (1688–1744) 'An Essay on Criticism'

9 He who can does. He who cannot teaches.
GEORGE BERNARD SHAW (1856–1950) *Man and Superman*

10 We conclude that – the psychology of human relationships being what it is – in adult education there is an inverse relationship between 'power' and 'learning'. Only the 'weak' can teach. If the teacher comes into too much power, he ceases to be a 'teacher' and becomes instead a religious or political (or other 'group') 'leader'.
THOMAS SZASZ *Psychoanalytic Training*, 1958

11 While I was listening eagerly to Freud's lectures I studied assiduously his technique of exposition with a view of modelling my own after him. I wondered how he succeeded in producing something unexpected and stupendous while his talk moved in simple terms, dispensing with the fireworks of baffling profundity or of glittering paradoxes. I found that he made use of Schopenhauer's recipe for a good style: 'Say extraordinary things by using ordinary words'.
HANS SACHS (1881–1947) cit. H. Peterson *Great Teachers*

12 To discover and teach are distinct functions; they are also distinct gifts, and are not commonly found united in the same person.
JOHN HENRY (CARDINAL) NEWMAN (1801–1890) *The Idea of a University*

13 It is difficult to find even a single study, ancient or modern, of what is retained from academic instruction. Given our expertise and the way we earn our livings, this omission can only be described as scandalous.
U. NEISSER *Memory Observed*, 1982

1 This child cannot read.
Because he cannot read
we must teach him.
He is little, so,
we break the job into little steps.
Because we break it into little steps
he can only learn in little steps.
I can only teach one-thing-at-a-time, so
he can only learn one-thing-at-a-time.
If he can only learn one-thing-at-a-time
then we can only teach one-thing-at-a-
time.
That is why I teach him this before that.
You must not teach him that before this
because that would upset my programme.
R.D. LAING *Knots*, 1970

2 Some experiences of popular
lecturing had convinced me that the
necessity of making things plain to
uninstructed people was one of the very
best means of clearing up the obscure
corners in one's own mind.
T.H. HUXLEY (1825–1885) *Man's Place in
Nature*

3 A professor is one who talks in
someone else's sleep.
W.H. AUDEN (1907–1973) attrib.

TELEVISION

4 Normally cats and dogs do not
respond to television pictures. This is
not because they are not interested in
the content of the pictures, but because
these are presented in a way that does
not match their sensory capacities....
The more like ours an animal's brain is
the more it will enjoy watching
television. Monkeys find it of some
interest; the Great Apes are gripped by
it almost as painfully as we are.
RICHARD LATTO in R.L. Gregory *et al. The
Artful Eye*, 1995

5 [Television] A box that has changed
children from an irresistible force to an
immovable object.
ANON.

6 Books are on their way out,
nowadays, didn't you know that? Words
are on their last legs. Words, print and

also thought. That's also for the high
jump. The sentence, that dignified entity
with subject and predicate, is shortly to
be made illegal. Wherever two or three
words are gathered together, you see,
there is a grave danger that thought
might be present. All assemblies of
words will be forbidden, in favour of
patterns of light, videotape, every man
his own telecine.
ALAN BENNETT *Getting On*, 1972

7 Thus technology has given us a
uniquely potent teacher [television] –
and in a complex society like our own,
effective teachers are much needed. At
the same time, though, the greater the
power of the teacher, the greater the
capacity to work for good or harm.
R.M. LIEBERT *et al. The Early Window:
Effects of Television on Children and Youth*,
1973

8 Reading is a creative art. Looking at
a television screen ... can be
extraordinarily educational. But what
the picture can never do for you, and
what the word can, is allow you to work
and exploit your own imagination.
PAUL BAILEY cit. N. Grey *Writer's Talking*,
1989

TESTS AND TESTING

9 Almost any kind of standardized
testing situation, even the type that
employs standard and structured
stimuli, may offer the clinician an
opportunity for projective interpretation.
In such instances the examiner does not
focus solely upon the subtler aspects of
the 'correctness' of the response.... He is
more concerned with the subtler
aspects of the response.... The subjects'
'cognitive style', manner of reasoning,
idiosyncratic content, and patterns of
successes and failures become grist to
the interpretative mill.
A.I. RABIN *Projective Techniques in Personality
Assessment*, 1968

1 While I am willing to agree that the role of 'tests' in modern psychological procedure is a very great and important one, I also think it obvious enough that no genuine problem of human behaviour is ever or ever can be solved in terms of tests alone.
F.C. BARTLETT *Proceedings of the 12th International Congress of Psychology, Edinburgh*, 1950

2 Attainment is a poor measure of capacity, and ignorance no proof of defect.
CYRIL BURT *Mental and Scholastic Tests*, 1921

3 The test is the ultimate scholastic invention.
HOWARD GARDNER *The Unschooled Mind*, 1993

4 If individuals can be given a score simply from putting them in rank order – and people can be put in rank order for anything under the sun – there is very little incentive to find the exact nature of the thing with respect to which they are being put in rank order.
R.B. CATTELL *Psychological Review*, 1944

5 Psychological tests are not simply to be regarded as good *in principle*. They are good only to the extent that they can serve useful and beneficial purposes and can do so more objectively, reliably and efficiently than other available means.
A.R. JENSEN *Bias in Mental Testing*, 1980

THEORY

6 A theory may be considered a way of binding together a multitude of facts so that one may comprehend them all at once. When the theory enables us to make reasonably precise predictions, one may call it scientific ... our anticipations of daily events, while not scientifically precise nevertheless surround our lives with an aura of meaning.... A theory provides a basis for an active approach to life, not merely a comfortable armchair to contemplate its vicissitudes with detached complaisance.
G.A. KELLY *The Psychology of Personal Constructs*, 1955

7 The history of acceptance of new theories frequently shows the following steps: At first the new idea is treated as pure nonsense, not worth looking at. Then comes a time when a multitude of contradictory objections are raised, such as: the new theory is too fancy, or merely a new terminology; it is not fruitful, or simply wrong. Finally a state is reached when everybody seems to claim that he had always followed this theory. This usually marks the last state before general acceptance.
KURT LEWIN *Psychological Review*, 1943

8 Why, sometimes I've believed as many as six impossible things before breakfast.
LEWIS CARROLL (1832–1898) *Alice Through the Looking Glass*

9 I must create a system or be enslaved by another man's.
WILLIAM BLAKE (1757–1827) 'Jerusalem'

10 It is a capital mistake to theorise before one has data.
ARTHUR CONAN DOYLE (1859–1930) *The Memoirs of Sherlock Holmes*

11 There is no more convincing proof of the truth of a comprehensive theory than its power of absorbing and finding a place for new facts, and its capability of interpreting phenomena which had been previously looked upon as unaccountable anomalies.
ARTHUR WALLACE *Westminster Review*, July 1876

12 A theory is both a *tool* and an *objective*.
M.H. MARX *Psychological Theory*, 1951

1 Yet Holmes was no Sensationalist. What sublimer confession of faith could any realist make than the remark in the *Study of Scarlet*: 'I ought to know by this time that when a fact appears to be opposed to a long train of deductions, it invariably proves to be capable of bearing some other interpretation.'?
RONALD KNOX (1888–1957) *Essays in Sature*

2 A scientific theory must, eventually, be able to convince the whole community of scientific sceptics by standing up to every rational and factual objection thrown at it. But that comes later, if it ever does. The inspired guess, the hypothesis, comes first. And often the joy of discovery stops there.
NICHOLAS HUMPHREY *The Inner Eye*, 1986

THERAPY

3 Psychotherapy rests on a very simple but fundamental assumption, i.e. human behavior is modifiable through psychological procedures.
ALBERT BANDURA *Psychological Bulletin*, 1961

4 To lighten the affliction of insanity by all human means is not to restore the greatest of the divine gifts; and those who devote themselves to the task do not pretend that it is.... Nevertheless, reader, if you do a little in any good direction – do it. It will be much some day.
CHARLES DICKENS (1812–1870) *Household Works*

5 The resemblance between the process of therapy and the phenomenon of play is, in fact, profound. Both occur within a delimited psychological frame, a spatial and temporal bounding of a set of interactive messages. In both play and therapy, the messages have a special and peculiar relationship to a more concrete or basic reality.
GREGORY BATESON *Steps Towards an Ecology of Mind*, 1972

6 Dark worries will be lessened by song.
HORACE (65–8 BC) *Odes IV*

7 I do my thing, and you do your thing
I am not in this world to live up to your expectations
And you are not in this world to live up to mine
You are you, and I am I,
And if by chance we find each other, its beautiful,
If not it can't be helped.
F.S. PERLS *Gestalt Theory Verbatim*, 1969

8 The sound of the flute will cure epilepsy and sciatic gout.
THEOPHRASTUS (c. 370–288 BC) *Physics*

9 The prevalent opinion in psychotherapy was that the victim fashioned his or her own torture. In particular, violent sexual crimes could be attributed to the victim's imagination. ... It was a comforting view for society, for Freud's interpretation – that sexual violence that so affected the lives of his women patients was nothing but fantasy – posed no threat to the existing social order. Therapists could thus remain on the side of the successful and the powerful, rather than of the miserable victims of family violence.
J.M. MASSON *Freud: The Assault on Truth*, 1984

10 The mystic sees the ineffable and the psycho-pathologist the unspeakable.
SOMERSET MAUGHAM (1874–1965) *The Moon and Sixpence*

11 As a whole, diagnosis may be described as the planning stage of therapy.
G.A. KELLY *The Psychology of Personal Constructs*, 1955

12 Because of this free mixing of the psychological and the spiritual in popular therapies and popular speech, one often gets a feeling at the best cocktail parties on the enlightenment circuit, ... that conversation merely refers to that which is inexpressible ... the peak experience, the ineffable revelation.... Their words don't belong to them so much as to the current guru of choice on the best selling self-help book.
R.D. ROSEN *Psychobabble*, 1978

1 Kinship is healing; we are physicians to each other.
OLIVER SACKS *Awakenings*, 1973

2 Why was he sent to England?
Why, because he was mad; he shall recover his wits there; or if he does not, 'tis no great matter there.
WILLIAM SHAKESPEARE (1564–1616) *Hamlet*

3 ... fundamentally psychotherapy cannot satisfactorily be cast in terms of anything other than a personal relation-ship, so that any attempt to standardize or technicize therapy is certain to detract from its proper understanding.
DAVID SMAIL in D. Pilgrim *Psychology and Psychotherapy*, 1983

4 Why waste money on psychotherapy when you can listen to the B Minor Mass.
MICHAEL TORKE *The Observer*, 23 September 1990

5 It may help the elderly if young people can include the elderly in conversation, unostentatiously update information about what is going on, realise the means for a slower pace, and provide some pauses for their remarks.
PATRICK RABBITT *New Scientist*, 1981

6 People go into counselling and never emerge. I wonder if counselling isn't the new religion.
RAJ PERSAUD cit. *The Independent*, 13 October 1997

7 Time is the great physician.
BENJAMIN DISRAELI (1804–1881) *Henrietta Temple*

8 Psychotherapy and dream analysis are, and always will be, arts rather than sciences, and in putting our work on a verifiable footing, we need not surrender the capacities for insight, compassion, and wisdom which personal commitment and long experience bring.
ANTHONY STEVENS *Private Myths*, 1995

9 It is indeed high time for the clergyman and the psychotherapist to join forces.
CARL JUNG (1875–1961) *Modern Man in Search of a Soul*

10 The wise, for cure, on exercise depend.
JOHN DRYDEN (1631–1700) *Epistles*

11 Applied behaviourism such as behaviour modification in the classroom and behaviour therapy as drugless tranquilliser, has fared poorly as a humane human science. It has invariably colluded with social norms in an unthinking manner.
DAVID PILGRIM *Psychology and Psychotherapy*, 1983

12 Canst thou not minster to a mind diseased,
Pluck from memory a rooted sorrow,
Raze out the written troubles of the brain
And with some sweet oblivious antidote
Cleanse the stuff'd bosom of that perilous stuff
Which weigh upon the heart?
WILLIAM SHAKESPEARE (1564–1616) *Macbeth*

13 The job of the feminist therapist is the subversion of patriarchy in the client, therapist and therapy session. The real client is the culture.
LAURA BROWNING cit. *The Observer*, 1 June 1997

14 Now what about 'behavior therapy', which is supposed to be at odds with humanistic psychology, and precisely so because it is 'rigorously scientific'? To my mind the only thing wrong with accounts of behavior therapy I have read is that they fail to mention who the principal investigator was. They call him a 'subject' while the fellow with the doctoral degree, who turns out to be only the technician in the project, is given credit for doing the experiment.
G.A. KELLY in D. Bannister *Perspectives in Personal Construct Theory*, 1971

15 Noble deeds and hot baths are the best cures for depression.
DODIE SMITH (1896–1990) *I Capture the Castle*

16 You can do very little with faith, but you can do nothing without it.
SAMUEL BUTLER (1835–1902) *The Note Books of Samuel Butler*

1 A merry heart doeth good like medicine.
Bible, Proverbs

2 End-points as well as starting-points differ greatly ... and make criteria of success and failure that much more difficult.
ROSEMARY DINNAGE *One to One: Experiences of Psychotherapy*, 1988

3 Harmless mirth is the best cordial against consumption of the spirits.
THOMAS FULLER (1608–1661) *The Holy and Profane State*

4 'Tis not enough to help the feeble up, But to support him after.
WILLIAM SHAKESPEARE (1564–1616) *Timon of Athens*

5 By drugging diseases many and grave in place of few and slight are wont to occur.
TIMAEUS (3rd cent. BC) *Dialogues*

6 The wonderful influence of the imagination in the cure of diseases is well known. A motion of the hand, or a glance of the eye, will throw a weak and credulous patient into a fit; and a pill made of bread, if taken with sufficient faith, will operate a cure better than all the drugs in the pharmacopaeia.
CHARLES MACKAY *Extraordinary Popular Delusions and the Madness of Crowds*, 1852

7 I live in a constant endeavour to fence against the infirmities of ill health, and other evils of life, by mirth.
LAURENCE STERNE (1713–1768) *Tristram Shandy*

8 A well chosen anthology is a complete dispensary of medicine for the more common mental disorders, and may be used as much for prevention as cure.
ROBERT GRAVES (1895–1985) *On English Poetry*

9 The best of healers is good cheer.
PINDAR (518–438 BC) *Nemean Ode*

10 And grew a seething bath, which yet men prove
Against strange maladies a sovereign cure.
WILLIAM SHAKESPEARE (1564–1616) *Sonnet*

11 The best way out is always through.
ROBERT FROST (1874–1963) 'A Servant to Servants'

12 It is then the essential task of the physician to help the patient to find the necessary new orientation toward life that acknowledges restriction.
KURT GOLDSTEIN (1878–1965) in *A History of Psychology in Autobiography*, Vol. 5, 1967

13 It is the confession, not the priest that gives us absolution.
OSCAR WILDE (1854–1900) *The Picture of Dorian Gray*

THINKING

14 In order to draw a limit to thinking, we should have to be able to think both sides of this limit.
LUDWIG WITTGENSTEIN (1889–1951) *Tractatus Logico-Philosophicus*

15 Thinking is to me the greatest fatigue in the world.
JAN VANBRUGH (1664–1726) *The Relapse*

16 Any general statement is like a cheque drawn on a bank. Its value depends on what there is to meet it.
EZRA POUND (1885–1972) *The ABC of Reading*

17 Thought always lags behind action and cooperation has to be practised for a long time before its consequences can be brought fully to light by reflective thought.
JEAN PIAGET *The Moral Judgement of the Child*, 1955

18 These two ways of thinking, the way of time and history, and the way of eternity and timelessness, are both part of man's efforts to comprehend the world in which he lives. Neither is comprehended in the other nor reducible to it ... each supplementing the other – neither telling the whole story.
ROBERT OPPENHEIMER *Science and the Human Understanding*, 1966

1 Never be afraid to sit awhile and think.
LORRAINE HANSBURY *A Raisin in the Sun*, 1959

2 Men suffer from thinking more than anything else.
LEO TOLSTOY (1828–1910) *Sevastopol*

3 The real question is not whether machines think but whether people do.
B.F. SKINNER *Contingencies of Reinforcement*, 1969

4 Man is only a reed, the weakest thing in nature; but he is a thinking reed.
BLAISE PASCAL (1623–1662) *Pensées*

5 Men fear thought as they fear nothing else on earth – more than ruin, more even than death. Thought is subversive and revolutionary, destructive and terrible; thought is merciless to privilege, established institutions and comfortable habits; thought is anarchic and lawless, indifferent to authority, careless of the well-tried wisdom of the ages.
BERTRAND RUSSELL (1872–1970) *Principles of Social Reconstruction*

6 The more we examine the mechanisms of thought, the more we shall see that the automatic, unconscious action of the mind enters largely into all its processes.
OLIVER WENDELL HOLMES (1809–1894) *Mechanism in Thought and Morals*

7 Whatever withdraws us from the powers of our senses; whatever makes the past, the distant or the future, predominate over the present, advances us in the dignity of thinking beings.
SAMUEL JOHNSON (1709–1784) *Inch Kenneth*

8 Thinking too little about things or thinking too much both make us obstinate and fanatical.
BLAISE PASCAL (1623–1662) *Pensées*

9 The human mind tends always and everywhere to think alike.
J.S. LINCOLN *The Dream in Primitive Society*, 1935

10 The whole of science is nothing more than a refinement of everyday thinking.
ALBERT EINSTEIN (1879–1955) *Out of My Later Years*, 1950

11 Think much, speak little, write less.
PROVERB

12 Thus we have two forms of thinking – *directed thinking* and *dreaming or phantasy thinking*. The first, working for communication with speech elements, is troublesome and exhausting; the latter, on the contrary, goes on without trouble, working spontaneously so to speak, with reminiscences.
CARL JUNG (1875–1961) *Psychology of the Unconscious*

13 Great talkers are so constituted that they do not know their own thoughts until, on the tide of their particular gift, they hear them issuing from their mouths.
THORNTON WILDER (1897–1975) *The Woman of Andros*

14 Categorical thinking is not just a reflection of individual experience but a shared experience that society can convey through its linguistic system.
A.R. LURIA *The Making of Mind*, 1979

15 The function of thinking is not just solving an actual problem, but discovering, envisaging, going into deeper questions. Often in a great discovery the most important thing is that a certain question is found. Envisaging, putting the productive question is often more important than the solution of a set question.
M. WERTHEIMER *Productive Thinking*, 1945

16 The psychical entities which seem to serve as elements in thought are certain signs and more or less clear images which can be 'voluntarily' reproduced and combined.... The above mentioned elements are, in my case, of visual and some muscular type. Conventional words or other signs have to be sought for laboriously only in a secondary state.
ALBERT EINSTEIN (1879–1955) cit. R.N. Shephard, L.A. Cooper *Mental Images and their Transformations*, 1982

1 Thinking is an activity in which we engage. We need our representational resources to make the activity effective, but the resources are varied, and they are not the same as the thought they sustain.
MARGARET DONALDSON *Human Minds*, 1992

2 Thought depends absolutely on the stomach, but in spite of that, those who have the best stomachs are not the best thinkers.
VOLTAIRE (1694–1778) letter to d'Alember, 20 August 1770

3 How can I know what I think till I see what I say?
G. WALLAS (1858–1932) in M. Wallas *The Art of Thought*, 1945

4 The profound thinker always suspects that he is superficial.
BENJAMIN DISRAELI (1804–1881) *Contarini Fleming*

5 The old metaphysical prejudice that man 'always thinks' has not yet entirely disappeared. I am myself inclined to hold that man really thinks very little and very seldom.
WILHELM WUNDT *Lectures on Human and Animal Psychology*, 1894

6 We are thinking beings, and we cannot exclude the intellect from participating in any of our functions.
WILLIAM JAMES *The Varieties of Religious Experience*, 1902

7 One thought fills immensity.
WILLIAM BLAKE (1757–1827) 'The Marriage of Heaven and Hell'

8 Man is master of his actions because of his ability to deliberate without them.
THOMAS AQUINAS (1225–1274) *Summa Theologica*

9 Amusement is the happiness of those who cannot think.
ALEXANDER POPE (1688–1744) *Thoughts on Various Subjects*

10 There is no expedient to which a man will not go to avoid the real labour of thinking.
THOMAS A. EDISON (1847–1931) posted on signs about the Edison Laboratory

11 The thoughts that come often unsought, and, as it were, drop into the mind, are commonly the most valuable of any we have.
JOHN LOCKE (1632–1704) letter to Samuel Bold, 16 May 1699

12 What the psychologists have hitherto called thought is nothing but talking to ourselves.
J.B. WATSON *Behaviorism*, 1924

13 One of the most fundamental properties of thought is its power of predicting events.
K.J.W. CRAIK *The Nature of Explanation*, 1943

14 I think that behaviourism makes the greatest possible contribution to an analysis of thinking.
B.F. SKINNER cit. D. Cohen *Psychologists on Psychology*, 1977

15 Form is the Golden vase wherein Thought, that fleeting essence, is preserved to posterity.
HORACE (65–8 BC) *Ars Poetica*

16 'You damn sadist,' said Mr. Cummings,
'you try to make people think.'
EZRA POUND (1885–1972) *Cantos*

17 I never could find any man who could think for two minutes together.
SYDNEY SMITH (1771–1845) *Sketches of Moral Philosophy*

TIME

18 In man's original view of the world, as we find among primitives, space and time have a very precarious existence. They become 'fixed' concepts only in the course of his mental development, thanks largely to the introduction of measurement. In themselves, space and time consist of *nothing*.
CARL JUNG (1875–1961) in R.E. Ornstein *The Nature of Human Consciousness*

19 An hour in the morning is worth two in the evening.
PROVERB

1 That period of time [the future] in which our affairs prosper, our friends are true, and our happiness is assured.
AMBROSE BIERCE (1842–1914) *The Cynic's Word Book*

2 The future is not what it used to be.
ANON.

3 The Future is something which everyone reaches at the rate of sixty minutes an hour, whatever he does, whoever his is.
C.S. LEWIS (1898–1963) *The Screwtape Letters*

4 The future is dark, the present burdensome, only the past, dead and buried, bears contemplation.
G.R. ELTON *The Practice of History*, 1967

5 Eternity's a terrible thought. I mean, where's it all going to end?
TOM STOPPARD *Rosencrantz and Guildenstern are Dead*, 1967

6 To every thing there is a season, and a time to every purpose under the heaven: A time to be born, and a time to die; a time to plant, and a time to pluck up that which is planted.
Bible, Ecclesiastes

7 The more we study the nature of time, the more we shall comprehend that duration means invention, the centre of forms, the continual elaboration of the absolutely now....
HENRI BERGSON *Creative Evolution*, 1911

8 ... a lifetime is not linear but instant ... inside the head everything happens at once.
PENELOPE LIVELY *Moon Tiger*, 1987

9 Misfortunes falling upon us and disease disturbing our happiness make the time of life, though short indeed, seem long.
HERODOTUS (484–424 BC) *Histories*

10 The present is only an imaginary dividing line between the past and the future.
E.H. CARR *What is History*, 1961

11 Many who find the day too long, think life too short.
CHARLES C. COLTON (1780–1832) *Lacon*

12 Time present and time past
Are both perhaps present in time future
And time future contained in time past.
T.S. ELIOT (1888–1965) 'Burnt Norton'

13 The obscurest epoch is today.
ROBERT LOUIS STEVENSON (1850–1894) *Across the Plains*

TRUTH

14 Truth does not lie beyond humanity, but is one of the products of human mind and feeling.
D.H. LAWRENCE (1885–1930) *The Rainbow*

15 Truth must necessarily be stranger than fiction: for fiction is the creation of the human mind and therefore congenial to it.
G.K. CHESTERTON (1874–1936) *The Club of Queer Trades*

16 In a culture which is constantly told lies, one wants to know not merely the truth but the *naked* truth.
P. SLOTENDIJK *Critique of Cynical Reason*, 1988

17 'Tis strange – but true, for truth is always strange;
Stranger than fiction.
LORD BYRON (1788–1824) *Don Juan*

18 A new scientific truth does not triumph by convincing its opponents and making them see the light, but rather because its opponents eventually die, and a new generation grows up that is familiar with it.
MAX PLANCK (1858–1947) *Scientific Autobiography and Other Papers*

19 That a lie which is all a lie may be met and fought with outright,
But a lie which is part a truth is a harder matter to fight.
ALFRED, LORD TENNYSON (1808–1892) 'The Grandmother'

20 The truth is rarely pure and never simple.
OSCAR WILDE (1854–1900) *The Importance of Being Earnest*

U

UNCONSCIOUS

1 Central to Freud's system is the concept of *unconscious motivation*.... His recourse to the concept was based on the need to discover a force or agency by which behavior might be controlled independently of the patient's will.
DANIEL ROBINSON *An Intellectual History of Psychology*, 1981

2 ... the unconscious ... not only binds the individuals among themselves to the race, but also unites them backwards with the peoples of the past and their psychology. Thus the unconscious, surpassing the individual in its generality, is, in the first place, the object of a true psychology, which claims not to be psychophysical.
CARL JUNG (1875–1961) *The Psychology of the Unconscious*

3 The most perfect humour and irony is generally quite unconscious.
SAMUEL BUTLER (1835–1902) *Life and Habit*

4 Our mind is so fortunately equipped, that it brings us the most important bases for our thoughts without our having the least knowledge of this work of elaboration. Only the results of it become unconscious.
WILHELM WUNDT cit. L.L. Whyte *The Unconscious Before Freud*, 1960

5 The elementary sensations directly making up our ordinary sensations are themselves compounded of sensations of less intensity and duration, and so on. Thus there is going on within us a subterranean process of infinite extent, its products alone are known to us, and are only known to us in the mass.
H.A. TAINE *On Intelligence*, 1871

6 The most important part of mental action, the essential process on which thinking depends, is unconscious mental activity.
HENRY MAUDSLEY (1835–1918) *Physiology and Pathology of the Mind*

7 To explore the most sacred depths of the unconscious, to labor on what I have just called the subsoil of consciousness, that will be the principal task of psychology in the century which is opening.
HENRI BERGSON *Independent* [New York], 30 October 1913

8 In the realms of the unconscious mental life there is no such thing as exhaustion.
C.G. CARUS *Psyche*, 1846

9 We know that, although individuals are widely separated by the differences in the contents of their consciousness, they are closely alike in their unconscious psychology.
CARL JUNG (1875–1961) *Psychology of the Unconscious*

10 I happen to regard the word 'unconscious' as peculiarly unfortunate – chosen as it is on the *lucus a non lucendo* principle. But let that pass. There it is and we must make the best of it – seeking to penetrate its dark wood.
C. LLOYD MORGAN *British Association for the Advancement of Science Reports*, 1921

11 ... depth psychology, for all its merits, may plunge too deep, and psychologists would do well to give full recognition to manifest motives before probing the unconscious.
G.W. ALLPORT in *A History of Psychology in Autobiography, Vol. 5*, 1967

UNDERSTANDING

12 ... the more I see the more I am aware of how much I do *not* understand.
N. TINBERGEN *Proceedings of the Royal Society London, B*, 1972

1 We do not love without seeking to understand and we do not even hate without a subtle use of judgement.
JEAN PIAGET *Play, Dreams and Imitation in Childhood*, 1951

2 There is no difficulty in investigating nature. To understand it means more a conquest of our own limitations of thought.
J.D. BERNAL interview *Science Journal*, March 1965

3 Now, my own suspicion is that the universe is not only queerer than we suppose, but queerer than we can suppose.
J.B.S. HALDANE *Possible Worlds*, 1928

4 A true and full understanding of another's thought is possible only when we understand its affective-volitional basis.
L.S. VYGOTSKY *Thought and Language*, 1962

5 The imagination that is raised in man, or any other creature indeed with the faculty of imagining, by words or other voluntary signs, is that we generally call 'understanding', and is common to man and beast.
THOMAS HOBBES (1588–1679) *Leviathan*

6 Sir, I have found you an argument; but I am not obliged to find you an understanding.
SAMUEL JOHNSON (1709–1784) cit. James Boswell *The Life of Samuel Johnson*

7 If scientists learn anything from their studies, it would be how *little*, not how much we know.
D. SUZUKI, P. KNUDSTON *Genethics: The Ethics of Engineering Life*, 1989

8 Not to let a word get in the way of its sentence
Nor to let a sentence get in the way of its intention,
But to send your mind out to meet the intention as a guest;
THAT is understanding.
CHINESE PROVERB

9 To understand another's speech, it is not sufficient to understand his words – we must also understand his thought.

But even that is not enough – we must also know its motivation. No psychological analysis of an utterance is complete until that plane is reached.
L.S. VYGOTSKY *Thought and Language*, 1962

10 Even for the physicist the description in plain language will be a criterion of the degree of understanding that has been reached.
WERNER HEISENBERG *Physics and Philosophy*, 1958

UNHAPPINESS

11 He's simply got the instinct for being unhappy highly developed.
SAKI (1870–1916) *Chronicles of Clovis*

12 Misery acquaints a man with strange bedfellows.
WILLIAM SHAKESPEARE (1564–1616) *The Tempest*

13 Those who weep lose more energy than they lose during any other act.
MICHAEL ONDAATJE *The English Patient*, 1992

14 Men who are unhappy, like men who sleep badly, are always proud of the fact.
BERTRAND RUSSELL (1872–1970) *The Conquest of Happiness*

15 Sorrow is tranquility remembered in emotion.
DOROTHY PARKER (1893–1967) 'Here Lies'

16 There is no greater pain than to remember a happy time when one is in misery.
DANTE (1265–1321) *Divine Comedy*

17 One cannot weep for the entire world, it is beyond human strength. One must choose.
JEAN ANOUILH (1910–1987) *Cecile*

18 The sole cause of man's unhappiness is that he does not know how to stay quietly in his room.
BLAISE PASCAL (1623–1662) *Pensées*

1   Unhappiness is best defined as the difference between our talents and our expectations.
EDWARD DE BONO *The Observer*, 12 June 1977

VALUES

2   ... alas, we are offered ... in the field of value-psychology the following definitions: Values and meanings are nothing but defence mechanisms and reaction formations. Well, as for myself I am not willing to live for the sake of my reaction formations, even less to die for the sake of my own defence mechanisms.
VIKTOR FRANKL *Beyond Reductionism*, 1969

3   Values are great habits, easily established and hard to change.
K.S. LASHLEY letter to W.A. Kepner, 14 May 1952 in G.A. Kimble *et al. Portraits of Pioneers in Psychology*, 1991

4   There is no room in the new value system for the equivalent of stoicism or fulfilment through suffering which may moderate the response to stress of those guided by the precepts of self-help, individual initiative and self-denial which are fostered by the old value system ... possessors of the new value system will tend to interpret relatively minor feelings of tension, anxiety, or depression, brought about by life-stresses, as evidence of mental disturbance, whereas individuals whose perceptions are governed by the old value system will define the same feelings as a morbid preoccupation or as indicating that they need to 'get a grip' on themselves.
R. COCHRANE *Acta Psychiatrica Scandinavica*, 1980

5   If the vicissitudes of the market are the judges of one's values, the sense of dignity and pride is destroyed.
ERICH FROMM *Man for Himself*, 1947

1 When people move to other cultures, value differences between them mean that previously established expectations and predictions are invalid. This poor fit between person and the environment may lead to distress and anxiety until the values of the new society are understood and internalised.
ADRIAN FURNHAM, STEPHEN BOCHNER *Culture Shock*, 1986

2 The modern educational emphasis on the scientific methods, combined with the deemphasis of spiritual, religious and philosophical concepts, has produced a distortion in our culture in which 'rational' materialistic values are exaggerated and the spiritual and emotional values are largely ignored or suppressed by the 'rational' mind.
G.E. PUGH *The Biological Origins of Human Values*, 1978

3 There are no genes for the values that matter for human living. These values were developed in our cultural evolution, biological evolution contributing the brain with its potentialities.
JOHN ECCLES *The Human Psyche* 1980

4 Values enter the world with life.
KARL POPPER cit. P.A. Schlipp *The Philosophy of Karl Popper*, 1974

5 One man means as much to me as a multitude, and a multitude only as much as one man.
DEMOCRITUS (5th cent. BC) *Fragments*

VANITY

6 Our vanity desires that what we do best should be considered what is hardest for us.
FRIEDRICH NIETZSCHE (1844–1900) *Beyond Good and Evil*

7 Flattery is all right – if you don't inhale.
ADALAI STEVENSON, speech, 1 February 1961

8 What is vanity but the longing to survive.
MIGUEL DE UNAMUNO *The Tragic Sense of Life*, 1913

9 How slight and insignificant is the thing which casts down or restores a mind greedy for praise.
HORACE (65–8 BC) *Epistles*

10 Conceit is the finest armour a man can wear.
JEROME K. JEROME (1859–1927) *Idle Thoughts of an Idle Fellow*

11 Virtue brings honour, and honour vanity.
THOMAS FULLER (1654–1734) *Gnomologia*

12 How many crimes are committed merely because their authors could not endure being wrong!
ALBERT CAMUS (1913–1960) *The Fall*

VARIABILITY

13 I soon learned that variety is not the spice of life, but the very stuff of life.
CHRISTOPHER BURNEY *Solitary Confinement*, 1952

14 Where order in variety we see,
And where, though all things differ, all agree.
ALEXANDER POPE (1688–1744) 'Windsor Forest'

15 Consistency is contrary to nature, contrary to life. The only completely consistent people are the dead.
ALDOUS HUXLEY (1894–1963) *Do What You Will*

VICE

16 'We all have flaws,' he said 'and mine is being wicked'.
JAMES THURBER (1894–1961) *The Thirteen Clocks*

1 It is the function of vice to keep virtue within reasonable bounds.
SAMUEL BUTLER (1835–1902) *The Notebooks of Samuel Butler*

2 I must talk of murders, rapes and
  massacres,
Acts of black nights, abominable deeds,
Complots of mischief, treason, villainies,
Ruthful to hear, yet piteously perform'd.
WILLIAM SHAKESPEARE (1564–1616) *Titus Andronicus*

3 Of all the causes which conspire to
  blind
Man's erring judgement, and misguide
  the mind,
What the weak head with strongest bias
  rules,
Is *Pride*, the never failing vice of fools.
ALEXANDER POPE (1688–1744) 'An Essay on Criticism'

4 By hating vices too much, they come to love men too little.
EDMUND BURKE (1729–1797) *Reflections on the French Revolution*

5 Hypocrisy is the most difficult and nerve-racking vice that any man can pursue; it needs an unceasing vigilance and a rare detachment of spirit. It cannot, like adultery or gluttony, be practised at spare moments; it is a whole-time job.
SOMERSET MAUGHAM (1874–1965) *Cakes and Ale*

6 Greed is excessive self-interest.
JACK MAHONY, interview, *Guardian Higher Education*, 30 September 1997

7 Vices are their own punishment.
AESOP (6th cent. BC) *Fables*

8 Half the vices which the world condemns most loudly have seeds of good in them and require moderate use rather than abstinence.
SAMUEL BUTLER (1835–1902) *The Way of All Flesh*

VIOLENCE

9 A person is more likely to be hit or killed in his or her own home by another family member than anywhere else or by anyone else.
R.J. GELLES, M.A. STRAUS *Journal of Social Issues*, 1979

10 What you get these days [in films], to a great extent, is a pornography of violence which is much more dangerous than a pornography of sex. I'd rather see people screwing each other than killing one another.... I've been a soldier, I know about the trauma of violence.
MICHAEL CAINE, interview, *The Guardian*, 8 February 1997

VIRTUE

11 Prosperity doth best discover vice, but adversity doth best discover virtue.
FRANCIS BACON (1561–1626) *Essays*

12 honesty is a good
thing but
it is not profitable to
its possessor
unless it is
kept under control
if you are not
honest at all
everybody hates you
and if you are
absolutely honest
you get martyred
don marquis (1878–1937) 'archygrams'

13 People seem to think there is something inherently noble and virtuous in the desire to go for a walk.
MAX BEERBOHM (1872–1956) *And Even Now*

14 How far that little candle throws
  his beams!
So shines a good deed in a naughty
  world.
WILLIAM SHAKESPEARE (1564–1616) *The Merchant of Venice*

1 It is better to be beautiful than good. But ... it is better to be good than to be ugly.
OSCAR WILDE (1854–1900) *The Picture of Dorian Gray*

2 Were infidelity and licentiousness to be prevalent among women, all would be corruption and disorder. Men are often restrained within the limits of morality, or at least of a decent appearance, from their attachment to virtuous women; and it cannot be denied that the infant mind receives its first moral tinge and virtuous bias from the watchful care and instruction of maternal affection.
JOSHUA COLLINS *A Practical Guide to Parents and Guardians*, 1802

3 Working out what it would take to program goodness into a robot shows not only how much machinery it takes to be good but how slippery the concept of goodness is to start with.
STEVEN PINKER *How the Mind Works*, 1997

4 Her virtue was probably her vice.
PATRICK WHITE (1912–1990) *The Vivisector*

5 Whenever there are great virtues, it's a sure sign that something's wrong.
BERTOLT BRECHT (1898–1956) *Mother Courage*

6 He who is too busy doing good finds no time to be good.
RABINDRANTH TAGORE (1861–1941) *Stray Birds*

7 Virtue is praised but hated. People run away from it, for it is ice-cold and in this world you must keep your feet warm.
DENIS DIDEROT (1713–1784) *Rameau's Nephew*

8 Virtue is more clearly shown in the performance of fine actions than in the nonperformance of base ones.
ARISTOTLE (384–322 BC) *Nicomachean Ethics*

9 When we are planning for posterity, we ought to remember that virtue is not hereditary.
THOMAS PAINE (1737–1809) *Common Sense*

10 A virtue to be serviceable must, like gold, be alloyed with some commoner but more durable metal.
SAMUEL BUTLER (1835–1902) *The Way of All Flesh*

VISION

11 ... the mind is the real instrument of sight and observation, the eyes act as a sort of vessel receiving and transmitting the visible portion of the consciousness.
PLINY THE ELDER (23–79) *Natural History*

12 We don't simply see, we look.
E.J. GIBSON *Annual Review of Psychology*, 1988

13 [Vision] is a process that produces from images of the external world a description that is useful to the viewer and not cluttered with irrelevant information.
DAVID MARR *Vision*, 1982

14 In 1872, Liebreich, who was ophthalmic surgeon to St. Thomas's Hospital ... suggested that colour-defective painters might be identified from the internal evidence of their paintings ... [and] that in later years colour values may change as a result of changes in the lens.... He was of the opinion that the changes in colour values and certain distortions present in the later work of Turner were due to a reduction in the transparency of the lenses and the development of lenticular astigmatism.
W.J.B. RIDDLE *Proceedings of the Royal Society of Medicine*, 1949

15 Nowadays we look upon visual perception as a piecemeal affair; our seemingly unified view of the world around us is really only a plausible hypothesis on the basis of fragmentary evidence. The transformations that go on in the retina and visual pathways are not merely reproductions, in high fidelity, of the visual image. At every stage a censor is at work, cutting with its scissors, and deleting with a red pencil, the unwanted visual messages.
COLIN BLAKEMORE in R.A. Hinde, J. Stevenson-Hinde *Constraints on Learning*, 1973

1 If anyone examines letters or small objects through the medium of a crystal or glass if it be shaped like the lesser segment of a sphere, with the convex side towards his eye, he will see the letters far better and larger. Such an instrument is useful to all persons.
ROGER BACON *Opus Majus*, 1268

2 So the techniques used by artists and the forms they select succeed because they exploit the properties of the visual system and through their work, artists have indirectly been defining the nature of visual processes, often before these processes have been investigated scientifically.
RICHARD LATTO in R.L. Gregory *et al. The Artful Eye*, 1995

3 It is certain by experience, that when we look at an object with both eyes, according as it approaches or recedes from us, we alter the disposition of our eyes, by lessening or widening the interval between the pupils. This disposition or turn of the eyes is attended with a sensation, which seems to me to be that which, in this case brings the idea of greater or lesser distance into the mind.
BISHOP GEORGE BERKELEY (1685–1753) in A.A. Luce, T.E. Jessop *The Works of George Berkeley*, 1949–1957

4 Colour vision has evolved because it is important ecologically. The basic categories and values of colour are products of brain evolution and brain embryology. Indeed, colour is nowhere else but in brains; the primary categories of colour could not have been learned.
COLWYN TREVARTHEN in R.L. Gregory *et al. The Artful Eye*, 1995

5 Vision is the art of seeing things invisible.
JONATHAN SWIFT (1667–1745) *Thoughts on Various Subjects*

6 The keenest of all our senses is the sense of sight.
CICERO (106–53 BC) *On the Orator*

7 The cubists, Picasso and Braque, who were obsessed with contours and boundaries, referred to this technique [irradiation] as Seurat's 'beautiful edges' and used it widely themselves. Irradiation then, is a technique developed independently by painters to sharpen edges and contours that is effective because it mimics a neural mechanism, lateral inhibition, which was identified many years later.
RICHARD LATTO in R.L. Gregory *et al. The Artful Eye*, 1995

WAR

1 As long as war is regarded as wicked, it will always have its fascination. When it is looked upon as vulgar, it will cease to be popular.
OSCAR WILDE (1854–1900) *The Critic as Artist*

2 ... the need to control, by wise rational responsibility, all our emotional allegiances to cultural values is as great as, if not greater than, the necessity of keeping our other instincts in check. None of them can ever have such devastating effects as unbridled military enthusiasm when it infects great masses and overrides all other considerations by its singlemindedness and its specious nobility.
KONRAD LORENZ *On Aggression*, 1963

3 A man's brains splattered on
A stretcher-bearer's face:
His shook shoulders slipped their load,
But when they bent to look again
The drowning soul was sunk too deep
For human tenderness.
They left this dead with the other dead,
Stretched at the cross roads.
ISAAC ROSENBERG (1890–1918) 'Dead Man's Dump'

4 Societies today are mostly much too complicated for it to be appropriate to compare their wars with the defence of territories by animals.
J.Z. YOUNG *An Introduction to the Study of Man*, 1970

5 If any question why we died
Tell them, because our fathers lied.
RUDYARD KIPLING (1865–1936) 'Common Form'

6 You say that a good cause will even sanctify war. I tell you, it is the good war that sanctifies every cause!
FRIEDRICH NIETZSCHE (1844–1900) *Thus Spoke Zarathustra*

7 I have never understood this liking for war. It panders to instincts already catered for within the scope of any respectable domestic establishment.
ALAN BENNETT *Forty Years On*, 1969

8 Here dead we lie because we did not choose
To live and shame the land from which we sprung.
Life, to be sure, is nothing much to lose;
But young men think it is, and we were young.
A.E. HOUSEMAN (1859–1936) 'Here Dead We Lie'

9 You must know then that there are two methods of fighting, the one by law, the other by force: the first method is that of men, the second that of beasts; but as the first method is often insufficient, one must have recourse to the second.
NICCOLO MACHIAVELLI (1469–1527) *The Prince*

10 War belongs, not to the Arts and Sciences, but to the province of social life.
KARL von CLAUSEWITZ (1780–1831) *On War*

11 The whole army experience is a nightmare to me. Never have I seen such incompetence, such extravagance, such a group of overbearing, inferior men.
J.B. WATSON in *A History of Psychology in Autobiography, Vol. 3*, 1936

12 War is primarily concerned with two sorts of activity – the delivering of energy and the communication of information.
N.F. DIXON *On the Psychology of Military Incompetence*, 1976

WILL

1 ... the terminus of the psychological process in volition, the point at which the will is clearly applied, is always an idea.... The only resistance which our will can possibly experience is the resistance which such an idea offers to being attended to at all. To attend to it is the volitional act, and the only inward volitional act which we ever perform.
WILLIAM JAMES *Text Book of Psychology*, 1892

2 The blink is provoked by irritation of the cornea. We cope with the irritation by closing the eyelid momentarily. But even this simple reflex activity shows the influence of other integrated neural centres.... Those who have seen cinema film of Mussolini may have noticed that his eyeblinks were infrequent but also astonishingly deliberate in appearance, as though his self-styled 'indomitable will' exerted itself in even this remote corner of his coping conduct.
G.W. ALLPORT *Pattern and Growth in Personality*, 1961

3 Fall seven times, stand up eight.
JAPANESE PROVERB

4 Thus ordered thinking arises out of the ordered course of nature in which man finds himself, and this thinking is from the beginning nothing more than the subjective reproduction of the regularity according to law of natural phenomena. On the other hand, this reproduction is only possible by means of the will that controls the concatenation of ideas.
WILHELM WUNDT *An Introduction to Psychology*, 1912

5 Will to the conceivability of all things: that is what *I* call your will! ... it is a will to power, and that is so even when you talk of good and evil and the assessment of values.
FRIEDRICH NIETZSCHE (1844–1900) *Thus Spoke Zarathustra*

6 The will is never free – it is always attached to an object, a purpose. It is simply the engine in the car – it can't steer.
JOYCE CARY (1888–1957) *Writers at Work: First Series*

7 It requires a much sharper Will, a much greater power of self-discipline, to govern a versatile intellect than one of less endowments.
NICHOLAS MORGAN *The Skull and Brain: Their Indications of Character and Anatomical Relations*, 1875

8 If we cannot do what we will, we must will what we can.
YIDDISH PROVERB

9 There is no such thing as a great talent without great will-power.
HONORÉ de BALZAC (1799–1850) *La Musée du Département*

WISDOM

10 Wise people know what they know and what they do not know as well as the limits of what can be known and what cannot be. They apply the processes of intellect in a way that eschews automatization.
R. STERNBERG *Wisdom*, 1990

11 Knowledge comes, but wisdom lingers.
ALFRED, LORD TENNYSON (1808–1892) 'Locksley Hall'

12 The wisdom of a learned man cometh by opportunity of leisure: and he that hath little business should become wise. How can he get wisdom that holdeth the plough, and that glorieth in the goad, that draweth the oxen, and is occupied in these labours and whose talk is of bullocks.
Bible, Wisdom

13 A word to the wise is infuriating.
ANON.

1 Men are wise in proportion, not to their experience, but to their capacity for experience.
GEORGE BERNARD SHAW (1856–1950) *Man and Superman*

2 A wise man hears one word and understands two.
JEWISH PROVERB

3 Wisdom is a balance between the opposing valencies of intense emotion and detachment, action and inaction, and knowledge and doubts. It tends to increase with experience and therefore age but is not exclusively found in old age.
J.E. BIRREN, L.M. FISHER in R.J. Sternberg *Wisdom*, 1990

4 The art of being wise is the art of knowing what to overlook.
WILLIAM JAMES *Principles of Psychology*, 1890

5 Wisdom differs from mere science in looking at things from a greater height. The same holds true in practical matters. Sometimes a decision has to be taken that cannot follow the common rules of procedure.
THOMAS AQUINAS (1225–1274) *Summa Theologica*

6 Wisdom may be the prototype of an area of cognitive functioning in which older adults, because of their age, have the opportunity to hold something akin to a world record.
P.B. BALTES, J. SMITH in R.J. Sternberg *Wisdom*, 1990

7 Happy is the man who findeth wisdom.
Bible, Proverbs

8 If only we could discover for certain the differences between those who, being given about the same opportunities, acquire wisdom and those who do not.
F.C. BARTLETT *The Mind at Work and Play*, 1951

9 Our knowledge is such that we could, if we chose to do so, direct our own evolutionary futures. Unfortunately our wisdom is all too poorly developed to trust ourselves to do this intelligently.
GEORGE BEADLE *Genetics and Modern Biology*, 1963

10 Contrary to the ancient myth, wisdom does not burst forth fully developed like Athena out of Zeus' head; it is built up, small step by small step, from most irrational beginnings.
BRUNO BETTELHEIM *The Uses of Enchantment*, 1978

11 As you are old and reverend, you should be wise.
WILLIAM SHAKESPEARE (1564–1616) *King Lear*

12 Organisms other than men have the 'wisdom of the body'; man has in addition the wisdom of humanity.
Th. DOBZHANSKY *The Biology of Ultimate Concern*, 1969

13 Fear not the anger of the wise to raise;
Those best can bear reproof who merit praise.
ALEXANDER POPE (1688–1744) 'An Essay on Criticism'

14 Wisdom is *expertise* in the domain of *fundamental life pragmatics*, such as, life planning or life review. It requires a rich factual knowledge about life matters, rich procedural knowledge about life problems, knowledge of different life contexts and values or priorities, and knowledge about the unpredictability of life.
P.B. BALTES, J. SMITH in R.J. Sternberg *Wisdom*, 1990

15 ... practical wisdom is more truly embodied in action than expressed in the rules of action.
MICHAEL POLYANI *Personal Knowledge*, 1958

16 Where is the wisdom we have lost in knowledge?
Where is the knowledge we have lost in information?
T.S. ELIOT (1888–1965) Choruses from 'The Rock'

1 ... nobody so far has discovered how by training to produce wisdom.
F.C. BARTLETT *The Mind at Work and Play*, 1951

2 Sciences may be learnt by rote, but wisdom not.
LAURENCE STERNE (1713–1768) *Tristram Shandy*

3 For one word a man is often deemed to be wise, and for one word he is often deemed to be foolish. We should be careful indeed what we say.
CONFUCIUS (c. 551–c. 478 BC) *Analects*

4 What is it to be wise?
'Tis but to know how little can be known;
To see all other's faults, and feel our own.
ALEXANDER POPE (1688–1744) 'An Essay on Man'

5 A fool sees not the same tree that a wise man sees.
WILLIAM BLAKE (1757–1827) 'The Marriage of Heaven and Hell'

6 Wisdom is a *metacognitive style* plus sagacity, knowing that one does not know everything, seeking truth to the extent that it is knowable.
R.J. STERNBERG *Wisdom*, 1990

7 When I have ceased to beat my wings
Against the faultiness of things,
And learned that compromises wait
Behind each partly opened gate,
When I can look life in the eyes,
Grown, calm and very coldly wise,
Life will have given me the truth,
And taken in exchange my youth.
SARA TEASDALE (1884–1933) 'Wisdom'

8 Wisdom comes with winters.
OSCAR WILDE (1854–1900) *A Florentine Tragedy*

9 A single conversation across the table with a wise man is better than ten years' mere study of books.
HENRY W. LONGFELLOW (1807–1882) 'Hyperion'

WIT

10 Wit is more often a shield than a lance.
ANON.

11 An ounce of a man's own wit is worth a ton of other people's.
LAWRENCE STERNE (1713–1768) *Tristram Shandy*

12 True Wit is Nature to advantage dress'd;
What oft was thought, but ne'er so well expressed.
ALEXANDER POPE (1688–1744) 'An Essay on Criticism'

13 For *wit* lying most in the assemblage of ideas, and putting those together with quickness and variety, wherein can be found any resemblance or congruity, thereby to make up pleasant pictures and agreeable visions in the fancies; *judgement*, on the contrary, lies quite on the other side, and separating carefully, one from another, ideas wherein can be found the least difference, thereby to avoid being misled by similitude, and by affinity to take one thing for another.
JOHN LOCKE (1632–1704) *An Essay Concerning Human Understanding*

14 Wit without employment is a disease.
ROBERT BURTON (1577–1640) *Anatomy of Melancholy*

WOMEN

15 The great and almost only comfort about being a woman is that one can always pretend to be more stupid than one is and no one is surprised.
FREYA STARK (1893–1993) *Valley of the Assassins*

16 The age of a woman doesn't mean a thing. The best tunes are played on the oldest fiddles.
S.Z. ENGEL cit. *Newsweek*, 4 July 1994

1 Frailty, thy name is woman!
WILLIAM SHAKESPEARE (1564–1616) *Hamlet*

2 The great question that has never been answered and which I have not yet been able to answer, despite my thirty years of research into the feminine soul, is 'What does a woman want?'
SIGMUND FREUD (1856–1939) cit. Ernest Jones *Life and Work of Sigmund Freud*

3 ... the need to comply, to be inwardly at one with the patriarchal order and its discourses is compelling, inscribing itself in the deepest level of the unconscious, ... I say this despite – indeed, because of – the obvious manifestations of change in the realm of women's power, position, and political consciousness brought about by the women's movement.
LINDA NOCHLIN *Women, Art and Power*, 1988

4 I do not wish them [women] to have power over men; but over themselves.
MARY WOLLSTONECROFT (1759–1797) *A Vindication of the Rights of Women*

5 A woman especially, if she have the misfortune of knowing any thing, should conceal it as well as she can.
JANE AUSTEN (1775–1817) *Northanger Abbey*

6 Women never have young minds. They are born three thousand years old.
SHELAGH DELANEY *A Taste of Honey*, 1959

7 Good women always think it is their fault when someone else is being offensive. Bad women never take the blame for anything.
ANITA BROOKNER *Hotel du Lac*, 1984

8 Ladies were ladies in those days; they did not do things themselves.
GWEN RAVERAT (1885–1957) *Period Piece*

9 A woman is like a teabag – only in hot water do you realise how strong she is.
NANCY REAGAN cit. *The Observer*, 29 March 1981

10 Women's rougher, simpler, more upright judgement embraces the whole truth, which their tact, their mistrust of masculine idealism, ever prevents them from speaking in its entirety.
JOSEPH CONRAD (1857–1924) *Chance*

11 Being a woman is of special interest to aspiring male transsexuals. To actual women it is simply an excuse not to play football.
FRAN LEBOWITZ *Metropolitan Life*, 1979

12 One is not born a woman, one becomes one.
SIMONE DE BEAUVOIR (1908–1986) *The Second Sex*

13 How sad it is to be a woman! Nothing on earth is held so cheap.
FU HSUAN (2nd cent. AD) 'Woman'

14 All over the world today more women suffer from reported psychiatric maladies than men. Social scientists have offered a hectic profusion of explanations for the apparent psychological frailty of females, but nobody has advanced much beyond the plausible assumption that women's numerical superiority among the ranks of the troubled and insane owes something to their subordination to men in the vast majority of human societies. Defective diagnoses, meaningless statistical comparisons, and crackpot moralizing characterize the most comprehensive surveys of the problem, and the best scholarship has concentrated on showing how the tyrannical pressure to conform to sex roles of specific countries and groups influences the detection and management of female insanity.
MICHAEL MACDONALD *Mystical Bedlam*, 1981

15 The happiest women like the happiest nations have no history.
GEORGE ELIOT (1819–1880) *Mill on the Floss*

WORDS

16 A word is a microcosm of human consciousness.
L.S. VYGOTSKY *Thought and Language*, 1962

1   Words strain
Crack and sometimes break, under the
    burden,
Under the tension, slip, slide, perish
Decay with imprecision, will not stay in
    place,
Will not stay still.
T.S. ELIOT (1888–1965) 'Burnt Norton'

2   The utter inadequacy of current
terminology, the need to reform it and,
in order to do that, to demonstrate what
sort of object language is, continually
spoil my pleasures in philology.
FERDINAND de SAUSSURE, letter, cit. J.
Culler, *Ferdinand de Sassure*, 1986

3   But words are things, and a small
    drop of ink,
Falling like dew, upon a thought,
    produces
That which makes thousands, perhaps
    millions think;
'Tis strange, the shortest letter which
    man uses
Instead of speech, may form a lasting
    ink
Of ages.
LORD BYRON (1788–1824) *Don Juan*

4   You must never be over-sure. You
    must say, when reporting:
At five o'clock in the centre section is a
    dozen
Of what appear to be animals: whatever
    you do,
Don't call the bleeders *sheep*.
HENRY REED (1914–1986) 'Lessons of the
War; Judging Distances'

5   Socrates: And is not naming a part
of speaking? For in giving names men
speak. And if speaking is a sort of
action and has a relation to acts, is not
naming also a sort of action?
PLATO (429–347 BC) *Cratylus*

6   Words are part of action and they
are equivalents to actions.
BRONISLAW MALINOWSKI *Coral Gardens
and their Magic*, 1935

7   Words, in their primary or immediate
signification, stand for nothing but the
ideas in the mind of him who uses them.
JOHN LOCKE (1632–1704) *An Essay
Concerning Human Understanding*

8   You can stroke people with words.
F. SCOTT FITZGERALD *The Crack-Up*, 1945

9   What's in a name? That which we
    call a rose
By any other name would smell as
    sweet.
WILLIAM SHAKESPEARE (1564–1616) *Romeo
and Juliet*

10   Words, as is well known, are the
great foes of reality.
JOSEPH CONRAD (1857–1924) *Under
Western Eyes*

11   'Well,' said Owl, 'the customary
procedure in such cases is as follows.'
'What does Crustimoney Proseedcake
mean?' said Pooh, 'For I am a bear of
Very Little Brain, and long words bother
me.'
A.A. MILNE (1882–1956) *Winnie-the-Pooh*

12   Without knowing the force of
words, it is impossible to know men.
CONFUCIUS (c. 551–c. 478 BC) *Analects*

13   Words are like leaves; and where
    they most abound,
Much fruit of sense beneath is rarely
    found.
ALEXANDER POPE (1688–1744) 'An Essay on
Criticism'

14   '*Un*important, of course, I meant,'
the King hastily said, and went on to
himself in an undertone, 'important–
unimportant–important –' as though he
were trying which word sounded best.
LEWIS CARROLL (1832–1898) *Alice's
Adventures in Wonderland*

15   By the words of others shall we,
using intelligence, know them; by our
own words do we, if we strive, know
ourselves.
ERIC PARTRIDGE (1894–1979) *Name into
Word*

16   A word devoid of thought is a dead
thing, and a thought unembodied in
words remains a shadow.
L.S. VYGOTSKY *Thought and Language*, 1962

17   We cannot prohibit what we cannot
name.
GEORGE STEINER *Extraterritorial*, 1972

1 Man is a creature who lives not upon bread alone, but principally by catchwords.
ROBERT LOUIS STEVENSON (1850–1894) *Virginibus Puerisque*

2 Words are plastic material with which one can do all kinds of things. There are words which have lost their original full meaning, but which can regain it in other connections. A joke of Lichtenberg's carefully singles out circumstances in which watered down words are bound to regain their full meaning:
'How are you getting along?' the blind man asked the lame man. 'As you see,' the lame man replied to the blind man.
SIGMUND FREUD (1856–1939) *Jokes and their Relation to the Unconscious*

WORK

3 Work banishes those three great evils: boredom, vice and poverty.
VOLTAIRE (1694–1778) *Candide*

4 In a hierarchy every employee tends to rise to his level of incompetence.
L.J. PETER, R. HULL *The Peter Principle*, 1969

5 When work is a pleasure, life is a joy! When work is a duty, life is slavery.
MAXIM GORKY (1868–1936) *The Lower Depths*

6 When in a state of hunger, one ought not to undertake labour.
HIPPOCRATES (c. 460–377 BC) *Aphorisms*

7 Lord Finchley tried to mend the electric Light
Himself. It struck him dead: And serve him right.
It is the business of the wealthy man
To give employment to the artisan.
HILAIRE BELLOC (1870–1953) *Cautionary Tales*

8 Why should I let the toad work Squat on my life.
PHILIP LARKIN (1922–1985) 'Toads'

10 Perhaps until one starts, at the age of seventy, to live on borrowed time, no year will seem again quite so ominous as the one when formal education ends and the moment arrives to find employment and bear physical responsibility for the whole future.
GRAHAM GREENE (1904–1991) *A Sort of Life*

11 Go to the ant, thou sluggard; consider her ways, and be wise.
Bible, Proverbs

12 Work is of two kinds: first, altering the position of matter at or near the earth's surface relative to other such matter; second, telling other people to do so. The first kind is unpleasant and ill paid; the second is pleasant and highly paid.
BERTRAND RUSSELL (1872–1970) *In Praise of Idleness and Other Essays*

13 A man willing to work, and unable to find work, is perhaps the saddest sight that fortune's inequality exhibits under the sun.
THOMAS CARLYLE (1795–1881) *Chartism*

14 One of the saddest things is that the only thing that a man can do for eight hours a day, day after day, is work. You can't eat eight hours a day, nor drink for eight hours a day nor make love for eight hours.
WILLIAM FAULKNER (1897–1962) *Writers at Home: First Series*

15 I paint just as I breathe. When I work, I relax: not doing anything or entertaining visitors makes me tired.
PABLO PICASSO (1881–1973) cit. E. Beyeler *Picasso*, 1968

16 Extreme busyness, whether at school or college, kirk or market, is a symptom of deficient vitality.
ROBERT LOUIS STEVENSON (1850–1894) *Virginibus Puerisque*

17 I like work: it fascinates me. I can sit and look at it for hours. I love to keep it by me: the idea of getting rid of it nearly breaks my heart.
JEROME K. JEROME (1859–1927) *Idle Thoughts of an Idle Fellow*

1 Overwork, n. A dangerous disorder affecting high public functionaries who want to go fishing.
AMBROSE BIERCE (1842–1914) *The Devil's Dictionary*

2 At work, people are a part of a complex set of complimentary relationships which convey identity and status. All this is lost in unemployment.
MICHAEL ARGYLE *The Psychology of Interpersonal Behaviour*, 1969

3 We live in the age of the overworked, and the under-educated; the age in which people are so industrious that they become absolutely stupid.
OSCAR WILDE (1854–1900) *The Critic as Artist*

4 Normally everybody works at any task a good long way below his maximum efficiency. If we did not then when the course of life made an extra demand we should crack and collapse.
F.C. BARTLETT *The Problem of Noise*, 1934

5 Whether our work is art or science or the daily work of society, it is only the form in which we explore our experience which is different.
J. BRONOWSKI *Science and Human Values*, 1956

6 Work expands to fill the time available for its completion.
C. NORTHCOTE PARKINSON *Parkinson's Law*, 1958

7 Complete explanations of why any of us do anything for an entire working lifetime are uninteresting because, if they are truthful, they are plotless catalogues of random accidents.
PAT RABBITT *The Psychologist*, 1999

WORRY

8 Fundamentally I am a worrier whom only work can relieve.
JEAN PIAGET cit. R.I. Evans *Jean Piaget: The Man and His Ideas*, 1973

9 It is not work that kills, but worry.
PROVERB

10 Worrying is the most natural and spontaneous of all human functions. It is time to acknowledge this, perhaps even to learn to do it better.
LEWIS THOMAS *The Medusa and the Snail*, 1979

11 I am the self-consumer of my woes
They rise and vanish in oblivious host.
JOHN CLARE (1793–1864) 'I Am'

12 Worrying implies a future, a way of looking forward to things. It is a conscious conviction that a future exists, one in which something terrible might happen, which is of course ultimately true. So worrying is an ironic form of hope.
ADAM PHILLIPS *On Kissing, Tickling and Being Bored*, 1993

XENOPHOBIA

1 The American people, taking one with another, constitute the most timorous, snivelling, poltroonish, ignominious mob of serfs and goosesteppers ever gathered under one flag in Christendom since the end of the Middle Ages.
H.L. MENCKEN (1880–1956) *Prejudices*

2 The dislike for all that is unlike.
ISRAEL ZANGWILL (1864–1926) *The Liberal Review*, 1901

3 Xenophobia looks like becoming the mass ideology of the 20th century fin-de-siecle. What holds humanity together today is the denial of what the human race has in common.
ERIC HOBSBAWM, lecture to the American Association of Anthropology, cit. *New Statesman*, 24 April 1992

4 Abroad is bloody.
KING GEORGE VI (1895–1952) cit. W.H. Auden *A Certain World*, 1970

5 They spell it Vinci, and pronounce it Vinchi. Foreigners always spell better than they pronounce.
MARK TWAIN (1835–1910) *The Innocents Abroad*

6 Meanwhile write up in letters of gold round your office *England knows nothing of phonetics, hates education, but will do anything for money.*
GEORGE BERNARD SHAW, letter to Sir James Pitman, 7 August 1947, cit. J. Pitman and J. St. John *Alphabets and Reading*, 1969

7 I am not the greatest conductor in this country. On the other hand I'm better than any damn foreigner.
THOMAS BEECHAM (1879–1961), interview, *Daily Express*, 9 March 1961

8 In my view, many of the problems of interfacing the neural sciences with the cognitive sciences are more sociological than scientific, i.e. professional xenophobia and infatuation with one's own discipline are the greatest barriers to adaptation.
N. GESCHWIND in D. Norman *Perspectives on Cognitive Science*, 1981

Y

Z

YOUTH

1 The youth of America is their oldest tradition. It has been going on now for three hundred years.
OSCAR WILDE (1854–1900) *A Woman of No Importance*

2 I'm not young enough to know everything.
J.M. BARRIE (1860–1937) *The Admirable Crichton*

3 Bliss was it in that dawn to be alive,
But to be young was very heaven!
WILLIAM WORDSWORTH (1770–1850) 'The Prelude'

4 It is a very widespread opinion that youth, which belongs, strictly speaking, only to the higher orders, is for the purpose of giving the animal time to adjust itself to the complicated tasks of life to which its instincts are not adequate.
KARL GROOS *The Play of Animals*, 1898

5 No young man believes he shall ever die.
WILLIAM HAZLITT (1778–1830) *The Monthly Magazine*, 1827

6 Youth seems a sad mistake – when one is no longer young.
ALEXANDRE DUMAS (1802–1870) *Twenty Years After*

7 Oh as I was young and easy in the mercy of his means,
Time held me green and dying
Though I sang in my chains like the sea.
DYLAN THOMAS (1914–1953) 'Fern Hill'

ZEAL

8 We are sometimes stirred by emotion and take it for zeal.
THOMAS à KEMPIS (1380–1471) *The Imitation of Christ*

9 Zeal for the deserving is quite compatible with coldness of nature.
MAX BEERBOHM (1872–1956) *A Peep into the Past*

10 Fanatics have their dreams, wherewith they weave
A paradise for a sect.
JOHN KEATS (1795–1821) 'The Fall of Hyperion'

ZYGARNIK EFFECT

11 Some men never think of it.
You did. You'd come along
And say you'd nearly brought me flowers
But something had gone wrong.
...
It made me smile and hug you then.
Now I can only smile.
But, look, the flowers you nearly bought
Have lasted all this while.
WENDY COPE 'Flowers', 1992

12 It is unfortunately true of the clergy, as of so many other categories of people, that one individual who fails to reach an expected standard is remembered and quoted, to the detriment of many who are all that could be desired but who in consequence receive less than justice.
B. SEEBOHM ROWNTREE, G.R. LAVERS
English Life and Leisure, 1951

1 Strephon kissed me in the spring,
Robin in the fall,
But Colin only looked at me
And never kissed at all.

Strephon's kiss was lost in jest,
Robin's lost in play,
But the kiss in Colin's eyes
Haunts me night and day.
SARAH TEASDALE (1884–1993) 'The Look'

Subject index

Entries in upper case refer to topic headings within the text, with page numbers for that topic shown in bold. Other topics appear in lower case. The page number is given before the raised point, followed by the quotation number on that page.

Author index

Page numbers are given before the raised point, folllowed by the quotation number on that page.

A

Abrams, Dominic 40·2

Abu Al-Ala Al-Ma'arri 116·12

Adams, Douglas 134·20

Addison, Joseph 67·6; 100·4; 217·11

Adler, Alfred 19·12; 68·5; 82·7; 103·1; 147·2; 156·7; 158·4; 164·11; 165·5; 184·9; 194·5

Adler, P.S. 53·6

Aeschylus 9·11; 85·11; 113·5

Aesop 249·7

Agassiz, Louis 78·11

Agathon 79·13

Aiken, Conrad 64·13

Ailred of Rievaulx 124·3

Aimee, Anouk 25·13

Akhmatova, Anna 146·10

Alexander, R.D. 77·1

Ali Ibn-Abi-Talib 163·4

Allan, Woody 7·2; 29·16; 46·4; 56·7

Allport, G.W. 32·13; 102·14; 120·4; 152·12; 159·8; 177·10; 179·3; 194·10; 225·1; 245·11; 253·2

Alvarez, A. 57·15

Amiel, H.F. 64·4; 212·15

Amis, Kingsley 6·15

Ammons, R.B. 79·18; 204·7

Anderson, P. 187·3

Anderson, P.W. 44·3

Andreski, Stanislav 171·12

Annan, Noel 6·2

Anon. 9·5; 28·8; 34·1; 44·11; 58·6; 62·9; 66·15; 69·2; 85·3; 96·11; 124·2; 132·14; 168·9; 172·7; 178·5; 184·10; 188·11; 189·1; 194·4,12; 205·9; 209·3; 223·2,8; 237·5; 244·2; 253·13; 255·10

Anouilh, Jean 25·15; 140·7; 246·17

Anscombe, G.E.M. 120·2; 158·8

Antrim, Minna 79·8

Aquinas, Thomas 16·4; 243·8; 254·5

Archimedes 114·9

Argyle, Michael 100·1; 188·7; 206·9; 212·7; 259·2

Ariosto, Ludovico 111·8

Aristotle 3·12; 6·8; 11·14; 13·2; 15·8; 16·5; 60·4; 68·7; 69·7; 90·2; 92·8; 99·6; 110·11; 111·6; 133·13; 144·5; 152·6; 158·5; 214·9; 229·1; 250·8

Armstrong, Sir Robert 57·2

Arnheim, Rudolph 142·11; 195·9; 232·10

Arnold, Matthew 87·13; 202·2; 223·3; 229·12

Arnold, M.B. 3·9

Arnold, Thomas 69·9

Aron, Raymond 31·1

Asch, S.E. 22·8; 200·11

Ascham, Roger 65·6; 199·12; 200·3

Ashby, W. Ross 133·2

Asher, Richard 59·1

Assaglio, R. 121·7

Astell, Mary 217·6

Attneave, Fred 114·2,7

Auden, W.H. 1·4; 5·6; 27·7; 58·3; 61·12; 73·9; 83·8; 89·1; 99·10; 109·10; 112·10; 141·9; 142·5; 157·5; 166·9; 192·12; 198·8; 200·5; 202·5; 226·5; 226·11; 229·11· 231·8; 235·13; 237·3

Augustine, St 76·3; 117·8; 128·1; 187·17

Aurelius, Marcus 49·6; 55·12; 75·2; 205·7

Austen, Jane 7·5; 8·3; 23·5; 100·16; 104·6; 111·14; 143·16; 149·2; 153·10; 181·2; 198·3; 217·5; 256·5

Austin, G.A. 198·2

Austin, J.L. 25·9

Ayckbourn, Alan 1·13; 50·11

B

Bachelard, Gaston 16·10

Bacon, Francis 2·3; 7·1; 26·2,7; 28·8; 32·8; 38·5; 43·5; 56·17; 62·14; 68·6; 83·13; 89·13; 125·6; 141·1; 143·10; 174·6; 226·8; 249·11